International Case Studies
of Dyslexia

Routledge Research in Education

For a full list of titles in this series please visit www.routledge.com

International Case Studies of Dyslexia

Edited by Peggy L. Anderson
and Regine Meier-Hedde

Routledge
Taylor & Francis Group
New York   London

First published 2011
by Routledge
711 Third Avenue, New York, NY 10017

Simultaneously published in the UK
by Routledge
2 Park Square, Milton Park, Abingdon, Oxon OX14 4RN

Routledge is an imprint of the Taylor & Francis Group, an informa business

Typeset in Sabon by IBT Global.
Printed and bound in the United States of America on acid-free paper by IBT Global.

Library of Congress Cataloging-in-Publication Data

International case studies of dyslexia / edited by Peggy L. Anderson and Regine Meier-Hedde.
    p. cm. — (Routledge research in education ; v. 56)
Includes bibliographical references and index.
1. Dyslexic children—Education—Case studies.   I. Anderson, Peggy L.
II. Meier-Hedde, Regine.
    LC4708.I585 2011
    371.91'44—dc22
    2010044074

ISBN13: 978-0-415-88437-2 (hbk)
ISBN13: 978-0-203-81840-4 (ebk)

This book is dedicated to the remarkable children who relived their experiences and feelings in the following pages so that others may better understand the challenges of dyslexia.

Contents

Tables

Foreword

"The only disability in life is a bad attitude." —Scott Hamilton

International Case Studies of Dyslexia presents a compendium of case studies from 17 countries all around the world. In exploring the lives of these children with dyslexia, the reader will appreciate that so many issues peculiar to the phenomenon of dyslexia are shared worldwide. The book reminds us that family dynamics, especially when a less-than–supportive school system is involved, are remarkably similar and familiar across oceans, language, and culture. Equally important, the book identifies the distinct ways that dyslexia is enculturated and institutionalized in different countries. The international comparisons represent a kind of cultural anthropological approach to dyslexia. Both similarities and differences exist from one case to another. Factors ranging from linguistic and psychological processing to educational, social and political forces all play roles in defining the interface of dyslexia and culture in various countries.

These case studies provide evidence that dyslexia is a world-wide challenge. The personal stories framed in the cultural context and analyses provided by the authors transcend individual languages and cultures from Sweden to China. In other words, there are people the world over who, in spite of sound intelligence, struggle with reading for no visible reason. In spite of sharp cultural/social/educational/political differences in the constructs of intelligence and learning, dyslexia exists as a universally recognized phenomenon.

The stories of 17 children with dyslexia offer a number of positive messages. As a parent of a child with dyslexia, I have witnessed many of the challenges faced by the children in this book in my own family's life. Of course, much of what unites persons with dyslexia the world over is pain and frustration, in many cases because of the ignorance and lack of sensitivity on the part of some schools. Sadness is inexorably connected to many of these stories. But the reader will not take away sadness as the central theme of this work. From my perspective as an ethnographer who has researched how persons with learning disabilities and dyslexia become successful, I cannot help but feel that all these children will find success. In spite of the obstacles thrown at them, they are amazingly resilient. They do not give up. They find an upside where many of us would find a downside. Such an approach to life lies at the foundation of the success process. Persistence and resilience are major players in success stories. And many individuals with learning disabilities and dyslexia credit the struggles they faced as children with making them more determined and focused to achieve as adults. If the reader comes away with the impression that these kids are winners, it may be because they are—and will be.

Little research has taken a cross-cultural approach to dyslexia, and even less has emphasized a holistic perspective about persons with dyslexia. Peggy Anderson, Regine Meier-Hedde and their colleagues provide an essential addition to the literature base and a critical imperative to the reader. We waste so much human capital through ignorance and misunderstanding. Exposing dyslexia for what it is—a significant condition to be sure, but not a terminal exclusion from a meaningful and satisfying life—is the strongest antidote to "the only disability in life—a bad attitude."

Henry B. Reiff

Preface

> *"Reading begins in first grade. She* [the teacher] *could have helped me with my written assignments because if you mess up first grade, you mess up the rest of your life."*
>
> —Christian, a German boy with dyslexia

In the course of our long careers as special educators, we have often been challenged by the various obligations of our profession. Many times it has been unclear how to choose and implement an appropriate intervention for a particular child or how to best prepare teachers to ensure the most significant achievement gains for their students. Our attempts to uncover specific strategies that are preferable have sometimes resembled a cross between a scavenger hunt and an obstacle course competition. Yet, there has always been one obligation that has remained crystal clear, and that is our responsibility to the children we serve. And little can be accomplished *for* a child without attempting to understand feelings and needs. This is particularly true for children with dyslexia, who are often made to feel that those who could help have instead turned their backs to them. This was certainly the case for Christian, a highly introspective and very bright child, who wanted, more than anything, for his teacher to pay attention to him and teach him to read. As a six-year-old-child, he faced feelings of failure on a daily basis at school, which gave way to the fear that his whole life would be ruined because he could not read. Was Christian neglected because his teacher was ignorant of differentiated teaching practices or was he neglected because his teacher was indifferent to his needs? The answer cannot be known, but the lessons of this child's story and that of 16 others, which are reported in this volume, resonate clearly: they are asking for help and it is their right to receive it. For schools to ignore the problems of these children or to blame the children and their families is unacceptable and unconscionable. There is a moral mandate for society to respond to the instructional needs of these children. This is a pressing need, the neglect of which has far reaching implications not only for these children, but also their families, and ultimately society.

Research in the last two decades has verified that dyslexia is a global challenge that is complicated by various linguistic demands and intervention problems. In order to move forward, it is imperative that information is shared across countries and continents. As a global community, we have far greater potential to address dyslexia than any one country could accomplish separately.

P.L.A.
R.M-H.

Acknowledgments

We are grateful, not only to the children who participated in this study, but to their mothers who spent countless hours detailing their families' experiences with dyslexia. We were continually amazed at the mothers' insight, commitment, and perseverance in efforts to secure appropriate help for their children. As we sifted through the mountains of meticulous interview data, we were reminded of the words of the renowned American pediatrician and child rearing expert, Dr. Benjamin Spock, who explained his vast knowledge of children with these simple words, "I really learned it all from mothers."

1 Introduction to the Study

Peggy L. Anderson and Regine Meier-Hedde

> "*We are interested in them for both their uniqueness and commonality. We seek to understand them. We would like to hear their stories. We may have reservations about some things the people . . . tell us, just as they will question some of the things we will tell about them.*"
>
> (Stake, 1995, p. 1).

EARLY CASE REPORTS OF DYSLEXIA

The earliest research devoted to children with dyslexia was based on case reports that were published in medical journals. There are probably few professionals in this field who are unfamiliar with the case of Percy F., the 14-year-old who could not read in spite of the fact that he was "always a bright and intelligent boy, quick at games, and in no way inferior to others of his own age" (Morgan, 1896, p. 1378). These early case reports of dyslexia proliferated in Europe and quickly spread to America (Anderson & Meier-Hedde, 2001) where the method was eventually supplanted with case study collections based on the clinical work of Fernald, Monroe, and Orton as well as many others (see Hallahan & Mercer, 2002). The shift from single case reports to case study collections was a logical progression that fostered the evolution of dyslexia research. These single and collective case reports are of particular interest as they provide an historical link between our present understanding of dyslexia and the scientific foundation of this disorder. Although today the large-scale group comparison method that relies on statistical analysis of data is the predominant research method for studying characteristics and treatments for dyslexia, case studies continue to have legitimacy especially for areas in which there is a limited knowledge base. As Miles and Miles (1999) suggested, there is particular value in examining individual case histories as a starting point, which is certainly where we currently stand with respect to international dyslexia research. Although there is a growing body of literature devoted to crosslinguistic orthographic aspects of dyslexia, there is a paucity of international research that focuses on the lives of children with this condition and their families. The goal of the current study is to attempt to bridge this gap in the literature and to provide some understanding of how dyslexia variously impacts children and families around the globe.

CASE STUDY RESEARCH

Qualitative research focuses on listening to people and describing experiences and phenomena. It "seeks to understand the world from the perspectives of those living in it" (Hatch, 2002, p. 7), which is an undervalued agenda in the study of individual differences, particularly those involving exceptionality. All too often individuals with exceptional needs or disabilities are involved in research that depersonalizes them to the extent that participants are made to feel more like specimens than individuals (Roach, 2003). This has been particularly true for children whose voices have been ignored or neglected by academic research even though the right for children to be heard is considered to be so fundamental that it is recognized by a special set of United Nations Convention articles (i.e., the Rights of the Child). These articles speak to the importance of respecting children's voices in many different contexts including school settings (Hart, 2002) and have far reaching implications for research. Qualitative research methods, such as ethnographies and case studies, have the potential to support these rights and lend credibility to the views of all children, including those whose disabilities or individual differences may have left them feeling marginalized.

There are varied perceptions about the case study approach to research, perhaps due to the fact that they have been implemented in different ways across disciplines. For example, a case study in science bears little resemblance to a case study in the social sciences. In the social sciences, this method has often been misunderstood by researchers and underrepresented in the literature, which reflects a strong preference for statistical studies (Chima, 2005). Not too long ago, conventional wisdom among experts relegated case study research to the "methodological trash heap" (Flyvbjerg, 2004, p. 420). Thus, it is not surprising that many of the earlier social science research texts failed to provide consideration to the case study as a formal method (Yin, 2009). In the past 20 years, there has been a gradual movement toward acceptance of case study methodology and general recanting of previous criticism by experts now turned advocates of this research method. Case study research today can be conceptualized as an approach that is based on a core of acceptable (and usually) clearly defined procedures that can be defended as well as any other research methodology. As space does not provide the opportunity to review all of the merits of this research method, the reader is referred to other resources for extensive discussion (see Merriam, 1998, 2009; Stake, 1995; Yin, 1994, 2009).

In spite of the vast differences in case study methodology, according to Hatch (2002) consensus can generally be reached on a few important characteristics that define this type of research, which are explained in reference to the current study. First, most case study research focuses on individuals representing specific groups or a phenomenon. In the case of the current study, the phenomenon is dyslexia and the groups are the children and their mothers. Second, Hatch noted that the phenomenon is studied within its natural context that is defined by space and time (i.e., the age range of the children, their school and social experiences and the countries they represent). In other words, the researcher is allowed to demarcate or as Merriam (1998) stated "fence-in" what will and will not be studied, thereby providing natural boundaries. And finally, the case study provides a depth of description that is typically not possible with other types of research. Using multiple interview tools with the children and their mothers provided researchers with ample data to construct meaningful interpretive narratives. The perspectives of the children, mothers and researchers provided the triangulation to enhance authenticity of the case studies.

THE STUDY DESIGN

In an effort to understand the experiences of those living with dyslexia, a constructivist paradigm (Hatch, 2002) that explored the realities of the child, mother, and researcher was used as the foundation for the study. This study relied on a multiple-case design with a cross-case analysis (Yin, 2009), which is also referred to as a collective case study approach (Stake, 1995). Although all prominent case researchers have varying ideas about the conceptual development of the case design, there seems to be agreement with regard to the importance of establishing a rigorous protocol that is not to be confused with a survey technique. As Yin (2009) suggested, a case study protocol has only one commonality with a survey questionnaire (i.e., both begin with a single data point). A case study protocol clearly defines exactly what will be researched and how it will be accomplished. It is the ultimate road map that will guide the research effort; therefore, it must be followed with minimal deviation. In order to increase the reliability of case study research, it is important that investigators are carefully guided in their data collection and analysis efforts (Yin, 2009). This was particularly important for the current research project because most of the researchers did not use English as a first language. The potential for misunderstanding and miscommunication was, in effect, multiplied by the number of different languages involved in this project. This study followed Yin's (1994; 2009) recommendations for study protocol requirements, which included the development of the following: (1) overview of the case study project with objectives; (2) field procedures (explanation of human subject requirements/guidelines, specific instructions for data collection); (3) case study instruments and procedures (questionnaires, scales, data collection scripts, and translation requirements); and (4) a case study report guide (sample case study report developed from pilot study).

OVERVIEW OF CASE STUDY PROJECT WITH OBJECTIVE

Researchers were provided with an abstract of the study that contained the rationale as well as the objective. This abstract emphasized the importance of dyslexia as a world-wide concern for children, parents and professionals in the educational, psychological and medical communities as well as the need for information that focused on the child and family's social, emotional, and cultural perceptions of this condition. The general objective of the study was to research the influence of dyslexia on children and their families from various countries around the world, to be addressed through the collection and analysis of the following data:

1. Medical and developmental history (birth, health, and early development);
2. Educational history (school achievement, dyslexia diagnosis and treatment);
3. Child perceptions of dyslexia (structured interview);
4. Parent perceptions of dyslexia (structured interview).

Eighteen dyslexic children between the ages of 10 and 12 years of age, representing 15 languages and 18 countries were selected for this research project. The principal investigators were researchers for their respective countries (i.e., the United States and Germany). Sixteen additional researchers from selected countries were invited to participate. The decision to limit the number of cases to 18 was based on practical considerations, primarily length of the study results. Country selection was influenced by several factors including the desire to provide wide global coverage. Consideration was also given to areas of the world that have higher prevalence of dyslexia and more research, which is why there was heavy emphasis on European countries. The major criterion for selecting researchers from respective countries was that the individuals had a record of research and publication in the area of dyslexia. A secondary criterion was that the individuals had published in the area of social and emotional aspects of dyslexia. However, given the fact that social and emotional aspects of dyslexia are not well represented in the literature, only approximately half of the investigators had this type of background. These researchers were identified either through recommendations by international dyslexia experts and/or a literature review. Of the final cohort, researchers from only one country did not complete the project; thus, the current study includes 17 cases.

The research population for this study included males between 10 to 12 years of age. Although age of identification varies around the world, the majority of children are diagnosed by 10 years of age. In the past, dyslexia case study literature has favored males over females (Riddick, 2010; Edwards, 1994), reflecting the overrepresentation of boys with this condition. Historically there has been a general consensus that a disproportionate number of males are affected by dyslexia while some research has found fewer gender differences (Shaywitz, Shaywitz, Fletcher, & Escobar, 1990) and other research has confirmed the higher prevalence of boys with this condition (Hawke, Olson, Willcut, Wadsworth, & DeFries, 2009; Rutter et al., 2004). As this study focused on sociocultural perspectives of dyslexia, it was decided that including both males and females would complicate the interpretation of case data. Thus, the variable of gender was controlled by interviewing only males. From a broad cultural perspective, there are vast differences with regard to achievement expectations for males and females. It would be beyond the scope of this study to attempt to analyze these with any degree of confidence. However, it should be noted that the absence of case study research on girls with dyslexia represents a significant need in this field.

There was no attempt to control for socioeconomic status of the subjects for this study. Admittedly, most research that has examined dyslexia has a socioeconomic bias in favor of the middle class and the current study is no exception. In the United States, vocal parent advocacy groups led the charge to establish the category of learning disabilities so their children would be served in special education programs (Hallahan & Mercer, 2002). Political clout that results in legislative educational change is rarely associated with low socioeconomic status. In fact it has been suggested that the category of learning disabilities in the U.S. was developed for purposes of allowing middle class parents to protect their underachieving children from lower class children (Sleeter, 1987). Though this conjecture was considered highly controversial, it helps to explain the influence of class on this disability category. Although the sample for the current study includes children from the lower socioeconomic class (e.g., one family could not afford child care, which necessitated sending the boy to live with relatives for many years) and upper class (e.g., one child had a chauffeur to drive him to tutoring classes), the majority of cases are from the middle class.

Other than age and sex, subject selection for this research was based on the single criterion of dyslexia diagnosis as verified by the researcher from that particular country. Obviously, there is little agreement and considerable discord regarding a preferable term to describe reading problems in children. In most cases, the various researchers for this study explained dyslexia as referring to unexpected reading underachievement in light of average to above average cognitive potential. Although IQ data were collected when available, it was not a subject requirement for this study as it is questionable whether examination of a child's intellect as measured by a test is beneficial for dyslexia diagnosis (Vellutino, Fletcher, Snowling & Scanlon, 2004). In fact, as far as discrepancy identification is concerned, it may be detrimental as characteristics associated with dyslexia, such as slower rate of processing visual information and/ or memory problems may depress the IQ and thereby decrease the difference between potential and achievement. Dyslexia is a term that is more commonly used in Europe, but less so in North America where the condition is frequently referred to as a learning disability or reading disability as in the United States and Canada. Yet, even though these terms may be more common, the International Dyslexia Association headquartered in the United States is one of the largest dyslexia organizations in the world. In Germany, where the term dyslexia was originally coined by Rudolph Berlin in 1877, it is more likely that the term Lese-Rechtschreibstörung would be used to describe this condition. In other countries, there are variants of these terms and politico-cultural influences that largely determine their use. As the current research project sought to connect children by studying the common thread of reading failure, it was considered unnecessary to impose arbitrary diagnostic criteria, which would likely be culturally biased. It was a necessary and sufficient condition that these dyslexia experts from their respective countries identified the subjects as having this condition.

FIELD PROCEDURES, INSTRUMENTATION REQUIREMENTS AND REPORT GUIDE

The Assessment Protocol included five instruments: Parent Interview, Parent Perception Scale, Child Perception Scale, Sentence Completion and Elaboration, (see Appendix) and the Child Interview, the latter of which is reported at the end of each case study chapter. The instrumentation was developed for this study and pilot tested prior to establishing the final materials for the protocol. Initially, a Picture Perception instrument was included in the protocol. This instrument included 20 pictures that children were asked to interpret (e.g., "can you tell me what is happening in the picture?"). However, after the pilot study it was concluded that the pictures were too leading, and therefore subject to bias and misinterpretation. Extensive study was devoted to the development of the questions for the protocol. With regard to the Child Interview, many references were consulted to determine how to approach children in an interview situation. In particular, the work of Garbarino and Stott (1989) from the Erickson Institute, Graue and Walsh (1998) and Greenspan (1981) was extremely helpful in terms of providing background knowledge for developmentally appropriate techniques for eliciting information from children.

In addition to the five instruments, all researchers were provided with a script to explain the study to the mother and the child. The researchers were instructed to translate all instrumentation and scripting into the native language of their country. They were also instructed to use an audio tape player to record the responses of the mother and the child. Additional instructions specified that the mother and the child should be interviewed separately. The time required for the interview varied significantly. The interviews for the children were generally accomplished within 90 minutes. However, the mothers' interviews took longer, usually closer to two hours or more. Sometimes, the researchers had to return for a second interview with the mother to gather additional information (e.g., school records, evaluation records, etc.). Once the interviews were completed, they were transcribed, and then translated into English and forwarded to the principal investigators along with the narrative case study that the researcher had developed.

All of the materials including consent forms for the mother and child for this research project were approved by the Human Subjects Review Board at the College where the principal investigator is employed.

The report guide for the study was a sample case study that was developed from the pilot testing and included as part of the detailed research protocol. This sample case study was organized according to data collection areas, such as medical history, family background, early development, etc. Thus, researchers developed their cases within this system to achieve continuity in result reporting.

DATA ANALYSIS AND INTERPRETATION

This study used both qualitative and quantitative data analysis with the emphasis on the former. The qualitative analysis was based on the constructivist research paradigm that was used for the study. As Hatch (2002) noted, the qualitative researcher attempts to construct the multiple realities of the case by describing the unique reality of individuals who were all interpreting the world from their vantage point. Thus, for this study, researchers were asked to construct an interpretive narrative of the child's experiences based on the perspectives of both the mother and the child. In effect, there were three parties engaged in the interpretive experience as the child and mother were describing their realities, and the researchers were interpreting data in reference to their backgrounds and expertise in dyslexia. It should also be noted that the editorial process potentially influenced these interpretations. The editing process was accomplished via email with an average of five revisions for each case study. The greatest number of revisions was necessitated because of linguistic and/or socio-cultural miscommunication and/or misperception. Even though all of the contributors have excellent English skills, there was considerable misunderstanding that arose because of differences in educational/psychological terminology, school system structure, and assessment/treatment methods, as well as other aspects. Great lengths were taken to avoid inadvertent cultural contamination imposed by editing.

Quantitative analyses of data are also provided, mostly in the form of frequencies. Inevitably, the sharing of such data suggests that generalization can be supported, but case study research has been criticized for its limited potential in this area. However, this criticism reflects a misunderstanding of its primary purpose. It should not be misconstrued as sampling research as "we do not study a case primarily to understand other cases" because the obligation of the researcher is to understand the case at hand (Stake, 1995, p. 4). Stake believes that value of a case study cannot be measured in terms of its typicality and even a collective case study design, such as the current one, would be difficult to defend as representational. He concluded that while generalizations can and do occur in case study research, they are not of the same magnitude uncovered in comparative or correlation studies. After all, it would be difficult to make far reaching generalizations on the basis of 17 children and their mothers, all from different countries and cultures. Although Yin (2009) admitted that there is no simple answer to the generalization question, he pointed out that it is also difficult to generalize the results of a single experimental study. And just as scientific fact is usually born out of multiple experiments, the same can be said for multiple-case studies. In speaking to the value of case study research, Fly-vbjerg (2004) suggested that formal generalization whether based on large samples or single cases might well be overrated and not necessarily the sole basis for acquisition of knowledge. Indeed there are times when the generalization argument can be used as a sledge hammer to quell scientific contributions as those in some academic fields have a bias against this type of research (Connor & Ferri, 2010).

It was never the intention of the current research project to identify cases of dyslexia that were representative of the condition in any given country. There are obvious reasons why this was not attempted, one of which is that it is well beyond the experience and expertise of the principal researchers to design a study that could control for all of the variables involved in dyslexia in 17 different countries. However, it may well be that individual contributors from these countries could conclude that some of these cases are representative while others might conclude that they are not. In any event, data frequencies were included in the cross-case analysis as a means of intra-group data analysis. It is the opinion of the researchers that certain quantitative results from this study can be generalized as they have consistently appeared in the dyslexia literature while others cannot. Yet even the results that cannot be generalized may be beneficial for researchers who wish to use this information to formulate hypotheses for future cross-cultural studies.

REFERENCES

Anderson, P.L., & Meier-Hedde, R. (2001). Early case reports of dyslexia in the United States and Europe. *Journal of Learning Disabilities, 34*, 9–21.

Chima, J. S. (2005, September). *What's the utility of the case-study method for social science research? A response to critiques from the qualitative/statistical perspective.* Paper presented at the annual meeting of the American Political Science Association, Washington, DC. Retrieved from http://www.allacademic.com/meta/p41952_index.html

Connor, D.J., & Ferri, B. (2010). Introduction to DSQ Special issue: "Why is there learning disabilities?"—Revisiting Christine Sleeter's socio-political construction of disability two decades on. *Disability Studies Quarterly, 30* (2). Retrieved from http//www.dsq-sd.org/article/view/1229/1276

Edwards, J. (1994). *The scars of dyslexia*. London: Cassell.

Flyvbjerg, B. (2004). Five misunderstandings about case-study research. In C.Seale, G. Gobo, J.F. Gubrium, & D. Silverman (Eds.), *Qualitative research practice* (pp. 420–434). Thousand Oaks, CA: Sage.

Garbarino, J., & Stott, F.M. (1989). *What children can tell us*. San Francisco: Jossey-Bass.

Graue, M.E., & Walsh, D.J. (1998). *Studying children in context: Theories, methods, & ethics*. Thousand Oaks, CA: Sage.

Greenspan, S.I. (1981). *The clinical interview of the child*. New York: McGraw-Hill.

Hallahan, D.P., & Mercer, C.D. (2002). Learning disabilities: Historical perspectives. In R. Bradley, L. Danielson, & D.P. Hallahan (Eds.) *Identification of learning disabilities: Research to practice* (pp. 1–68). Mahwah, NJ: Lawrence Erlbaum Associates.

Hart, S.N. (2002). Making sure the child's voice is heard. *International Review of Education, 48*, 251–258.

Hatch, J.A. (2002). *Doing qualitative research in education settings*. Albany, NY: State University of New York Press.

Hawke, J.L., Olson, R.K., Willcut, E.G., Wadsworth, S.J., & DeFries, J.C. (2009). Gender ratios for reading difficulties. *Dyslexia, 15*, 239–242. doi: 10.1002/dys.389

Merriam, S.B. (1998). *Qualitative research and case study applications in education*. San Francisco: Jossey-Bass.

Merriam, S.B. (2009). *Qualitative research: A guide to design and implementation*. San Francisco: Jossey-Bass.

Miles, T.R., & Miles, E. (1999) *Dyslexia: A hundred years on*, (2nd ed.). Berkshire, UK: Open University Press.

Morgan, P. (1896). A case of congenital word blindness. *British Medical Journal*, 1378.

Roach, A.T. (2003). In search of a paradigm shift: What disability studies can contribute to school psychology? *Disability Studies Quarterly, 23*, (3/4). Retrieved from http//www.dsq-sds.org/article/view/438/615

Riddick, B. (2010). *Living with dyslexia* (2nd ed.). Oxon, UK: Routledge.

Rutter, M., Caspi, A., Fergusson, D., Horwood, L.J., Goodman, R., Maughan, B., Moffitt, T.E., Meltzer, H., & Carroll, J. (2004). Sex differences in developmental reading disability. *Journal of American Medical Association, 291*, 2007–2012.

Shaywitz, S.E., Shaywitz, B.A., Fletcher, J.M., & Escobar, M.D. (1990). Prevalence of reading disability in boys and girls: Results of the Connecticut longitudinal study. *Journal of American Medical Association, 264*, 998–1002.

Sleeter, C. (1987). Why is there learning disabilities? A critical analysis of the birth of the field with its social context. In T.S. Popkewitz (Ed.), *The formation of school subjects: The struggle for creating an American institution* (pp. 210–237). London: Palmer Press.

Stake, R.E. (1995). *The art of case study research*. Thousand Oaks, CA: Sage.

Vellutino, F.R., Fletcher, J.M., Snowling, M.J., & Scanlon, D.M. (2004). Specific reading disability (dyslexia): What have we learned in the past four decades? *Journal of Child Psychology and Psychiatry, 45*, 2–40.

Yin, R.K. (1994). *Case study research: Design and methods* (2nd ed.). Newbury Park, CA: Sage.

Yin, R.K. (2009). *Case study research: Design and methods* (4th ed). Thousand Oaks, CA: Sage.

2 Felix, a Case Study of Dyslexia in France

Gilles Leloup and Liliane Sprenger-Charolles

The definition of dyslexia used in the present chapter is the one presented by Lyon, Shaywitz, and Shaywitz in a seminal paper (2003). That definition, currently used by the International Dyslexia Association (http://www.dys-add.com/define.html#revised) and based on the last 30 years of research on typical and atypical reading acquisition (for reviews, see Lyon et al., 2003; Sprenger-Charolles, Colé, & Serniclaes, 2006; Ziegler & Goswami, 2005, 2006) describes dyslexia as being a specific learning disability that results in unexpected reading difficulty characterized by problems with accurate and/or fluent word recognition which typically results from a phonological deficit. Felix's case is an excellent illustration of that definition.

Felix is an 11-year-old child who was identified as being at risk for dyslexia at the age of 6 and was subsequently diagnosed at the age of 8. His current reading level is similar to that of a 7-year-old. Felix is described as a cheerful child who is aware of his learning difficulties and is working to overcome them. In the interview he came across as a very mature child who is sometimes on the defensive about his severe reading disorder.

BACKGROUND

Family History

Felix is the second child in a middle-class family with three children. He lives with his parents and his older sister (Lara, age 14) and his younger brother (Hugo, age 9) in a residential suburb near Paris. His mother first attended a school in which she studied for a diploma in film editing (two years), and then a school to become a pattern maker for clothing (three years). She worked in the latter capacity for a short period of time, and then stopped in order to devote herself to caring for her three children. She reported that her school results were often not commensurate with her level of effort. She says she still needs to read uncommon words aloud. However, despite her initial difficulties, she made progress; and now she reads newspapers and books with pleasure. The father, who works in sales has a diploma in business, obtained after two years of vocational training.

Unlike his wife, he never encountered problems at school, nor did other members of his family.

The mother reported that Lara's learning difficulties (Felix's older sister) were first mentioned in kindergarten. At the end of first grade, she was unable to read, but she was diagnosed as dyslexic only in the middle of second grade, because in France dyslexia is usually only established after 18 to 24 months of reading instruction. As was his sister, Hugo was diagnosed as dyslexic in the middle of his second grade. In addition, the mother's brother apparently also had learning difficulties and would probably have been diagnosed as dyslexic. His eldest son was recently diagnosed as dyslexic and his youngest daughter is currently experiencing academic difficulties.

Medical History

Felix was born by Caesarean section after delivery was induced three weeks before term because of early contractions and the fact that the baby was in the breech position. Since birth, he has experienced a healthy childhood. The mother reported that his only significant childhood illness was chronic sinusitis from age 5 to age 7 and that he never suffered from otitis media (that could have caused a hearing loss and thus learning difficulties). However, he is thought to have had vision problems, and has received orthoptic training.

Early Development

Felix's infancy was normal, although he was somewhat slow in achieving developmental milestones, especially at the motor level. He started taking his first steps at 18 months. He had difficulty going up and down stairs and finally managed to learn to ride a bike at the age of 9½. He also runs in a rather ungainly fashion. However, his sport educators have never identified any specific problems, and Felix has participated in at least two sports: judo and archery. He has been particularly successful at the latter. He likes to disassemble and assemble a variety of electronic devices, with success. He also enjoys drawing and coloring.

Another noteworthy aspect of Felix's development is his slowness. He strongly resists being rushed. He is not yet independent, either at school or at home. He must be encouraged to dress, wash, and eat. Even now, he has difficulties managing daily activities. His mother acknowledges that she is perhaps overly protective of him.

Felix is said to be a nice social child, who does not initiate conflicts. His mother says that when he was young, he liked to be alone, which is still the case. However, this has not prevented him from developing social relationships. He is liked by his classmates and has genuine friendships with some of them. Finally, according to his mother, Felix's spoken language development was normal, without any delay. His comprehension was good and his verbal production was intelligible. In addition, he was curious, and asked questions about everything.

SCHOOL HISTORY

In France, school entry begins with kindergarten at the age of 3 and lasts for three years (from age 3 to age 6). The last year of kindergarten is the beginning of Cycle 2 (the cycle of basic learning), which includes the two first grades of Primary School. The true beginning of learning to read is in grade 1 (which begins in September of the year when the child turns 6), and not before. Children can be retained in the same grade once per cycle.

To summarize Felix's school history, at age 3 he was enrolled in a school where he remained until the beginning of his second grade; afterwards, he was transferred to another school in which he remained until the end of his primary grades (grade 5). Felix repeated grade 2. Because of his birth date (November 18), before repeating that grade, he was among the youngest in his class.

Kindergarten

Felix started kindergarten in a neighborhood public school when he was 3 years old. The first year was chaotic, with the teacher being absent regularly (because she was pregnant). An assistant (whom Felix's mother referred to as the "cleaning lady" because she was not an accredited teacher) was in charge of the children. However, Felix was happy, easily accepted separation from his parents in the morning, and had lots of friends. The second year, the teacher found that Felix was slow, attributing this to the fact that he was among the youngest in the class. The mother reported to the teacher that her eldest child had had learning difficulties and that Felix's slowness might be the result of a similar problem rather than immaturity, but the teacher ignored this information. The third year, according to Felix's mother, was a disaster. Like her predecessor, the new teacher found Felix a very slow worker, and attributed this to his young age as well as a lack of motivation. Therefore, she kept him in class during play-time to finish his work as a form of punishment. Felix did not understand why he wasn't treated like the other children, and went to school reluctantly. His parents asked to meet the teacher and, once again, they explained that Felix's slowness could be due to a learning disability. Their intervention had a very limited effect as the teacher agreed with the parents and refrained from punishing Felix for a couple of days, and then reverted back to her practice of withholding pleasant activities until his work was completed.

During these three years, the school proposed no specific aid and no consultation with a specialist. In the end it was Felix's sister's speech therapist who advised his parents to contact the "Centre Médico-Psycho-Pédagogique"

(Pedagogical and Psychological Medical Centre, or CMPP), which is a public institution devoted to a geographical area with specialists (e.g., psychiatrists, psychologists, social workers, psychomotor-therapists, speech therapists and educators) providing free consultations. In France, psychiatrists and psychologists have been deeply influenced by the theories of psychoanalysis, especially those enrolled in CMPP. Therefore, a psychoanalytically oriented therapy is often provided to children with reading disabilities, which was the case for both Felix and his sister. A psychomotor assessment was also carried out, but the parents received no report.

First Grade

When Felix was 6 years old, he started first grade in the same school and was thus able to keep his friends. His new teacher had not been made aware of his difficulties with school tasks when he was in kindergarten. This teacher, who was "friendly" and caring towards Felix, noted, like her previous colleagues, that he was very slow, and easily tired, which she too attributed to his young age. At the end of the first trimester, she also noted that Felix mixed up letters more than is normal in the early steps of reading acquisition, and that he had difficulty learning to read and to write.

In February, the mother was worried about Felix's results, and spoke again to her daughter's speech therapist, who advised her to consult a colleague. This colleague, another speech therapist, performed a reading assessment that highlighted phonological deficits (i.e., difficulties with phonological awareness tasks, confusion between phonemes such as /p/-/b/ or /b/-/d /); and a strong reading deficit (he read only short syllables, like "pa", not words or sentences). The speech therapist also noted that Felix was slow, whatever the type of task. Based on her diagnosis of a phonological deficit, she initiated a reading remediation based on phonological training (twice a week). In addition, she referred Felix to an orthoptist to have his vision checked. The orthoptist provided him with oculo-motor training for six months. According to Felix's mother, this training seems not to have helped him.

In spite of the therapy he had received, Felix was one of the few children in his class who was still unable to read at the end of first grade. Pointing out that children have two years to learn to read, and saying that Felix would eventually accomplish this task, the teacher proposed that he continue on to grade 2.

Second Grade

During the summer holiday, the parents had worked with Felix on first grade reading and spelling skills. Although he did benefit from this instruction, Felix continued to be unable to read. His new teacher, who had not been informed of his reading difficulties, suggested classroom exercises based on written instructions, which Felix was unable to process. This teacher thought that it was because Felix refused to work. She did not consider the possibility that he simply could not read. This period was very painful for Felix: he slept poorly, ate little, and lost self-confidence. Therefore, his parents quickly initiated an application process to allow Felix to enter a private school offering pedagogy adapted to children with special needs (a school in which his sister was already enrolled).

Felix was transferred to this new school in November. This abrupt transition could have been expected to be a source of stress and anxiety, but this was not the case. Felix adapted quickly to his new class, became friends with his new classmates, and regained his appetite and normal sleep patterns. That school offered him a personalized schooling project. A teacher who specialized in helping children with special needs saw Felix twice a week outside the class, with other children. This teacher basically provided repetition of the classroom exercises. He was also seen twice a week in his class by the specialized teacher, who focused Felix's training on French language and mathematics. In addition, a classroom assistant was assigned to facilitate his integration in the class by helping him organize his work, and by explaining written instructions aloud, for instance.

Felix also spent a half-day per week in a class for children with severe disorders (e.g., Down syndrome). The underlying idea was to show him that he was not the only one facing academic difficulties, and that he could even help some other children. Initially Felix was very happy with this solution. However, he quickly reported to his parents that despite their disabilities, the children enrolled in this class read better than he did. After a few months, he stopped attending this class.

Outside of school, Felix still received the help of the speech therapist (one hour biweekly of remedial reading based on phonics, sight word recognition, and phonological awareness exercises) and the psychotherapist (45 minutes weekly: psychoanalytically oriented therapy). Despite all these aids, Felix's reading and spelling skills did not improve. The educational team thus suggested that he repeat second grade.

Grade 2 (Repeated)

Felix had the same teacher as the previous year, at the teacher's own request. Unfortunately, she fell ill two months after the start of the school year. She was replaced by a new teacher who was unable to manage the class. After a few months that teacher was replaced by yet another teacher, who reportedly did not have the time to address Felix's difficulties. At the end of the year, the educational team proposed that Felix be integrated into grade 3 for the areas in which he excelled (i.e., history and science), at least when he did not have to read.

During this time, Felix was happy to go to school. In class, he was less passive, more attentive, and sought the assistance he needed. He became motivated to read and write. His understanding of instructions and his writing improved. At that time, he was no longer aided by the classroom assistant. However, the speech therapist and psychologist continued to offer him support. All the persons in charge of him noted that Felix was making progress. At home, like in school, he became more confident and more cheerful. However, he was still unable to do his homework alone.

Third Grade

For the first time, Felix seemed to be able to read independently, but his reading speed was still far below that of a third-grader. In addition, his teacher reported that it was often necessary to orally summarize the material that Felix had read before he really understood the text. However, because Felix seemed to be able to read independently, the teacher specialized in helping children with special needs gradually decreased the time she spent with him. However, out-of-school training continued with the same frequency as before.

Fourth Grade

By the age of 10, Felix began, to recognize that school was quite difficult for him, but his attitude was influenced tremendously by the demands of the assigned tasks (i.e., whether the tasks were written or oral). Faced with written tasks, he showed little autonomy or efficiency. For instance, when given long written words, he invented the answer, and since identifying written words was very laborious for him, he stopped reading after a few lines. This was why his school assessments were administered orally, and why Felix was provided with the accommodation of dictating his answers to the teachers. Faced with tasks involving spoken language, on the other hand, he provided relevant answers demonstrating a good mastery of linguistic subtleties, such as those involved in making inferences or in understanding humor.

The educational team said that Felix had developed compensatory strategies, which they hoped would allow him to obtain a greater autonomy in written language processing. At the same time, the speech therapist became very concerned with the stagnation of Felix's performance, and the fact that he seemed to be becoming unmotivated and sad. The consultation of another speech therapist was thus suggested. This new speech therapist initiated a different therapeutic approach which was based on studies with aphasic patients conducted by a French neurologist (Gelbert, 1989). At the same time, Felix continued his ongoing work with his previous speech therapist. In spite of all this assistance, Felix's parents did not notice any significant increase in his performance during this school year, unlike the previous one.

Fifth Grade

Felix "loves" his fifth grade teacher and seems happy in school; however, the teacher is worried about his slowness, and the severity of his written language disorder. At the beginning of grade 5 (age 11), his reading age was that of a child at the end of grade 1 (age 7). At the same time, however, he obtained a high level in a school assessment (mean of the scores he obtained on tests that measure basic academic skills: 15/20) because he was evaluated orally and allowed to dictate his responses.

The educational and medical teams noted that Felix was less passive during this time. However, while the speech therapist reported that he was more motivated than he had been previously, she also said he was pessimistic about his reading potential, assuming that it was not possible to improve his reading level. In addition, Felix's teacher worried because it was now necessary to make recommendations for future schooling (as he was at the end of the primary grades), which would include the consideration of a special school for adolescents with specific reading disorders.

DYSLEXIA DIAGNOSIS AND TREATMENT ISSUES

As specified in a number of recent French laws and regulations, especially those published following two reports on specific language and reading impairments (Ringard, 2000; Weber & Ringard, 2001) a dyslexic child can be recognized as being a disabled person (in French "handicapé") when his/her reading deficit is severe, as is the case for Felix (see MEN [Ministry of National Education], 2002; MENSR [Ministry of National Education, Higher Education, and Research], 2006a, 2006b; see also MENSR, 2009). In order to facilitate the schooling of a disabled person, a "Projet Personnalisé de Scolarisation" (Personalized project for schooling) is drawn up to address the child's needs. This project includes integration into mainstream classrooms or in classes for children with special needs; adaptation of the time spent in school to facilitate relevant out-of-school activities (e.g., speech therapy, psychotherapy); modification of the in-class time devoted to specific curricula (e.g., increase in the time devoted to reading); support for a specialized teacher providing help with classroom exercises, inside and outside the classroom; help from a classroom assistant who for instance aids the child by reading written instructions aloud to him/her; provision of adapted pedagogical devices (e. g., computer); as well as special arrangements for exams. An educational committee, headed by a qualified teacher, examines the appropriateness of the chosen forms of educational guidance. The school teacher(s), the school physician, the school psychologist, the speech therapist, and the child's parents participate in this committee. The qualified teacher at the head of the educational committee is also in contact with the Departmental House of the Disabled, an institution that houses the human rights commission for people with disabilities. The Departmental House of the Disabled is the institution that, on the basis of diagnoses made by physicians, psychologists and/or speech therapists, decides whether a student will be recognized as being a disabled person, and thus qualify for special accommodations in and out of school.

Another French specificity is the presence of two main types of schools: public schools (from the French state, without school fees) and private schools (mainly confessional schools, such as Catholic schools, for instance, with school fees). Private schools have a contract with the state and commit to following the same rules as public schools (for instance, same curricula, and same qualification requirements for teachers, who are paid by the state). The parents are free to register their children in such schools, but they receive no financial support from the government. At the difference of a public school, a private school can refuse to register a child.

An additional French specificity is that speech therapy be provided outside of the school, like other remedial training (from psychologists and orthoptists), including psychoanalytically oriented therapy (which is often provided to children with reading disabilities in France). These forms of therapy are paid for by the parents, with some (in particular speech therapy) being reimbursed by Social Security. It is also noteworthy that French speech therapists are trained to work on reading (phonics and whole word recognition, reading comprehension) in addition to spoken language (from low-level skills such as phonology and syntax to high-level skills such as spoken language comprehension).

As previously explained (see the section on School History), Felix has benefited extensively from all the school arrangements set up to allow disabled children to maintain continuity in their school education. He has also largely received different out-of-school therapies: speech therapy, oculomotor training, and psychoanalytically oriented therapy.

Felix's First Assessment

A diagnosis of dyslexia cannot be established before reading acquisition. However, early deficits, particularly in spoken language, as well as the history of the child's family, can help to anticipate future reading difficulties. Felix's family history offered such a clue, although his spoken language development did not, at least according to the mother's reports. On the other hand, a developmental disorder could have been suspected based on the fact that, from the age of 4 years on, atypical developmental patterns had been reported both by the school and the family: in particular, Felix was reported to be slow and to have psychomotor problems.

The first comprehensive exam was conducted by a speech therapist when Felix was 6 years old. Assessment of non-verbal skills as measured by the Rey-Osterrieth Complex Figure Test (Rey, 1960) showed difficulty in visual-spatial processing for immediate, but not delayed, copying of a complex drawing with scores respectively at the 10th and 50th percentile. In the identification of reversed letters measured by the Jordan Left-Right Reversal Test—Revised (Jordan, 1990), Felix was slow and imprecise. His scores on a visual-attentional test, The Bells Test (Gauthier, Dehaut, & Joanette, 1989) were within the normal range. In terms of reading-related skills, Felix's scores in phonological awareness as measured by the Nouvelles Epreuves pour l'Examen du Langage (N-EEL; Chevrie-Muller & Plaza, 2001) were weak and a deficiency in short-term memory was observed. On the other hand, his scores on the rapid naming task were within the normal range, as were those for semantic fluency. On a widely-used French standardized test, l'Alouette (Lefavrais, 2005), Felix was designated as a non-reader (he was able to decipher only a few simple syllables). The Alouette test involves the reading aloud of a 265-word text which includes rare words and misleading contextual information (e.g. the word 'poison' [poison] rather than 'poisson' [fish] after 'lac' [lake]). Therefore, this test is useful to diagnose dyslexia, because dyslexic children make heavier use of contextual information than average readers.

Markers of deviancy in phonological information processing were therefore found, and Felix's reading deficit seemed to be very significant. However, a visual-spatial impairment due to poor processing of visual-motor information was also observed. Thus, the speech therapist directed Felix to an orthoptist to have his vision checked and trained. At that time, no other special educational arrangements were proposed. The speech therapist did, however, take the problems that had been identified into account, initiating phonological awareness training based on both spoken and written language.

Felix's Second Diagnosis

At age 8, when Felix was in grade 3, a new reading assessment using the Batterie Prédictive de l'apprentissage de la lecture et Batterie de Lecture (BP-BL; Inizan, 2000), corroborated the diagnosis of dyslexia: Felix's reading level did not differ from that of a child at the very beginning of the first grade (after 3 months of reading instruction). Compared to previous results, he had improved his memory for digit span, but his scores on phonological awareness tests remained deficient at the syllabic and phonemic levels. His scores for serial color naming were within the normal range for accuracy, but not for speed. These pieces of information reinforced the phonological hypothesis as an explanation of Felix's reading disorder.

Felix's Third Diagnosis

When Felix was 11 years old, he was given a comprehensive assessment by teams from different institutions. The psychologist who assessed his IQ

(WISC III; Wechsler, 1990) once again noted his slowness. Felix's full-scale IQ was 122, with a discrepancy between Performance IQ (107) and Verbal IQ (130), which was mainly the consequence of the fact that there were more timed measures for non-verbal than for verbal IQ. It is note-worthy that Felix managed to solve arithmetic problems even when he had to read them, which he did using a very laborious and slow decoding process. The fact that, in spite of that, he succeeded to solve arithmetic problems is probably due to his level of intelligence, associated with a high level of attention.

For visual skills, in contrast to the results obtained in the first assessments, Felix's scores were within normal range in visual-spatial processing for both immediate and delayed copying of a complex drawing; in the identification of reversed letters, his scores were only borderline.

At the same time, Felix's reading age was 7 years as determined by l'Alouette (Lefavrais, 2005). His reading skills were also assessed in greater depth using EVALEC (Sprenger-Charolles, Colé, Béchennec, & Piquard-Kipffer, 2005; Sprenger-Charolles, Colé, Piquard-Kipffer, & Leloup, 2010), a battery of tests based on Coltheart's dual-route model (e.g., Coltheart, Rastle, Perry, Langdon, & Ziegler, 2001). EVALEC thus includes reading-aloud tasks assumed to assess the efficiency of the lexical reading route (high frequency irregular word reading) and of the sublexical (or phonological) reading route (reading of unknown words, called pseudowords). For these tasks, accuracy and speed (latency of vocal responses) are taken into account. Developmental dyslexics are also assumed to suffer from deficits in phonological reading-related skills such as phonemic awareness, phonological short-term memory, and rapid automatic naming (Ramus, 2003; Ramus et al., 2003). Therefore, EVALEC includes tasks aimed at assessing phonological reading-related skills: phonemic awareness (phonemic and syllabic deletion); phonological short-term memory (repetition of three-to-six-syllable pseudowords); and Rapid Automatic Naming for colors (with a control task involving written names of colors). Accuracy and speed are taken into account.

For reading-related skills, Felix's accuracy scores were within the normal range in comparison with either same chronological age controls (CAC) or younger children of the same reading level (RLC). Alternatively, his scores for speed were below those of CAC in all the phonological awareness tasks and naming tasks and even below those of RLC on the phonemic deletion task, not the syllabic deletion task.

For reading skills, Felix's scores were consistently below the normal range, both for irregular word and pseudoword reading and both for speed and accuracy in the comparison with CAC, but only for speed in the comparison with RLC. Therefore, whatever the control group used for the comparison (CAC and RLC), Felix appeared to have a mixed profile, with an impairment of both phonological and lexical reading routes.

Reading comprehension was assessed by the standardized reading test Lire avec Epreuves pour évaluer la capacité de lecture (D-OR-LEC; Lobrot,

1973) that involved reading a story aloud twice with speed recorded followed by oral questioning. Felix's scores were within the lower quartile for speed while they were within the higher quartile for comprehension. These results indicated that Felix was able to compensate for his deficit in written word identification, and to understand a written text, but arriving at a good understanding was costly for him in terms of time.

The Relevance of Accuracy and Speed to Diagnose Dyslexia

In the previous sections of this chapter it was reported that there were strong differences between accuracy and speed in Felix's reading and reading-related skills. According to accuracy measures alone, Felix's reading level at age 11 is that of a child after one year of reading instruction (see the results of the comparison with younger children of the same reading level), suggesting that he has established basic grapheme-phoneme-correspondences, and set up a basic orthographic lexicon. However, his processing speed indicates that the mechanisms he relies on to convert graphemes into phonemes, as well as the access to his written lexicon, are far from being automatic. This result shows the importance of taking processing speed into account in reading tasks for an assessment of dyslexia, which is very often done in languages that have a more regular orthography than English. This is because in languages with a shallow orthography, accuracy scores reach a ceiling level very early (e.g., for results with French-speaking children see Sprenger-Charolles, Siegel, Béchennec, & Serniclaes, 2003; for reviews, see Share, 2008; Sprenger-Charolles et al., 2006; Ziegler & Goswami, 2005, 2006).

These results also point to the importance of taking processing speed into account in the assessment of reading-related skills, which is rarely done. This can induce diagnostic errors. Indeed, only processing speed indicates that Felix's phonological awareness scores are lower than those of a 7-year-old child—at least in the most difficult task, which involves the manipulation of phonemes, results that suggest that Felix's slowness is not general.

PARENT PERSPECTIVES

The mother clearly understands Felix's difficulties as she herself worked hard at school to achieve only average results. She is also well aware of the academic difficulties of her son, and of the consequences they could have on his academic and professional achievement. The mother thinks he should find a job where "It is not necessary to go fast." She acknowledges that, if Felix's dyslexia has had little impact on his academic results, it is because he was always evaluated orally. Felix's mother also says that her son's dyslexia has had little impact on family life, apart from the fact that she has had to accompany him (like her other children) to various therapy sessions. She acknowledges, however, that currently she does not spend enough time reading stories to him, as she (and her husband) did in the past. If she spends less time on Felix's homework, it is because she wants him to become more autonomous. She also reported some improvements: Felix now communicates via the net with his friends and does not refuse to see subtitled movies, even if he can only decode a few words.

Both parents say that they are very happy with the school arrangements made for Felix. They also both say that his teachers, at least from the private schools he has attended, have always tried to best help their son. They understood the importance of new laws for the "handicapped," and the importance of the educational team. They also have confidence in the various therapists, and understand the difficulty of treating their son's dyslexia.

CHILD PERSPECTIVES

Felix agreed to participate in this study without hesitation. He often responded to our questions, some of which he found surprising, with much subtlety. For instance, when asked about what one has to do to become a good reader, he answered "Well, I don't know, if I knew I would have done the same thing!" He also replied that computers cannot help him to read, as they do not do the reading for him. Felix also shows subtlety in not giving some expected answers: for example, the wishes he articulates do not include not suffering from dyslexia, because he thinks that this does not depend on a wish. Similarly, he does not report, among things or events that make him sad, being unable to read. He says that reading is difficult for him, that this is why he does not read, and he adds that he is not "a monster" for all that.

Felix seems to conceive reading as being mainly a functional competence, useful to answer a letter, for instance. He also misunderstands the literacy demands of different situations (e.g., indicating that he would like to be a cancer researcher because "it has nothing to do with reading and writing"). He seems not able to understand that one can read to learn, perhaps because he benefited from the fact that there is always someone who reads for him: at school, teachers, and even his classmates; at home, his mother and his older sister. Knowing that his reading difficulties are huge (according to him, 9/10 on a scale of difficulties), he probably makes as much use of the help that is available to him as he can. He also says that he is happy to go to school because he learns many things and has good grades. He does not perceive that he is failing at school even though he knows that his reading problem significantly influences school success (rating the magnitude of the problem as 8/10). Perhaps this confirms the effectiveness of the educational arrangements he has benefited from.

He speaks little about his dyslexia, except with his friends, and rarely with his parents. He believes his parents are proud of him when he reads and that they expect him to succeed so he must "hang on." Since his brother and sister are suffering from dyslexia, the question whether he speaks about dyslexia with them made him laugh. The worst thing about school for Felix is "when I have to read." He is very appreciative of his teacher's willingness to "do things instead of me . . . it's nice of her to write for me." Felix perceives the various educational and family interventions he has received quite positively. When asked who has helped him the most, he identifies his first speech therapist; he seems to be very clear about the support she has given him. He adds that without her assistance, plus the help of the educational team and his family, he would not have made any progress. He also explains that he greatly appreciates that his teacher, his friends, his parents, and his sister relieve him from the burden of reading, by reading for him.

Finally, his perception responses indicate that he is a well-adjusted child who is very social. For instance, even though the best thing about school for Felix is "play time" he says he is happy to go there because he has friends there and no one makes fun of him. He is a quiet child who rarely gets angry or complains about his friends or his relatives with the possible exception of his young brother whom he wishes were "less energetic."

CASE COMMENTARY

Felix's IQ is well above average and he was identified as being at risk for dyslexia in the first grade. He was immediately enrolled in speech therapy that included remedial reading. Special arrangements for his schooling were also established very early (starting in grade 2). In spite of this, at age 11, Felix is still facing severe reading difficulties: his reading scores are those of a child at the end of grade 1 (age 7) for accuracy, and even lower for processing speed. Therefore, his written word identification mechanisms are far from being automatic, as they usually would be at that age. As is often observed in such cases, many of his relatives also suffer from reading impairments (or more generally from learning disabilities): his mother, his sister, and his brother; the brother of his mother and *his* two children.

Felix's case also illustrates the need, for a diagnosis of dyslexia, of longitudinal data. Indeed, Felix's deficits in reading and phonology-related skills (especially, phonemic awareness) are long-lasting, a result which confirms that his reading impairment has a phonological basis. However, this deficit may have been aggravated by other problems, in visuo-motor skills, for instance. Felix's motor development was observed to be slow and a first exam (at age 6 years) revealed deficits in tasks involving visuo-motor coordination, but not in tasks involving visuo-attentional skills. However, these deficits were no longer present at age 11. In this respect, then, there can be no more than the suspicion of a delay in the development of visuo-motor skills that is now compensated, at least according to the tasks and measures taken into account.

According to some of the people responsible for Felix's education (parents, educational team, speech therapists), the persistence of his reading impairment may plausibly be explained by the fact that he was not "forced to read" enough. Indeed, from the second grade on, teachers almost always read and wrote for him, as did his classmates and his parents. In addition, his speech therapist reported that in spite of her insistence, it was very difficult to motivate Felix to read and write as he was resistant. Paradoxically, then, too much help could be a hindrance. After having correctly diagnosed the nature of the reading disorder and organized specialized schooling and therapy, then, the issue is to work out the level of effort to require from a child who fails to learn to read—and to get him/her to do what is needed to make progress, overcoming refusals and avoidance strategies. This case also illustrates the fact that, in spite of the use of appropriate forms of training—at least according to the diagnosis—results are far from what was expected.

The results of a large-scale training study with children with specific reading disorders (no children with limited intellectual ability, severe vision or hearing problems, or with English as a second language, see Vellutino, Scanlon, Sipay, Small, Pratt, Chen, & Denckla, 1996) can help us to understand Felix's case. These children received 15 weeks of training in phonemic awareness, phonics, sight word recognition, and reading comprehension in grade 1 (70 to 80 sessions lasting 30 minutes). Children who did not reach the 40th percentile in a reading test after the initial training received an additional 8-to-10 weeks of training in grade 2. Compared to a control group of average readers who received no specific training, reading achievement in most of the children with specific reading disorders was found to be at least within the average range after one semester of remediation. However, the scores of a subgroup of these children (19 out of 74 trained children) were below those of the two other groups (normal readers and poor readers readily remediated) on kindergarten and first grade measures of phonological skills, but not on measures of visual, syntactic and semantic skills. The last result is "consistent with convergent findings from previous research suggesting that reading problems in some poor readers may be caused primarily by phonological deficits" (Vellutino et al., 1996, p. 601). Another result, particularly relevant for our purpose, is that the reading difficulties of these poor readers—as is the case for Felix—are very difficult to remediate.

CONCLUSION

Despite his reading deficit, which is severe, specific and long-lasting, Felix is not experiencing severe difficulties in school. There is a large difference between his reading scores (which are very low) and his scores on tests that do not require reading (which are very high). Felix has thus benefited from help provided to children with dyslexia both inside and outside the classroom, as recommended by a number of recent French laws and regulations, and he knows how to deal with both his weaknesses and his strengths.

REFERENCES

Chevrie-Muller, C. & Plaza, M. (2001). *Nouvelles épreuves pour l'examen du langage* [New tests for language assessment]. Paris: Les Editions du Centre de Psychologie Appliquée (ECPA).

Coltheart M., Rastle K., Perry C., Langdon R., & Ziegler J. (2001). DRC: A dual route cascaded model of visual word recognition and reading aloud. *Psychological Review, 108,* 204–256.

Gauthier, L., Dehaut, F., & Joanette, Y. (1989). The Bells Test: A quantitative and qualitative test for visual neglect. *International Journal of Clinical Neuropsychology, 11,* 49–54.

Gelbert, G. (1989). Étude d'un cas d'un enfant "non-lecteur": Application de méthodes aphasiologiques [A case-study of a nonreader child using a therapy for patients with aphasia]. *Psychiatrie de l'enfant, 32* (1), 123–160.

Inizan, A. (2000). *Batterie Prédictive de l'apprentissage de la lecture et Batterie de Lecture* [BP-BL, Battery with predictive tests of reading and reading tests]. Paris: Les Editions du Centre de Psychologie Appliquée (ECPA).

Jordan, B.T. (1990). *Jordan Left-Right Reversal Test—Revised.* Hydesville: Psychological and Educational Publication.

Lefavrais, P. (2005). *Test de l'Alouette (Test de lecture standardisé)* [Test of the Lark (A standardized reading test)]. Paris: Les Editions du Centre de Psychologie Appliquée (ECPA).

Lobrot, M. (1973). *Lire avec épreuves pour évaluer la capacité de lecture (D-OR-LEC)* [Reading: Tests to assess reading skills]. Paris: Les Editions ESF.

Lyon, G.R., Shaywitz, S.E., & Shaywitz, B.A. (2003). Defining dyslexia, comorbidity, teachers' knowledge of language and reading: A definition of dyslexia. *Annals of Dyslexia, 53,* 1–14.

MEN [Ministry of National Education] (2002). Mise en œuvre d'un plan d'action pour les enfants atteints d'un trouble spécifique du langage oral ou écrit [Implementation of the Action plan for children suffering from a Specific Language Impairment or a Specific Reading Impairment]. *Bulletin officiel, 6.* Retrieved from: http://www.education.gouv.fr/bo/2002/6/default.htm.

MENSR [Ministry of National Education, Higher Education, and Research] (2006a). Programme personnalisé de réussite éducative: Mise en œuvre à l'école et au collège [Implementation of a personalized program for educational success in primary and secondary education]. *Bulletin officiel, 31.* Retrieved from: http://www.education.gouv.fr/bo/2006/31/MENE0601969C.htm.

MENSR (2006b). Mise en œuvre et suivi du projet personnalisé de scolarisation: Enseignements élémentaire et secondaire (Elèves handicapés) [Implementation and monitoring of a personalized educational project for students with disabilities (Primary and secondary education)]. *Bulletin officiel, 32.* Retrieved from: http://www.education.gouv.fr/bo/2006/32/MENE0602187C.htm.

MENSR (2009). Continuité de l'accompagnement scolaire des élèves handicapés (Enseignements élémentaire et secondaire) [Continuity of school program for students with disabilities (Primary and secondary education)]. *Bulletin officiel, 39.* Retrieved from: http://www.lemosdedys.org/ext/http://www.education. gouv.fr/cid49300/mene0922380c.html.

Ramus, F. (2003). Developmental dyslexia: Specific phonological deficit or general sensorimotor dysfunction? *Current Opinion in Neurobiology, 13*(2), 212–218.

Ramus, F., Rosen, S., Dakin, S.C., Day, B.L., Castellote, J.M., White, S., & Frith, U. (2003). Theories of developmental dyslexia: Insights from a multiple case study of dyslexic adults. *Brain, 126*, 841–865.

Rey, A. (1960). *Test de copie d'une figure complexe* [Rey-Osterrieth Complex Figure Test]. Paris: ECPA.

Ringard, J.C. (2000, Février). *A propos de l'enfant dysphasique et de l'enfant dyslexique*: Rapport [Report about the Dysphasic and Dyslexic child]. Retreived from: http://www.education.gouv.fr/cid1944/a-propos-de-l-enfant-dysphasique-et-de-l-enfant-dyslexique.html.

Share, D.L. (2008). On the Anglocentrism of current reading research and practice: The perils of overreliance on an "outlier orthography". *Psychological Bulletin, 134*, 584–615.

Sprenger-Charolles, L., Colé, P., Béchennec, D., & Kipffer-Piquard, A. (2005). French normative data on reading and related skills from EVALEC, a new computarized battery of tests. *European Review of Applied Psychology, 55*, 157–186.

Sprenger-Charolles, L., Colé, P., Piquard-Kipffer, A. & Leloup, G. (2010). *Une batterie informatisée d'évaluation diagnostique des troubles spécifiques d'apprentissage de la lecture* [A Computerized battery of diagnostic tests to assess specific reading impairment]. Isbergues: Ortho-Edition.

Sprenger-Charolles, L., Colé, P., & Serniclaes, W. (2006). *Reading acquisition and developmental dyslexia*. Hove and New-York: Psychology Press (Essays in Developmental Psychology).

Sprenger-Charolles, L., Siegel, L.S., Béchennec, D, & Serniclaes, W. (2003). Development of phonological and orthographic processing in reading aloud, in silent reading and in spelling: A four year longitudinal study. *Journal of Experimental Child Psychology, 84*, 194–217.

Vellutino, F.R., Scanlon, D.M., Sipay, E.R., Small, S.G., Pratt, A., Chen, R., & Denckla, M.B. (1996). Cognitive profiles of difficult-to-remediate and readily remediated poor-readers: Early intervention as a vehicle for distinguishing between cognitive and experiential deficits as basic causes of specific reading disability. *Journal of Educational Psychology, 88*, 601–638.

Weber, F. & Ringard, J.C. (2001, March). *Plan d'action pour les enfants atteints d'un trouble spécifique du langage* [Action plan for children suffering from Specific Language Impairments], *remis à Jack Lang (Ministre de l'Education Nationale), Bernard Kouchner (Ministre délégué à la Santé) et Dominique Gillot (Secrétaire d'État aux personnes âgées et aux personnes handicapée).* Retrieved from http://www.apedys.com/rapport_gouv.htm#plan.

Wechsler, D. (1990). *Echelle d'intelligence de Wechsler pour enfants, forme révisée.* Paris: Editions du Centre de Psychologie Appliquée (ECPA).

Ziegler, J., & Goswami, U. (2005). Reading acquisition, developmental dyslexia and skilled reading across languages: A psycholinguistic grain size theory. *Psychological Bulletin, 131*, 3–29.

Ziegler, J. C., & Goswami, U. (2006). Becoming literate in different languages: Similar problems, different solutions. *Developmental Science, 9*, 429–436.

FELIX'S INTERVIEW

1. What do you want to be when you grow up?
   I'd like to be a researcher to find a treatment for cancer.

Why do you think you would be good at that job?

I don't know because I like it . . . it has nothing to do with reading nor writing, which are too hard for me . . . with science you don't have to write all the time.

2. Tell me about a teacher who has been really important to you or one who has helped you: what did the teacher do to help you?

    As a matter of fact, almost all my teachers have helped me. Mrs. E. [speech therapist] helped me to improve in reading and writing.

3. Tell me about a teacher who didn't really help you that much or one who did not give you the help you needed. What did you want the teacher to do to help you?

    I don't remember very well, I think I was in grade 2 and I was not allowed to go to playtime because I was too slow. It happened in another school I think.

4. Tell me what your mother thinks about your dyslexia. Does she talk to you about the problem? What does she say?

    Sometimes we talk about it. She says it's ok if I can't do it sometimes. She says I have to hold on . . . well, she doesn't complain.

5. Tell me what your father thinks about your dyslexia. Does he talk to you about the problem?

    Dad, I don't know, we don't talk about that. As a matter of fact both tell me I must hold on and I must not give up.

6. Tell me about something that makes you really happy.

    I'd rather go to the swimming pool than read . . . there are some things I like . . . well . . . I like to go to the swimming pool, and racing sports like motorbike or quad. I also like going to summer camp during holidays.

7. Tell me about something that makes you really sad.

    Sad? If someone dies in my family I would be sad.

8. When the work gets very hard at school and you think you can't do it, what do you do?

    I often try . . . it is always difficult but I am not going to give up because it's hard.

9. What kinds of books do you like to read?

    As a matter of fact I don't really read books. . . . . . heroic fantasy books.

    Do you read to yourself?

    No.

    Who else reads to you?

    Most of the time it's Mom. But it's Dad who read Spiderwick to me.

10. Do your friends know that you have dyslexia?

    Yes.

Do you talk to them about it?
Uh, no . . .

What do your friends say to you about dyslexia?
They don't say anything because we don't talk about it. They live with it.

11. Do your siblings know that you have dyslexia?
Because (He laughs, his brother and his sister also have dyslexia).

Do you talk to them about it?
Well, no . . .

12. Name three things you are really good at:
Math . . . but really, there is nothing I am very good at . . . maybe in science. There was something else but I don't remember what.

[interviewer asks about swimming]
Yes, but that's not a school thing.

13. Name three things you are not so good at:
French, it depends and then [long pause] writing and conjugation as well.

14. If you are feeling bad about your reading, is there one person you can talk to who makes you feel better?
Sometimes I can talk about it with my friends but that's all.

15. Do computers help you with your reading?
No, they don't read for me.

16. Do you usually have problems with your homework?
Yes and no. Sometimes I forget my notebooks or sometimes I forget to write my homework.

Can you do your homework independently or does someone help you?
There are some things I can do by myself and some I can't.

Is homework a big problem or just a little one?
Before it was hard, but now it's OK. For me homework is not a big deal! For sure I'd rather do something else.

17. If there was one thing you could change about school, what would it be?
[Pause] No, it's ok.

18. If you could have three wishes, what would they be?
(1) It wouldn't be not to be dyslexic any more.
(2) Maybe that there won't be disease in the world anymore.
(3) Well, I wish not to be sad sometimes.

19. Tell me three things you would like your teacher to do to help you with your dyslexia?
As I said before when I have to dictate my answers to my teacher and when I have to read instructions.

20. Who is the best reader in your class?
    I don't know, they are all good at reading.

    How did he/she get to be such a good reader?
    Well, I don't know, if I knew I would have done the same thing!

21. Is it important to learn how to read?
    Well, yes it is! If you want to read road signs . . . when you receive a letter for your work for example or things like that, you must read it, it's important.

3   Hassan, a Case Study of Dyslexia in Egypt

Soad A. Shahin

Hassan is a 10-year-old boy, who was diagnosed as dyslexic at the age of 7. He is a healthy, good-looking child who is polite and has an excellent sense of humor. Hassan is a bright child who was very cooperative throughout the interview, answering all questions. However, during the interview Hassan was observed looking to his mother frequently as he was responding to the questions. When the interviewer asked him why he was doing this, he did not answer, but smiled. The mother interjected that Hassan likes to see approval in his mother's expression.

BACKGROUND

Family History

Hassan lives with his parents and 5-year-old sister, Randa, in an upper-middle-class suburb of Cairo. His father is a civil engineer and his mother is an economic researcher. Hassan's father did not experience any difficulty in school; however, he has a nephew who was diagnosed as dyslexic at the age of 8. Hassan's mother thinks that she has mild dyslexia, as she had a very difficult time learning English. She doesn't like to write emails or letters in English. Her sister, Hassan's aunt, left school before obtaining a high school diploma because of difficulties in learning languages and math. The family could not find any professional to assess her learning problems in Egypt, but when she was 19 she was finally tested in England and subsequently diagnosed as dyslexic. Hassan's uncle (his mother's brother) could not obtain the certificate of primary school; he could only read and write well enough to work in a store. At that time there was little awareness of learning disabilities in Egypt and the general perception was that the uncle was spoiled when he was growing up as he was the only brother of five sisters.

Medical History

Hassan was born by Caesarean delivery at 38 weeks gestation. The mother's narrow pelvis precluded the possibility of a typical delivery. He was a healthy baby, but cried more than usual. There was always a problem during feeding as he had sucking difficulty. In spite of the feeding problem, his mother continued to breast feed him for two years with supplementary bottle feeding. Hassan suffered from frequent ear infections since he was 2-years-old. These infections occurred almost on a monthly basis and were treated with antibiotics and ear drops. Along with the ear infections, he had upper respiratory viruses that were treated with medication, tonsil inflammation, and asthma. As Hassan became older, these infections and colds decreased until they disappeared when he was between 6 and 7 years of age.

Early Development

Hassan's mother reported that he continued to cry excessively without reason throughout his first year of birth. He started teething at 6 months, which may have been related to the crying. Hassan demonstrated unusual early motor development as he did not crawl. At the age of 1 year he stood up. He walked at 15 months. His language development was delayed as he did not speak his first words until the age of 18 months and began using sentences much later. Hassan had other peculiarities in his language development. For example, he referred to every meal as *dinner* and he could not discriminate between the names of different meals until he was 9 years old. His mother reported that he also had unusual memory problems related to events. He could not remember his birthday, the sequence of months of the year or the sequence of years. He also could not remember important holidays or religious events, such as feasts and prayer times, especially Dohr, Asr and Maghreb. Only recently, at the age of 10, has he started to become more aware of the sequence of these occasions. At the age of 2 Hassan started playing with paper and a pencil, pretending that he was drawing or writing. His mother believes that this early drawing was perhaps related to his interest in the artwork in the many books she exposed him to as a young child. She spent a good deal of time reading stories to him. Hassan continued to experience eating problems during childhood. He had a poor appetite and ate very little. He typically vomited more than once a day even though he was not eating much. Riding in a car presented particular difficulty as this increased the vomiting. Hassan also had sleep problems; it was very hard for him to sleep unless his mother held him and sang lullabies.

His mother had to watch him constantly as a young child as Hassan had a problem with pica. He put everything in his mouth regardless of his mother's attentive care. That was the reason she decided to put him in nursery school when he was 2½ years of age. He stayed there almost two years. In nursery school, he loved coloring, drawing, listening to music and swimming, but it was clear that he had a very difficult time playing with the other children. He loved his toys and was so attached to them that he refused to let other children play with them. His mother thought that this may have been the reason why he could not get along with the other children. He started swimming lessons at the age of 3½, but he never learned to ride a bike.

In nursery school he began to show a talent in painting. He drew lots of whales, crabs and other types of fish. His drawings were not detailed, but accurately illustrated the current posture of the characters. Hassan also started using computers at a very early age and was playing computer games at the age of four.

SCHOOL HISTORY

Kindergarten

There are two types of schools in Egypt: Arabic schools (public schools) that teach all subjects in Arabic, and provide English, French or German as second languages, and Language schools that teach all subjects in English, French or German, in addition to providing Arabic language classes. Children are accepted in the first primary grade at age 6–7 years. Before primary school children usually spend two years in kindergarten (i.e., kindergarten 1 and kindergarten 2). According to the recommendations from the Ministry of Education, public school children are not required to read and write at these early education levels. All of the material in the kindergarten curriculum is illustrated by pictures. In Language schools, the second language (English, French, or German) is started in the first year of kindergarten and reading and writing are required in both levels of kindergarten.

Hassan started kindergarten at an English school at the age of 3 years and 8 months. In kindergarten 1, the school taught Hassan both Arabic and English letters and numbers. Identifying letters and numbers was a huge problem for him. The teachers concentrated on teaching the English capital letters. After a few months they taught him to identify and write easy English words. Spelling proved to be the greatest challenge for him. His mother reported that the school was not supportive or sensitive to the children's needs. She had to help him every day at home with his schoolwork. Finally, she became so frustrated with the lack of support from the teachers that she decided to change schools. Hassan began a new English school when he was 4 years and 8 months old. But the new school was a disappointment. It was not a good experience for him as the methods of teaching did not provide Hassan with the help he needed, and the school did not seem to support and nurture the children. Spelling continued to present significant problems for Hassan. The teacher did not teach all Arabic letters and again concentrated on capital English letters. His mother continued to help him daily, but without the support of his teachers, he did poorly. The mother decided once again that she needed to find a new school for Hassan. His mother reported that it was during this time that Hassan became particularly fond of cartoons and animated films, especially those that featured whales, gorillas and dinosaurs. He also became very interested in insects and has continued to be fascinated with them, trying to learn about them on television programs, such as the "Magic School Bus."

First Grade

Hassan started first grade in a new English Language school when he was 5 years and 8 months, which was young compared to the other children, whose ages ranged from 6½ to 7½ years. His mother had wanted Hassan to repeat kindergarten 2 as she felt his learning had been insufficient, but his father insisted on placing him in first grade even though he was the youngest child in the class. In this school, the demands of the homework were unreasonable. The first grade curriculum included all of the Arabic and English letters, numbers and spelling. The mother reported that she helped him a lot every day and used a variety of different computer programs for the English and Arabic alphabets, but the help was insufficient for his learning needs. It wasn't a good experience for the child and the mother began to suspect that Hassan had a learning problem. She discussed this problem with the father, but he refused to allow Hassan to be taken to a clinic for evaluation. The father believed that Hassan was completely normal and that the school was responsible for any problems he was experiencing. As a result, the mother once again decided to move Hassan to another school.

Second Grade

Hassan started his new school in second grade at the age of 6 years and 8 months. This school was a very good English Language school that was more responsive to his needs. In the middle of the first semester, a British teacher referred him for assessment. The mother reported that Hassan was subsequently diagnosed as dyslexic. She did not receive any of the assessment reports so was unaware of the specifics of the diagnosis. The teacher explained Hassan's problem to the mother as a type of learning disability and told her it could be attributed to genetics. She recommended that the mother make letters from clay and use these to teach Hassan. She also referred the mother to the Egyptian Dyslexia Association for additional materials and support. The father refused to listen to the explanation and would not allow Hassan to go to the Association. He insisted that Hassan needed to work harder and receive more help from the mother. It appeared that this situation caused a lot of pressure for Hassan and his mother. The mother made the clay letters and continued to help Hassan with his reading. In general, she was satisfied with the new school as she felt they used sound methods of teaching for all of the children. Hassan started to identify letters by making body movements to associate with these letters. He imagined Arabic letters in reference to body movements and posture. For example, Hassan would say that the Arabic letter ق is sitting on the floor but the Arabic letter ﺐ is lying on his side. Whenever his mother asked about one of these letters he asked "which one—is it the one that is sitting on the floor or the one that is lying on its side?" The teachers were very knowledgeable about dyslexia and professional in their instructional approach and Hassan was beginning to show improvement. Unfortunately, the school suddenly closed, and this left the family with no option except to look for another school for Hassan.

Third and Fourth Grades

At the age of 7 years and 8 months, Hassan was transferred to a new Language school for the third grade. Hassan's mother reported that this level was a good experience for her son because the previous school had addressed his dyslexia and Hassan was showing improvement. The mother also continued to work with Hassan, which was also helpful. However, a new problem arose in third grade because he had to learn a third language. The mother chose French for Hassan's third language but it was very difficult for him and the mother could not offer her son any help because she did not know this language. So she hired a special teacher. The new teacher initially complained about Hassan, but then began to help him as she recognized that he was actually very bright, but had a learning problem. At this point, the mother decided to come to the Egyptian Dyslexia Association alone to obtain more information about dyslexia. She attended one of the training courses that provided a comprehensive explanation of dyslexia, which included an explanation of symptoms, causes, learning strategies, teaching strategies as well as assessment practices, homework issues, and related math problems and technology assistance.

The mother started to use everything she learned about dyslexia to help her child. This same year, Hassan started to attract his teacher's attention to his talent in music; he became accomplished in playing the flute. The music teacher trained him frequently until he could play different pieces of music. During third grade, he started to take many different subjects including Arabic, English, science, mathematics, social science, French, music, art, religion and other activities. Hassan had a difficult time with organization and he could not remember the materials he needed for his classes or the schedule. Every day he carried all of his books and notes with him to school to avoid forgetting any of them. Hassan continued fourth grade in the same school, which accepted him even though he had learning problems. He proved himself quite capable in art, music and basketball. The physical education teacher chose him to be on the basketball team. Hassan won an award in basketball and started to improve in reading and writing. However, he continued to have problems with organization and his schedule, which he still experiences today.

During fourth grade, the mother was very attentive to Hassan's school performance and homework. She was careful to keep the telephone numbers of a few students in his class to check with them about homework or any activities needed for her son. She also met with the Arabic language teacher, and explained Hassan's spelling problem and politely requested that she not put pressure on him. Fortunately, the teacher was sensitive to Hassan's learning difficulties and started to address his specific instructional needs. In spite of all of the mother's efforts, some of the teachers accused Hassan of being careless, which resulted in a detention warning. The director of the school gave Hassan the detention warning letter for his parents when he was standing in the morning line. The letter stated that if he continued to be careless and did not complete his work, he would be punished by staying in class during every break until his work was finished. If the work was not finished by the end of the school week, Hassan would have to stay late every Thursday (the last day of the school week in Egypt). Before he distributed the letters, the school director announced the names of all students, including Hassan, who were to be punished. His cousins, who attended that same school, heard his name and that caused Hassan to become very embarrassed. He did not tell his mother anything about the incident for two weeks, until Feast time when he refused to go to his cousins' house to celebrate. After Hassan told his mother the whole story, she asked to meet with the school director. At this meeting she explained everything she had learned about dyslexia and asked the director to contact the Egyptian Dyslexia Association to provide training for Hassan's school. The director was supportive and made arrangements for the Association to provide the training course at the school. Both the director and Hassan's father attended that course. The director, after hearing the course information about dyslexia, asked the teachers to make photocopies of all class materials for Hassan to take home and permitted him to have extra time in any school exams except those from the Ministry of Education. The director told the teachers to address Hassan's instructional needs. She did everything possible to compensate for the announcement of his detention in the morning line that had caused so much embarrassment. Hassan gained confidence and he received good marks for fourth grade. He obtained the highest grade possible in science, which reflected his interest in this area. Hassan was particularly interested in plants and animals. He owned an aloe plant and two pets (a cat and a turtle), which he carefully tended.

In addition to Hassan's reading problems, he also experienced social difficulty. He had few friends and those he did have were considerably younger than Hassan. His mother started to think about ways to make age appropriate friends for him. She invited the polite students to his birthday and also invited them to special parties she arranged for Hassan. She made him bring presents to children at school. The mother's objectives were to increase his social circle and to have contacts that Hassan could call about homework assignments. The mother asked the father for permission to bring Hassan to the Egyptian Dyslexia Association to talk to someone familiar with dyslexia because he was experiencing self-esteem problems related to his school performance. Hassan had written derogatory names on most of his school books referring to himself as "bad boy," "donkey," and "stupid." It was apparent to the mother that Hassan had come to the conclusion that he was unintelligent. When Hassan finally visited the Egyptian Dyslexia Association, he was encouraged to talk about his strengths, such as the award he won in basketball and his talent in music. He told the Association staff that whenever they had a party at his school, he was always chosen to play the flute for the guests. In this interview, the staff encouraged Hassan to focus on his abilities rather than his problems.

DYSLEXIA DIAGNOSIS AND TREATMENT ISSUES

At the age of 7 years, while in second grade, Hassan was assessed and subsequently diagnosed as dyslexic. This is a very young age to be diagnosed as dyslexic; however, it should be noted that Hassan had experienced three years of school failure and had changed schools three times because of difficulty before he received this diagnosis. The Egyptian language school system is quite demanding in that children are expected to begin to identify letters when they are in the first grade of kindergarten. Hassan was not even 4 years old when letters were first introduced to him. He experienced a great deal of difficulty for both years of kindergarten as well as first and second grades. It was not until mid-year in second grade that he was finally assessed and diagnosed as dyslexic. The mother did not receive any written reports of the assessment or diagnosis. She was provided only with an oral report, explaining that Hassan had a learning disability that was genetically based. The school was closed shortly after this time and the family was not able to access the written diagnostic report. Hassan struggled in school for three and a half years because of the unusual demands of the curriculum in Egypt (i.e., the requirement of children at the ages of 4 and 5 to begin reading).

Hassan represents a very special case in dyslexia as he was learning two written language systems simultaneously (i.e., English and Arabic) and then added a third (French). Research has reported that primary grade children in Egypt who are bilingual experience more difficulties in learning to read and write than do peers who are monolingual Arabic speakers (Mousa, 2006). In fact, Arabic appeared to be the easiest language of the three for Hassan. Arabic has a 28-letter alphabet (i.e., 17 characters with diacritical markings that provide the complete alphabet) that is phonemic with almost every letter representing consistent individual sounds so spelling is easier than it is for English. However, in colloquial Arabic, the diacritical marks that represent various short vowels are not used, which can lead to misunderstandings of the text. The frequency of inflectional morphemes, the irregularity of verb conjugation, and the elaborate use of dots to differentiate graphemes bear responsibility for dyslexia in monolingual Arabic speakers (Elbeheri, 2004). All Arabic is written in cursive, which helps children as there is only one system that they need to learn, but as Elbeheri (2004) noted, this can also be a drawback as independent characters cannot be written. In spite of the irregular linguistic characteristics of the Arabic language, its challenges are minimal compared to the English language with its characteristic low transparency and requisite high degree of memorization. It has been suggested that English may in fact be one of the most difficult languages for dyslexic children to acquire (Spencer, 2000). Thus, it is not surprising that Hassan had many more difficulties in English than Arabic. His literacy problems were compounded in third grade when he started to learn French, which was also a very difficult language with low transparency. His reading, writing and spelling problems became even more pronounced in this language.

Although all of Hassan's teachers noticed his reading problems, it is interesting to note that this child did not receive direct remediation services for this difficulty. Some of the teachers provided accommodation for his needs and recommendations for the mother to support his instruction, but he did not receive direct instruction for his dyslexia from any of the schools he attended. Perhaps if his second grade English Language School had not closed abruptly, there would have been assistance forthcoming from those teachers who appeared to be the most knowledgeable about dyslexia.

There were also family variables that influenced Hassan's diagnosis and treatment as the parents were in disagreement about their son's problems. The father felt that Hassan's problems were the result of the child being overly gratified by the mother. He did not believe that his son had a bona fide learning problem. The mother has been a tremendous source of support for Hassan throughout his development. She was keenly aware of his problems from the beginning of his school experience and has sought resourceful ways of providing him with assistance. Her contact with the Egyptian Dyslexia Association was particularly beneficial and led to positive changes in many different areas of Hassan's life. The father began to accept Hassan's learning difficulties only after he attended meetings at the Association. Hassan's support at school increased substantially after the Director arranged to have the training course on instructional methods for dyslexia presented to all of the teachers. After that point, many significant changes were made to Hassan's curriculum, which in turn allowed him to experience success. Hassan also received counseling at the Association that helped him to better understand his disability in light of other talents and strengths he possessed.

PARENT PERSPECTIVES

Hassan's mother describes him as a "polite, talented, and innocent" child. She noted that he has special talent in art and music; he is quite accomplished in drawing and playing the flute. He reads fictional stories and magazines independently, but his mother reads to him for studying purposes. She noted that she reads to him at home approximately 28 hours per week to help him study. Hassan enjoys watching cartoons on television and does this for over eight hours per day when he is on vacation and an hour a day on school days.

His mother reported that Hassan has always been socially immature for his age. He currently has only one friend. He is often rejected by peers because his behavior seems very childish compared to that of the other children. When he was young, he had a strong desire to play football with other children; however, once he tried this, he became very frightened of the ball. He ended up crying and the children teased and laughed at him. The mother noted that Hassan has always seemed different from other children, at least in terms of what others think of him. Even though Hassan has cousins that are the same age, who have lived in the same house, and attended the same school, they did not play together. According to the mother, the cousins seemed very different in their social development compared to Hassan. The mother has repeatedly tried to address these social problems by arranging social activities, but these efforts have resulted in limited success in this area. On the Parent Perception Scale, she identified Hassan's social life as the area that is the most significantly affected by his dyslexia.

The mother thinks that her child's life will be different because he can't read easily and he hates doing his homework. The mother perceives Hassan's dyslexia to be significant (rating 7/10). She also believes that the problem will significantly affect school success and family life (rating each of these as a 7 also).

The mother indicated that the most difficult aspect of Hassan's reading problem is the fact that he is very slow. Homework is a significant problem because the assignments are too long and Hassan works so slowly. She helps him most of the time, but it is still an arduous and frustrating experience for both of them. Hassan doesn't seem to have a normal sense of time; he has confusion with weekly, monthly and yearly calendar dates and hours of the day. He also has problems paying attention. He can read by himself with relatively good comprehension, but he seems to miss quite a bit of information. When the mother reads to him, he understands and retains the information better. The mother thinks that it is useless to let him read by himself so she continues to read to him while he is studying. She is very concerned that his inability to read independently will significantly interfere with his school success.

The mother is somewhat satisfied with the progress that Hassan has made with his dyslexia thus far, but she continues to hope for more improvement. She does not feel that the Egyptian government has sufficient awareness of dyslexia and therefore the teachers do not have the knowledge to help these children in the classrooms. The mother is also concerned about the way dyslexic students are treated in the schools today. She believes that it is important that these children be respected instead of punished as they have no control over their learning problems.

CHILD PERSPECTIVES

In spite of the fact that Hassan does not have a satisfying social life, he has strong ties with his family and hobbies that he enjoys. Every week he goes to sport club with his father, mother and sister where he swims and plays basketball. He has experienced some measure of success in both of these sports. Hassan has also enjoyed accomplishment in music with his flute performances. His mother has supported him throughout all of his struggles and remains a strong advocate for him. However, it is interesting to note that Hassan's perceptions regarding the influence of dyslexia are very different from those of his mother. For example, he does not believe that his reading problem is significant (rating it a 3/10). Neither does he believe that it interferes significantly with school success, family life or social life. In spite of Hassan's reading difficulties, he reports that he reads a lot and thinks that the most difficult thing about having a problem with reading is being slow in the comprehension of text, which leads to difficulties in answering the questions within the time provided for exams.

From Hassan's responses on the Sentence Completion questions, it appeared that the main problem in his social life is lack of friendships, and the major problem in his school life is the homework. In the Egyptian educational system, homework is one of the most significant factors for many students. Most families complain about homework and it is a huge challenge for most students, especially those with learning problems. Hassan considers the worst thing in school to be the amount of homework, which causes pressure on him. He stated that when he does his homework, he feels "exhausted." Hassan's mother helps him by reading to him so the homework will take less time. Hassan stated:

> Understanding and pronouncing words is very difficult for me, but when Mother reads for me I could understand, but if I was trying to read I wound up skipping over a hard word and nothing made sense after that. I can do well with easy stuff, but if it gets harder my mother reads to me. When I read something other than school stuff, I find it easier or maybe it is more interesting to me.

Hassan's Sentence Completion responses for socialization appeared to be somewhat inconsistent, as he said that the best thing about school is "having lots of friends," which is interesting in light of the fact that he only has one friend and is rejected by most of the other students. However, when completing the sentence "sometimes I wish my friends would . . ." he responded "be closer to me" revealing a desire to have stronger friendships. He appreciates the relationship he has with his best friend and feels happy when he helps him, and sad when the friend faces any problem. Hassan pointed out that he doesn't like it when teachers deduct points for something he didn't do. He explained this as occurring when a teacher, for example, gives dictation or math and deducts points for poor handwriting.

According to Hassan, his classmates perceive him to be a hard worker and, like any student, he likes having bonus points for his work. Hassan enjoys drawing, which is his favorite thing to do. He stated that other kids like him because he is nice to them, but they make fun of him because he gets "worried about exams." Hassan seems to be a very ambitious child who strives to earn high grades, which is not always possible because of his dyslexia. He feels that his parents expect him to study well and they are proud of him when he gets high grades, and on the contrary, they are disappointed when he gets bad grades. Hassan may be feeling pressure from his parents as he stated that they always expect him to study hard and he would like them to leave him alone. He also wishes that his little sister would be more understanding.

As indicated in the interview of the child, Hassan likes his teachers to help him with his dyslexia by allowing him to talk to them during their break times to receive additional explanation for work. He also wants them to help him by giving additional time for exams and extending homework assignments. He wishes there was a way to decrease the amount of homework in school. When work gets too hard for him, he tries to concentrate as much as possible. He also tries to relax and sometimes he takes a break and then returns to work.

In spite of Hassan's learning difficulties and bad experience in schools, he is very optimistic and ambitious. He wants to be an engineer when he grows up because he loves math and drawing. Hassan's father is an engineer and his career aspiration may be related to his affection and admiration for him. He loves his family and his best friend, noting that if anything happened to them it would make him very sad. Hassan is enthusiastic about the teacher who inspired his interest in math. This was his teacher in third and fourth grades, who gave him the highest grade possible in math. In sharp contrast to his experience with the math teacher, Hassan complained that his first grade teacher did not explain anything to the children and gave them too much homework. He clearly recognizes the importance of reading and understands it is key to increasing "knowledge about anything." Hassan likes to read horror stories and science fiction books, both of which he reads independently. He prefers to read from the computer as it is easier for him than reading from books.

Hassan apparently does not confide in anyone about his dyslexia, except his only friend. As indicated in his interview, he does not speak with his mother, father or sister about his reading problems. Hassan is not embarrassed of being dyslexic; he explained dyslexia to his only friend in reference to a long list of famous accomplished people with whom he shared this disability, including Walt Disney, Einstein and Leonardo de Vinci.

CASE COMMENTARY

In Hassan's case, there were a number of relatives in his family suspected of having dyslexia, including his uncle, aunt, and his mother, suggesting that genetics played a role in the transmission of the reading problem. Hassan had frequent ear infections when he was young, which may also be associated with his dyslexia. He had difficulties with spelling as well as phonological processing that are common problems exhibited by Arabic dyslexic children (Mannai & Everatt, 2005; Elbeheri & Everatt, 2007).

From an early age, Hassan demonstrated a number of different language, motor and socialization problems that interfered with his functioning. His case was further complicated by the demands of the school system, (i.e., requiring him to begin learning and writing letters at the age of three in two different languages) and the fact that he changed schools three times in his first three years. Hassan was fortunate to meet the British teacher who was knowledgeable about dyslexia and concerned enough to provide a formal assessment for him. After he was diagnosed as dyslexic, this teacher also provided appropriate instructional recommendations to the mother who followed through with these. His mother was very active in her support of him, helping him learn his letters with different methods that created strong visual and tactile memories. As a result of this support, Hassan was able to make progress in the area of reading. Hassan is a very hard worker and over the years he has developed some good strategies for dealing with the stress he faces in the classroom, such as trying to relax and taking short breaks to improve concentration.

Hassan also has an excellent imagination, which probably helps him in drawing and writing fiction. His mother proudly shared the following story as a reflection of his creative imagination. When the interviewer asked about the lack of spelling and grammatical errors, the mother indicated that his English teacher had corrected it. Hassan declined to share the original as he was ashamed of his spelling mistakes.

> *Today, as I was walking from school, a spaceship landed right in front of me! An alien with eyes like a cat and long spidery legs walked out.*
>
> *"I am hungry," he said "I have come to your planet in search of books to eat."*
>
> *"Books aren't food," I said.*
>
> *"That's the craziest thing I ever heard" said the alien. "I love good books! Right now I am craving a big fat math book." He started to walk towards me and started staring at me.*
>
> *"Where do you come from?" I asked.*
>
> *"I came from the fifth Galaxy," he answered.*
>
> *"Why did you come to earth?" I asked.*
>
> *"I came to earth to eat books all over the seven Galaxies," he answered.*
>
> *"How long have you been here?" I asked.*
>
> *"One hour and 30 minutes and half second," he answered.*
>
> *"Have you ever been in that Galaxy before?" I asked.*
>
> *"I came once 1000000 years ago," he answered.*

"How are you getting along with the language?" I asked.

"Your language is easy and it consists of 24 letters only, in my language we have 180000 letters," he answered.

" What do you like here?" I asked.

"The taste of French books, they taste delicious," he answered.

"What do you hate here?" I asked.

"German books they cause allergy," he answered.

"What are your plans for the future?"

"I am planning to taste all books in the universe," he said.

"I hope you achieve what you want."

Hassan is a very bright and ambitious child who wants to be an engineer, but he may later change his mind and decide on a career that is more creative and consistent with his strengths in the area of creative arts (design, graphics, advertising, etc.) or he may choose to do something that is related to his strong interest in plants and animals. In any event, he will need continued support from his teachers to succeed to the best of his capability.

Hassan's case is only one of hundreds of cases of dyslexia in Egyptian schools. Lack of awareness of dyslexia is the main reason that teachers treat dyslexic children as if they were spoiled, stupid or sometimes slow learners, recommending their transfer to special need schools for students with intellectual disabilities as a solution for addressing reading problems. There are many special education learning centers in Cairo and other cities in Egypt, many of which provide support for disabilities such as mental retardation, but there are few services for dyslexia. There is also a lack of qualified individuals who can administer diagnostic assessment for children suspected of having dyslexia and until recently there were no tests that focus specifically on this disability. Although various intellectual measures (e.g., the Stanford Binet and Wechsler Scales) have been translated and standardized for the Egyptian community, there are no available funds to administer these. Additionally, there is no formal teacher training that deals strictly with dyslexia. Although during their professional training at the university, the topic of learning disabilities is discussed in general terms, pre-service teachers are not provided with specific information that focuses on dyslexia (Elbeheri, 2004). Thus, it is not surprising that teachers misinterpret behaviors associated with dyslexia and punish children instead of providing the support needed to be successful.

At the current time there are no laws or regulations in support of dyslexics, so it is very difficult for these students to be granted special accommodations (e.g., extended time for examinations, particularly for Certificate exams that come from the Ministry of Education). Such accommodations would encourage successful achievement in schools, and things are slowly improving in Egypt as there are developing projects that are beginning to address dyslexia in the schools. The Egyptian Dyslexia Association was founded in Cairo in 2005. It's a non-profit association that serves dyslexic students of all ages as well as their families and communities. The Association provides diagnoses, educational therapy and training courses in dyslexia for teachers, parents and psychologists. In 2009, the Egyptian Dyslexia Association in collaboration with the Kuwait Dyslexia Association implemented a pilot program for dyslexia screening in the Gawad Housney Primary Public School in North Giza Arabic. This screening involved the administration of the Cognitive Profiling System (CoPS; Singleton & Leedale, 2001), which is a computerized psychometric assessment system developed for dyslexia screening for children from 4 years to 8 years-11 months. This assessment system was translated and standardized to the Arabic culture by the Kuwait Dyslexia Association (Qatamy, 2007). The results of this pilot program revealed that 9.8% of the 305 children (63% males and 37% females) who were screened were determined to be at risk for dyslexia. This high incidence of students at risk for dyslexia has attracted significant attention to this problem in Egypt.

The Egyptian Dyslexia Association has submitted several projects to increase dyslexia awareness and to address dyslexia in the schools, such as the "dyslexia friendly schools project." In cooperation with the Kuwait Dyslexia Association, the Egyptian Dyslexia Association is working toward the implementation of this model. There are four important steps required for a school to achieve the status of *dyslexia friendly*. These steps include (1) screening for dyslexia, (2) providing dyslexia training courses for school faculty, (3) implementing diagnostic techniques for referred cases, and (4) providing effective dyslexia treatment. As Egypt continues to move forward with its commitment to supporting those with dyslexia, there is reason to be hopeful that Hassan and other children like him will experience improved services and increased opportunities for success.

REFERENCES

Elbeheri, G. (2004). Dyslexia in Egypt. In I. Smythe, J, Everatt & R. Salter (Eds.) *International book of dyslexia: A guide to practice and resources*. West Sussex: John Wiley & Sons, Ltd.

Elbeheri, G. & Everatt, J. (2007). Literacy ability and phonological processing skills amongst dyslexic and non-dyslexic speakers of Arabic. *Reading and Writing, 20*, 273–294.

Mannai, H., & Everatt, J. (2005). Phonological processing skills as predictors of literacy amongst Arabic speaking Bahraini children. *Dyslexia, 11* (4), 269–291.

Mousa D.A. (2006). صعوبات تعلم القراءة والكتابة باللغة العربية في كل من الأطفال مدارس الابتدائية (دراسة مقارنة) ثنائي اللغة والمتعلمين باللغة العربية في أطفال مدارس الابتدائية (دراسة مقارنة) [Difficulties in learning to read and write Arabic in both bilingual and Arabic learners within primary school children (a comparative study)]. Unpublished Master's thesis. Ein Shams University, Cairo, Institute of Childhood Studies.

Qatamay, M.Y. (2007, November 19). *Arabic Cognitive Profiling System (CoPS)*. Paper presented at the Regional Conference of Psychology, Cairo.

Singleton. H., Thomas, K.V. & Leedale, R.C. (2001). *Cognitive Profiling System (CoPS) Teacher's manuel* (2nd ed.). East Yorkshire: Lucid Research Limited.
Spencer, K. (2000). Is English a dyslexic language? *Dyslexia*, 6, 152–162.

HASSAN'S INTERVIEW

1. What do you want to be when you grow up?
   An engineer.
   Why do you think you would be good at that job?
   Because I love arithmetic and drawing.

2. Tell me about a teacher who has been really important to you or one who has helped you: what did the teacher do to help you?
   Mr. A., he was my math teacher for two years and with his help I always took the highest grade in math and he was the one that made me love math.

3. Tell me about a teacher who didn't really help you that much or one who did not give you the help you needed. What did you want the teacher to do to help you?
   The teacher who taught me in first grade, she didn't explain anything and gave a lot of homework.

4. Tell me what your mother thinks about your dyslexia. Does she talk to you about the problem?
   No.

5. Tell me what your father thinks about your dyslexia. Does he talk to you about the problem?
   No.

6. Tell me about something that makes you really happy.
   Drawing, meeting my friend and playing sports.

7. Tell me about something that makes you really sad.
   Something bad that happened to one of my family or to my friend.

8. When the work gets very hard at school and you think you can't do it, what do you do?
   I try to concentrate and be relaxed and sometimes I take a break and then come back to work.

9. What kinds of books do you like to read?
   Science fiction and horror stories.
   What is your favorite book?
   Harry Potter.
   Do you read to yourself?
   Yes.

Who else reads to you?
Nobody.

10. Do your friends know that you have dyslexia?
    No, my colleagues don't know.

    Do you talk to them about it?
    Sometimes.

    What do you say?
    I have only one friend, I tell him I'm dyslexic and explain to him what it is, but I don't tell anyone else.

    What do your friends say to you about dyslexia?
    I don't talk with my colleagues about it, and they don't know about it.

11. Do your siblings know that you have dyslexia?
    No.

    Do you talk to them about it?
    No.

12. Name three things you are really good at:
    Drawing, basketball and swimming.

13. Name three things you are not so good at:
    Football and volleyball.

14. If you are feeling bad about your reading, is there one person you can talk to who makes you feel better?
    No.

15. Do computers help you with your reading?
    Yes.

    If yes, how do they help you?
    When I read from computers I find it easier than reading from a book.

16. Do you usually have problems with your homework?
    Sometimes.

    Can you do your homework independently or does someone help you?
    Sometimes my mother helps me.

    Is homework a big problem or just a little one?
    A big problem.

17. If there was one thing you could change about school, what would it be?
    Decreasing the amount of homework during exam time.

18. If you could have three wishes, what would they be?
    Having a lot of friends and being successful in school.

19. Tell me three things you would like your teacher to do to help you with your dyslexia.

    Allowing me to come to him in break times to explain for me what I don't understand and giving me more time in exams and in handing in my homework.

20. Who is the best reader in your class?

    Lila.

    How did he/she get to be such a good reader?

    I don't know.

21. Is it important to learn how to read?

    Yes.

    Why or why not?

    Because by reading we know about our history and it is also a good way to spend time in reading to know more knowledge about anything.

4 Ka-ho, a Case Study of Dyslexia in China

Steven S.W. Chu, Kevin K.H. Chung and Fuk-chuen Ho[1]

Ka-ho is a 10-year-old boy who was diagnosed as dyslexic at the age of 7. Throughout the interview, he appeared to be an optimistic, obedient and caring child. At home, Ka-ho reported that he spends most of his spare time watching TV and chatting with friends on Facebook. He told the interviewer that he seldom reads at home because it is difficult for him, making him feel frustrated because of his reading and writing disabilities.

BACKGROUND

Family History

Ka-ho lives with his parents and 2-year-old brother in a socially disadvantaged suburb of Hong Kong. His father is a technician who works for a bus company and his mother is a secretary for a communications company. The father and mother left school in grades 11 and 9 respectively. The mother reported that neither she nor her husband had difficulties in reading and writing while in school. However, Ka-ho's cousin, aged 12, was referred for assessment in third grade because of his continued failures in reading and writing, and was subsequently diagnosed as dyslexic.

Since his birth, Ka-ho has lived with relatives because his parents both worked and could not afford day care for him. When Ka-ho was in grade 2, his mother became pregnant with Ka-ho's younger brother. In light of this, she quit her job and took Ka-ho home to live with them. At present, the parents have been able to hire a Filipina maid to take care of the children when they are at work. Although the maid is from the Philippines, the family communicates with her in Cantonese, which is the dialect of daily communication in Hong Kong.

Medical History

The mother reported that Ka-ho was born after a normal full-term pregnancy. However, complications arose during delivery when the mother experienced a high fever and an extended labor of almost 21 hours. After the baby was born, he was sent to the Intensive Care Unit for special care and medication for three days because he had inhaled placental fluid during delivery. Although the doctor did not discuss possible side effects of this difficult delivery in terms of the child's future development, the mother was very concerned. After staying at the hospital for a week, the mother and the baby were discharged without follow-up medication. Nevertheless, Ka-ho has had a healthy childhood, with no other significant illness. He was, however, diagnosed with far-sightedness during a regular medical checkup in the second grade and has worn corrective lenses ever since.

Early Development

Ka-ho lived with his grandmother (from birth to age 3), an aunt's family (while in kindergarten), and another aunt's family (while in grades 1 and 2). Thus, his mother admitted that she had not witnessed his entire early development. She also noted that as a young child Ka-ho felt anxious about his living situation and frequently asked when he could go home to live with his parents. Despite the fact that the mother could only partially capture Ka-ho's early development, she remembered that Ka-ho started speaking his first words and making his first steps when he was 10 months old. Ka-ho's mother noted that his language development was characterized by speech dysfluency as well as object naming problems. For example, the child repeatedly stuttered over the first word of phrases and also exhibited a lisp. Although Ka-ho has received speech therapy in a government subsidized health clinic beginning at age 4, his stuttering problem continues to affect him today. He also experienced problems naming colors and shapes, such as circles and squares, which his mother attributed to "absent-mindedness." With regard to early motor development, his mother observed that he had some problems with fine motor skills, noting that Ka-ho did not like drawing and coloring because he found it difficult to hold crayons. In addition, he often dropped his spoon, chopsticks or fork when he ate.

Chinese Reading-Related Skills

Before discussing Ka-ho's school history and the difficulties he faced, it seems beneficial to provide an explanation of the unique characteristics of the Chinese language in reference to the challenges they impose on dyslexic readers.

Orthographically, Chinese characters are visually complicated. Characters are made up of strokes instead of a string of alphabetic letters. A character can be structured differently according to some conventional "rules" (regularities), which determine their lexicality. A character is lexically "illegal" if the components (i.e., radicals) are positioned incorrectly. Generally, 90% of the common characters used are semantic-phonetic compounds (Kang, 1993), which are usually left-right configured (e.g., 清 [cing1] clear) or top-down structured (e.g., 花 [faa1] flower). Most likely, the left and the top ones are semantic radicals whereas phonetic cues are placed on the right or the bottom. Given the fact that characters are composed of different strokes, they are more visually complicated with a greater number of strokes. A recent study (Pun & Hong, 2003) found that a real Chinese character could have up to 32 strokes such as 籲 [jyu6] (call). Another earlier study proposes that approximately 620 stroke-patterns comprise all of the Chinese characters (Hoosain, 1991). Hence, readers of Chinese should master complete orthographic knowledge such as character structure orientation and radical regularities in order to learn how to read Chinese fluently (Ho, Yau & Au, 2003). However, Ho, Chan, Tsang, and Lee (2002) demonstrated that Chinese dyslexic children experienced significant orthographic-related deficits such as identifying the correct orientation and deciding the lexicality between legal and illegal character structure.

In addition to its graphic feature, the Chinese script is syllabic-and-meaning-based which is different from English. An English word such as "farmer" could have more than one syllable and be constituted by two morphemes, the root word "farm" and the inflectional suffix "-er". However, each Chinese character represents only one syllable and one morpheme (the smallest unit of meaning). Based on the limitations of this monosyllabic feature at the character level, two individual characters will be compounded to form compound-characters that are composed of two syllables and two morphemes (Anderson, Ngay, & Zhang, 2002) like 冰水 [bing1 seoi2] (iced water) 熱水 [jit6 seoi2] (hot water) with the same root (morpheme) 水 [seoi2] (water). In the Chinese language, almost 70% of the characters are compound, with two or more characters (Zhou et al., 1999). However, the formation of compound characters could be opaque and arbitrary. For instance, 女子 [neoi5 zi2] (girl) and 女婿 [neoi5 sai3] (son-in-law) share the same root word 女 [neoi5] (girl) but the former refers to a female whereas the latter to a male. To become fluent readers of Chinese, learners should have the morphological awareness and ability to manipulate Chinese morphological structures (Ngay et al., 2002). Yet recent research studies (e.g., Ho et al., 2004; Luan, 2005) have shown that Chinese dyslexic children performed worse on tasks measuring their morphological awareness, and these findings indicated that these Chinese dyslexic children experienced deficits in distinguishing meanings among morpheme homophones, manipulating and accessing morphemes in words (characters) with two or more morphemes (Chung et al., 2010). Shu et al. (2006) also proposed that one of the best tools for screening children with and without dyslexia is morphological awareness.

Phonologically, the phonetic cues embedded in Chinese characters are less reliable than those in English. Only 23 to 26% of the characters could be accurately pronounced according to the embedded phonetic cues when tone is taken into consideration (Zhou, 1978). In addition, the spoken form (Cantonese) and the written language (Modern Standard Chinese) do not correspond in terms of syntax and phonology. For example, the word "arms" is pronounced as 手瓜 [sau2 gwaa1] in Cantonese whereas the standard written form is 手肱 [sau2 gwang1] or 手臂 [sau2 bei3]. The pronunciation system of Cantonese is rather complex: some Chinese characters could have nine different tones as well as meanings in which some are pronounceable without meaning, although they have the same syllable. Given that the pronunciation system is rather complex, Hong Kong Chinese teachers commonly adopt a "look-and-say" approach to teach reading in which learners are not explicitly taught the skills in segmenting the phonemic structures (e.g., onset and rime) of characters. Hence, Chinese children learn pronunciations by rote learning and drilling (Holm & Dodd, 1996). Developmentally, students are drilled and rehearsed to memorize the pronunciations of characters.

SCHOOL HISTORY

Kindergarten

In Hong Kong, parents conceptualize pre-primary education as a tool to equip elementary learners with the necessary knowledge for primary education (Li & Rao, 2000). With this in mind, the foci of the curriculum are inclined towards preparing kindergarten children with some standard knowledge before primary education (Curriculum Development Council, 2006). Children are expected to start learning Chinese characters in the first year of the three years of kindergarten.

As reported by Ka-ho's mother, since most teachers emphasized rote learning, Ka-ho was required to memorize the orthographic feature, meaning, and pronunciation of Chinese characters starting from the age of three years. However, the mother reported that Ka-ho could not remember the stroke-patterns. For example, he could not distinguish some visually similar characters like 未 [mei6] (not yet) and 末 [mut6] (end). Also, he had significant difficulties in word association. For example, Ka-ho read 天堂 [tin1 tong4] (heaven) instead of 大堂 [daai6 tong4] (concourse). According to the mother's observation, Ka-ho did not like reading and writing because he thought he was not good at them. In his interview, Ka-ho explained that reading gives him a headache and is a frustrating experience because of his continuous failures in recognizing characters and remembering the complex stroke-patterns. The mother added that her child had difficulties reading short stories because he could not recognize and memorize some characters he had learned.

At the completion of the third year in kindergarten, children are expected to be able to read and write 200 Chinese characters (Ho et al., 2003). However, Ka-ho was very slow in copying and writing these characters. When he copied from textbooks, he always missed some strokes. Consequently, the mother noted that Ka-ho hated doing drills. Having struggled with the demanding drilling exercises, Ka-ho often asked his caregiver to complete homework for him because he felt tired of writing the characters over and over. The mother sought help from the class teacher who told her that Ka-ho might have specific learning difficulties in reading and writing. Although the mother understood that her child might need help from professionals, she did not immediately seek assistance. She attributed her son's reading and writing difficulties to his laziness. The mother told the interviewer that she had expected her child would make progress when he grew older or became "more hard-working."

In summary, Ka-ho exhibited some specific learning difficulties in reading and writing such as slow handwriting, poor memory, difficulties in word association, and visual discrimination of words. Although he continuously struggled throughout kindergarten, neither his parents nor the school came to his rescue despite the fact that both his mother and teacher were aware of his difficulties. However, Ka-ho was promoted to the first grade as the mother and his teachers expected that he would do better if he worked harder. In Hong Kong, it is an unusual practice to retain children in their last year of kindergarten.

First Grade

In Hong Kong, it is expected that primary school children learn about 3,000 characters in the first six years of elementary schooling (Pun & Hong, 2003). Thus, students learn about 500 characters in each grade. At grade 1, the characters usually have strong positional regularities and simple stroke-patterns with fewer strokes (Shu et al., 2003). These characters tend to be transparent and regular in terms of semantic category and phonetic cues, and left-right or top-bottom structured characters are taught, such as 明 [ming4] (light), 洋 [joeng4] (ocean), 花 [faa1] (flower), and 草 [cou2] (grass).

At the age of 6, Ka-ho entered first grade where he continued to struggle with his slow handwriting and problems discriminating similar stroke-patterns. The mother reported that he always missed one or two strokes when he wrote. He had to be explicitly taught how two visually similar characters were different in one individual stroke as in the previously mentioned example 未 [mei6] (not yet) and 末 [mut6] (end). Although Ka-ho had deficits in discriminating visually similar stroke-patterns, he could tell the differences when the strokes were highlighted. Because grade 1 is a transition period for young learners, most teachers tend to tolerate learners' errors in reading and writing. However, Ka-ho's teacher always complained to his mother about his untidy work and required him to correct those characters that were incorrectly copied many times (at least five times). To Ka-ho, the worst nightmare about school was doing homework and completing the corrections because of the amount of time and effort required, which did not result in successful performance.

Though Ka-ho had problems in his studies, he still enjoyed playing with his classmates. He reported he had no problems with his peers. For example, he liked running on the playground and playing hide-and-seek with friends at recess time. In addition, his friends helped him with homework.

At home, Ka-ho seldom had time to review what he had learned because homework required an excessive amount of time. If he had extra time, he would prefer reading comics and watching TV alone. Since Ka-ho did not live with his parents, he received little support other than the shelter and food provided by the caregiver's family. At school, no teacher's support was provided either even though the Chinese language teacher kept complaining about Ka-ho's untidy work. Although his classroom teacher recommended that Ka-ho be retained in first grade hoping that the child could make better progress, the parents rejected this suggestion because they continued to believe that their son could have done better if he had worked harder.

Second Grade

When Ka-ho was promoted to the second grade at the age of 7, his difficulties at school progressively increased. His homework problem worsened because the curriculum became more demanding, requiring him to memorize and practice more characters. Ka-ho's mother reported that he performed poorly in Chinese dictation (similar to English spelling drills) that required him to repeat the exercise every week. This dictation practice is common among Hong Kong's primary and junior secondary schools as teachers conceptualize it as a tool to help learners consolidate what they have learned. However, Ka-ho had great difficulties in retaining what he had learned; he could not recall and dictate what he had revised although he had spent many hours on revision. According to Ka-ho's report, the most pressing challenge was recalling the correct positions of the stroke-patterns. When he read, he could only see the outline of the characters. Discriminating and manipulating the correct visual-configuration or the stroke-patterns was a challenge for him. For example, when he wrote the character 很 [han2] (very), he would miss writing the first stroke 丿. Consequently, the semantic radical becomes 亻 instead of the correct semantic radical 彳 and that should be attached to the phonetic radical 艮. Or, he would reverse the radicals, putting the radical-pattern 艮 on the left and the semantic radical 彳 on the right. In the first term, Ka-ho had ten dictation drills. Unfortunately, he received a zero on every dictation assignment. During the second term, Ka-ho refused to submit homework. He told the interviewer that he hated doing homework and learning. He said, "No matter how hard I tried, I still failed." His frustration was obvious but still no assistance was forthcoming from his parents or school.

In grade 2 Ka-ho's performance on his Chinese tests and examinations was very unsatisfactory, which made the classroom teacher suspect that Ka-ho might have learning difficulties. Hence, all the teachers working with Ka-ho completed *The Hong Kong Specific Learning Difficulties Behaviour Checklist* (Ho et al., 2000). The results showed that Ka-ho was obviously at-risk for dyslexia. Thus, the classroom teacher referred Ka-ho to an educational psychologist for a full assessment.

Ka-ho was given two tests: (1) *Raven's Standard Progressive Matrices*, and (2) *The Hong Kong Test of Specific Learning Difficulties in Reading and Writing for Primary School Children (2nd edition)* (HKT-SpLD (II)). The Raven's results showed that Ka-ho's nonverbal intelligence was within the normal range (i.e., 98 IQ). However, the HKT-SpLD results showed that he had significant deficits in Chinese word reading, rapid naming, and orthographic processing. His performance in these measures was one standard deviation below the local norms. Thus, Ka-ho was classified as a child with developmental dyslexia. The mother reported that she met with the psychologist who provided a brief explanation about the assessment results. No teachers attended this meeting, but the school was officially informed of Ka-ho's assessment results when the report was sent by the Education Bureau of the Government of the Hong Kong Special Administrative Region.

Third and Fourth Grades

Starting from third grade, Ka-ho moved home to live with his parents because his mother recognized that her child should be given more parental support. After being diagnosed as dyslexic, Ka-ho was given some accommodations on homework and school examinations based on the educational psychologist's suggestions. According to the assessment report, Ka-ho was slow in completing copying tasks. For this reason, he was only required to finish half the amount of work. In addition, Ka-ho was assigned to a separate room to take the examinations to avoid disturbance. The examinations were reproduced on enlarged papers, and an extra 15 minutes for each test were given, hoping that the child would be able to read the exams clearly and have more time to finish them. Furthermore, Ka-ho was enrolled in a two-hour remedial class held after school in which he would be given support for homework. He has continuously received these adjustments since the third grade.

In grades 3 and 4, Ka-ho met with more academic difficulties, but continued to socialize well with peers. Although he spent less time on homework because of the allowances and support given by teachers, his performance in Chinese reading and writing was still unsatisfactory. His challenges increased as he advanced in grade level, with the most significant stressor resulting from memorizing Chinese characters for reading and writing. For new vocabulary, he required excessive time for memorization as he did not know how different stroke-patterns and radicals were constructed to form Chinese characters. As he reported, he would copy the words he learned many times before dictation. However, this method often failed because he typically forgot those characters a week later without the support of continual drilling. In light of this, it appears that Ka-ho has weak memory in orthographic knowledge. In addition, he also has difficulties in written Chinese language expression. When asked to write a short passage (e.g., 80 to 100 words), he is unable to organize his ideas and recall the necessary Chinese vocabulary to express himself in written form. However, he can express his ideas when he is asked to present orally.

Although Ka-ho encountered different Chinese reading problems in grades 3 and 4, the mother reported that he could finish almost all his homework before going home. This helped reduce the tension and conflicts between Ka-ho and his mother. While attending the remedial class, he spent one hour each day completing his homework. For the rest of the time, the teacher taught Chinese reading skills to Ka-ho and the fourteen other children in this remedial class. For example, Ka-ho and his classmates were taught how to decode ideo-phonetic compound characters. They were also taught how to identify the phonetic radicals and the semantic radicals. As semantic radicals are more frequent in Chinese reading, the teacher summarized some characters that shared the same radical. Ka-ho learned that there are a number of characters like 找 [zaau2] (find), 控 [hung3] (control), 拯 [cing2] (save), 持 [ci4] (hold) that share the same semantic radical 才 (hand). In addition, characters that share the same phonetic radicals were also taught like 青 [cing1] (green) in 清 [cing1] (clear), 請 [cing2] (please), and 晴 [cing4] (sunny). Ka-ho thought that this kind of "concentrated character learning method" 集中識字法 [zaap6 zung1 sik1 zi6 faat3] (Tian, 1987) helped him learn Chinese characters' semantic and phonetic regularities.

By the end of grade 3, Ka-ho told his mother that he "loved" attending the remedial class because his teacher understood his problems and gave him a lot of encouragement and support. In the fourth grade, the remedial teacher became his class teacher, which meant she would also be teaching him Chinese. Ka-ho was excited about this. In the meantime, his mother noticed that he was making progress, but she was concerned that he did not have any support at home. Therefore, she hired a private tutor to help him with his homework on Saturdays for two hours. Starting from the second term in grade 4, Ka-ho made further achievements. The mother reported that he passed almost all subjects, except English, in the final examinations.

DYSLEXIA DIAGNOSIS AND TREATMENT ISSUES

Ka-ho struggled for some time before he was diagnosed dyslexic and received treatment. As discussed previously, this investigation has highlighted related issues about early diagnosis and treatment. His teachers did not refer him for assessment until the end of the second semester of grade 2, which suggests that they may have lacked training in identifying dyslexia. In addition, parents' awareness is also influential for early identification. Commonly, it is assumed that parents are in a position to observe early development, but such was not the case for Ka-ho who did not actually live with his parents until the third grade. Thus, they were not in a position to monitor school achievement from a firsthand perspective. Further, his mother did not understand the term dyslexia as she believed that is was related to a short attention span, which would improve as age advanced. Had his mother understood the nature of dyslexia, she might have sought professional help immediately. Thus, Ka-ho was not provided with critical early intervention.

Fortunately, Ka-ho's reading problems were diagnosed when his teachers referred him for assessment by the end of grade 2. At present, school teachers refer poor academic achievers to professional psychologists for assessment if the identification tool, The Hong Kong Specific Learning Difficulties Behaviour Checklist (For Primary School Pupils) (Ho, Chan, Tsang, & Lee, 2000), shows that further professional assessment is needed. Locally, the Education Bureau of the Hong Kong Special Administrative Region encourages schools to identify children with dyslexia at grade 1 by using The Hong Kong Specific Learning Difficulties Behaviour Checklist (Ho et al., 2000). However, some dyslexic children may still go undetected at grade 1 if teachers are not aware of children's reading problems, which was the case for Ka-ho who experienced continual failures before his referral to the educational psychologist. In Hong Kong, it was common that many dyslexic children were not diagnosed given that there were no standardized and reliable identification and assessment tools before 2000 (Hong Kong Education Department, 2002). However, this situation has since been improving as the Hong Kong Specific Learning Difficulties Research Team (http://web.hku.hk/~hksld/index_e.html) has developed a set of local tools for screening and assessing Cantonese-speaking children with dyslexia.

According to Ka-ho and his mother's report, some progress in reading and writing has occurred since enrolling in the remedial class. The examination allowance and homework assistance have also helped him. Currently many primary schools in Hong Kong adopt adjustments such as those offered by Ka-ho's school. If children are diagnosed dyslexics, for example, the amount of homework will be reduced and extra examination time will be given. These policies are most likely school-based and depend on children's needs and situations.

Other than giving homework and examination allowances, this case has also highlighted the issue of empowering teachers with the skills in teaching children with special educational needs. In Ka-ho's case, it appears only a few of his teachers were able to identify his reading problems and give him support. At present, there exists, perhaps, a mismatch in which teacher training has lagged behind the increasing number of confirmed cases of dyslexic children (Apple Daily, 2009). That is, there was a five-fold increase from the school year 2003–2004 to 2007–2008 as highlighted in the 21st Annual Report of The Ombudsman (Office of the Ombudsman, 2009). In the academic year 2007–2008, there were 76% of secondary school teachers and 30% of primary school teachers who had not received any training related to special education. Before the school year 2007–2008, the Education Bureau (formerly the Hong Kong Education Department), perhaps, did not have a comprehensive policy on teacher training with which to focus on equipping teachers with skills and knowledge in catering to students' diverse educational needs. Since September 2007, the Education Bureau in Hong Kong has formulated a 5-year teacher professional development framework to provide teacher training in supporting children with special educational needs at a three-tier level (Education Bureau, 2007). With this in mind, it is expected that a small proportion of teachers (10%) will have completed the Basic Course within the five years from the 2007–2008 school year (Education Bureau, 2007).

In Hong Kong, parents seldom fight for special requests that should be arranged for their children with special educational needs, and that was also true in this case. As reported by the mother, she also expected that Ka-ho should be pulled out from the mainstream classroom and be taught by teachers who have received special education training. However, it appears that she has never voiced her opinions and asked for that. As cited in the 21st Annual Report of The Ombudsman (Office of the Ombudsman, 2009):

> Some parents dare not stand up to the school management in their quest for support for their children. The Education Bureau's records show that only one parent used its mediation service during the school years 2005–2006 to 2007–2008. (p. 60)

In 2008, the Office of the Ombudsman also criticized the Hong Kong Examinations and Assessment Authority (HKEAA) for inconsistency in policies for examinations for students with specific learning difficulties (SpLD). Although HKEAA has provided some guidelines for schools, "practices may vary significantly from school to school" (Office of the Ombudsman, 2008, p.71) because of teachers' lack of knowledge in making special examination arrangements and psychologists' increasing caseload. In short, whether a dyslexic child can succeed depends greatly on how much support is provided by parents, teachers, and schools.

PARENT PERSPECTIVES

Ka-ho's mother thinks that her child is friendly, caring, and sociable. She believes that he could perform better in reading and writing if he were given time and the school was less demanding. In the interview, she constantly mentioned that Ka-ho would enjoy life more if he could manage his studies. As she emphasized, the most significant stressor and challenges come from homework. She believes her child could explore his full potential if Ka-ho was provided with suitable curricula and assessments based on his special educational needs in language learning. According to her, Ka-ho's reading problems have reached the extent that they not only affect his academic performances, but have also become a topic of family conflicts.

The mother also worries that Ka-ho will be less competitive compared with other children without dyslexia and thus will perform badly in public examinations. She believes this may hinder Ka-ho from getting a better job in the future. Furthermore, she commented that the Education Bureau had not provided sufficient information to parents for helping them understand dyslexic children's needs. She hinted that she would have understood her child's needs if extra resources were given on parent education. Therefore, she suggested that the government should provide parents with workshops to equip them with the knowledge required to serve the needs of dyslexic children. Given that the mother was so intent on learning more about dyslexia, it came as a surprise that when she was asked what she knew about the subject, she was unsure of the meaning of the term. The mother reported,

> I am not sure what dyslexia means. To my understanding, I think dyslexic children are not attentive. They are not good at reading, but they are good at speaking.

In addition, the mother wonders whether her child and other dyslexic children should be removed from normal classes and taught by a specialist with special-education training. She believes that her child might benefit more if the teacher was equipped with the necessary skills and knowledge in teaching children with developmental dyslexia. If appropriate support was provided, she expects that Ka-ho would not suffer from reading and writing difficulties after leaving school. The mother clearly attributes Ka-ho's Chinese reading problems to external factors such as the curricula, examinations, and lack of support from teachers.

CHILD PERSPECTIVES

Throughout the interview, Ka-ho emphasized that he had not had any problems socializing with his peers. At school, he has a few best friends who always help him with homework. He reported that his classmates like him because he is a cheerful person, and his personality helps him get along well with peers. He also enjoys visiting his friends and studying with them. Despite his insistence his reading problems do not interfere with his social life, Ka-ho stated that he knows "that some students do not like to make friends with me because I perform badly in my studies."

As revealed in the Sentence Completion questions, Ka-ho emphasized that he has encountered a lot of problems related to homework and studying. He clearly indicated that, "the worst thing about school is doing homework." When he does homework, he feels "frustrated because the homework and Chinese reading are getting more demanding and difficult." Ka-ho also reported that his Chinese reading problems have affected his family life to a certain extent. For example, during the interview, Ka-ho emphasized that he wants to make progress in his studies so he can please his parents. He indicated, "My parents expect me to be smart and obedient, and they also want me to do as well as what my normal achieving peers do." Throughout his interview he mentioned the importance of his parents' approval with regard to their achievement expectations. He believes that his parents would be disappointed if he failed some subjects, and he also thinks of himself as "useless." It appears that Ka-ho has a very close relationship with his parents, but that this relationship is characterized by stress related to his dyslexia.

Ka-ho knows how important reading is because he believes reading helps him understand the world more. However, he thinks his Chinese reading problems hinder him from knowing and remembering more characters. He reported:

> The most difficult thing about having a reading problem is to understand and recognize Chinese characters that are complexly configured. It is difficult for me to remember the stroke-patterns and the pronunciation of those words.

Although Ka-ho has tried hard, he still finds reading difficult. When he was asked if there was one thing he could change about school, he wished he could use information technology (e.g., computers) to help him read and write in class and examinations. Provided with the help of information technology (e.g., using the spelling checker on a word processing tool), he expects he would do better in reading and writing. Regarding his perceptions of school, he indicated, "I do not like school when my teacher scolds me because of my untidy writing. On the contrary, I like going to school when my teachers teach me to read." Based on the above discussion, it appears that Ka-ho has ambivalent feelings about school.

Apart from reading and writing, Ka-ho conceptualizes himself as "useful," (i.e., being able to contribute to his school in other ways). He said,

> The best thing about school is attending extra-curricular activities. I like running and doing sport. I have also won several gold medals in running. Therefore, I want to be an athlete when I grow up because being an athlete does not require me to be good at reading and writing.

In short, Ka-ho has met severe difficulties in his studies at school. To a certain extent, his Chinese reading problems have also caused tensions between him and his parents. Fortunately, he possesses a cheerful personality that helps him get along with peers and overcome many of the problems he has met.

CASE COMMENTARY

Family genetic transmission is often seen in the families of children with dyslexia, and though neither the mother nor father reported any reading and writing difficulties, Ka-ho's older cousin has been diagnosed with dyslexia. It is unclear whether Ka-ho's difficult delivery may have affected his development.

Prior to grade 3 Ka-ho received very little family support, and help was not immediately sought although his mother was informed that her son might be dyslexic in Kindergarten 3. This period of Ka-ho's education was marked by an ignorance of his problems and a lack of understanding of dyslexia. Ka-ho's perceptions of the significance of dyslexia are consistent with those of his mother, in that both perceive Chinese reading and writing problems as interfering significantly with school success. To some extent, his reading and writing problems have also affected his family life. Consistently, it should be noted that both the mother and the child perceive that his reading problems have caused significantly more negative effects on school success and family life than they have imposed on his socialization with peers.

It is noted that Ka-ho has faced a lot of problems related to reading and homework. In an early stage of development, Ka-ho could still manage his homework given that the curricula were not that demanding for him. However, when Ka-ho was in grade 2, he was facing an increasing amount of homework and difficulty with the language curriculum. Obviously, Ka-ho's performance in school improved after he moved home during grade 3, allowing the family to establish a closer relationship. His mother noticed that he also was less anxious after the provision of adjustments by the school. To this end, perhaps, the school and parents' support may have played a role in helping Ka-ho improve. If Ka-ho had been able to move home during the kindergarten period and his school had provided adjustments earlier, perhaps he would have made more progress in reading as well as in his overall studies.

Despite the fact that Ka-ho has performed poorly in school he still enjoys going because he likes his teachers and classmates. Ka-ho mentioned in the interview that he would especially like to thank one particular teacher who taught him patiently and helped him with his homework in the remedial class when he was in grades 3 and 4. He thinks the teacher's effort has helped him become more confident. In addition, he also mentioned that his friends are always helpful in that they never treat him differently even though he is dyslexic. Therefore, Ka-ho's positive attitude toward his life has helped him face many dyslexia-related challenges.

Ka-ho is accepted and supported by his parents, teachers, and classmates, but as reflected in this case, there is still room for improvement in relation to treatment. In Hong Kong, there is no curriculum or assessment that is specifically tailored to meet the needs of those Chinese dyslexic children. In a normal classroom, both dyslexic children and their achieving peers learn the same materials and take the same tests. Although schools provide adjustments for dyslexic children, these strategies only reduce the workload and provide more time for examinations. When Ka-ho was asked whether these adjustments helped, he reported that he would prefer a tailor-made curriculum that was different from that which non-dyslexic students receive as this would help him learn more effectively. He further added that he would also prefer other examination methods that do not require him to write (e.g., completing exams on a computer). It is highly possible that these Hong Kong Chinese dyslexic children would perform better if they were given suitable curricula and assessments that do not require them to read and write using the conventional methods such as pen and paper tests.

This case highlights the need for more government resources to support the needs of dyslexic learners. As Ka-ho's mother reported, she would have sent her child for assessment earlier if she had known more about dyslexia. Furthermore, Ka-ho might have received an educational psychologist's assessment sooner if his reading problems had been detected by the teachers in grade 1. Ka-ho's performance in school, before and after the identification of his developmental dyslexia and appropriate intervention, illustrates the importance of teachers' and parents' awareness, knowledge and skills in catering to the needs of Chinese children with dyslexia. At present, although the Education Bureau has advocated early identification and provided a five-year training framework for teachers, it is undeniable that there still exists a lag between the increasing number of detected cases and teacher training. For example, by the end of 2013, only a total of 10% of teachers will have been equipped with the training necessary to provide for the needs of children with special education requirements (Office of the Ombudsman, 2009).

On the other hand, as mentioned by Chung (2008), Hong Kong has made reasonable progress in producing reliable and standardized identification and assessment instruments for the use of teachers and educational psychologists. In addition, with the support of specialists, an additional identification instrument, *The Hong Kong Learning Behaviour Checklist for Preschool Children (Parent Version)*, was developed for use by parents to identify kindergarteners with developmental dyslexia (Wong & Hong Kong Specific Learning Difficulties Research Team, 2006).

While this case may or may not be representative of a Chinese child with developmental dyslexia, it is clear that Ka-ho performed differently before and after his diagnosis of dyslexia and treatment. Hence, early identification and diagnosis are important. Apart from that, parent and school support is also important in addressing dyslexic children's needs.

In this case, Ka-ho had to come a long way before making some small progress at school in grade 4. Yet, in spite of this, Ka-ho demonstrates optimism and resilience that will likely help him surmount the obstacles ahead. It is hoped that in the future teachers and the government will extend the support that Chinese dyslexic children need to reach their achievement potential.

NOTES

1. In this paper, pronunciation notes are used to indicate the characters' Cantonese pronunciations. For example, in the syllable [bing1], /b/ is the onset, / ing/ is the rime, and "1" means that the syllable is in the first tone, i.e., a high level tone.

REFERENCES

Anderson, R.C., Li, W., Ku, Y.-M., Shu, H., & Wu, N. (2003). Use of partial information in learning to read Chinese characters. *Journal of Educational Psychology*, 95, 52–57.

Apple Daily. (2009, March 27). *The detected number of children with special educational needs increases five folds: Teacher training cannot catch up*, p. A18. (In Chinese).

Chung, K.K.H. (2008). Supporting Chinese learners with developmental dyslexia. In C. Forlin (Ed.), *Catering for learners with diverse needs: An Asia-Pacific focus* (pp. 61–70). Hong Kong: HKIEd.

Chung, K.K.H., Ho, C.S.H., Chan, D.W., Tsang, S.M., & Lee, S.H. (2010). Cognitive profiles of Chinese adolescents with dyslexia. *Dyslexia*, 16, 2–23.

Curriculum Development Council. (2006). *Guide to the pre-primary curriculum*. Hong Kong: The Curriculum Development Council.

Education Bureau. (2007). Teacher professional development framework on integrated education. Retrieved from http://www.edb.gov.hk/index. aspx?nodeID=6567&langno=1

Hong Kong Education Department. (2002). Understanding and helping students with special educational needs: A guide to teaching. Retrieved from http://www. edb.gov.hk/UtilityManager/Publication/upload/sen_guide_e.pdf

Ho, C.S.-H., Chan, D.W., Tsang, S., & Lee, S. (2000). The Hong Kong specific learning difficulties behaviour checklist (for primary school pupils). Hong Kong: Hong Kong Specific Learning Difficulties Research Team.

Ho, C.S.-H., Chan, D., Tsang, S.-M., & Lee, S.-H. (2002). The cognitive profile and multiple-deficit hypothesis in Chinese developmental dyslexia. *Developmental Psychology*, 38, 543–553.

Ho, C.S., Chan, D.W., Lee, S., Tsang, S., & Luan, V.H. (2004). Cognitive profiling and preliminary subtyping in Chinese developmental dyslexia. *Cognition*, 91(1), 43–75. doi:DOI: 10.1016/S0010–0277(03)00163-X

Ho, C.S., Yau, P. W.-Y., & Au, A. (2003). Development of orthographic knowledge and its relationship with reading and spelling among Chinese kindergarten and primary school children. In Mcbride-Chang, C., & Chen, H. (Eds.). *Reading development in Chinese children*. Westport, CT: Praeger.

Holm, A., & Dodd, B. (1996). The effect of first written language on the acquisition of English literacy. *Cognition*, 59, 119–147.

Hoosain, R. (1991). *Psycholinguistic implications for linguistic relatively: A case study of Chinese*. Hillsdale, NJ: Lawrence Erlbaum Associates.

Kang, J.S. (1993). Analysis of semantics of semantic-phonetics compound characters in modern Chinese. In Y. Chen (Ed.), *Information analysis of usage of characters in modern Chinese* (pp. 68–83, in Chinese). Shanghai: Shanghai Education.

Li, H., & Rao, N. (2000). Parental influences on Chinese literacy development: A comparison of preschoolers in Beijing, Hong Kong, and Singapore. *International Journal of Behavioral Development*, 24 (1), 82–90. doi:10.1080/016502500383502

Luan, H. (2005). *The role of morphological awareness among Mandarin-speaking and Cantonese-speaking children*. PhD dissertation, The University of Hong Kong.

Ngay, W.E., Kuo-Kealoha, A., Wu, X., Li, W., Anderson, R.C., Chen, X. (2002). The role of morphological awareness in learning to read Chinese. In Li, W., Gaffney, J. S., & Packard, J. L. (Eds.), *Chinese children's reading acquisition-Theoretical and pedagogical issues* (pp. 59–86). The Netherlands: The Kluwer Academic Publishes.

Office of the Ombudsman. (2008). *20th Annual report of the Ombudsman*. Hong Kong: Office of the Ombudsman.

Office of the Ombudsman. (2009). *21st Annual report of the Ombudsman*. Hong Kong: Office of the Ombudsman.

Pun, W.Y., & Hong, P.M. (2003). *A study of the Chinese characters recommended for the subject of Chinese language in primary schools*. Hong Kong: Hong Kong Baptist University Language Centre.

Shu, H., Chen, X., Anderson, R.C., Wu, N., & Xuan, Y. (2003). Properties of school Chinese: Implications for learning to read. *Child Development*, 74(1), 27–47.

Shu, H., McBride-Chang, C., Wu, S., & Liu, H. (2006). Understanding Chinese developmental dyslexia: Morphological awareness as a core cognitive construct. *Journal of Educational Psychology*, 98, 122–133.

Tian, B.-N. (1987, December). *The concentrated character learning method: A primary school reading instruction reform project*. The Proceedings of the Third International Conference of the Language Education Institute. Hong Kong. (In Chinese).

Wong, Y. F., & Hong Kong Specific Learning Difficulties Research Team. (2006). *The Hong Kong learning behaviour checklist for preschool children (Parent Version)*. Hong Kong: Hong Kong Specific Learning Difficulties Research Team.

Zhou, Y.G. (1978). To what degree are the "phonetics" of present-day Chinese characters still phonetics? *Zhougguo Yuwen*, 146, 172–177. (In Chinese).

Zhou, X., Marslen-Wilson, W., Taft, M., & Shu, H. (1999). Morphology, orthography, and phonology in the Chinese mental lexicon. *Language and Cognitive Processes*, 14, 525–565.

KA-HO'S INTERVIEW

1. What do you want to be when you grow up?
   An athlete.

   Why do you think you would be good at that job?
   It is because I am strong enough and I like doing sport.

2. Tell me about a teacher who has been really important to you or one who has helped you.
   I think Miss Y. is an important teacher to me.

What did the teacher do to help you?

> *She has taught me in the remedial class since grade 3. She was also my class teacher when I was in grade 4. When I had problems, she would explain those problems clearly, and she would also call my mum to discuss how to help me at home.*

3. Tell me about a teacher who didn't really help you that much or one who did not give you the help you needed.

> *No, I think all the teachers are nice and they have given me a lot of support.*

4. Tell me what your mother thinks about your dyslexia. Does she talk to you about the problem?

> *Yes.*

What does she say?

> *She wishes I was not dyslexic. She wants me to be the same as my normal achieving peers in which I don't need any allowances adjustments on homework and examinations. She was upset when she knew that I was dyslexic.*

5. Tell me what your father thinks about your dyslexia. Does he talk to you about the problem?

> *No.*

What does he say?

> *He is worried about my marked difficulties in reading and writing. He shares what my mum thinks.*

6. Tell me about something that makes you really happy.

> *I feel happy when I go out to eat with my whole family. My mum and dad are always busy with their work so I usually have dinner myself. I hope they can stay with me all the time and have dinner together.*

7. Tell me about something that makes you really sad.

> *When I know that my school results are not good, I feel sad. I think I am useless. I hope I can work harder. I am disappointed, although I have worked very hard. I tried but I still failed. Among all, I think Chinese reading is the most difficult one. I had never passed this subject before grade 4.*

8. When the work gets very hard at school and you think you can't do it, what do you do?

> *I will ask my mum and dad by calling them. If they can't help, I will solve the problems by myself. More importantly, I will also ask my teachers after school if I really don't understand the work that I need to do.*

9. What kinds of books do you like to read?

> *Story books.*

What is your favorite book?
> *Three Little Pigs.*

Do you read to yourself?
> *Yes.*

Who else reads to you?
> *I read by myself.*

10. Do your friends know that you have dyslexia?
    > *Yes.*

    Do you talk to them about it?
    > *Yes.*

    What do you say?
    > *I am dyslexic. Actually, they do not understand what dyslexia is, I just told them I am unable to read and write well.*

    What do your friends say to you about dyslexia?
    > *I have never mentioned my reading problem directly, but my class teacher put a label on my student handbook, indicating that I have some special allowances for homework. That is, I just have to finish half of the amount of homework. Although they have said nothing about my problem, but they are still willing to give me support, especially when I don't know how to do homework.*

11. Do your siblings know that you have dyslexia?
    > *No.*

    Do you talk to them about it?
    > *No, I have said nothing.*

    What do your siblings say to you about dyslexia?
    > *My little brother is only a 2-year-old baby so he does not understand what my problem is.*

12. Name three things you are really good at:
    > *Doing sport, story telling, willing to help others*

13. Name three things you are not so good at:
    > *Learning English, doing homework, spelling*

14. If you are feeling bad about your reading, is there one person you can talk to who makes you feel better?
    > *No.*

    What does that person say to you?
    > *I wish my mum and dad would encourage me and give me support. They are too busy, however. I know they are willing to help me, but they don't know what to do and how to help.*

15. Do computers help you with your reading?
    > *Yes.*

If yes, how do they help you?

> *When I don't understand some vocabulary, I will go online to check the meanings.*

16. Do you usually have problems with your homework?

> *Yes, I do. I need a lot of help from others.*

Can you do your homework independently or does someone help you?

> *Sometimes I can finish my homework independently provided the tasks are very easy. If I really don't understand, I will look up the words in the dictionary. Luckily, I have enrolled in the remedial class since grade 4 so that the remedial class teacher has given me a lot of support on homework.*

Is homework a big problem or just a little one?

> *It is a big problem for me because I am really weak in reading and writing, and my parents do not know how to teach me.*

17. If there was one thing you could change about school, what would it be?

> *I wish I could change the curriculum that I could not have to read and write. When I do homework, I can ask my parents, classmates, and teachers. But nobody will be able to help when I take the examinations. When I fail, both my parents and I will be very upset.*

18. If you could have three wishes, what would they be?

> *I wish I could read and write well. In other words, I wish I was not dyslexic.*
> *I wish I could always stay with my parents.*
> *I wish my baby brother could grow up healthily.*

19. Tell me three things you would like your teacher to do to help you with your dyslexia

> *When I don't know some words, they would help me.*
> *My teachers teach me how to understand the main points of the text.*
> *My teachers help me do revision before examinations.*

20. Who is the best reader in your class?

> *Wing-sze.*

How did he/she get to be such a good reader?

> *She knows a lot of words because she reads different kinds of books regularly.*

21. Is it important to learn how to read?

> *Yes.*

Why or why not?

> *When I know how to read the questions in the examinations or quizzes and the text, I can understand how to answer questions in examinations. Besides, I can understand the world more. I can learn more by reading.*

5   Percy, a Case Study of Dyslexia in India

Sunil Karande and Rukhshana F. Sholapurwala

Percy, a 10-year-old Parsi (Zoroastrian) boy in the fifth grade, was diagnosed as dyslexic at the age of 8 years 11 months, when he had just begun the fourth grade. He is a bright child who enjoys the support of his close-knit family. During the interview Percy cooperated fully. He was quite excited that he was being interviewed; he communicated willingly, freely expressing his feelings and opinions.

BACKGROUND

Family History

Percy lives in an upper-middle-class neighborhood in Mumbai (formerly known as Bombay), which is a cosmopolitan mega-city in the west of India, with his parents and older brother. Percy's parents are both college graduates from programs that required English as the medium of instruction. Percy's father works as a creative director in an advertising agency and his mother is a homemaker. Although Gujarati is the language of their Parsi (Zoroastrian) community, both parents speak English to their two children and, for the most part, between themselves, too. Percy is an English speaker, but understands Gujarati to some extent.

Percy's 14-year-old brother exhibited the same learning difficulties that Percy has experienced, and was also diagnosed as having specific learning disability (SpLD), which included dyslexia, dysgraphia, and dyscalculia as well as attention-deficit/hyperactivity disorder (ADHD). The mother did not experience any school difficulties. Percy's father wrote very slowly and had problems finishing his papers as a child, but was never evaluated because at that time there was no awareness of dyslexia. The mother also stated that Percy's father was left-handed as a child and was forced by his teacher to become right-handed. Even today he writes with both hands and has very poor handwriting; he is also very self-conscious if others watch him while he is writing. The father was always easily distracted and often daydreamed, but he was not considered to be hyperactive.

In spite of both their sons having SpLD and ADHD the parents have accepted their situation in life remarkably well. The family is very close and enjoys spending time together.

Medical History

Percy was born after a full-term pregnancy. Although his mother experienced spotting when she was about seven to eight months pregnant and was advised complete bed rest, the birth was without complications. When Percy was about 5 years old he developed an allergy to dust, for which he was prescribed Salbutamol meter dose inhaler that he continues to take today. In spite of the medication his breathing becomes heavy during colds. When he was about 6 years old he became ill and received nebulization in the hospital and an injection for his fever. He never had ear infections or serious illnesses, but when he was about 7 years old he had a fall at his friend's house for which he received about five stitches on his head. When he was 8 years old, he was admitted to the hospital for four days for complaints of acute gastroenteritis. He currently takes Attentrol (Methylphenidate) for management of ADHD symptoms.

Early Development

Percy's mother remembers him as a talkative child who attained all his developmental language milestones on time. His mother also stated that his language was clear and that he had no difficulty in naming objects, colors or anything else. Percy started walking when he was 1 year old. Between the ages of 7 and 8, he mastered riding a two-wheel bicycle without any difficulty. He started coloring and drawing pictures at an early age (less than 5 years), which he thoroughly enjoyed. However, his drawings were not good and appeared to be scribbles. He held the crayons tightly in an awkward grip with his fingers positioned too closely to the tip of the writing instrument.

Since an early age he was a mischievous child who was somewhat hyperactive, but he also had an extremely pleasant and friendly temperament. His activity level and mischievousness did not bother his parents as they felt this was characteristic of most young boys. During these years he enjoyed the company of other children and never had any problems making friends.

SCHOOL HISTORY

Kindergarten

Percy was 3 years old when he entered English-medium kindergarten (i.e., a kindergarten that uses English as the primary language of instruction). India is a large multilingual country with up to 29 languages spoken by more than a million native speakers. Hindi is the official national language and English is a subsidiary official language. In Mumbai, which is the capital of the state of Maharashtra, Marathi is the official regional language. However, in Mumbai parents irrespective of their own linguistic background (commonly Marathi or Hindi, or Gujarati or English) prefer to educate their children in English-medium schools. Hence, a large part of kindergarten is dedicated to familiarizing children with the English language and preparing them for the first grade. In the first term (first six months) of junior kindergarten the curriculum focuses only on oral language activities; and in the second term the children start learning to write alphabets. By the end of the junior kindergarten year children are expected to learn to write two to three letter words. In the senior kindergarten they begin learning to write and read simple sentences and by the end of the year to write and read small paragraphs of four to five lines.

Percy attended kindergarten for two years when he was 3 to 5 years of age. Since he was quite bright with good oral language, teachers did not notice any problems even though he was hyperactive and very mischievous.

First Grade

Percy's mother remembered that he enjoyed going to school (an Indian Certificate of Secondary Education board affiliated school) when he was in the first grade. His school teachers did not inform her about any difficulties that Percy might have faced in learning. The mother feels that problems might have been there, but the school teachers either "did not notice them" or "just did not care to inform her."

In the first grade children should be able to learn to demonstrate beginning reading and writing skills. Percy's mother did not notice any problems in his reading. But she did notice that his handwriting was "not up to the mark"; he was skipping words while writing; and his writing work in school was often incomplete.

Second Grade

Percy's second school year was also described by his mother as enjoyable. Again, his teachers did not report any learning problems that Percy might have faced, but by this point the mother was certain that he was having learning difficulties in school because she was finding it difficult to teach him at home. She continued to notice the problems that he had in writing; Percy would throw tantrums when she asked him to write. She also noticed that his reading was laborious and that he was hesitant to read. He was very happy when she tutored him by reading his lessons to him. Since there were no complaints from the school his mother did not bother to pursue an evaluation.

Third Grade

Third grade was the first time Percy's classroom teacher noticed that he had problems with writing and reported this to his mother. This teacher complained that Percy's handwriting was poor; he wrote very slowly, with tiny words without spaces and was unable to write complete sentences. His mother observed that his class work was usually incomplete because he could not copy from the blackboard. Percy coped with this problem by photocopying his classmates' books and then copying the material. His reading problems had also worsened and by now had become obvious. In spite of this, the school authorities did not advise any evaluation. Percy's mother believed that his problems were not taken seriously by the school authorities since there were no curricular standards for young children. In Percy's school, the policy is not to have any comprehensive evaluations until fifth grade and to promote every student up to this point irrespective of the child's academic progress.

Fourth Grade

When Percy was in fourth grade, although his understanding of the subjects was not too bad, he was reluctant to read and to write. However, his difficulties in writing were worse than his difficulties in reading. He had problems writing sentences and essays, and his spelling was generally poor. Because of his writing problems, Percy wanted to be given only oral tests. His reading was very slow and he would skip words, substitute words, and read without understanding the meaning. His class work continued to be incomplete; he had to finish it during recess or take it home and copy his classmates' books. Sometimes his mother helped him to complete it at home. The school still did not advise any evaluation and Percy continued to enjoy his schooling as his limitations were not considered as significant or alarming by the school authorities. He did not face any criticism from his teachers or problems with his classmates.

Percy's mother clearly remembered that the school authorities did not offer her any guidance for his problems. However, her elder son, who is now studying in ninth grade in the same school, had experienced similar problems. Her elder son's problems had been totally overlooked until he reached fifth grade at which point the school authorities provided the mandatory referral letter for evaluation at the state government-recognized learning disability clinic; wherein he was diagnosed as having SpLD. Without this referral letter from the school this learning disability clinic, which is situated in a municipal medical college, will not evaluate and certify disabilities. (Please note: It is a clinic situated in a municipal medical college run by the Municipal Corporation of Greater Mumbai which is an autonomous quasi-government body.)

Because Percy was still in his fourth grade, his mother knew from past experience that the school authorities would not support an evaluation of his academic problems at the municipal clinic. Since she did not want to wait for another year to have his problems addressed she pursued an evaluation at a private clinic, which did not require the official school letter.

As part of this evaluation, Percy was given the WISC (MC Bhatt version standardized for Indian Children; Bhatt, 1971) which indicated that he had bright normal intellectual functioning (Full-scale IQ= 118, Performance IQ= 122, Verbal IQ=109). The ACID (Arithmetic, Coding, Information and Digit Span) profile, which is associated with learning disabilities revealed three positive indicators.

For his educational assessment, Percy was given a locally devised Curriculum-Based Test (CBT). In the CBT evaluation Percy used his finger to assist his reading. He read phonetically, but with numerous additions, omissions, and substitutions, frequently mispronouncing words and ignoring punctuation. His comprehension was adequate as he was able to answer simple literal questions. When asked to write an essay he had difficulty with expression of ideation. His handwriting and letter formation were developmentally immature; he held the pen in an awkward grip and had numerous letter reversal and spacing problems. Percy was very reluctant to write and would have preferred to answer orally. His spelling age was that of an 8-year-old, which was approximately one year below expectancy. Percy could do simple computational sums, but with calculation errors. His mental math computation skills were good. The educational testing results on CBT evaluation were clearly indicative of SpLD (dyslexia, dysgraphia and dyscalculia). The WRAT-3 (Wilkinson, 1993) was also given as a supplementary test. The results indicated that Percy was functioning at the 23rd percentile in reading, the 32nd in spelling, and the 39th in math. Percy's reading was interpreted as 'low average' while his spelling and math were 'average'.

It was also noted that Percy displayed behaviors suggestive of ADHD, thus, an evaluation by a pediatric neurologist/child psychiatrist was recommended. However, the parents did not wish to consult any doctor at this time.

Within two months since entering fourth grade, Percy's parents on their own decided to send him for: (1) remedial sessions with a remedial teacher (special educator) at a private clinic for learning disabilities and (2) private tuitions (tutoring) for all his regular school subjects. Percy's daily schedule became extremely hectic as he attended school all day, followed by remedial lessons twice a week and tutoring sessions five days a week. In the private tutoring classes there were only ten students in the classroom as opposed to the 35 students in his school classroom. The school curriculum was re-taught in the private tuition classes by regular teachers (not special educators). The trend of sending a child for private tuitions, which is much more expensive than the school fees, is well entrenched in Mumbai. Parents generally believe that their children will be able to learn the school subject(s) which they find difficult if they are provided with private teachers who are able to give more individual attention. Since his parents felt that

Percy was not doing "too well" in all his school subjects he was started private tutoring for all of them.

Percy's mother showed his psycho-educational test reports to the school principal a few weeks after starting remedial sessions. The principal appeared to be indifferent and did not discuss the reports with Percy's mother. Without explaining the term dyslexia or the meaning of remedial education he told the mother that Percy could start attending remedial classes in the school library twice a week. However, Percy did not want to attend these classes so she did not force him as he was already receiving remedial training from the private learning disability clinic.

In general, Percy was very receptive to his private remedial tutoring, the focus of which was to improve his specific problems in reading, writing, spelling, and arithmetic skills. As his handwriting was illegible, the private remedial teacher began with patterning exercises and continued until he mastered letters, which took approximately four to five months. Spelling instruction focused on phonics, beginning with vowels and moving to consonants. After six months Percy learned the alphabet and began mastering blends, moving on to one syllable words. His reading instruction was coordinated with the spelling remediation. Percy was taught words through color-coded segmentation (e.g., bot/tle), word formation games, and sight word identification. After six months of instruction he started reading story books with five to six lines of text. Since Percy hated writing, the private remedial teacher developed a behavioral program that provided a reward system for successive approximations toward the goal of improved legibility. This program emphasized letter formation within the context of copying exercises. The private remedial teacher also addressed math weaknesses by working on math calculations and mathematical language.

Since Percy's attention problems were hampering his progress, the private remedial teacher again requested that Percy's parents consult a pediatric neurologist/child psychiatrist. About 6 months after beginning remedial education, Percy was evaluated by a child psychiatrist who diagnosed him as having ADHD-combined type as per DSM-IV-TR criteria (American Psychiatric Association, 2000). Percy began a daily dosage of 10 mg of Methylphenidate (to be omitted on school holidays).

Percy's mother recalled that it took about eight months of remedial education (along with two months of medication for ADHD) for improvement in handwriting and spelling. However, she could not comment on his school performance since there are no examinations in fourth grade and no test scores for comparison.

Toward the end of the year, Percy's mother requested that the school principal refer her son to a municipal clinic (whose reports are recognized by the state government) to secure his official learning disability certificate. Even after the referral letter is written by the school it can take another two months for the evaluation to begin because there is a long waiting list. Hence, she took an appointment two months in advance so that Percy could get evaluated during his vacation after he had completed fourth grade. Only when a child is diagnosed as having SpLD by a government recognized center and issued an "official" disability certificate are the school authorities duty bound to provide provisions/accommodations to the child. The principal obliged and she considered herself "very lucky" to have obtained the school referral letter without any delay as she knew some parents had been refused. School authorities are often reluctant to issue the mandatory referral letter (which describes the problems noticed in the child when he/she is reading, writing or doing mathematics and the child's behavior in the classroom) because of bureaucratic problems.

Fifth Grade

Since Percy has been officially diagnosed as having a specific learning disability his spelling mistakes are now condoned. He has not yet been allowed to drop Hindi (his second language) as a subject in school although the state government rules permit this accommodation. The school principal again asked him to attend remedial classes in the school library. This time Percy agreed as he now perceives these classes to be a form of recreation that offers an enjoyable break from academics. The remedial classes are conducted by the school special educator twice a week for an hour each. Percy attends them during his craft and value education (character education) class periods so that he doesn't miss content area instruction. However, Percy's mother and private remedial teacher are both unaware of the nature of the remedial exercises that are provided by these special education classes as this information is not provided to the family.

Percy is also continuing the same schedule of private tuition and remedial classes. His mother reported that he enjoys the private remedial sessions "because for him they are just another form of play," but he does not like the private tuitions because of the academic demands imposed. The private remedial teacher has observed that his attention to his work has increased since he has started the medication for ADHD. He has made slow, but steady gains in handwriting and reading. The private remedial teacher continues to use segmentation and color coding for teaching vocabulary. Percy's arithmetic has improved to the extent that he no longer needs support in this academic area.

DYSLEXIA DIAGNOSIS AND TREATMENT ISSUES

Percy's difficulties were noticed by his school teacher early, when he was in third grade (8 years old). His teacher informally told Percy's mother about his poor handwriting skills, but the school authorities did not take any initiative to have him evaluated nor did they provide counseling or recommendations to the mother. Luckily for Percy his mother was aware of

SpLD because of the problems her eldest child experienced. After she independently secured an evaluation and his diagnosis was confirmed, Percy started remedial education with a private remedial teacher (special educator). He did not access special education services from his school until fifth grade although these were offered to him in fourth grade.

In Mumbai, awareness of SpLD among parents, teachers and doctors is still less than optimum (Karande, 2008). In 1996, the state government of Maharashtra was the first in India to formally grant children with dyslexia the benefit of availing necessary provisions/accommodations to enable them to complete education in regular mainstream schools (Karande & Kulkarni, 2005). Initially from 1996 to 1999 children with SpLD were given provisions/accommodations only during their ninth grade school examination and tenth grade state board examination. The state government realized that this was grossly inadequate and subsequently in the year 2000, children with SpLD were given provisions/accommodations throughout their schooling years, namely, from first grade to twelfth grade (Karande & Kulkarni, 2005). In 2003 the state government of Maharashtra extended the provisions to college courses; seats were even reserved for adolescents in the physically handicapped category (Karande & Kulkarni, 2005). A recent judgment of the Mumbai High Court has clearly stated that in Maharashtra it is mandatory for the school and college authorities to provide these provisions as denial would be regarded as contempt of court resulting in possible prosecution of school/college authorities who would be considered liable (Anonymous, 2006). As a result of this ruling, awareness of the needs of these children has grown in India. Since 1999, the national Educational Boards which conduct the Indian Certificate of Secondary Education and the Central Board of Secondary Education examinations have also formally granted children with dyslexia the benefit of availing the necessary provisions/accommodations (Karande & Kulkarni, 2005). Subsequently, in the last few years the state governments of Karnataka, Tamil Nadu, Kerala, Gujarat, and Goa have also granted these provisions/accommodations (Karande, 2008).

The municipal learning disability clinic where Percy was evaluated was established in 1996 and was the only "certification center" recognized by the Maharashtra state government as a competent authority until 2007 when a second clinic in the city was authorized. Considering the number of children in Mumbai and state of Maharashtra, there is a need for many more government recognized centers to be established in other cities and towns of the state. Ironically, Percy was lucky to have an elder brother diagnosed with the same problem as this led to his early diagnosis, which occurred prior to school's awareness of the problem. If Percy's mother had not taken the initiative, his problems would not have been addressed until he was in the fifth grade (when he would have probably started failing in his school examinations) or even later. Most dyslexic children, including those with co-morbid ADHD, are referred late after having suffered chronic academic underachievement or even class detainment (Karande & Kulkarni, 2005; Karande, Satam, Kulkarni, Sholapurwala, Chitre & Shah, 2007). For example, the mean age of children who are diagnosed as having SpLD in the clinic where Percy was evaluated is approximately 12 years (Karande et al., 2007; Karande, Bhosrekar, Kulkarni & Thakker, 2009).

At present, remedial education is still not available in many schools even in a mega-city like Mumbai and many parents cannot afford the services of remedial teachers (special educators) working in the private sector (one session costs about Rupees 250; 1 US$ = 50 Rupees; Karande, 2008). There is no law in Maharashtra or India that mandates that a school should provide remedial education within its premises (Karande, 2008). Percy is also fortunate that he attends a school that offers remedial education within its premises. In India, there are no guidelines regarding the way remedial education should be done. Special education teachers have the option of choosing any method they believe will best aid the child. As seen in Percy's case, the school remedial teacher (special educator) has not informed his mother of the methods she has selected for him and she will not communicate or cooperate with his private remedial teacher.

Another problem faced by dyslexic children in India is coping with the language learning demands. The education system in India comprises three streams; namely the two national Educational Boards: the Indian Certificate of Secondary Education (ICSE) board and the Central Board of Secondary Education (CBSE) board; and the Secondary School Certificate (SSC) board which is run by each state government. If the child is attending a CBSE or ICSE board affiliated school he/she must learn three languages from second to eighth grades; and in the ninth and tenth grades only two languages. In a SSC board affiliated school the child does all 3 languages from second grade to the board examinations in tenth grade. Children with dyslexia find it extremely difficult to cope with these language learning demands. These second and third languages (Marathi and Hindi) create near insurmountable problems especially for dyslexic children who come from English-speaking backgrounds (as in Percy's case). These dyslexic children find it difficult to learn the grammar and writing in these second and third languages. Reading is difficult and laborious as they read word by word without understanding the meaning; and writing is difficult as these children primarily tend to think in English and then translate the content in their mind to write in the second or third language.

PARENT PERSPECTIVES

Percy's mother described him as a very loving, caring child who is full of life and always on the run. She stressed that since Percy's nature is very affable he makes friends easily. Percy is always happy; he loves company and wants to play all the time. He is good at sports: swimming, billiards, and skating. Knowing Percy's love for sports, his mother has ensured that every day in the evening after he finishes his tuition classes he goes to the local gym-khana (club) to play billiards with his friends for an hour before returning home. She makes efforts to improve his general knowledge by ensuring that he watches educative programs such as National Geographic's Animal Planet on television. The mother also describes Percy as a sensitive child. Since he saw the terror attacks on Mumbai on television, he refuses to sleep alone or with his brother as he only feels safe with his parents or grandmother.

Percy's mother is aware of the meaning and significance of his learning disability and ADHD. In spite of both her sons having these conditions she has faced the situation remarkably well. As indicated by the mother's response on the Parent Perception Scale, she is aware that Percy's reading problem is significant and greatly interferes with school success, but she does not believe that the problem has affected his family life or friendships. The mother believes that Percy has made significant progress as a result of remedial education and medication even though "he still hates to read and write." She reads to Percy very little as she wants him to read independently, which she has found to be "impossible" since he will only comply when tuition teachers require him to do so.

She is quite sure that Percy (like his elder brother) over a few years will be able to largely overcome his academic problems. Hence, she insists that Percy attends his remedial classes regularly and also takes his medication for ADHD without fail. She is positive about Percy's future and does not worry about it.

However, Percy's mother does not believe that remedial education and medication are sufficient to help Percy overcome his academic problems. She believes that private tuitions for his regular school subjects are also very important for achieving academic competence. Therefore she has thrust a vigorous schedule of private tuitions (up to 11 hours per week) onto him. She is aware that Percy does not like attending these classes as the teachers are strict and demanding; especially the arithmetic tuition teacher. The mother reported that Percy is scared of his tuition teachers as he always completes the homework given by them (at times by getting up at 6 a.m. to complete the work).

Percy's mother is aware of his hectic daily schedule (from Monday to Friday) and its repercussions as she admits that "He is busy from morning to night and this often results in his school homework, especially the school arithmetic homework, remaining incomplete." To help Percy cope with his hectic schedule his parents have ensured that he travels all day in a chauffeur-driven car (i.e., from home to school to private remedial classes/ tuition classes to the club and back home by 8 p.m.). After dinner Percy's mother, if necessary, also helps him finish his school homework before he goes to sleep by 10 p.m.

She is a bit upset that the school authorities did not guide her to have Percy evaluated. She is also dismayed that in spite of both her sons being afflicted, the school authorities have never counseled the family or explained the meaning of the term dyslexia. However, she appreciates that when she made a request the school principal promptly helped her obtain an official learning disability certificate and that Percy's spelling mistakes are now condoned. She is dissatisfied that the school authorities have not allowed Percy to drop Hindi language as a subject. She faced lots of problems getting Hindi language dropped as a subject for her elder son, who was finally allowed to drop the requirement in grade eight when his private remedial tutor (who is also currently Percy's tutor) threatened the school authorities with contempt of court. As per government rules this accommodation should have been provided as soon as his dyslexia was diagnosed.

Percy's mother admitted that she is not fully aware of the laws and regulations that the state has made regarding SpLD, but she has no major grouse against his school authorities, teachers or his classmates. She believes her child's school treats dyslexic students relatively well and has heard that this may not be the case in other schools.

CHILD PERSPECTIVES

Percy does not like to study and would prefer to play games with his friends, play on his own (video games, puzzles), or watch television. He believes that other children like him because he is playful and is a good friend. He is keenly aware of his reading and writing problems in school and admits that he finds it extremely difficult to read in class. This is apparent by his comment "I read only in school when asked to; and then I stand and read with my head put down." However, interestingly enough, in contrast to his mother's perception, he does not believe that the problem interferes with school success. He complained that he doesn't like it when his teacher gives a lot of work to write and when she erases material on the blackboard before he can copy it. Yet, he enjoys going to school as his teachers (all except his Hindi language teacher) and classmates are good to him. However, he is aware that if his teachers were to be strict then he would be facing lots of problems in school.

Both his mother and his private remedial teacher have explained dyslexia to him. He is aware that his elder brother has the same problem, but they do not talk about this with each other. Although he has never discussed his dyslexia with his school classmates, he is not ashamed of his problem. When classmates ask him why he goes to the school library he does not hesitate to explain it is because he has a problem with his reading and writing.

Percy enjoys going to private remedial classes; this is apparent because he never complained about them even once during his interview. He admits that he does not like attending the tuition classes, saying "The best thing about school is I don't have to go to tuitions in the morning." His daily hectic schedule irritates him. This is apparent as two of his three wishes are (1) no tuitions and (2) no traveling long journeys in car in traffic jam. The traffic in Mumbai is very heavy and this does not allow Percy to come home to rest after school hours are over. He has to travel directly after school to his grandmother's house where he rests before attending his private reme- dial and tuition classes. However, Percy does not feel any anger or dissatis- faction towards any of his tuition teachers. Although he becomes worried when he has not done his tuition teacher's homework, he also admits that this teacher is also the only one he can talk to, and who makes him feel better about his reading problem.

Percy adores his mother. He admits that he feels "really sad" when his mother gets annoyed with his behavior and stops talking with him. He immediately apologizes because he cannot bear being ignored by his mother. Percy becomes easily irritated while interacting with his elder brother and often fights with him. He wishes that he would become stronger or that his elder brother would become weak so that he could beat him. He is aware that his parents do not approve of this sibling rivalry, but he is unable to resist fighting with his elder brother. Regarding his parents, Percy says that they are proud of him when he gets good marks (in his tuition classes) or when he wins in swimming or skating competition.

When the work at school becomes very difficult, Percy's strategy is to "leave it" for his mother to complete later or to get a friend's work to copy. Percy could not identify the best reader in his class. He is unsure about the significance of learning to read, remarking that he thinks "it is not so important." He justified his opinion by explaining that there are many things one does in life that don't require reading, particularly after finishing school. Percy does not demonstrate any understanding of the relation that reading has to success in other areas of school and adult life. He doesn't really have any idea what he will become when he grows up as he has "not thought about it" at this point.

CASE COMMENTARY

Since 1996, children with specific learning disability (dyslexia, dysgraphia, and dyscalculia) have been granted the benefit of provisions and accom- modations by the state of Maharashtra. However, at the current time there is no law that specifies the state's obligation towards these children and stipulates what support they should be given (Karande, 2008). Hence, most schools in Mumbai and Maharashtra do not have remedial centers within the school premises. Most parents have to spend money from their own pockets and travel long distances with their child after school hours to attend private remedial classes. Sadly, awareness about specific learning disability only exists in a few good schools. As can be seen in Percy's case, in spite of having a special educator on the school premises, the school authorities did not take any initiative to evaluate his academic problems. The main reason for this apathy is that there is no law that penalizes the school authorities for not detecting dyslexia on time or at an early stage. Another glaring omission in Percy's case is that the school authorities have never explained to his parents the meaning of dyslexia and why he has been instructed to attend remedial classes in the school library. Also, there is no communication between the school remedial teacher and the family or his private remedial teacher.

Percy has begun overcoming his academic difficulties because of the initiative taken by his mother to obtain an evaluation and subsequent remedial sessions. He still needs to continue remedial classes for some years to address his problems. The school has inadvertently helped Percy by not imposing demands on him until the fifth grade. The struggle will now begin in school as he will be facing examinations and his promotion to the sixth grade will depend on his academic performance. The school principal has allowed some accommodations, but time will tell whether Percy will be allowed to avail other provisions, which are mandated by law (e.g., extra time for written examinations, getting a writer during examinations, and dropping of second language (Hindi) for a work experience subject). As Percy's case demonstrates, school authorities do not willingly allow the learning disabled children to avail all the benefits as soon as the diagnosis is made. There is a general tendency to have a patronizing attitude and to allow only a few provisions and accommodations.

Percy's parents have provided him with a secure home life and he's faced his disabilities most positively. In spite of both sons being similarly afflicted, the parents have ensured that their family life and social life are active and enjoyable. Percy's parents express no negativity about his disabilities, future academic progress or prospects in life. This outlook is reflected in Percy's behavior and attitudes, (i.e., he is a happy and friendly child who enjoys his school and social life). Although he is aware of his academic problems, he has a healthy self-esteem. The only possible criticism of Percy's parents concerns their insistence on private tuition classes. In India, there is a large majority of parents of dyslexic children who want to continue with private tuitions along with remedial education to help their child. This appears to be the result of the general trend of most parents sending their children for private tuitions, even if their child is not learning-disabled and already doing well in school.

The problems faced by children with SpLD in India can and must be addressed at a national level (Karande, 2008). Firstly, awareness of this hidden disability has to be increased and the topic of SpLD should be compulsorily taught to doctors, school teachers, counselors, and general public (who are the future parents) during their undergraduate studies. Secondly, an evaluation for SpLD should be considered for all children presenting with learning problems in preschool/school. At present many children with SpLD studying in non-English (vernacular) medium schools, and especially in rural areas, are undetected because of non-availability of standardized psychological and educational tests. This lacuna needs to be corrected by developing standardized psychological and educational tests in all Indian languages (Karande, 2008). Also, few special educators are available to do the educational testing necessary for diagnosing SpLD. Many more universities in our country should develop and offer special education degrees at the undergraduate and graduate levels. Regular school teachers should be encouraged to take up the additional responsibility of becoming remedial teachers (Karande, 2008). Thirdly, SpLD should be recognized as a disability by the central (national) government of India. Since the late 1990s, the national Educational Boards which conduct the Indian Certificate of Secondary Education (ICSE) and the Central Board of Secondary Education (CBSE) examinations; and the state governments of Maharashtra, Tamil Nadu, Karnataka, Kerala, Gujarat, and Goa have formally granted children with SpLD the benefit of availing the necessary provisions/accommodations from first to twelfth grades. However, a large majority of children with SpLD who study in other state government-affiliated schools cannot avail any provisions or accommodations for their disability. In an effort to obtain this, advocacy groups will have to convince the policy makers to amend the Persons with Disabilities (Equal Opportunities, Protection of Rights and Full Participation) Act, 1995, to include SpLD as an official disability. At present this national Act recognizes only the following as disabilities: visual impairment, hearing impairment, locomotor disability, mental retardation, leprosy-cured and mental illness (Karande, 2008). The government of India since 2001 has launched the Sarva Shiksha Abhiyan ('Education for All' Movement) which is a comprehensive and integrated flagship program whose mission is to attain universal elementary education in the country (Karande, 2008). Launched in partnership with the state governments, the program aims to provide useful and relevant education to all children, including children with disabilities. Once SpLD is recognized as a disability by the government of India, children with SpLD studying in every school in every state of the country would be able to benefit significantly. Funds from the Sarva Shiksha Abhiyan would be available to set up detection centers in every city/town/district headquarter; and remediation centers in each school all over the country (Karande, 2008). Once this is accomplished, the outlook for all dyslexic children in India will be greatly improved.

REFERENCES

American Psychiatric Association. (2000). *Diagnostic and statistical manual of mental disorders* (4th ed.). Washington, DC: Author.
Anonymous. (2006, July 22). HC boost for dyslexic students. *The Times of India*. Retreived from http://www.timesofindia.com articleshow/1789910.cms.
Bhatt, M.C. (1971). *Adaptation of the Wechsler Intelligence Scale for Children for Gujarati population* (Doctoral dissertation). University of Gujarat.

Karande, S. (2008). Current challenges in managing specific learning disability in Indian children. *Journal of Postgraduate Medicine, 54,* (2), 75–77. PMid: 18480515

Karande, S., Bhosrekar, K., Kulkarni, M., & Thakker, A. (2009). Health-related quality of life of children with newly diagnosed specific learning disability. *Journal of Tropical Pediatrics, 55* (3), 160–169. PMid: 19042966

Karande, S., & Kulkarni, M. (2005). Specific learning disability: the invisible handicap. *Indian Pediatrics, 42* (4), 315–319. PMid: 15876592

Karande, S., Satam, N., Kulkarni, M., Sholapurwala, R., Chitre, A., & Shah, N. (2007). Clinical and psychoeducational profile of children with specific learning disability and co-occurring attention-deficit hyperactivity disorder. *Indian Journal of Medical Sciences, 61* (12), 639–647. PMid: 118174633

Wilkinson, G.S. (1993). *The Wide Range Achievement Test: manual.* (3rd ed.). Wilmington, DE: Wide Range.

PERCY'S INTERVIEW

1. What do you want to be when you grow up?
   I don't know. I have not thought about it. But I will become something.

2. Tell me about a teacher who has been really important to you or one who has helped you: what did the teacher do to help you?
   My maths teacher. About a month ago, I had not understood how to solve something and I told her that. She called me in the lunch recess and explained it again on the blackboard for about ten minutes.

3. Tell me about a teacher who didn't really help you that much or one who did not give you the help you needed.
   All my teachers have helped me.

4. Tell me what your mother thinks about your dyslexia. Does she talk to you about the problem? What does she say?
   I don't know. She does not talk about my problem.
   Sometimes she asks me whether I have attended my remedial classes in the school library.

5. Tell me what your father thinks about your dyslexia.
   I don't know.
   Does he talk to you about the problem?
   No, he never says anything about it.

6. Tell me about something that makes you really happy.
   If I have to leave writing or studies and get to play then I am really happy.

7. Tell me about something that makes you really sad.

When my mother does not talk to me: when I irritate her, or yell at my brother. I tell her "sorry" and then she talks with me. This happens often.

8. When the work gets very hard at school and you think you can't do it, what do you do?
    I leave it. I don't do anything. Then Mummy writes it. I get the book from my friend.

9. What kinds of books do you like to read?
    I don't like to read any book. I read only in school when asked to and then I stand and read with my head put down.

   What is your favorite book?
    I don't have any favorite book.

   Do you read to yourself?
    No.

   Who else reads to you?
    My grandmother and my father often read a book to me.

10. Do your friends know that you have dyslexia?
    Yes. I have 3 to 4 friends who have dyslexia and many friends who don't have it.

   Do you talk to them about it?
    No.

   What do your friends say to you about dyslexia?
    They ask me why I have to go to the library. I say I go because I have a problem.

11. *Does your sibling know that you have dyslexia?*
    Yes, he also has it.

   Do you talk to him about it?
    Never.

12. *Name three things you are really good at:*
    Skating, swimming, table tennis.

13. *Name three things you are not so good at:*
    Studies, tennis, running.

14. If you are feeling bad about your reading, is there one person you can talk to who makes you feel better?
    My tuition teacher.

   What does that person say to you?
    She reads it to me. She explains it to me.

15. Do computers help you with your reading?

Not at all. I write on computer. I find that easy. But reading from computer is difficult. I don't check what I have typed.

16. Do you usually have problems with your homework?
    Yes, I cannot finish it.

    Can you do your homework independently or does someone help you?
    My mother sits with me, tells me, and helps me concentrate.

    Is homework a big problem or just a little one?
    Little. But if my teachers were strict then it would be a big problem. All my teachers are nice.

17. If there was one thing you could change about school, what would it be?
    I would change my Hindi teacher. I don't like her at all. Out of 43 of us only ten may like her.

18. If you could have three wishes, what would they be?
    1) *I wish I could be very strong.*
    2) *No tuition.*
    3) *No traveling long journeys in car in traffic jam.*

19. Tell me three things you would like your teacher to do to help you with your dyslexia.
    1) *Read the whole story to me.*
    2) *Help me when I cannot figure out jumbled words.*
    3) *Not give me lots of things to write.*

20. Who is the best reader in your class?
    I don't know.

21. Is it important to learn how to read?
    Not so important.

    Why or why not?
    Because for many things you don't have to read; especially after you finish school.

6　Johan, a Case Study of Dyslexia in Sweden

Gunnel Ingesson

Johan was diagnosed as dyslexic nine months ago when he had just turned ten years old. He is a very charming child who is unusually open about his dyslexia. During the interview, he impressed the researcher as a highly verbal child who is quite social and possesses a great sense of humor.

BACKGROUND

Family History

Johan lives with his parents and two siblings in a city in southern Sweden. He is the second child of three siblings. His older sister Jessica is also dyslexic and was diagnosed in fifth grade. He has a younger brother who has not started school yet. Johan's father is a counselor who works with female teenagers in a reformatory. He, too, is dyslexic, but was diagnosed as an adult. Johan's mother, who does not have any reading or writing problems, is a lay worker in a local church community. She does not work full time because of the two children's dyslexic difficulties. She must help them a lot with reading, writing, and homework, for which she receives some financial support from the government. In Sweden, one parent in a family with a disabled child can receive a care allowance from the state health care insurance equivalent to half a salary, or in less severe cases, a quarter of a salary. The object of this is to ensure that the parent can afford to work part-time, since having a disabled child involves a great deal of additional time and effort. In cases that involve dyslexic children this arrangement is rather unusual, unless there are extenuating circumstances. Johan's mother receives an allowance equivalent to a quarter of her salary since she has two children with dyslexia and a dyslexic husband who cannot help out as much as would be expected.

When Johan's sister initially showed signs of reading and writing difficulties, the parents asked her teachers for an evaluation. The teachers were very reluctant to comply as they wanted to "wait and see" how she developed. The parents then took their daughter to a private clinic where she was diagnosed as dyslexic. The teachers did not acknowledge the diagnosis, but two years later she was referred by the school and eventually diagnosed as dyslexic once more. As a result of this experience the parents wanted to make sure that Johan received the help he needed as soon as his difficulties became apparent. They did not want to repeat the circumstances of their daughter's experience.

Medical History

The mother experienced a normal full term pregnancy, but Johan's birth was difficult as there was a problem related to a short umbilical cord that interfered with his heart. When his heart beat could not be detected during labor, he was delivered with a vacuum extractor. Johan came out lifeless and required emergency resuscitation. Mother and child stayed longer than usual at the maternity ward, but after that everything was normal and additional care was not deemed necessary. The mother feels that the shortened umbilical cord was symbolic because she and Johan have always had a close relationship.

During early childhood Johan had infantile febrile seizures on two occasions, so whenever he was sick the parents worried that these would reoccur. The first occurred when he was nine months, but after the second it never happened again. The parents have been to the hospital several times because he has broken his arm and collarbone on separate occasions, and has had many minor injuries involving sprained feet and hands as well as concussions. His mother says that he does not think ahead; he thinks afterwards. As an example, he and his schoolmates on one occasion had a competition in the schoolyard over who could fall most gracefully to the ground, and it was then he broke his collarbone. Johan has never had a serious accident though and has only had the normal childhood diseases.

Early Development

Johan spoke his first words around the age of 1 year, but after that he seemed somewhat delayed in his language development as he experienced specific problems related to articulation and word finding. Initially his nursery school teachers reported that he was delayed, but after the summer holidays when he was almost 2½ years he started to put words together to make sentences. After that his verbal development was explosive and his parents felt they could hardly silence him. In the beginning, he did not articulate very well, but family members understood him. The mother reported that it took Johan an unusually long time to learn the names of colors. While his word retrieval problems did not seem to be particularly significant when he was younger, his mother believes that these have become increasingly obvious as he has developed.

Johan's gross motor development was typical, but he experienced problems with fine motor tasks. He took his first steps around 1 year of age and had no problems walking and learning to ride a bicycle. Johan has been exceptionally good at swimming, for which he recently received a medal for the 200-meter competition for the fifth consecutive year. Johan's mother, being afraid that he would encounter the same difficulties as his older sister and father, had read that it is important for dyslexic children to train balance and gross motor skills so she took him for long walks on rough terrain for training purposes. His fine motor ability developed more slowly and was characterized by problems. The mother reported that he was very late in learning to draw and did not like this activity. Johan was ambidextrous until he started school so he experienced confusion with drawing and writing. He used his left hand for using a hammer and eating, but did not know which hand to use for school activities. He had trouble learning to use writing utensils and scissors.

On the whole, Johan was a happy and easygoing child who also liked to play with other children. Sometimes, there would be conflicts with his friends though, if he felt they did not stick to the rules when playing. His mother described him as a child who is somewhat lacking in flexibility.

SCHOOL HISTORY

Nursery School/Kindergarten

Johan started nursery school early at the age of 1 year since both his parents worked. He had a very good time there, and also in kindergarten later on. He enjoyed playing, especially outdoor activities, such as digging in the sand and land hockey. However, in the last year of kindergarten, which is called preschool class, there were activities designed to prepare the children for school, which he disliked. These activities involved learning simple mathematics, including basic concepts related to quantity, size, and contrasts. Children were also taught to write numbers and letters, and to recognize short words. Holding a pencil correctly, sitting still, taking turns, and so forth, were other important elements of the preschool class. In spite of the pre-academic tasks he disliked, he was also free to do many things that he enjoyed.

First Grade

Johan's difficulties became obvious in first grade when he could not put together letters to identify words and, therefore, did not learn to read. He was behind the other children from the start. Moreover, he had difficulties following directions and understanding what he was supposed to do. Johan realized almost from the beginning that he could not make it like the other children in his class when it came to reading and writing. Very early on he told his mother that "reading and writing is not for me." However, there were other subjects in which he succeeded, such as math and music, and then he said "Mom, this is something for me." Johan's mother and father, knowing that dyslexia is hereditary, asked for an assessment at this point, but the teacher wanted to "wait and see."

Johan's initial reading problems were related to phonological processing and matching letters with sound combinations. Swedish orthography builds on four principles, of which the phonemathic principle is the most important (Cederfjärd & Sandström, 2005). This principle, also called the sound principle, means that each letter represents a sound (phoneme). However, since there are more sounds (phonemes) in the Swedish language than there are letters, there are some systematic exceptions to the rule, and these exceptions are sounds that are written in quite a few different letter combinations. The morpheme principle, also called the meaning principle, means that the significant part of a word is spelled in the same way in different words although they are pronounced differently. Also, there are word pronunciations that have to be learned specifically, such as in many older Swedish words and in loan words. The final principle is that vowels can be pronounced differently, depending on the number of consonants that follow it. Elbro (2004) stated that the more important the non-phonemathic principles are in a language, the deeper is its orthography, or spelling system.

When children have reached the "alphabetical" or "phonological" stage, they are using letter sounds for decoding purposes, which means that they can read new words by identifying letters representing these sounds (Lundberg, 2006). Children in Sweden are expected to have reached this stage by the end of the first grade. Since Johan had not mastered this beginning reading skill, he started to receive some supplementary instructional support toward the end of first grade, every other day, for approximately 20 minutes. He had to leave his classroom for this remediation, something he disliked very much as he felt this singled him out as different so he always considered this to be a punishment. Johan's parents were not very happy with this arrangement either because it turned out that this support consisted of the remedial teacher reading aloud to Johan. The parents felt that they could do that at home and expected school help to be more professional. They also thought that if it was established that Johan's difficulties were indicative of dyslexia, he would receive appropriate instruction specific to his needs.

Eventually the remedial teacher discontinued the reading aloud and began to train Johan in reading and spelling. However, the mother felt that the extra help had not made a difference as Johan failed to make any progress. It was a frustrating time for both Johan and his family; his mother felt it was awful to see Johan fall behind his classmates and become disillusioned about his abilities. This was a sad experience for her and her son.

Second Grade

By the time Johan reached second grade, he no longer wanted to attend school. It became more and more difficult for the parents to motivate him in the mornings. The supplementary instruction he received in school was very similar to that he had received in first grade. He had great difficulties focusing on what he was supposed to do in school. Also, he had problems comprehending the meaning of school and his self-confidence became even more adversely affected. He was not making any progress in reading and writing. The parents, keenly aware of the hereditary link in dyslexia, once again requested an evaluation of Johan's reading difficulties. The teachers, however, did not think that an assessment was necessary since he was already receiving special instructional assistance. Even though Johan's classroom teacher was generally supportive, she seemed uncertain about her responsibility and was content to let the remedial teacher handle everything. The mother felt that the school did not take any extra interest in Johan's difficulties. The fact that he was provided extra support relieved their conscience regarding obligations they might have to this child who was not succeeding. She also feels that her knowledge of dyslexia has always exceeded that of the teachers in school.

Third Grade

After additional pressure from the parents, the assessment was finally carried out in the third grade by the remedial teacher, the school psychologist, and a speech therapist at a local hospital. This is a rather common arrangement for diagnosing dyslexia in Sweden. In most cases, it is considered necessary that the child be evaluated by these three professionals, but it would be uncommon for schools to have their own speech therapists. The assessment procedure is often delayed because of long waiting lists for school psychologists and even longer for speech therapists. Therefore, it is not unusual that, when it is finally decided that an assessment would be desirable, the child may wait for at least one and often two years. In Johan's case, the process was hastened only because his parents agreed to allow the speech therapist to video-tape Johan during the testing. The therapist, who taught speech therapy students at the university, needed a film to demonstrate dyslexia assessment. Parents in Sweden are not generally open to exposing their children to strangers, so she had trouble finding a child suitable for this video recording. Therefore, when Johan's parents agreed, she made an exception and placed him at the top of the waiting list.

The remedial teacher did not use any standardized tests, but rather gave a more descriptive account of his abilities. Her assessment indicated that Johan could read "easy to read books" where the text comprehension was supported by pictures. He was able to proficiently understand and discuss texts in social science as long as he did not have to read the material. Johan's gross motor development was good, but his fine motor skills were weak. His difficulties with hand and finger functioning affected his ability to draw figures and write legibly. His writing was characterized by numerous omissions of letters and words, and he could not read much of what he had written. However, he demonstrated age appropriate mathematics skills with the exception of problems related to denominate numbers. Johan also had problems comprehending and memorizing oral instructions, requiring the support of pictures or other visual memory cues.

The intelligence test (WISC-III) revealed normal cognitive potential (FSIQ of 107) with a significant discrepancy between verbal (VIQ of 116) and performance abilities (PIQ of 95). Johan's score on the Raven's Matrices, a nonverbal logical test, resulted in placement at the 65–70th percentile, which was above average. The speech therapist found that receptive and expressive abilities in oral speech were normal for his age. Yet, Johan was slow in rapid naming and he demonstrated great difficulty with his phonological abilities when he read and spelled. His spelling test results placed him at the third stanine. Johan's text comprehension was affected by his extremely slow reading speed. He could read a very easy text, but the speech therapist concluded that Johan needed CD books to be able to 'read' texts that were age appropriate with respect to content and theme. She also found that he had difficulties with oral sequences because of impaired auditory working memory.

In summary, the assessment showed all the signs of phonological difficulty that are specific to reading and writing difficulties associated with dyslexia. Johan demonstrated unexpected reading achievement problems in reference to his overall cognitive ability.

Fourth Grade

Johan has gradually realized that he must attend school, but is still very reluctant to do so. His mother feels school constantly reminds him of his shortcomings and that it continues to erode his self-confidence. Johan himself says that of all things, he likes school vacation best, an opinion reflecting his mostly negative school experiences. He continues to enjoy math and music, but he is only able to read and write very simple texts that are not age appropriate. The academic expectations are rising and Johan is lagging further behind his classmates. When all the other pupils in his class are assigned to read a novel, his mother must find the same book in a CD format for Johan since he cannot read such difficult texts. She thinks that it would be natural for the teachers to do this for him, but requiring such things, she is afraid that the teachers think she is tedious and says,

Before I dare to ask for such things, I have sleepless nights. It is so tiresome to have to be the one who questions their way of teaching. Therefore, I do it on my own.

Recently the teacher told the class that everyone would be reading aloud sections of a book that had been assigned. Since Johan had listened to the book and knew he could not read aloud, he asked the teacher what he should do. The teacher replied, "it will solve itself." Johan didn't understand how, but finally told his mother he had found a solution to this problem: "I won't go to school tomorrow." So, of course, the mother continues to be frustrated that his teachers do not understand his problem. Apart from his dyslexic difficulties, he finds it very difficult to structure an assignment. For example, if he is to write an essay on a subject like "describe your family," he has no idea how to even start.

Another problem that Johan has recently begun to face is learning English, which starts in the fourth grade. Swedish orthography is generally believed to be deep with medium complexity, as compared with Spanish and Italian that are considered to have a less complex syllabic structure. Swedish is considered to have the same complexity level as Dutch (Seymour, Aro & Erskine, 2003). On the other hand, English is much more complex and almost always poses a great problem for dyslexic children in Sweden. The English words are much more difficult to read and write than the Swedish. Johan complains that "English words are a great problem for me; the others in my class just have to repeat them once and I have to rehearse them every day."

In spite of the mother's general dissatisfaction with Johan's school, she has seen some improvements since his dyslexia diagnosis. He has been provided with a laptop computer that he can use in the classroom, for remedial sessions, and at home, which has been a positive change. On his laptop he has a spelling program designed for dyslexic children and a word prediction program. There is also a synthetic speech program that can read a text for him. He now receives individual instruction for several hours a week. His special education teacher sometimes assists in the classroom, too. She encourages him to remember what to do, asking such questions as "Did you bring your books, are they in your bag?" She also makes him write down his assignments. There is better coordination between classroom work and remedial work. The teachers collaborate more now. However, as illustrated above by the teacher's suggestion that Johan's problem would "solve itself," not all teachers in school understand dyslexia and its implications for practice.

DYSLEXIA DIAGNOSIS AND TREATMENT ISSUES

Johan's mother thinks that the best thing about the assessment was that Johan became aware that he was not less intelligent than his classmates, since he had felt stupid before. He realized that his difficulties are specific and only affect his reading and writing. He has relaxed after the diagnosis and has been brave enough to tell his classmates about his dyslexic problems.

In Sweden there are no established common standards for either identification or remediation of developmental dyslexia. Schools have their own regulations and guidelines, so there can be great differences depending on which school a child attends. In the last decade assessment procedures that were used in Johan's case have become more common, but in many places the assessment is carried out by a specially trained teacher alone, or the school psychologist, or a speech therapist. While there is not unanimous agreement about the diagnostic criteria, the majority of professionals agree that dyslexic difficulties typically result from a deficit in the phonological component of language that is often unexpected in relation to other cognitive abilities (i.e., the definition adopted by the board of directors of the International Dyslexia Association (2002). As a rule, the school remediation teacher assesses the reading and spelling levels when a child is suspected of having dyslexia. The school psychologist then investigates cognitive strengths and weaknesses to determine whether the reading and writing difficulties are unexpected in relation to the child's intelligence. It is common that a speech therapist completes that last piece of the assessment through the examination of the child's language, including possible phonological difficulties and word retrieval ability, to determine whether the child should be diagnosed as dyslexic.

Remediation and training programs in Sweden differ a lot, depending on the teachers' training, interests and experience. In many cities, courses in dyslexia are provided for teachers, but they are voluntary and differ in content and quality. Most schools have at least one special education teacher who is usually more qualified in dyslexia than the regular teachers, but there is great disparity in remedial methods. Some teachers focus on phonological training and others on general improvement of reading and writing.

While there are no federal laws dealing specifically with the treatment of dyslexia, the schools are required to address student achievement problems when "it has become known by the school staff, the student or the student's parents that the student needs extra support in school, the school headmaster shall see to that a remediation program is established" (Grundskoleförordningen, kap 5, §1) [Compulsory School Ordinance, Chapter 5, §1]. Moreover, this ordinance states that "a student shall be provided with supportive education, if there is an apprehension that the student will not reach the goals in the fifth or the ninth school year," and "special support shall be given to students that are in need of it" (Grundskoleförordningen, kap 4, §4 [Compulsory School Ordinance, Chapter 4, §4]. Legislation places responsibility on schools to provide the interventions needed, but there is no legal right for students to request these. Thus, the parents have no legal grounds to insist on an assessment or any special type of intervention.

PARENT PERSPECTIVES

Johan's mother described him as lively, imaginative, and funny. He is also very friendly and empathic. She perceives him to be socially gifted and does not believe that dyslexia exerts much influence on his friendships. Johan is musically gifted and likes to sing. He also enjoys helping out in the kitchen.

Since Johan's father and older sister are also dyslexic, everyone in the family is well acquainted with the associated difficulties. Yet, his mother feels that dyslexia can manifest itself in different ways as Johan and his sister do not share all the problems in the same fashion. She feels that Johan has more difficulties with concentration than his sister, but on the other hand, he is smarter. She perceives his reading difficulties to be substantial, imposing significant limitations on school success. Yet, she is convinced that he will find his own way when he grows up, but she very much wants him "to get help now so he can handle it as an adult." She is philosophic about his challenges, believing "all people are limited in some way or other, and this will be his limitation." The mother is concerned that Johan's dyslexia might have an impact on his capacity to learn other languages though, as Johan has great trouble with English. At universities in Sweden most of the literature is in English. Johan's father has rather recently completed several courses at the university. He wanted to show that this was possible in spite of dyslexia, and hopes that Johan will benefit from his example.

The mother feels that her family endured much hardship in the efforts to obtain a diagnosis in spite of the fact that both his sister and father are dyslexic. The teachers did not think it necessary since Johan received some instructional assistance anyway. However, since the diagnosis, the teachers have thanked the parents for being so persistent and fully admit that the assessment, which would not have happened without parental pressures, has had a positive influence on Johan's life.

The mother thinks that Johan's and his sister's dyslexic problems affect family life a great deal. The parents cannot leave it up to their children to take care of the schoolwork like many others who have children who are 10 and 13 years old. The mother must help out several hours every day, not only with homework, but keeping up with what happens in school for both of them, but mostly for Johan. They have to plan in advance since both children need more time to keep up with the other children. Also, since Johan's father is dyslexic too, he cannot help with many of the reading-related activities.

Johan's mother is unsure how much all the individual instruction has helped him. The parents have asked the teacher to set up short-term goals and evaluate these continually, at the very least to keep Johan motivated, but this has never been done. She is critical about the school in the sense that not all teachers have knowledge of dyslexia, and they do not try to understand Johan's specific difficulties. Homework is a very significant problem as she must assist him throughout the process as he "never does anything automatically or voluntarily." During the past fall, Johan's classmates had a lot of homework, at least three assignments each week, which Johan did not have. When the mother asked the teachers about this, they explained they were not requiring Johan to do any homework because of his reading difficulties. After their discussion with the mother, the teachers reconsidered their original accommodation and rather abruptly decided they should be requiring Johan to do the same homework as the other children. Since by this time it was close to Christmas, the teachers decided Johan could complete all of the homework assignments from the first term over the holidays. This was rather shocking to the mother. Although the teachers might have believed this would be in the best interest of the child, it would have been punitive to Johan who greatly enjoys his holidays and needs a break from the stress associated with academics. The mother flatly refused and from that point on, she has decided that she will make all decisions regarding the amount of homework Johan will complete each week. In general, she feels that she has too great a responsibility for his school achievements and she must fight too much to get the help he needs. Sometimes she feels "like a lion mother who has to defend him" because nobody really understands him at school. This, of course, affects her and she feels that she can never "take a break from dyslexia."

The mother clearly understands the nature of dyslexia and its associated problems. As a matter of fact, she seemed particularly insightful of the nature of this condition as she indicated "it is easy to say that it is reading and writing difficulties, but it is so much more," including "concentration to comprehend situations." She also believes that "low self-esteem can be a secondary effect of the dyslexia." The mother expressed concern that Johan is such a positive and lively child at home, and yet when visiting school, she has observed him to be "shy, reserved, and uptight," sometimes sitting on a fence by himself appearing to be very insecure.

Although the mother isn't familiar with the country's regulations for serving children with dyslexia, she was surprised and disappointed that Johan's diagnosis seemed to have little impact on the resources and professional support that he receives at school. She is also concerned that school does not receive extra funds for dyslexic students and that there may be too many children with learning difficulties in classes. If there was one thing the mother would change about the way the school treats children with dyslexia it would be to treat them more individually, "that is, I wish they would take my son more seriously" and try to determine his specific needs. As the parent of a dyslexic, she believes that her most difficult challenge concerning his reading problems is to understand what her expectations for performance should be.

CHILD PERSPECTIVES

Johan is a very engaging child who is also insightful about the influence of dyslexia on his life. Like his mother, he realistically perceives his dyslexia to be a significant problem that greatly interferes with school success.

Given three wishes, his first would be to "wish my dyslexia away." While he is distressed about the problems that dyslexia poses at school, it seems to have minimal influence on his home and social life. He appears to be very content with listening to CD-books that interest him and does not seem to mind that he cannot read the books himself. Asking him why it is important to be able to read, he thinks quite a while and then says, quite practically, "if you need medicine because you have an allergy, it is not good if you cannot read the label on the bottle." In Sweden, the majority of television programs are broadcast in English with Swedish subtitles that Johan cannot read, but that doesn't appear to concern him as he is more interested in Swedish programs about home renovation that he watches with his father. It seems his reading difficulties would not have any great impact on his life if it were not for school requirements.

Johan has self-confidence with respect to other subjects in school and other personal domains. He thinks he is good at mathematics and sports, such as swimming and jujitsu, and he enjoys scouting. He likes playing with his three best friends whom he has known for a long time.

Johan is rather vague about his future career aspirations. At one time he wanted to become a policeman, but has since realized that is childish. He also mentioned that he wanted to be the same as his father, but interestingly enough he said he didn't remember what his father did, and referred the interviewer to the mother for this information.

Johan expressed few negative feelings about school in the interview. If there was one thing he could change, he mentioned that he would like everyone to have better teachers. He also described a situation in which another child had complained that it was unfair that Johan had a computer at school; however, the teacher reprimanded the child, who never complained again. He does not like it when teachers become angry and yell at the class or when his friends treat him as if he were "different or strange, but it is not very often." He has not had any specific bad experiences and does not feel that teachers or children have been mean to him at school. He is very certain though, that the thing he likes best is school vacation, especially the beginning of a long summer vacation (children in Sweden have at least nine weeks of vacation in summer). Asking what makes him sad, he jokes first and says "end of vacation," but then he says "a lot of homework."

As opposed to his mother, Johan does not think that his dyslexia affects family life very much. He is aware though that his mother thinks it is tiresome to have two children with dyslexia, and that it means a lot of extra work for her to help out with homework, reading and English. However, it seems that it has been helpful for him that both his father and sister are dyslexic. He compares his reading ability to his father's and states smilingly that "he reads better than me, but I am not far behind." Johan believes that he inherited his dyslexia from his father and seems to be very sensitive to the challenges his father faces as he struggles to improve his reading. Johan may take some measure of comfort in the fact that his family has a heightened understanding of the nature of this condition and therefore can lend considerable support to one another.

He could not think of anything that made him worried, but mentioned homework on five separate instances in the interview. One of these was in relation to his parents: he stated that his parents were proud of him when he has done his homework, and disappointed when he doesn't do it. He also said that when he does his homework he "feels proud, but uneasy," perhaps indicating that he is insecure about the outcome. Apparently, this is one area of school that continues to have somewhat of a negative influence on his home life as there is quite a bit of associated stress.

CASE COMMENTARY

The case of Johan is rather typical for children with developmental dyslexia in Sweden, especially considering his school experiences. It is not uncommon that the disability is present in close relatives and in Johan's case both his father and his sister had been diagnosed some years before Johan's difficulties became apparent. Thus, the parents were very observant of early signs of dyslexia in Johan and were persistent in efforts to secure an early evaluation for him. Nonetheless, it wasn't until Johan was ten years old that he was diagnosed. Most experts in Scandinavia agree that early identification is important for several reasons even though most children wait much longer for an assessment than Johan did in this case (Höien & Lundberg, 1999). There is a tendency for teachers to delay evaluation of children with possible dyslexia in spite of obvious signs and the presence of heredity indicators. Unfortunately, when teachers finally realize that an evaluation is necessary, the waiting lists for psychologists and speech therapists result in the child having to wait for an unreasonably long time before testing. The result is that children are left with the feeling of confusion and embarrassment since they cannot cope with the things that everyone else in the class seems to master. It is not long before self-confidence is affected. Johan's mother described this very vividly when she explained how her lively and friendly little boy turned into a shy and uptight child in school. Beginning as early as first grade, Johan developed an aversion to school.

Apart from the unnecessary and unfortunate delays of assessment procedures, Johan's case is also typical, in the sense that once a child is diagnosed with dyslexia in Sweden, it is not certain that appropriate remediation will be forthcoming. It is up to the schools to provide dyslexic students with proper instruction and therapy, the quantity, and quality of which will vary according to individual teachers' commitment and education. Johan's mother was unsure whether all the individual instruction he received had any effect at all. The instruction seems to have been carried out in a routine fashion, with no special consideration of Johan's individual needs. It is surprising that teachers seem to have little interest in evaluating their methods or using research findings in order to improve their teaching methods. Johan's mother had become a reluctant expert on dyslexia, and yet she feels that she has had little influence on the programs provided for her children.

Considering Johan individually, his dyslexic difficulties seem typical in many ways. His intelligence is average and verbal skills are above average. He shows the typical phonological difficulties and impaired auditory working memory. Also, as most dyslexic children in Sweden, English is extraordinarily difficult for him to learn to read and spell. This is especially troublesome for many dyslexic students because admission to university requires passing grades in English. Children in Sweden start learning English very early on, at the latest in fourth grade, and the requirements for passing examinations are high. In some schools, teachers are allowed to disregard spelling when evaluating the students' performance in English, but it is up to the individual school to make this determination.

Johan is not typical in the sense that he is very open about his reading and writing problems as most dyslexic children try to conceal their difficulties. There could be two reasons for this, the first being that his father and sister are dyslexic. It is likely there has been a lot of talk about dyslexia in the family, which makes the condition seem more usual than unusual. The other reason might have to do with the relief he experienced after diagnosis, since he then felt that he was not stupid, which he had feared.

Johan is an intelligent child with a lot of potential. He is very social and has a great sense of humor as well as a highly supportive family. He is also well acquainted with compensatory devices, such as CD-books and assistive software programs. All these factors are favorable and indicate that he will do well in the future. Hopefully over time he will also feel more comfortable in school when he realizes that his dyslexia does not have to be an obstacle to success.

REFERENCES

Cederfjärd, C., & Sandström, E. (2005). *Barns begynnande ordavkodning -från bokstavsnamn till automatisering* [Children's beginning word decoding—from name of letters to automation]. Unpublished master's thesis. Umeå University, Umeå, Dept of Psychology. Master's thesis.

Elbro, C. (2004). *Läsning och läsundervisning.* [Reading and reading instruction]. Malmö, Sweden: Liber AB.

Grundskoleförordningen Grf, (1994). [Nine-year compulsory school ordinance]. Stockholm: Fritzes.

Höien, T., & Lundberg, I. (1999). *Dyslexi: från teori till praktik.* [Dyslexia: From theory to practice]. Stockholm: NoK.

International Dyslexia Association (IDA). Retrieved from: http://www.interdys.org.

Lundberg, I. (2006). Ingvar Lundberg. In B. Kullberg & E. Åkesson (Eds.), *Emergent literacy: femton svenska forskares tankar om barns skriftspråkslärande.* [Emergent literacy: Fifteen Swedish researchers' thoughts about children learning written language]. Göteborg University, Dept of Teaching Methodology.

Seymour, P.H.K., Aro, M., & Erskine, J.M. (2003). Foundation of literacy acquisition in European orthographies. *British Journal of Psychology, 94,* 143–174.

JOHAN'S INTERVIEW

1. What do you want to be when you grow up?

   I don't know, I haven't thought so much about that. When I was little I wanted to become a policeman, but not now, not any longer. Maybe I want to work with the same as my daddy does. Oh, what is it now? He is also dyslexic, and my sister too. She is older and in the sixth grade. I don't remember what my daddy works with, but he takes care of girls. I don't remember. You must ask Mom later what he does.

   Why do you think you would be good at that job?

   [He couldn't answer this question as he didn't seem to know what to say.]

2. Tell me about a teacher who has been really important to you or one who has helped you: what did the teacher do to help you?

   The one I had from first year to third year, she was very good at dyslexia. She helped me after school. Now I have one named Mr. R. and he is rather good, too. Sometimes I get to sit outside the classroom to do math, and that is good because it is quieter there. I am good at math, but I want to be there because it is not as noisy.

3. Tell me about a teacher who didn't really help you that much or one who did not give you the help you needed. What did you want the teacher to do to help you?

   No, I have only had two teachers, but none of them was mean to me.

4. Tell me what your mother thinks about your dyslexia. Does she talk to you about the problem? What does she say?

   She doesn't like that I got homework over the Christmas holidays. But then she can think it is extra tiresome to have two children with dyslexia. She helps so that I read two pages and she reads four in a funny book. She helps me with English because we don't have so many other home assignments.

5. Tell me what your father thinks about your dyslexia. Does he talk to you about the problem? What does he say?

   Because he is dyslexic, too, I think I got it from him. He doesn't like having dyslexia, he must read, too, now and then and he thinks it is a big nuisance. When I went to jujitsu he used to go with me and he sat and read there. I go to jujitsu once a week and scouting once a week. I used to play baryton, but I had too much homework so I quit that because I didn't have time. But I go to a music class in school so we have music four times a week and now we have a Beatles theme and we have learned four or five songs. My favorite instruments are bass and drums.

6. Tell me about something that makes you really happy.
    Vacations, especially in the beginning, mostly summer vacation.

7. Tell me about something that makes you really sad.
    End of school vacations, (ha, ha), I don't know, maybe a lot of homework. The friends I have, we don't fight, we keep the peace.

8. When the work gets very hard at school and you think you can't do it, what do you do?
    I ask if I can do less, or if I can do it at home. I must do a lot at school anyway.

9. What kinds of books do you like to read?
    I listen to books, I don't read. Just now I listen to Harry Potter 7, and I have read [listened] to all the others before.

    What is your favorite book?
    The Petrini detective stories. I like detective stories and fantasy most.

    Do you read to yourself?
    No.

    Who else reads to you?
    Mom usually reads to me, but when she is at work Daddy reads to me, some simpler book then. He reads better than me, but I am not far behind [laughing].

10. Do your friends know that you have dyslexia?
    Yes, all of them know. I have told them myself, that feels good. Some of the new ones in my class maybe don't know, but since I have a computer they ask and then I think everyone knows.

    Do you talk to them about it? What do you say? What do your friends say to you about dyslexia?
    Some of them think it is unfair that I have a computer at school, one of them yelled that it was unfair and then the teacher got very angry at him. He was quiet after that.

11. Do your siblings know that you have dyslexia? Do you talk to them about it? What do you say? What do your siblings say to you about dyslexia?
    My sister has dyslexia, too, and I have two friends in her class and they have it, too. In her class they are three with dyslexia.

12. Name three things you are really good at:
    Math, jujitsu, making chocolate cake. I can help with cooking, too.

13. Name three things you are not so good at:
    English, reading, and writing.

14. If you are feeling bad about your reading, is there one person you can talk to who makes you feel better?
    My teacher, the special teacher that I have; mom and dad think that she is very good.

What does that person say to you?
Talk to your teacher, you can read here.

15. Do computers help you with your reading? If yes, how do they help you?
Yes, but it is a little tough too, because it takes such a long time to start up. I make good use of it because the text becomes much easier. Now we work specifically with Sweden as a topic and then I go to Mary, my special teacher, and she helps me with the text and then I transfer it to my computer. I don't fetch texts on the internet, but pictures. I also have a program named Vital that reads aloud, so I can listen to texts on the computer and also I have a spelling program so I can get help with the spelling.

16. Do you usually have problems with your homework? Can you do your homework independently or does someone help you?
Mom always reminds me. She must tell me to do my homework, even math, although I can do that on my own. Most of the time, if I have homework in math, I go home after school and do it, and then I can go with my friends to the club, a recreational club, where I play games, pool or ping pong.

Is homework a big problem or just a little one?
Somewhere in between, it depends what kind of homework. If we have a reading assignment, I listen to it in my headphones, but English words are a great problem for me. The others in my class just have to repeat them once, and I have to rehearse them every day. Also I have more homework than the others, because I have to read a hundred words [Swedish]. It is homework that I do for my special teacher.

17. If there was one thing you could change about school, what would it be?
That everybody had better teachers if they aren't good. That it would be easier for me with English.

18. If you could have three wishes, what would they be?
Maybe wish my dyslexia away. That we would win a lot of money on the numbers game, better environment. Or peace on earth, I take away "win a lot of money" and change it to peace on earth.

19. Tell me three things you would like your teacher to do to help you with your dyslexia
That I don't have to do as many texts as the others in the Sweden project. I can't think of anything else. Yes, maybe if I could have an extra teacher in English, that would be good. I have English together with the others now.

20. Who is the best reader in your class?
Maybe Freddy, he is rather smart too, maybe Charlie, too.

How did he/she get to be such a good reader?

They have elder brothers and started to read in kindergarten, and then they continued and they don't have dyslexia.

21. Is it important to learn how to read? Why or why not?

Yes, it is. Let's say you have some allergy and couldn't read on the label what is in it, that wouldn't be good.

7 Alon, a Case Study of Dyslexia in Israel

Talya Gur and David Share

Alon, a 10-year-old boy in the fourth grade, was diagnosed as dyslexic at the age of 8, prior to entering the grade 3. Alon is a bright child who enjoys the support of his close-knit family. During the interview Alon cooperated fully with the interviewer. Nevertheless, he did not communicate easily and although he opened up more in later stages of the interview, he continued to respond to the questions in an abbreviated manner.

BACKGROUND

Family History

Alon lives in a middle class neighborhood in a large city in the north of Israel with his parents and younger sister. Alon's parents were both born in Russia and moved to Israel in 1991 when they were 19 years old. Both studied for academic degrees in Hebrew in Israel and thus speak Hebrew to their two children and, for the most part, between themselves, too. Alon is a Hebrew speaker, but understands Russian to some extent. His 4-year-old sister Dana attends kindergarten, but does not exhibit the sort of difficulties that Alon demonstrated at this age. Alon's father is a detective in the police force and his mother is a social worker who works in a child development center. The mother did not experience academic difficulties as a student, but Alon's father reported struggling with various learning problems as a child and still, today, writes somewhat slowly, with spelling errors. The family enjoys playing games and taking trips together.

Medical History

Alon was born without complications after a normal full-term pregnancy. However, Alon had a congenital orthopedic condition that required his foot to be put in a splint until the age of 4 months. When Alon was several months old, he began suffering from skin eczema for which he was treated until age 3 when the condition resolved. From age 2, Alon suffered from ear infections and was given homeopathic treatment until the infections stopped. Alon was never admitted to hospital, nor seriously ill. In the middle of the third grade, he was diagnosed with attention deficit disorder and, since the beginning of grade 4, has been treated with Ritalin. He takes a tablet a day on school days, but does not take medication during school holidays or weekends.

Early Development

Alon was born to Russian-speaking parents and until the age of 2 years heard and spoke Russian at home. His mother remembers him as a talkative infant who attained all his developmental milestones in language on time. At 1 year, he began speaking his first words and joining words to create short sentences at the age of a year and a half. At the age of 2, Alon entered a (Hebrew-language) kindergarten and his mother reported that in a short time (about one month) he started understanding and speaking Hebrew. At around the age of 4 years, Alon's parents noticed that he had difficulties "finding" words he wanted to use and when he was 5 he was diagnosed by a speech therapist as suffering from a word retrieval problem. Alon's mother emphasized that at no stage was it suggested that the onset of her son's language problems was connected to the fact that Hebrew was a second language for him.

Alon started walking at the age of 1 year. At about the age of 2 years he started riding a tricycle, but was never able to master riding a two-wheel bicycle. His mother remembered that at an early age he enjoyed scribbling although the way he held the crayons was "immature." At about the age of 3½ Alon started avoiding any activity that involved drawing or cutting with scissors. His mother explained that he is a perfectionist and avoids activities in which he had problems. Alon's mother stated that he was an irritable baby who was relatively hard to pacify. During these years he enjoyed the company of other toddlers and had no difficulty playing with them.

SCHOOL HISTORY

Preschool

At the age of 3 Alon attended a small pre-nursery play group. At this stage no questions regarding his cognitive and motor function arose. When he was 4 years old he entered the first year of nursery school and after a few months the teacher called the mother and reported that Alon had problems cutting and coloring and that he tried to avoid taking part in small work groups in which these activities were used. In addition she said that his oral expression was not articulate and that many times while talking he seemed to be "searching" for words. As a consequence, Alon's mother started to devote more time to him, trying to develop her son's motor abilities: she would initiate games and activities that included coloring, drawing and cutting.

Kindergarten

Alon was 5 years old when he entered (compulsory) kindergarten. A large part of the kindergarten year in Israel is dedicated to preparing the children for the first grade by focusing mainly on language and visual-motor activities. As a consequence, Alon's motor difficulties and word retrieval problems became more apparent. Based on the preschool teacher's report and on her own perceptions, the mother asked the kindergarten teacher to closely observe Alon's functioning. The teacher subsequently called the mother and recommended professional help for the child. At this point, Alon started receiving occupational and speech therapy, the latter of which focused on speech sounds and letter identification. These therapies were provided by a university clinic, but were paid for by their health maintenance organization. It was at this time that the mother stated that Alon became aware of his problems and emotional difficulties developed.

His mother stated that a lot of pressure was put on the family regarding the issue of readiness for the first grade and, as a consequence, she remembers this year as a very stressful one. She recalled that the family was continually being told that there was "something wrong with the boy." It was very hard for her to accept this idea and that she too put a lot of pressure on Alon. The mother noted that during this period she was "more a teacher than a mother." At this stage Alon started exhibiting resistance by saying "I don't know" in response to questions even though she knew that he really *did* know the answers. Alon's speech therapist prepared the parents for the possibility that he would encounter difficulties in reading acquisition as a consequence of his phonological and naming difficulties.

First Grade

His first school year was described by Alon's mother as "one big nightmare." Adapting to school was very challenging. Alon did not understand what the teachers and the education system expected of him. For example, organization was a huge problem. He struggled with getting everything he needed into his backpack. He did not seem to understand what he was required to bring to school on a daily basis. He found it hard to follow the schedule and enter the classroom before the bell rang. In addition he did not understand that homework was obligatory and as a consequence many problems revolved around this issue. His mother started helping, but often lost her temper and could not cope so Alon's father took over, but he too soon felt unable to continue.

The mother gave birth to Alon's younger sister at the end of kindergarten so she was at home on maternity leave during his first-grade year. She was glad she could spend time at home and help her son with schoolwork. At the time, this seemed a good solution, but looking back, the mother feels it may have done more harm than good as she put a lot of pressure on her son.

Alon's first-grade teacher understood his needs and tried to assist and support him. She understood, for example, that it was important for Alon to sit alone near a table (and not with a partner as most children do). In addition, she accepted his request to be seated near the wall close to the class door. However, her hands were full as the class was a difficult one and included quite a few children with learning and behavior problems. Thus, she was not able to give additional, more personal, instructional support. The mother stated that Alon had no motivation to learn. As a consequence of the speech therapist's counseling, the mother anticipated that Alon would have difficulties in school and was not surprised when they quickly became apparent. The mother recalled that at the end of the first grade Alon still was unable to identify all the diacritic marks and letters that are part of the Hebrew orthography. He read very slowly and did his best to avoid reading whenever possible.

Hebrew orthography has several elements that differentiate it from English and are important in understanding the nature of dyslexia in Hebrew. First among these, is its derivational morphology (Berman, 1985). Almost all words in Hebrew consist of a consonantal "root" which is embedded in a "pattern" consisting of infixes, prefixes and suffixes. In this way, from the "root" KLT (טלק), for example, the words KALAT (טלק, he grasped) and MIKLAT (טלקמ, shelter) are formed (Share & Levine, 1999). Second, Hebrew can be written in either pointed (fully vowelized) or an unpointed (partly vowelized) script. Reading is taught in the first grade using the pointed form. Thus, the novice reader of Hebrew learns to read an extremely shallow orthography (Share & Levine, 1999). As a consequence, mastery of decoding is accomplished by most children by the end of first grade (Share & Levine, 1999). Thus, the fact that Alon was not able to master early reading skills in this system was an early warning of his problems.

Although the mother was aware of his difficulties in learning to read, she did not seek an assessment at this stage because she could not yet accept the situation. She also mentioned that school personnel did not bring up the possibility of assessment at this point. During this year Alon's mother heard about a book called "It's Hard For Me to Read." The story is related from the point of view of a young child who shares his thoughts about his dyslexia. After Alon read the book, his mother says that his eyes "lit up" as he understood that other children suffer from similar difficulties.

Second Grade

Alon's second school year was described by his mother as a restless year with many changes that caused adjustment problems for the child. Usually elementary teachers in Israel continue teaching the same class for two years but in Alon's case, for various reasons, his first-grade teacher left and a different teacher started teaching him in the second grade. This teacher found it hard to cope with the behavioral problems in the class. About a third of each lesson was devoted just to classroom management. This situation was detrimental to the class as they were missing valuable instructional time, which was particularly difficult for Alon.

Nevertheless, Alon became attached to this teacher and seemed to have more motivation. But after two or three months, his energy diminished and once again he was unenthusiastic about school work. In March this new teacher left on maternity leave and was replaced by yet another teacher, a transition that lowered Alon's motivation to learn even further. In June, his original homeroom teacher returned from her maternity leave and, once again, the change affected him negatively.

During this school year Alon started receiving private help from an educational therapist. This additional help, which was given at home after school hours, was initiated by his mother who felt she had to reduce the pressure at home. These lessons, involved the teacher working with Alon on his homework twice a week for one-hour sessions. This assistance partly relieved his parents of the task of coping with homework preparation. As a result, Alon's interaction with his parents improved.

Alon did not like these lessons and objected to them, but they continued nonetheless throughout the school year. Alon's mother felt that these lessons advanced him in small steps, although this progress was less apparent in school. In Israeli primary schools, grades are given on a scale of 1–100 in which the passing mark is 55 and 100 is considered "excellent." At the end of the second school year, Alon's grades in Hebrew reading, comprehension, and written and verbal expression were 60 ("satisfactory"). On the other hand, his math grade was 90, which is considered to be "very good." At this point, the school advised the parents to have Alon evaluated.

Third Grade

In order to qualify for assistance from the school, Alon was evaluated by the school psychologist during the summer holiday between the second and the third grades. The findings indicated that Alon's intelligence was above normal (Hebrew version of the WISC-R (Cahan, 1998); Full Scale IQ= 120, Performance IQ= 129, Verbal IQ=110). To assess Alon's reading, he was asked to read a short story at his class level aloud. The diagnostician listed the words that were read inaccurately and noted attention to reading rate. The spelling assessment included tests of copying and dictation. Because no reading and spelling norms for Hebrew existed at the point the assessment was administered, the evaluation of reading and spelling was impressionistic. Alon's reading was described in the evaluation as "partly accurate and extremely slow." When decoding a word, Alon was described as rereading the word again and again until he eventually managed to decode it correctly. In addition, he wrote with numerous homophonic spelling errors. As a result of this assessment, the psychologist diagnosed Alon as having a reading disability. Following this evaluation, he began receiving one 45-minute weekly lesson from the school reading specialist along with another student who had similar problems. The mother noted that this instruction focused on reading comprehension and writing skills, but she was unsure of the exact content of the lessons.

As part of the evaluation Alon underwent a general psychological assessment which, the mother reported, included various personality tests (the exact nature of these tests and a diagnosis, if given, are not available as the assessment was not revealed to the interviewer). After the psychological assessment the parents were given advice on how to deal with him. Following these conversations the mother understood that she must accept Alon's difficulties and stop struggling against them and him. For example, she stopped expecting him to do his homework independently or get his school bag ready on his own, a situation that always ended in a crisis. Now, she understood that she must sit with him on a daily basis, organize the school bag and do "their" homework.

One of the psychologist's recommendations was that Alon be sent for an evaluation regarding his attention problems. The findings from the neurological evaluation were not altogether clear. Although there was clearly a problem in maintaining attention, the neurologist could not determine if it was primary, or a product of his emotional difficulties. Nevertheless, the neurologist recommended that Alon start taking Ritalin. The mother, who was not convinced it would help, gave him the drug on an irregular basis.

For various reasons, in the third grade, the class was given yet another new teacher, which created an additional hurdle for Alon. In spite of this, the year started with great hopes that the remedial reading instruction he was going to receive at school would help. This support consisted of one weekly, 45-minute lesson, in a group of two pupils. The mother reported that although she could see that Alon made some progress as a result of these lessons, the remedial reading teacher insisted that Alon was behaving defiantly and was not deriving benefit from the lessons. Furthermore, Alon was missing nature studies in the hour he was withdrawn for the remedial work. As an accommodation, the school allowed him to give up this subject. In addition to the remedial reading lessons at school, Alon continued his homework assistance sessions once a week at home with the private teacher after school hours.

During this year his homeroom class studied many subjects in small groups (up to 16 children in a group). Although this system made it easier, at least in theory, for the teacher to answer to Alon's specific needs, his experience during this year was not positive. He felt he was continually getting lost: he kept getting confused about his class schedule and was continually missing or arriving late to lessons.

Towards the end of the year Alon's resistance to doing any kind of school work increased. He did not want to go to school and refused to participate in the reading remedial lessons because it made him feel different from his classmates. The mother stated that Alon "did not progress" with his reading during the third grade. The remedial reading teacher recommended that they speak to a "coach" specializing in work with children who have learning disabilities and attention deficit disorder. The emotional difficulties came to a peak in the summer holidays when Alon behaved defiantly and developed a fear of entering elevators and going back to school. As the family lives on the 6th floor of an apartment building, the fear of entering an elevator interfered immensely with daily life and was the cause of a great deal of concern and conflict. As a result, his parents sought emotional help for him by following the recommendation of the reading teacher and securing a coach for Alon.

Fourth Grade

Just before entering fourth grade, Alon started working with a special education teacher who studied and specialized in life coaching for children with learning problems. She was the first professional figure to whom Alon really responded. His mother said that the change in his self image was dramatic. The coach taught him not to be so hard on himself and to develop positive thinking skills. Today, for example, if he receives a test with the grade of 60, he is now able to see that he knows 60% of the material instead of just focusing on what he doesn't know. Alon also started taking Ritalin on a regular basis. The mother decided on this after Alon told her that the medication helped him read and write. In spite of Alon's perceptions of the benefit of medication, it is noteworthy that the mother does not attribute even a small part of the positive change to Ritalin.

Even with the benefits of the coaching and the medication, fourth grade presented both challenging and supportive school experiences. The three third-grade homeroom classes were combined to form two new fourth-grade classes. Once again, Alon was placed in a new class with a new teacher. Nevertheless, he coped with this change with the support of his coach. Also, his new teacher recognized his special needs and made accommodations for him. For example, she allowed him to answer fewer questions during class and reduced the homework load. She encouraged him and managed to give him the feeling that he could be successful with the learning challenges at school. She was very organized and structured, which helped Alon to function in the classroom. His motivation for learning increased as a result of the teacher's attitude and support. He continued taking part in the remedial reading classes once a week and the teacher reported progress although he lagged behind his classmates. Alon, according to his mother, still finds it very hard to read, copy from the blackboard and meet other class requirements. As no standardized measures of reading were used by the school, it is hard to determine how far behind Alon is in his reading achievement. Nevertheless, regarding his classroom requirements, his fourth-grade reading score is 80 (good) while the reading comprehension mark is below 65. There is a gap between his reading score of 80 and his mother's evaluation of his reading ability ("still finds it hard to read") which may stem from her inability to distinguish between his technical reading skills and his reading comprehension. An additional explanation may be that Alon's relatively high grade in reading was inaccurate because of the teacher's difficulty in getting a true assessment of his level. This could happen in a large fourth-grade class where most of the reading is done silently in contrast to lower classes where a lot of the reading is done aloud.

An additional problem concerns the lessons he misses in his homeroom class when he goes to the remedial reading lessons. The question of whether he has to make up the material he misses remains unclear. Although the teacher does not ask him to make up the material he misses, Alon has not been explicitly told he can skip this material.

DYSLEXIA DIAGNOSIS AND TREATMENT ISSUES

As the above description reveals, Alon's difficulties were apparent from an early age; word retrieval, visual-motor coordination, and attention problems were identified in kindergarten. Dyslexia in Israel is diagnosed as a discrepancy between scholastic achievement and intellectual ability with a minimum two-year gap between the child's achievements and those which are the norm for his age and grade. As a consequence, most children in Israel, just like Alon, are not diagnosed before the third grade (Alon was evaluated in the summer just prior to entering third grade).

The Israeli special education law (Special Education Law, 1988) and an amendment to the law which was accepted in 2002 ("integrating law" "*Hok hashiluv*"), allocates school hours ("integrating hours" *sha'ot shiluv*) to aid learning disabled pupils who learn within mainstream schools. In order to qualify for these hours a pupil must be assessed by an educational psychologist or "didactic diagnostician" (*me'avxenet didaktit*) and the case must be brought before an "integrating" committee (*va'adat shiluv*). The principal, school educational consultant, special education teacher, the child's homeroom teacher and his parents participate in this committee. On the basis of the child's evaluation and classroom functioning, a decision is made as to whether to provide additional assistance. Usually these are not individual lessons, but are given in small groups of not more than five children per group. These lessons are given during the school hours and, like Alon, the participating children miss the home-class lessons that are given at the same time.

Psychological and didactic evaluations are given in Israel either by private agencies, in which case they are financed by the parents, or by "learning centers" that are part of the educational system. In some cases the parents prefer having their children evaluated privately as it enables them to choose the diagnostician. Alon's parents, on the other hand, turned to the school and were referred to the school's educational psychologist for an evaluation. The reason they chose the school for the evaluation was that they felt that, in the years to come, they would still have many occasions in which there would be a need to interact with various school officials (teachers, remedial teachers, psychologists) and wanted the "system" to get to know Alon, his abilities and difficulties.

An additional reason that Alon's parents sought a psychological evaluation and not a didactic one is that they were seeking advice on how to cope with the behavioral and emotional aspects of his problems. This guidance is based on information which is collected in the psychological evaluation. While in Israel, a diagnosis of dyslexia can be given either by an educational psychologist or a special education teacher professionally trained to diagnose learning disabilities, the focus of each of these professionals is different to some extent. Whilst the latter focuses on evaluating learning abilities and underlying cognitive and linguistic processes, the former focuses on reading and writing skills in a less detailed way and relates to emotional aspects, too.

Once Alon was diagnosed and recognized by the "integrating committee" he immediately started receiving remedial help from a teacher specializing in learning disabilities. In Israel, there are state guidelines regarding the way reading should be taught. Furthermore, the Ministry of Education determines which of the existing reading instructional methods conform to these principles. Nevertheless, the remedial teacher has the option of choosing any method she thinks will best aid the child. The type of instruction that Alon received is unknown, but in any event, especially during the first year of therapy (third grade) it did not appear to be effective. The mother's explanation for this is that in addition to the didactic assistance, additional emotional support was needed so that he could make use of the tools he was being given. The help he received made him feel different and he expressed this feeling in questions such as "why do I have to get this kind of help and not other children in my class?" There are other reasons that may explain why this support was largely ineffective. Firstly, Alon received only a single 45-minute lesson each week. In addition, this lesson was given in small groups, consisting presumably of children with different needs. In the fourth grade, for example, Alon's learning group consisted of a group of five children, one of whom was very restless and hyperactive, which made it very difficult for Alon, who suffers from attention difficulties himself, to concentrate. Nevertheless, in the fourth grade, as a consequence of the emotional help he received, the mother noted that she saw a slight improvement in his ability to benefit from these lessons.

PARENT PERSPECTIVES

In describing her son, Alon's mother stressed his strengths. She described him as a wonderful, clever, and sensitive child. She stated that he has good logical thinking skills; a great ability to use logic strategically in games and riddles. She added that he has started learning tae-kwon-do and is progressing well. Nevertheless, she is aware of his weaknesses and of the complexity of his situation. She noted he is a challenging child, who demands a lot of introspective learning, thought and consideration from her as to how to deal with his specific needs. Her explanation of the term dyslexia was given through Alon's eyes:

> . . . when you read to me it's fun. I see pictures and understand. But when I read to myself, I am busy trying to read the words and it's no fun.

As one can see, Alon's mother is aware of her son's decoding difficulties. Nevertheless she stated that she does not fully understand what being "dyslexic" really means, but she does understand the significance of Alon's reading problem and how it affects school success as indicated in her ratings on the Parent Perception Scale. In addition, she thinks that his dyslexia significantly interferes with his social life, too; however, she thinks it interferes slightly less with family life. She believes that in elementary school, success is very important for one's self image, and Alon's poor school achievement interfered with the development of a positive self-concept and thus socialization opportunities. The mother sees Alon's difficulties as placing a lot of stress on the family, especially the continuous struggle with homework. Although she is aware of the effect his dyslexia has on different aspects of his life in the present, Alon's mother expressed hope that he will overcome his difficulties and that they will not influence him as an adult.

She is aware that it is her role, as a mother, to be involved with Alon's hardships. At the same time she is dissatisfied with the way the school deals with the situation. She feels that teachers do not give enough thought to Alon's difficulties and do not go out of their way to help or support him. She feels that although the state has laws and regulations regarding dyslexia and other learning disabilities, the parents have a very important role. If they are not aware of their child's needs and do not monitor the school situation and become very involved, the child will often not get what is his due.

CHILD PERSPECTIVES

Alon is a quiet and reserved child who is somewhat reticent to share his feelings. He frequently responded that he would "rather not say" or that he didn't know the answer to a number of interview questions relating to his school performance, friendships, and family life. However, his curiosity and intelligence are evident in his statement that the best thing in school is that one "learns things one didn't know before." Alon does not mention that his parents, or anybody at school explained to him, either before or after his evaluation, about his dyslexia, but says that he and his mother read to one another in order to improve his reading. It seems that Alon, lacks a somewhat deeper understanding of the nature of his difficulties. On the Child Perception Scale, he indicated that his reading problem does not interfere with his family life or social relationships. He rated his reading problem as moderate (i.e., 5 on a scale of 10), but indicated that the problem interferes minimally with school success. These perceptions are very different from those of his mother's who tended to rate the influence of Alon's reading problems as being much more significant.

If he feels any anger or dissatisfaction towards figures at school, (teachers, etc.), and the way he was treated, these feelings are not expressed. Actually, Alon appears to have repressed almost all feelings associated with his dyslexia. He reported that all his teachers, throughout his school years, helped him. Yet, when asked what type of help he was given during these years, he only mentioned the help that was given when taking exams, such as additional time and the use of a calculator.

Alon has two good friends who have been close to him since kindergarten and if there was one thing he could change at school, he says he would "like more friends." This thought is poignant as it shows that despite his poor academic achievement the thing that most disturbs Alon at school is not his academic status, but his social one. Despite the fact that these two boys have been his friends for some years he thinks that they, like the other children in his class, are not aware of his dyslexia. Even though he knows on some level that his social life is lacking, he apparently does not perceive that there is a relationship between his academic problems at school and this lack of friendships. Thus, he also thinks that his reading problems do not affect his social life in any way.

Alon feels happy when he succeeds in doing things that are hard for him and feels sad when he doesn't succeed. He reveals a practical approach to his difficulties and says that when schoolwork becomes very hard and he feels he can't cope he tries to find the answer in other places (in the book). When he grows up, Alon wants to build cars and other machines. He wants to do this because, as a younger child, he enjoyed building cars with his LEGOs.

When Alon described himself, he focused on his weaknesses (i.e., reading and bible lessons at school, particularly the archaic Hebrew in which the bible is written adds to the burden of decoding and understanding). On the other hand he describes playing computer games as his only area of strength, not mentioning the strengths his mother identified (i.e., logical thinking and tae-kwon-do).

Alon, like his mother, sees homework as his major problem. He stated that he cannot do it alone and has to have his parents' help. The fact that Alon says that the worst thing about school is that teachers give so much homework indicates that he is aware of how this influences his day to day life. Nevertheless, in the Child Perception Scale, Alon chose not to share his thoughts about the way this created tension in his family and responded that his reading problems do not affect his family life in any way.

Alon could not identify the best reader in his class, but said such a child probably became a good reader because "he learned at school." He stated that it is important to learn to read so that "you can read quicker and make less mistakes." One can see that he is aware of the importance of learning to read yet he does not demonstrate an understanding of the relationship between reading well and success in other areas of school and adult life. This may explain his response regarding the negligible influence his dyslexia has on his familial and social life and the relative low impact it has on his success at school.

Regarding his family, Alon says that they are proud of him when he succeeds in exams and they are disappointed if he wakes them up while they are napping. It is interesting that he did not mention failure at school as the cause for his parents' disappointment. These statements reveal the delicate balance his parents have managed to create in the last year between their ambition to see him do well at school and their attempts not to put too much pressure on Alon; success is seen as a cause for pride but failure is not seen as a source for disappointment. Alon says his younger sister annoys him when she makes unjust accusations, revealing a normal relationship with his younger sibling. Alon's insight regarding the hardships he has, and will continue encountering during his school years due to his disability, and his concern that his younger sister will have to cope with similar hardships is expressed in the sentence completion section. In this section he completed the sentence: "I wish my sister would . . ." with the words: "do well in school."

CASE COMMENTARY

Since 1988, the rights of Israeli learning-disabled pupils, as of other children with special needs, are protected by law. The "special education law" specifies the state's obligation towards these children and stipulates what support they should be given. As can be seen in Alon's case, the school worked "by the book" and once he was evaluated by the school psychologist he started receiving "integrating hours." The aim of these hours, as defined by the law, is to enable the child to function within the class curriculum. Although Alon has been participating in these "integrating hours" for the last one and a half years, sufficient progress has not yet been seen and today he still finds it very hard to cope in class. In particular, he finds it hard to read, comprehend, and copy from the blackboard. In most cases, he can neither work independently in class nor at home on his homework. Although math is his relative strength, his ability in this field is adversely influenced by his reading problem. His most recent report card, which says that his grade in verbal math problems is 75 ("almost good") while his grade in math that does not include a verbal component ranges between 90 ("very good") and 100 ("excellent"), demonstrates the influence linguistic difficulties have on his math achievement.

There may be several reasons for the fact that although Alon has been taking part in the reading remedial lessons for the last year and a half, sufficient progress has not yet been made. The mother's explanation is that Alon's emotional condition is an impediment to his achievement. She stated that Alon's belief in himself and in his abilities is so low that he has basically given up. The mother sees a direct connection between his emotional state and the difficulties he has had to cope with since kindergarten. Moreover, she assumes considerable responsibility for his emotional state as over the years she has imposed an enormous amount of pressure on Alon regarding his success in school. Alon's mother said that in the two instances in which she did get at least some parental guidance (from the school psychologist and from the current coach), she gained new insights that enabled her to cope better with her son. She reported that even the subtle changes she made in her parenting as a result of the guidance influenced Alon's behavior and the atmosphere at home.

An additional reason for the doubtful effectiveness of the remedial reading for Alon may be that this instruction is not individualized, but rather took place in small groups. Apart from the child's specific needs, many other variables have to be taken into account when creating these groups: the child's grade, the specific class he misses in his homeroom class (most children are not prepared to miss a sports class for example), the social aspects of the small group and so on. As a consequence, although an attempt is made to create homogeneous learning groups the result is not always ideal. For instance, Alon's mother was insistent that her son's learning group for the fourth grade was most unsatisfactory. This group consists of five fourth-grade pupils who need to work on different areas in different ways. This makes it very hard, if not impossible, for the teacher to cater to the students' different behavioral and instructional needs in a 45-minute lesson. Moreover, the school allocated Alon only a single 45-minute lesson per week in order to work on his severe difficulties. This amount of time is clearly inadequate. The school cannot be held completely responsible for this situation as it has a problem balancing budget restrictions with the necessity of providing extra hours for all those who need them. Current research emphasizes the need for intensive instruction if satisfactory progress is to be made (Torgesen et al., 2001). The task is seen by the authors as one which clearly extends beyond the educators who are charged with providing direct instructional services to higher political forces that must fight this battle.

Alon's mother said that if she could change one thing about school she would change the amount of the cooperation she got from everyone there. She said that she feels the need for ongoing collaboration with the teachers.

She would like to know if the remedial teacher defined goals for the work with Alon, and if she did, why these weren't shared with the parents. She would also like to know what the class and the remedial teachers did in order to achieve the goals, and if the goals have been accomplished. The mother emphatically spoke of her need to be apprised of measurable goals to monitor her child's progress. It is interesting that the mother raises this specific concern as this is one of the aims set out in the Israeli special education law. It may be that her experience as a social worker in a professional unit working with children who suffer from developmental problems helps her to see this so clearly. In any event, the law stipulates that the remedial teacher is responsible for building, together with the class teacher, an individual educational program for each child. This program must include measurable goals and an estimation of the period of time it will take for the goal to be reached. Moreover, the law determines that this program must not only be reported to the parents but must be clearly *explained* to them and that they have the right to remark and comment on the program. When asked if she was ever shown a working program, the mother recalled that one was sent to her in the post but no additional explanations or conversation on the issue was conducted. This raises the question of whether the school was actually adhering to the program or whether it was sent to her simply to comply with the law but is actually not regarded by the teacher as an obligating document.

The point the mother raised above aligns with her feeling that school, the class teacher, remedial teacher and principal, did not initiate contact with her. She would like to be invited to school meetings that provide information about Alon's progress instead of being the one to initiate contact. The mother feels that she is receiving the rights laid down by law, but that she still has to struggle for things that are beyond the letter of the law; especially the class teacher's understanding of Alon and his special needs and, as a result, her full cooperation. One may presume that an increase in the willingness of teachers to assist dyslexic children in their classes will come about only when they gain more knowledge about the phenomenon of dyslexia. This is a process that is more long term and will require a much greater effort than the one it took to formulate the law.

REFERENCES

Berman, R. (1985). Hebrew. In D.I. Slobin (Ed.), *The cross-linguistic study of language acquisition* (pp. 255–371). Hillsdale, NJ: Erlbaum.

Cahan, S. (1998). *Manual for the WISC-R95 Intelligence Test*. Jerusalem: The Psychological Service, Israeli Ministry of Education. (In Hebrew).

Share, L.D. & Levin, I. (1999). Learning to read and write in Hebrew. In M. Harris & G. Hatano (Eds.), *A cross-cultural perspective on learning to read* (pp. 95–129). Cambridge: Cambridge University Press.

Torgesen, J.K., Alexander, A.W., Wagner, R.K., Rashotte, C.A., Voeller, K.K.S., & Conway, T., (2001). Intensive remedial instruction for children with severe reading disabilities: Immediate and long-term outcomes from two instructional approaches. *Journal of Learning Disabilities*, 34 (1), 33–58.

ALON'S INTERVIEW

1. What do you want to be when you grow up?
    I want to build cars.

    Why do you think you would be good at that job?
    I used to do it with my LEGO and it was fun. I know how to do it.

2. Tell me about a teacher who has been really important to you or one who has helped you: what did the teacher do to help you?
    All my class teachers were all right. They gave me accommodations: this year for example I can use a calculator and I get more time in the tests.

3. Tell me about a teacher who didn't really help you that much or one who did not give you the help you needed.
    All the teachers help me.

4. Tell me what your mother thinks about your dyslexia. Does she talk to you about the problem? What does she say?
    She doesn't talk to me.

5. Tell me what your father thinks about your dyslexia. Does he talk to you about the problem?
    He doesn't talk to me about this.

6. Tell me about something that makes you really happy.
    I am happy when I succeed in things that are hard for me. When I get something I want and when I hear a good joke.

7. Tell me about something that makes you really sad.
    If I don't succeed in things I become a little sad.

8. When the work gets very hard at school and you think you can't do it, what do you do?
    I try and check where I can find the answer. I, for example, look for the answer in text.

9. What kinds of books do you like to read?
    I like adventure stories and stories about children.

    What is your favorite book?
    There is no special book. Whatever book I am reading at the time.

    Do you read to yourself?
    I read part of the book alone and part of it with my mom.

10. Do your friends know that you have dyslexia?
    They do not know.

11. Do your siblings know that you have dyslexia?
    No, my sister is small she does not know.

12. Name three things you are really good at:
    Computer games . . . I don't know what more . . .

13. Name three things you are not so good at:
    Bible lessons, reading, and that's it.

14. If you are feeling bad about your reading, is there one person you can talk to who makes you feel better?
    No, I don't speak to anyone.

15. Do computers help you with your reading?
    No, they do not help.

16. Do you usually have problems with your homework? Can you do your homework independently or does someone help you?
    Yes, I have a lot of problems. My parents help me.

    Is homework a big problem or just a little one?
    It's a big one.

17. If there was one thing you could change about school, what would it be?
    I would like more friends at school.

18. If you could have three wishes, what would they be?
    I would rather not say.

19. Tell me three things you would like your teacher to do to help you with your dyslexia.
    The things she is doing now are all right.

20. Who is the best reader in your class?
    I don't know.
    How did he/she get to be such a good reader?
    He learned at school.

21. Is it important to learn how to read?
    Yes.
    Why or why not?
    So you can read quicker and make less mistakes when you are reading.

8 Jacob, a Case Study of Dyslexia in Canada

Ronald W. Stringer, Barbara Bobrow and Brenda Linn

Jacob is a 10-year-old boy, who lives in a large multicultural city in Québec. He is an intelligent and active boy with many friends. He loves to engage in sports, particularly hockey. He can be very friendly and interactive, though certain subjects of conversation can turn him rather uncommunicative and avoidant. This is particularly the case when the topic turns to school and his reading problems. Jacob was assessed and identified with dyslexia at 7 years of age.

BACKGROUND

Family History

Jacob comes from an intact and closely-knit middle-class family, with two children, of whom Jacob is the elder. Jacob's father manages a business, and his mother is a Chartered Public Accountant. Both hold university degrees. Jacob's grandparents emigrated from Eastern Europe to the city in which the family now lives. Jacob's father attended a trilingual parochial school much like the school Jacob now attends, where he excelled in mathematics and computer science, but struggled with French and Hebrew. None of Jacob's immediate family has experienced problems with reading. However, Jacob's father was adopted, and has little information about his extended biological family.

The city in which Jacob lives is a complex mosaic of many cultures, faiths, and ethnicities. The family speaks English at home, French at work, and encounters Hebrew at the Synagogue. This tri-lingualism is not unusual among young people in Québec, where a very large proportion of the population are allophones, whose first language is neither French nor English. Most children, including Jacob, move fairly effortlessly from one language to another. However, the mastery of multiple languages places additional demands on children who have language or reading difficulties.

The particular exigencies of life in Québec have also played a large part in determining the nature of Jacob's school. Jacob's tri-lingual parochial

school is supported partly by tuition and partly by the provincial government (education is a provincial responsibility in Canada). Because Québec
is the only Canadian province in which French is the sole official language,
much of the instruction is in French. However, because the reality of life
in North America is that English is almost universally required, the school
also instructs in English. The school is founded on the tenets and beliefs
of Jewish faith and heritage, so Hebrew is taught as a third language, and
is used as the language of instruction in some classes. This use of three
languages at school is not common, but neither is it unique in this city. The
public school system, which until recently was divided along religious lines
(Catholic and Protestant) has been realigned on linguistic grounds: there is
now a French School Board in all jurisdictions, and an English School Board
where numbers warrant. Also, many allophone parents send their children
to schools where Greek or German or some other language and culture
are emphasized. This diversity is encouraged by government policies that
support private, as well as public schools, but all students must pass French
proficiency examinations in order to graduate from high school. The language program in the Jewish schools is probably unusually demanding,
especially for children who have specific difficulties in that area. Yet, the
classes are usually quite small, and individualized help is available.

Medical History

During the mother's pregnancy, doctors discovered that one of Jacob's kid-
neys was not functioning. Although the pregnancy continued to full term,
he was placed on antibiotics immediately after birth, and had successful
surgery at the age of 3 months. Other than this, Jacob's medical history
has been uneventful. He experienced four or five ear infections, had eye
therapy for a tracking problem, was diagnosed with mild sleep apnea several years ago, and had an allergy to tree nuts, all of which he appears to
have outgrown. His mother regards him as a very healthy child, as he has
experienced only the usual childhood illnesses and has not had any significant injuries.

Early Development

Jacob's motor milestones were achieved in the usual course of development.
He learned to walk at about the age of 1, and rode a bike, with no difficulty,
when he was 4 years of age. His fine motor control developed sufficiently
that he began coloring and drawing pictures between 2 and 3 years of
age. Jacob enjoyed playing with other children and had no problems with
socialization.

    In language development, Jacob reached the milestones within the nor-
mal time periods. He uttered his first words around the age of 1 and
phrases and sentences were produced soon thereafter. Jacob's mother

described him as very verbal, although his language was not always intelligible to everyone. He had some difficulty producing a few specific phonemes, notably /ch/ and /th/. Jacob received speech therapy for this problem, and overcame it with little difficulty. He has not had any further problems or peculiarities with his language and has never had any problems in naming objects. His mother summarized his early development by saying, "He was a very happy kid." The only thing that has consistently stood out for Jacob is his problem with learning to read, and the effects that has had on his life.

SCHOOL HISTORY

Kindergarten

Jacob began school at 5 years of age, as is typical in the Québec school system. Because his parents wished him to be schooled in the context of their religious faith, he was enrolled in a parochial school. Jacob's mother recalled kindergarten as a good experience for Jacob, a year in which he had no problems. She did remember, though, that Jacob was somewhat taller than the other children, and did not like to sit in the small classroom chairs. This may or may not have reflected a certain restlessness that has been noted in later reports, in which Jacob was described as sometimes inattentive and distractible. It also could have reflected the fact that the chairs signaled instructional time, when Jacob may have begun to realize that he was having difficulty with reading.

Grade 1

Jacob's particular academic problems became clearly apparent from the beginning of grade 1. According to his parents, learning to read, for Jacob, was "a great chore." First grade was full of frustration and Jacob cried frequently, even though his mother worked on reading with him at home, and he had no difficulty with the other parts of the program. In French and Hebrew, instruction still focused primarily on oral language. In English, however, his reading problems worsened, and Jacob's anxiety mounted.

Grade 2

In grade 2, presumably as a way of compensating for his learning difficulties, Jacob assumed the role of "class clown." Unfortunately, when the other children jumped on him (which apparently they enjoyed doing, despite his size and strength), Jacob would react emotionally and physically. Despite his clown persona, Jacob appeared agitated at times, and had particular difficulty with unstructured periods during the day. He was seen as impulsive, and as having problems with self-control. At home, during this period,

Jacob's parents were dealing with medical issues of their own. His mother recalls that period as having been a "tough" time for the whole family. She became concerned that her son would be labeled a troublemaker.

Although Jacob's school provided the best supportive resources it could, it was a small, independent entity, and it could not provide specialized psychological services. Despite an individualized education plan (IEP), by the middle of grade 2 Jacob's school situation had reached the point that his parents and teachers made the joint decision to arrange a formal assessment. This assessment was conducted at a unique, private, not-for-profit learning center that offered psychological/educational assessment by trained and licensed psychologists, as well as tutoring and other remedial resources.

During the testing sessions, the school psychologist noted that Jacob asked an unusual number of questions and sought a great deal of feedback, perhaps to help him manage his anxiety as the assessment became increasingly difficult. He also made comments such as, "That must be a high school question!" leading the psychologist to comment that there was a defensive quality to his interactions. In a valiant attempt at self-direction, Jacob engaged in lots of self-talk to get through the tasks, yet his frustration became increasingly obvious. After an hour-and-a-half, he had become too restless to sit still and had to occasionally walk around in order to answer the questions. The psychologist allowed him to take breaks, during which they played cards and had snacks, in order to continue.

Jacob's test results confirmed that his intelligence was in the high to superior range. Despite poor phonological awareness, Jacob's word attack score was normal for his age, a very unusual situation, which probably reflected good teaching on the part of the school, and very hard work on the part of the child. Jacob's spelling, however, was a standard deviation below the mean, his word identification was very nearly as low, and his phonological processing scores were weaker still. Jacob's reading comprehension, although in the low average range, was strikingly weak in comparison with his high-to-superior verbal IQ score, pointing to a very specific difficulty with written language (dyslexia). Jacob's difficulties with attention and behavior, were also noted, and may well have been implicated in his low scores in word reading and rapid color naming (RAN), both of which can be negatively affected by impulsivity. According to behavioral checklists, however, Jacob's difficulties in this area were relatively mild, and observed mainly in school situations. They were, therefore, suspected of being secondary to his learning difficulties and to the anxiety that those difficulties elicited.

When the school received the psychologist's report, they immediately set up a support program for Jacob. Jacob's school had a coordinator for student services, and a very knowledgeable and effective behavior therapist, who lectured in a university Faculty of Education and gave teacher workshops on learning-related behavior problems. The coordinator arranged individual help for Jacob, including one-to-one tutoring, twice a week, at school, first thing in the morning, when he was fresh. The tutoring followed a modified version of the reading program *Words in Colour* (Gattengo, 1968) a synthetic phonics program that uses color cues to indicate phonetic properties of letters. The program presents the phonemes of English systematically, first teaching basic spelling, and then introducing alternative spelling for each sound. All the common spellings of each phoneme are represented on one large chart. The chart is used for "visual dictation," in which the child analyzes the word, one phoneme at a time, pointing to the corresponding grapheme. The idea is that the motor activity helps to consolidate the grapheme-phoneme correspondence in the child's memory. During grade 2, Jacob mastered the basic spellings of all the English sounds, and practiced applying them to the decoding and encoding of phonetically regular words. In French and Hebrew, program modifications continued, emphasizing oral language skills and reducing written demands. When these supports were in place, Jacob found school to be a less noxious experience. The real turning point for Jacob, however, seems to have been the summer reading camp, which he attended during the summer between grades 2 and 3. This was a three-week intensive reading intervention program offered by the learning center where his assessment had taken place. The reading summer camp was a supportive, warm, fun-oriented environment, which nevertheless approached reading in a systematic, intensive way. Children received individual attention from lead teachers (experienced tutors from the center) and from summer staff, mostly pre-service teachers who had completed special training in the instructional approaches of the center. The reading camp program was also based on *Words in Colour*, but drew on a wide variety of complementary synthetic phonics resources. Children were introduced to "Letter Families" and engaged in a variety of reading and writing activities and games, including phonics through poetry. They worked with Sound Flash Cards from the Wilson Reading Program, as well as phonics workbooks, word searches, crosswords and computer games designed to reinforce computing skills. Campers also played card games in which they built words, changed vowels within words, and manipulated letters and sounds in other ways. They developed fluency through repeated readings of words and stories.

The children attending the summer reading camp were a culturally diverse group, who shared a common difficulty with phonological processing and reading. Jacob related easily to the other children and participated willingly in the activities. The self-esteem building components of the reading camp were complemented by a cooperative arrangement with an existing basketball camp, led by a professional player who is much admired in the community. The basketball camp, like the reading camp, was a non-profit initiative, with many bursaries (scholarships) available to children from inner-city schools. Children who attended the reading camp in the morning took part in the basketball camp in the afternoon.

Grade 3

When Jacob returned to school in September, his reading and his self-confidence had improved to the extent that teachers said that he was "not the same kid." Jacob's mother reported that third grade was "a great year" for him. His tutoring was reduced to once per week. Having learned to apply the alphabetic principle in English, with its complex, relatively opaque orthography, Jacob was much better prepared to tackle French and Hebrew, both of which have more regular orthographies. French spelling depends heavily on an understanding of syntax, and can prove particularly challenging for children whose difficulties are not purely phonological, but extend to other aspects of language. This seems not to be the case for Jacob, whose dyslexia appears to stem entirely from what Stanovich (1998) called the phonological "core deficit," without complications. Nevertheless, Jacob continues to dislike both French and Hebrew, and given a choice, he would eliminate them from the curriculum.

The summer following grade 3, Jacob again applied to the reading camp. In pre-camp screening, both his reading and his spelling scores were now average or above average. Comprehension remained his greatest strength. Returning to the camp was a very positive experience and he felt "great," because that summer he was the strongest reader in his group.

Grade 4

Currently in fourth grade, Jacob is doing very well. His weekly tutoring continues, focusing on reading comprehension, writing, editing, and math facts. His teachers described him as "happy-go-lucky" and his mother sees him as "a leader." Jacob enjoys English and the sciences. His mother noted that as his schoolwork was becoming more conceptual, Jacob was finding it more engaging. Despite all his progress, however, Jacob still indicates that he does not like school, and feels that the school day is too long (in fact, at this school the day is actually somewhat longer than other schools, from 8 a.m. to 4 p.m., approximately). When he returns at 4:30, Jacob is often very tired and wants to relax. His evenings are especially hectic when he has hockey practice, as he has to coordinate his homework with his sports schedule. The learning center had recommended to the parents that they should never take away his hockey if they find the schoolwork is too much for him. Instead, they should negotiate with the school to limit the amount of homework and concentrate on essentials, indicating, for example, which questions are most important if he cannot finish them all. The staff of the learning center has found that curtailing participation in enjoyable extra-curricular activities can be very detrimental to a student's well being. A balanced approach is considered the best option, and in this case, the school has proven to be cooperative and understanding about the homework load.

Jacob particularly expresses a dislike for the additional languages he is required to learn. On the other hand, precisely because the three-language system presents challenges, the teachers and staff at Jacob's school are very knowledgeable and dedicated. Jacob's final report card was excellent, and his marks were above the class average.

DYSLEXIA DIAGNOSIS AND TREATMENT ISSUES

Although Jacob clearly has had problems with written language from the beginning of his schooling, he was not diagnosed until the middle of grade 2. Even at that, Jacob's difficulties were identified much earlier than is the case for many children, since many educators still hold to the unsubstantiated view that each child progresses at his or her own rate, and that while some may need more time than others, they will catch up in the end. One of the unfortunate results of this approach is that students are often not identified until after the point at which remediation would be most effective. In Québec, identification is complicated by the fact that Ministry of Education guidelines are primarily intended to be applied in a francophone context, in which dyslexia is assumed to be part of a broader language impairment. However, the assumption that dyslexia is simply one manifestation of broader language impairment (beyond phonological awareness) is in direct contradiction to the assumption of specificity that is central to dyslexia research in North America (Stanovich, 1998, 1999, 2005; Siegel, 1999) and in the United Kingdom (British Psychological Society, 1999). Its application to English speaking students in Québec is clearly problematic. In recognition of this fact, in June of 2010, the Québec ministry of education revised its conditions for exemption from schooling in French (i.e., permission to attend an English public school) for children who would not otherwise qualify for such an exemption because neither parent was educated in an English Canadian school (Government du Québec, 2010). The revision extended the right to attend an English public school to children diagnosed with dyslexia, dyscalculia, or dysgraphia, who continue to lag at least one year behind in language or mathematics, despite remedial help from a teacher with special education qualifications or experience. Unlike earlier ministry stipulations regarding the diagnosis of dyslexia, this new exemption policy stipulates that the determination of dyslexia be made by a registered psychologist (rather than a speech and language pathologist).

The new ruling is significant because it permits children like Jacob, who have no significant oral language impairment, to be diagnosed with dyslexia. However, in neither the English nor the French school system in Québec does a diagnosis of dyslexia in the absence of more global impairments exempt children from meeting curriculum expectations in written French. In reading, this may not pose a serious problem, since for the purposes of decoding (that is, going from grapheme to phoneme) French orthography is more transparent than English orthography. In writing, however, the phoneme to grapheme relationship is complicated by syntactic and morphological factors. For students still struggling with the basic code, this additional layer of complexity makes the traditional *dictée* something of a nightmare. Even in reading, many dyslexic children require more explicit instruction in French phoneme-grapheme relationships, and more practice in their application, than is ordinarily emphasized in French as a Second Language instruction. The problems posed by French language requirements come to a head, for children like Jacob, when they face the ministry examinations required to obtain a secondary school graduation diploma. These requirements will pose a very serious challenge for Jacob, and will require that support remain in place in French as well as English, throughout the course of his schooling.

Although dyslexia is now coming to be recognized in Québec as a specific learning disability that can exist in the absence of global language impairment, it cannot be diagnosed unless a child's written language is a full year below expectations. This does not necessarily mean that the child must "wait to fail" before receiving remedial intervention. Instead, children who demonstrate "certain vulnerabilities" may be designated as being "at risk," and be provided with extra support to prevent their falling behind (Government du Québec, 2007). In principle, this approach should ensure that a child not be diagnosed as learning disabled if his or her learning difficulties are primarily the product of inadequate or inappropriate instruction. In practice, however, schools often lack both the resources and the knowledge of reading disability to put appropriate preventative measures in place. In the authors' experience, preventative measures are frequently motivational—time may be spent looking at books, practicing high-frequency words, and modeling the use of multiple-cues, particularly prediction from context. Complete, letter-by-letter decoding may even be actively discouraged. Under these circumstances, the child's inherent difficulty with reading will continue to be apparent, while the role of instruction is likely to be missed. In this situation, children will be diagnosed despite the instructional inadequacies, but not until they have fallen further behind. Fortunately, Jacob's school fast-forwarded the identification process, recognizing that their first attempt at intervention was not working, encouraging a psychological assessment, and acting immediately upon the psychologist's diagnosis and recommendations. The support the school was able to offer did not include the computer assistive devices that are provided in the Québec public system to children with severe learning impairments diagnosed by speech and language pathologists. Instead, and perhaps more to the point, Jacob received immediate behavioral interventions, and tutoring in reading. (Fortunately, Jacob's parents were able to provide him with a computer, and there were also many available at school.)

The Québec policy of diagnosing learning disabilities on the basis of the discrepancy between age and achievement level, rather than the discrepancy between IQ and achievement level has a good deal to recommend it. It is consistent with current research, which has established that the underlying deficits in dyslexia are essentially the same, regardless of IQ or other measures of general cognitive ability (Siegel, 1988, 1992; Stanovich, 1998, 2005). Jacob, as we noted earlier, has a very high verbal IQ. However, even if Jacob's general cognitive ability had been very much in line with his reading scores, the Québec guidelines would have permitted a diagnosis of dyslexia, based on the absolute low level of his reading and phonological processing scores. Elsewhere in Canada, Jacob's situation would have been a little different. In many Canadian provinces, some form of IQ-achievement discrepancy is central to the definition of learning disabilities, including reading disability. Although learning disabilities are now assessed in terms of specific underlying psychological processes, most provinces continue to insist that the child's specific difficulties be "unexpected," where unexpected means out of line with the child's overall ability in "thinking and reasoning" (Learning Disabilities Association of Ontario, 2001). The assumption, here, is that word level reading difficulties are "expected" in children with modest ability in thinking and reasoning. This assumption flies in the face of solid research evidence to the contrary (e.g., Siegel, 1999; Stanovich, 1999, 2005; Stuebing, 2002). However, the Ontario working group responsible for the definition of learning disabilities used widely in Canada and beyond was "not prepared to apply research findings related primarily to reading disabilities to the whole field of learning disabilities," or in fact, even to the field of reading disability (Learning Disabilities Association of Ontario, 2001, p. 5). The result was that, in most jurisdictions, a discrepancy, often defined as two standard deviations, between general cognitive ability and reading measures remains a contiuing requirement of any learning disability diagnosis, even for children who clearly demonstrate the specific deficits characteristic of dyslexia. The Ontario approach to diagnosis would have worked to Jacob's advantage, but continues to disadvantage many other children whose specific difficulties with reading are all the more disabling because of their other intellectual challenges.

Jacob was fortunate in that the interventions he received were appropriate to his needs, and have since proved effective. He is also fortunate that his classroom teachers understood and complied with the recommendations of Jacob's psychological assessment. (This is by no means always the case, in Québec or in the rest of Canada, since many mainstream classroom teachers still believe that over-reliance on phonics is a cause of poor reading, and that good readers owe their fluency to their skill in context-based guessing.) There are, however, two respects in which Jacob's situation remains less than optimal. One concerns the demands of his school program in languages other than English. The other concerns the way in which dyslexia has been explained to Jacob, and the way he feels about his disability. These concerns are explored in the following sections.

PARENT PERSPECTIVES

Jacob's mother's affection for, and confidence in, her son were evident throughout her interview. She described him as having "great empathy" and creativity, as being friendly and social, and a natural leader. She stated that he has special friends, but will play with anyone. She does not feel that his reading problem has impacted his social life (rating this 1/10 on the Perception Scale). Jacob's mother reported that he is becoming a good athlete, and showing considerable musical ability, but "does not like to practice." She said that Jacob enjoys *The Hardy Boys*, mysteries and adventure stories. Although he only reads under duress, an hour and a half a week, he enjoys having his parents read to him. Both parents read to him, though his mother does so more frequently. Jacob's preferred relaxation is television, which has had to be limited to three hours a week. He likes watching wrestling and comedies best, but also enjoys The Treehouse Channel. Jacob has not suffered from childhood fears or phobias. He does experience some anxiety, particularly when his mother yells at him, or he is worried about making mistakes. On the Perception Scale, the mother rated the impact of dyslexia on family life to be 2/10.

Jacob's mother is delighted with the way that school tutoring and reading camp have helped Jacob. She is clearly proud of his achievements, both academic and athletic, but places even more value on his human qualities. The fact that Jacob's family regards kindness, empathy, loyalty and friendship as core values, more important, than grades and goals, may in part explain why Jacob has overcome the social problems that threatened to develop in grade 1, and are so often characteristic of children with learning disabilities (Wiener & Schneider, 2002). She recognizes that Jacob has had intense school related anxiety, but she thinks that he is now comfortable at school. In the past, she would have rated the significance of his reading problem to 8/10, but today she believes it is much less problematic (2 or 3/10) and therefore has less impact on school success (2/10). She takes a rather global view of dyslexia as something that makes her son's brain pathways "not the same as anyone else's." She notes, "He sees the world a little differently." In keeping with the "gift of dyslexia" view, Jacob's mother seems to have come to accept this as yet something else to be proud of in her son. When asked how she thinks dyslexia will influence her son's life, she replied that he knows "his brain is different both positively and negatively, and he will use the positive side." She explained that, from her perspective as a mother, the biggest challenge was to make "sure that he knows he's smart and good enough" in spite of the difficulties he faces.

CHILD PERSPECTIVES

Jacob's responses during the interview and on the sentence completion suggest that, in most respects, his mother knows him very well. He identified the things that he is good at as "hockey, protecting people, in hockey and real life, and skiing." He confirms that he loves sports, and is indeed becoming a good athlete, practicing a lot, and playing on the A-level hockey team. Although he doesn't point this out, playing on the A team is a significant achievement. Jacob says that when he grows up he would like to be either a hockey player or a wrestler. Unsurprisingly, what makes him really happy is watching wrestling on TV, or playing hockey. Scoring goals also makes him really happy, but he points out that he plays all positions on the team, not only those in which he is most likely to score. Jacob has many friends and enjoys a rich social life. Jacob doesn't believe his dyslexia has any impact on his friendships. When asked what he would change about his friends, he replied that they were fine as they were. His little sister, on the other hand, could talk less, and be "a bit nicer."

Jacob described dyslexia as having a significant effect on his schoolwork (7/10 on the Perception Scale), but no impact on other dimensions of his life. He concluded that the amount of reading he does is average (5/10) and confirmed that *Hardy Boys* and the Jack Stalwart mysteries are his favorite books. He said he reads independently, and that his parents also read to him (his mother more than his father). Jacob's enjoyment of stories extends to writing as well as reading. His favorite teacher, the one he feels helped him the most, was the teacher who taught him to write longer stories, to add more details to his characters, and to use "proper language" (grammar). Jacob was unwilling to single out any teacher who had not been supportive. He commented, though, that he wished teachers would push him, and not let him quit the first time. Jacob explained that he dealt with teachers who don't help him by putting the work on the corner of his desk and falling asleep, though he later admitted he really just relaxed with his eyes closed. Jacob mentioned that the French teacher frequently refuses to help, and acknowledged that often he can, in fact, complete his French independently when he really tries.

Jacob's positive attitude and coping skills notwithstanding, what makes him really sad is "going to school," as he finds it boring and a waste of his time. His three wishes included no school, knowledge that could be programmed directly into our brains, and unlimited vacations. Asked what he would change about school, he replied, "no French, no Hebrew, or math." What he likes best about school is "going home." It is interesting that his response to a question about what he found most difficult was, "Reading is not too hard—spelling is OK, too," after which he became very silent. He said that he doesn't talk to anyone about his reading, but then added that his mother "says stuff that doesn't help," and then "She's not talking to me about it really." What exactly Jacob meant by this is not clear. Perhaps he meant that he didn't like her to talk about it, but he may also have meant that he felt his mother was mainly reassuring herself. When questioned further, he said that he did not like to talk about his reading problems as, "It's not fun to talk about . . .

there's nothing to be said." Echoing what his mother said about his fears, he added, "I also don't like to talk about getting into trouble." Jacob mentioned frequently that his parents want him to try harder, that they are proud of him when he does well on a test, and disappointed when he does poorly. He adds, though, "they are proud of me anyway." On the Perception Scale, Jacob indicated that his reading problem does not interfere with his family life (1/10).

Despite his reluctance to talk about it, and his comment that he "just wants to get over it," Jacob is clearly puzzled by his difficulty with reading. He says, when his mother talks about dyslexia, he doesn't really "understand the concept of having dyslexia" and asks, "What do I have that other people don't have?" Developmental psychology would strongly suggest that, to a 10-year-old, being told that "his brain is different" and that he "sees the world . . . differently" from his peers is likely to cause considerable anxiety and distress, even if he is assured that the difference has a positive side. Asked about the best reader in his class, he explained that this boy excels because "he is smart and he likes to read." He added, "I practice, but I don't want to do it, but HE DOES." This suggests that despite whatever he may have been told to the contrary, Jacob still suspects his reading problems are related to intelligence or motivation. He is not willing or able to talk about strategies for dealing with his problem. He knows that his teachers have helped him, but says he doesn't understand how. Similarly, when his friends ask him how dyslexia affects his reading and writing, he replies that he doesn't know.

In describing his dyslexia, neither Jacob nor his mother made any reference to this condition being a specific difficulty that only affected the ability to distinguish and manipulate speech sounds. They seemed not to have considered the similarity of a specific phonological deficit to other very specific deficits, such as trouble carrying a tune (tone-deafness) or color-blindness, nor do they seem aware that the phonological deficits of dyslexics only interfere with learning because of the way our spelling system operates (see McGuinness, 2005). Interestingly, though, the computer resource that Jacob reported as being most helpful was the ClickNRead website that his father had found, in which, as he explained to the interviewer, "They say the sounds and you click on a letter." This was significant as the one and only instance in which Jacob demonstrated an understanding that segmenting words into phonemes, and linking those phonemes to graphemes, is the key to dealing with his reading problem. This resource may also have pleased him particularly because his father found it. Jacob explained that, in general, dealing with dyslexia is his mother's project and that his father "lets my mom take care of it."

Jacob said that reading is important to get jobs and to succeed in life, something he clearly intends to do. As far as Jacob is concerned, the most difficult thing about having a reading problem is simply "not being able to read as well as other people."

CASE COMMENTARY

Jacob's case is in many ways a "best case" scenario. His dyslexia is not complicated by the other motor, language or social difficulties that so frequently accompany it. In fact, his outstanding athletic ability may have served to mitigate the effects of his school problems. Jacob's reading disability was diagnosed relatively early, though identification in kindergarten would have been ideal. He has had the support of caring, creative, pro-active parents, and a well-informed school. He also had access to private professional diagnostic services, whose report the school took seriously. Jacob's intelligence meant that his dyslexia could be diagnosed on the basis of an IQ-reading level discrepancy, whereas a child with a lower IQ and identical phonological processing difficulties might not have been so diagnosed. The value that Jacob's family places on empathy, loyalty and friendship, and the timely intervention of a behavioral therapist, has protected him against the isolation that frequently accompanies a serious learning disability. Jacob's own courage and resilience also played an important part in enabling him to meet the challenges that dyslexia inevitably brings, even when it is managed in an optimal way. After only fifteen months of twice-weekly tutoring, and four weeks of intensive instruction at summer reading camp, Jacob's standard scores in reading and spelling were average for his age (103 and 100 respectively).

Even though Jacob seems almost to have attained his goal of "just getting over" his dyslexia, it will be important that his situation continues to be closely monitored, especially as the reading load, and the amount of written work, increase. In addition, it will be important to monitor the demands of French and Hebrew, and the effect of those demands on Jacob's self-esteem and on his attitude toward school. It will be especially important that Jacob receive actual remedial reading instruction in French, rather than simply receiving accommodations. Lowering expectations would leave him unprepared for the ministry final exams, on which he qualifies for extra time, but not for any other special consideration. Addressing his specific dyslexia-related problems with decoding and spelling in French and Hebrew, with its clear, unambiguous grapheme-phoneme correspondences could also help develop the metalinguistic awareness that Jacob needs in order to understand the nature of his disability. Although it will be tempting to bolster Jacob's self-esteem by assuring him that only children with high IQs can have dyslexia, it would be more accurate, and more respectful of children with other learning challenges, to stress to Jacob that dyslexia, like color-blindness, has nothing to do with intelligence, but that it often plagues very bright students, making them question their overall ability. It will be also vitally important that Jacob's subject-area teachers understand both his ability and his disability, so that they maintain high expectations, but recognize how much more effortful and time consuming the basics of reading and spelling are for Jacob than for most other children. It is to be hoped that Jacob's family will continue to read together, but it will also be important to find books Jacob is motivated to read for himself, since Matthew Effects (e.g. Stanovich, 1986) will play an increasing role in all aspects of his intellectual growth.

So far, Jacob, his family, his school, and the learning center professionals have shown themselves more than equal to the challenges that dyslexia has posed. With continued instructional and emotional support, there is every reason to expect that Jacob will maintain his hard-won gains.

REFERENCES

British Psychological Society. (1999). *Dyslexia, literacy and psychological assessment*. Leicester: BPS.

Gattengo, C. (1968). *Words in colour*. Reading, U.K.: Cuisenaire.

Gouvernement du Québec. (2007). *Organisation of educational services for at-risk students and students with handicaps, social maladjustments or learning difficulties*. Québec: Ministère de l'Education, du Loisir et du Sport.

Governement du Québec (2010). Regulation respecting the exemption from the application of the first paragraph of section 72 of the Charter of the French Language which may be granted to children having serious learning disabilities. *Charter of the French Language*. Law C 11, section r.6.

Learning Disabilities Association of Ontario (2001). *Promoting early intervention for learning disabilities 1999–2002, Draft definition of learning disabilities*. Retrieved from www.ldao.ca/aboutLDs/Definitions_of_LDs.php

McGuinness, D. (2004) *Early reading instruction. What science really tells us about how to teach reading*. Cambridge: MIT Press.

Siegel, L.S. (1989). IQ is irrelevant to the definition of learning disabilities. *Journal of Learning Disabilities, 22*, 469–479.

Siegel, L.S. (1992). An evaluation of the discrepancy definition of dyslexia. *Journal of Learning Disabilities, 25*, 618–629.

Siegel, L.S. (1999). Issues in the definition and diagnosis of learning disabilities: A perspective on Gluckenberger v. Boston University. *Journal of Learning Disabilities, 32*, 304–320.

Stanovich, K.E. (1986). Matthew Effects in Reading: Some consequences of individual differences in the acquisition of literacy. *Reading Research Quarterly, 21* (4), 360–407.

Stanovich, K.E. (1996). Toward a more inclusive definition of dyslexia. *Dyslexia, 2*, 154–166.

Stanovich, K.E. (1998) Refining the phonological core deficit model. *Child Psychology & Psychiatry Review, 3*, 17–21.

Stanovich, K.E. (1999). The sociopsychometrics of learning disabilities. *Journal of Learning Disabilities, 32*, 350–361. Stanovich, K.E. (2005). The future of a mistake: Will discrepancy measurement continue to make the learning disabilities field a pseudoscience? *Learning Disability Quarterly, 28* (2), 103–106.

Stuebing, K., Fletcher, J.M., LeDoux, J.M., Lyon, G.R., Shaywitz, S.E., & Shaywitz, B.A. (2002). Validity of IQ-discrepancy classification of reading difficulties: A meta-analysis. *American Educational Research Journal, 39*, 469–518.

Wiener J, & Schneider B. H. (2002). A multisource exploration of the friendship patterns of children with and without learning disabilities. *Journal of Abnormal Psychology, 30* (2), 127–141.

JACOB'S INTERVIEW

1. What do you want to be when you grow up?
   A wrestler or a hockey player.

   Why do you think you would be good at that job?
   I'm strong and I'm good at acting. For hockey, I practice a lot and I'm on the "A" Team for Cote St- Luc.

2. Tell me about a teacher who has been really important to you or one who has helped you: what did the teacher do to help you?
   Helene, the Grade 2 and English teacher. She helped me to write longer stories, she'd tell me to add more details to my characters and she helped me to learn proper language, like I and not me, like "Could me and Jacob go outside?"

3. Tell me about a teacher who didn't really help you that much or one who did not give you the help you needed. What did you want the teacher to do to help you?
   All my teachers helped me.

4. Tell me what your mother thinks about your dyslexia. Does she talk to you about the problem?
   Not really.

   What does she say?
   She talks to me, but I don't really understand—the concept of having dyslexia. What do I have that other people don't have—I just want to get over with it.

   [To get better?]
   Yeah.

5. Tell me what your father thinks about your dyslexia. Does he talk to you about the problem?
   No.

   What does he say?
   He doesn't do anything. My mom's the one who does things. He lets my mom take care of it.

6. Tell me about something that makes you really happy.
   Watching wrestling on TV, playing hockey. I like scoring goals. I play all positions on the team.

7. Tell me about something that makes you really sad.

    Going to school. It's boring. I'm wasting my time—they don't teach me anything. Grade 4 is a review of grade 3—it's not that fun.

8. When the work gets very hard at school and you think you can't do it, what do you do?

    I ask the teacher and if she refuses to help me, I put it at the corner of my desk and fall asleep. She says I have to do it myself.

9. What kinds of books do you like to read?

    Mysteries, Hardy Boys

    What is your favorite book?

    Jack Stalwart—about a kid who works for a special agency and goes about helping others around the world and solves mysteries.

    Do you read to yourself?

    Yes.

    Who else reads to you?

    My dad a little and my mom.

10. Do your friends know that you have dyslexia?

    Some of them.

    Do you talk to them about it?

    No.

    What do you say?

    Some ask me and I say that I have trouble reading and writing.

    What do your friends say to you about dyslexia?

    They ask how it is harder for you to read and write and I say I don't know.

11. Do your siblings know that you have dyslexia?

    I don't know.

    Do you talk to them about it?

    No, she is much younger.

12. Name three things you are really good at:

    Hockey, protecting people—in hockey and in real life, skiing

13. Name three things you are not so good at:

    Reading is not so hard: spelling is OK too. [He became silent and said he could not think of anything else to say for the other two.]

14. If you are feeling bad about your reading, is there one person you can talk to who makes you feel better?

    No one.

    What does that person say to you?

    My mom says stuff that doesn't help. She's not talking to me about it really . . . it's not fun to talk about. There's nothing to be said. I also don't like to talk about getting into trouble.

15. Do computers help you with your reading?
    Yes.

    If yes, how do they help you?
    Dad found a website where they say the sounds and you click on a letter.

16. Do you usually have problems with your homework?
    No.

    Can you do your homework independently or does someone help you?
    They only help me for Mad Minute [Math] and spelling.

    Is homework a big problem or just a little one?
    A little one—I don't want to do it sometimes. I get it over with and then I have supper and watch TV and play video games, but I don't play them a lot.

17. If there was one thing you could change about school, what would it be?
    I would have only gym and recess, no Hebrew, French or math.

18. If you could have three wishes, what would they be?
    NO school . . . when you are born you could be programmed in your head.
    I could go on as many vacations as I wanted.
    That I could fly.

19. Tell me three things you would like your teacher to do to help you with your dyslexia.
    I don't know. I already said that they help me but I don't know HOW they help me. I find a difference but I don't know what it is that helps me. [He could not think of any other things].

20. Who is the best reader in your class?
    Jesse

    How did he/she get to be such a good reader?
    He's smart and he likes to read—I practice, but I don't want to, but he DOES.

21. Is it important to learn how to read?
    YES.

    Why or why not?
    You need to read to get jobs and be successful in your life.

9   Christian, a Case Study of Dyslexia in Germany

Regine Meier-Hedde

Christian is a 12-year-old child who lives with his mother and father in a small village in Mecklenburg-Vorpommern (Neue Bundesländer, formerly the Deutsche Demokratische Republik), Germany. He was diagnosed as dyslexic at the age of 9 in the second grade. Christian is a delightful child who is highly verbal and socially engaging.

BACKGROUND

Family History

Christian is the youngest child in the family of four. He lives alone with his parents as his 27-year-old sister has a family of her own that includes two young children. Christian proudly noted that even though he is only twelve, he is already an uncle. Christian's sister has a different father; however, the two siblings are very close and Christian visits her often. His sister, Sabine, did not experience any academic difficulty in school and has a college degree in environmental science. Christian's father is a hydraulic machinist who works for a large company. He did not have any problems with school, but the mother reported that she had reading and spelling difficulties as did her mother, Christian's grandmother. The mother completed ten years of schooling and received a Realschulabschluss, which is a certificate that qualifies for a practical rather than an academic career. She later completed a three-year apprenticeship as a book seller and passed the exams for a master book seller. She currently owns two small book stores in local villages. In spite of her history of significant reading problems and the persistence of this difficulty, she continues to be an avid reader.

Medical History

The pregnancy and delivery were normal, and Christian was a healthy baby. However, at the age of 1½, he was rushed to the hospital with severe abdominal pain. Christian was diagnosed with a blockage of the colon and received emergency surgery. He experienced a full recovery and has had no other remarkable illnesses or hospitalizations. Christian had sleeping problems as a child, awaking most nights for a period of two to three hours. His hearing is normal, but he has worn glasses since the age of 7 to correct astigmatism.

Early Development

Christian had a typical infancy with early acquisition of language milestones: at the age of 2 he was speaking in complete sentences. He was a highly verbal child. His motor development was initially normal with walking occurring at 1 year of age, but later the mother noted that Christian experienced motor difficulties. He had a very difficult time learning to ride a bike because of balance problems. When Christian was a baby, his grandmother took care of him while his mother worked and he was later placed in day care.

SCHOOL HISTORY

Kindergarten

Christian started nursery school at the age of 2 and kindergarten at the age of 3. The German kindergarten curriculum focuses on language, visual motor, and play activities. Christian began to experience problems at the age of 4. He had particular difficulty with fine motor activities, such as cutting and pasting. This was the first time Christian and his family knew that he could not accomplish the same tasks as peers. The teachers repeatedly told the mother that Christian was very slow and had major difficulties in fine motor tasks, but they provided no assistance or recommendations. The mother assumed that the problems would resolve themselves without intervention so she was not overly concerned. He stayed in kindergarten for three years and went to first grade at the age of almost 7.

First Grade

Christian entered first grade in a very small school with approximately 65 students. He loved this school as all of the teachers and students were residents of his village. However, from the beginning, Christian's teacher expressed disappointment in his lack of achievement. She frequently castigated him for not being able to perform the class work and told him that he was really "stupid." This was a very small class of 14 students, which should have presented an ideal situation for extra assistance from the teacher. Instead, the teacher offered no help whatsoever. She ridiculed Christian in front of his peers for his problems, particularly his inability to identify easy c/v/c words. Christian noted that the teacher praised her favorite students frequently and called attention to his problems. As the classroom situation continued to deteriorate, Christian became depressed. It was apparent to him that he was failing first grade. He remembers thinking, "if I mess up first grade, I will mess up my whole life," which is a very astute observation for a 7-year-old. As his depression worsened, the mother became more concerned. Every six months, she attended a parent teacher conference in which the reports were similar to those in kindergarten: Christian was extremely slow and could not achieve the same work as peers. It appeared to the mother that Christian had some neurological problem that was influencing him to become slower and slower in his schoolwork. She finally decided to take him to the family doctor to obtain recommendations. The doctor referred Christian to a psychologist, who subsequently tested his IQ and reported that he was above average. The mother did not receive any other information. She gave this report to the teacher, but received no reaction. Christian continued to do poorly in first grade and exhibit symptoms of depression. In his report card at the end of the year, Christian's teacher stated that he had severe problems in reading (phoneme blending) and spelling, but had an extensive vocabulary and was able to make adequate comments in content area subjects. It is hard to understand why Christian's teacher described the problems, but didn't investigate the cause of the severe difficulties or offer any specific support. Perhaps the teacher was waiting because of the regulations that were in effect at that time. According to the administrative instructions for the remediation of students with specific difficulties in reading, spelling and arithmetic issued by the Ministry of Education, Research and Culture of the state of Mecklenburg-Vorpommern in 1996, children with reading and spelling problems were not to be officially evaluated for risk until the end of second grade. In 2005 new administrative instruction moved the evaluation time to the end of first grade.

Second Grade

Christian had the same teacher in the second grade as it is typical to remain with the same teacher for four years in German elementary schools. He also repeated the same demoralizing experience, only it had worsened as the other children were increasing their reading achievement and Christian was continuing to do poorly. The gap between Christian and his peers was widening. The teacher expressed increased frustration at his inability to learn. Finally, at the end of the second grade year, she recognized that something was wrong and things were not getting better. She called the mother and recommended that Christian be evaluated for possible placement in a classroom for students with dyslexia. Christian was sent for a day-long evaluation to a school with a dyslexia program in a different village.

The evaluation revealed that Christian was at risk for dyslexia, which is referred to as Lese-Rechtschreib-Schwierigkeiten (LRS) and therefore qualified for placement in the special education class at that school. To assess reading, the school administered the Züricher Lesetest (ZLT; Linder & Grissemann, 2000), which included subtests in letter and word identification as well as oral passage reading. Christian refused to complete the full oral passage reading section, because he was totally exhausted after having read two passages. With regard to letter identification and word reading, the test results showed that Christian had fewer problems with accuracy (26–50th percentile) than with speed (1st percentile). The mother as well as his teachers reported that Christian tried to avoid making mistakes and always worked very slowly and accurately. The tests used for the assessment of spelling were the Lory Rechtschreibtest and Sätze nach Bauer (see Kultusministerium, 1996). For both tests he scored at the 5th percentile. His errors included phonetically and orthographically incorrect spellings. The Worttafel nach Kossakowsky (see Kossow, 1985) was also administered to examine Christian's spelling performance, which placed him in the category of a severe LRS. He performed at the 29th percentile on the Lautwortoperationsverfahren (LWOV; Kossow, 2000), which assessed spelling subskills. For measurement of overall intellectual ability, the Hamburg-Wechsler-Intelligenztest für Kinder (Hawik-III; Tewes, Rossmann, & Schallberger, 1999) was administered. The results indicated that Christian's overall IQ fell within the superior range (FSIQ =121, VIQ=123, PIQ=114).

This evaluation led to the decision that Christian would transfer to the school with the dyslexia program so he had to leave his neighborhood school with all of his friends and was bused to the larger school with 400 students, none of whom he knew. Christian was sad to leave his friends, but was not sad to leave his teacher.

As part of the new placement, Christian had to repeat second grade. This was a requirement of every child accepted into the program for dyslexia. In this special education classroom, there were approximately 12–14 students. Instruction focused on phonics and spelling skills for students with dyslexia. Christian had three teachers (i.e., a math teacher, a reading teacher, and a remedial teacher, the latter of whom provided one to one instruction). His math curriculum was the same as the general education students obtained. He did not like his math teacher because she frequently lost her temper and shouted at him, especially when he forgot his homework. From Christian's report, the math teacher told him that he should give up because he was incapable of learning the content. Christian reported that the reading teacher did not provide him sufficient help as he did not make any progress with her instruction in spite of the effort he was extending. Christian was one of the few students who received individual intervention from his remedial teacher as he demonstrated more significant need. However, this remedial instruction was only for one to two hours per week. For whatever reason, Christian did not learn to read during the first year in the dyslexia classroom even though most of the other children were making progress. As Christian is a very bright child, he was aware of his lack of progress. He desperately missed his old friends from his former school and experienced continuing depression. This time the depression was worse as he was beginning to give up hope that he would ever learn to read. The mother reported that he was becoming withdrawn from his family and friends.

Third Grade

In third grade, Christian continued with the same teachers in the special education classroom. By the middle of third grade, it became obvious to the special education classroom teachers that Christian was making little, if any, progress. The teachers told the mother that they could not help him and suggested sending him to a special education clinic associated with a medical university 200 kilometers away. This was a clinic for psychiatric, neurological, psychosomatic, and psychological problems of children and young adults. Although Christian was referred to the clinic for the evaluation of dyslexia, this clinic served many children and adolescents with severe psychiatric problems, such as schizophrenia and manic-depressive disorders. Christian was put on a waiting list and admitted several months later as an inpatient in this hospital for two months, during which time he was placed in a ward with children with severe emotional disturbance. The clinical report referred to Christian as being shy, overly adaptive, with very low self-esteem and some compulsive tendencies. He was given a series of psychological and educational tests to determine why he could not learn to read. The clinical diagnosis included three disabilities: social functioning, dyslexia, and fine and gross motor deficits as per the World Health Organization, International Classification of Diseases. Following his diagnosis, he was referred to dyslexia, behavioral, music, and perceptual therapies. Christian reported that in spite of the fact that he was with children with severe emotional disturbances, he liked the hospital because "for the first time someone helped me and I was so happy about that." He received dyslexia therapy for two hours per day, which focused on multisensory phonics, spelling, and grammar instruction. The clinician's report indicated that after ten weeks, Christian had made significant progress in decoding. The clinician also recommended that the program should be continued during the summer break, and that he be given small group instruction in school. In addition, she recommended that the parents apply for LRS status for Christian for fourth grade. Christian did not have any summer remediation as the mother wanted him to have some free time to enjoy himself.

Fourth Grade

In fourth grade, Christian was sent to another elementary school as the LRS program was limited to two years. Christian could not go back to the school in his small village as it had closed. He was glad to leave the LRS school as he felt it had not been beneficial to him and he missed his friends. At his new school Christian basically received the general education curriculum with the support of biweekly remediation for English and occupational therapy.

Although the school accepted the mother's application for LRS status, Christian did not receive any supplementary services in spite of the fact that the dyslexia therapist had made specific recommendations (i.e., perceptual training, large print text and materials, less homework, fewer exercises to accommodate his slow completion rate, and more weight on oral performance rather than written work). The mother stated that the school ignored all of these recommendations. Christian received his official LRS status in the second half of the school year after another spelling, reading, and intelligence test was administered. The test results of the Lory Rechtschreibtest revealed that his spelling performance was lower than that of 95% of his classmates. He was reading at the 1st percentile while his intellectual ability as measured by the Grundintelligenztest Skala 2 (CFT 20; Weiß, 1998) was in the average range of performance (IQ= 104). Spelling improvement was observed as his errors were no longer dysphonetic. Although Christian had also made some progress in reading, his working speed was extremely slow. Another evaluation of his intellectual abilities with the Hamburg-Wechsler-Intelligenztest für Kinder (Hawik IV; Petermann & Petermann, 2008) identified a significant discrepancy between his Verbal Comprehension Index (VCI 124) and his Processing Speed Index (PSI 74), indicating visual processing weakness.

Fifth Grade

Christian moved to another school for fifth grade as German elementary schools only include grades 1–4. Here again, Christian received very little special instruction that was adapted to his reading level. He was in a group remedial session once a week for an hour with students from different grades with varying degrees of reading and spelling problems. Christian had a difficult time in fifth grade as his reading was so slow that he couldn't cope with the tasks.

DYSLEXIA DIAGNOSIS AND TREATMENT ISSUES

It is important to understand that there are 16 states in Germany, which all have individual regulations for the identification and treatment of dyslexia. The Kultusministerkonferenz (KMK) under the Ministry of Education provides national recommendations for identification and treatment of dyslexia; however, each state then develops its own guidelines for practice because of the sovereignty of the states in all educational and cultural affairs. Consequently, some states provide dyslexic students with excellent services whereas other states do not see this as a priority. Thus, local services are determined by that state's regulations. In general the KMK considers at least three areas to be important for the dyslexic student: (1) counseling and remediation, (2) accommodation of dyslexia in grading policies regarding tests and report cards, and (3) compensation for disadvantages in tests and final exams.

In Mecklenburg-Vorpommern, according to the latest administrative instructions for the remediation of students with specific difficulties in reading, spelling, and arithmetic (Ministerium für Bildung, Wissenschaft und Kultur des Land Mecklenburg-Vorpommern, 2005), students should be screened for possible difficulties in reading and spelling before the end of first grade. If they have a percentile rank of 15 or below on an informal spelling test, they will be referred for further evaluation. Eligibility of services and official recognition, which occur in fourth grade, require a percentile rank of 10% and below in reading and spelling, and an IQ of at least 90. As previously indicated, Christian demonstrated severe characteristics of dyslexia from an early age. Although his first-grade teacher noted his reading and spelling problems after the first six months, she did not consider him to be at risk for developing a reading and spelling disability. Before Christian was evaluated at the end of second grade, his classroom teacher had to fill out a questionnaire to judge Christian's achievement, which required the teacher to provide explanations about the support given and the results. It is interesting to note that Christian's weakness in reading and spelling and working speed as well as his strength in vocabulary, abstract thinking and general knowledge and listening comprehension were described while questions concerning the treatment that was offered and the success of the remediation were simply not answered. If Christian's teacher had been more sensitive and more highly educated in this area, she would have suspected that this was a child with severe reading problems and provided him with some intervention in the first grade.

It was only after Christian's pediatrician referred him to a psychologist, who assessed his cognition to be normal, that his teacher apparently began to consider other possibilities. At that point, she could no longer attribute Christian's lack of reading progress to lower cognitive ability. Referring him for dyslexia evaluation was a step in the right direction, but it should be noted that she continued to castigate him for lack of progress even though she knew that dyslexia was a possibility. The results of the evaluation clearly indicated that Christian had severe reading and spelling problems despite above average intelligence. He attended the LRS class and one to two remedial sessions per week with little, if any, progress. His teachers did not provide explanation of this insufficient progress or change their remedial approach. Only a ten-week stay at a university-affiliated psychiatric clinic led to reading progress as a result of an individualized highly structured phonics approach.

PARENT PERSPECTIVES

Christian's mother feels that he is a well-adjusted child with a lot of potential. She described him as having a good sense of humor, an open mind and many interests, but she also noted that he is somewhat controlling. He enjoys playing football, using the computer, and watching educational programs on television, particularly those focusing on history and geography. Christian and his mother read together every evening for approximately 45 minutes. Usually Christian chooses books on trains or history while the mother reads adventure stories. The mother reported that she chooses only large print books with pictures for him to read. He prefers to read silently as he says it is easier for him. The mother is impressed with the manner in which he can bring his wealth of knowledge on different subjects to the reading process to aid in his comprehension. She reported that Christian had a friendly way of communicating with others. He is currently president of his class, which attests to his popularity. Also, there are usually friends at his home as he has no social problems. He's a good team player and enjoys playing football, although he is not very good because of motor problems. The mother stated that Christian has fears of failure (i.e., he is very concerned about how others perceive his problems and accomplishments). She doesn't really understand why he is so insecure as he has so many positive attributes. He spends considerable time and energy focusing on others' opinions of him. It's very perplexing to the mother why he feels this way, but she thinks it may be related to the other children teasing him about his reading problems and jealousy about his reduced homework load. She described dyslexia as a condition in which the ears and eyes take information to the brain, where it is misperceived and, therefore, results in a slow processing speed. When asked how dyslexia might influence Christian's life, she commented that it would affect every aspect including all subject areas and ability to perform well. She feels that the most difficult aspect of his reading problem is the suffering he must endure as a result.

Homework often presents a great deal of stress because Christian cannot complete it independently and the mother has a full time job. As an example of this difficulty, the mother recounted a situation in which Christian called her at the book store to inform her of math homework that involved word problems, which he couldn't read. She told him to start the homework and she would help when she got home. When she returned home, she discovered that he had not written anything. After the mother began to read the problems to him, Christian's face lit up: he grasped the problems immediately and quickly finished them. This example emphasizes the frustration that children with dyslexia face when they try to work independently and it further shows the lack of self-esteem they may experience as a result of always having to depend on others.

On the Parent Perception Scale, the mother acknowledged the seriousness of Christian's problem with dyslexia (8/10) and the impact it has on school success (9/10). However, she views this problem as having a lesser impact on his family (5/10) and social life (4/10). She perceives school as the most negative aspect of her son's life, indeed almost a stumbling block to his potential success. His past struggles and the ongoing challenges of increasing amounts of homework were identified as significant stressors to Christian and his family. The mother does not express bitterness, but she is dissatisfied with the school's efforts (or lack thereof). She noted that she has frequently asked the teachers to give her a progress report. With some frustration, she recently asked Christian's teacher "where is the ship going?" to which the teacher answered "what ship?" The mother interpreted this as another avoidance response. The mother believes that if the teachers had identified the problem earlier and addressed it with intensive remediation, the result would have been different. She stated that it would have saved the family and Christian from a lot of the emotional problems that they had experienced. She feels that if her child would have received at least two hours a week from a teacher, similar to the instruction provided by the university clinic, then he would have made more progress. It is her opinion that the teachers in Christian's school did not have an adequate education in reading and, therefore, could not help her child. But she doesn't blame them as she perceives they do not have the training support they need from the administration. The mother noted that the State's regulations are actually very good because they provide support for individual adaptation beyond the fourth grade, but unfortunately the current fifth-grade teacher has declined to implement these as she believes that all children should be treated the same. When the mother complained that all children are not alike, some have reading and spelling problems and some don't, the teacher did not respond. If she could change one thing about the way the school treated children with dyslexia, she recommended that intervention should begin early and that children with dyslexia and their teachers should be provided with support to help them deal with this disability in the classroom.

CHILD PERSPECTIVES

In spite of the fact that Christian had a very poor academic school experience, he has enjoyed a good social life with friends and relatives. He reported that his friends know a lot about him and accept him the way he is. On the Child Perception Scale, Christian rated the influence of his problem on his social life to be minimal (1/10). He is really happy about having good friends, but regrets living in an isolated village where it is difficult to meet his school friends who live further away. Christian enjoys football although he admits that he doesn't play well. He feels strongly supported by his family, especially his mother who listens to him when he feels frustrated at school and who addresses his problems with his teachers. Christian also perceives the influence of his problems on his family life to be minimal (3/10). His father and sister don't talk about his reading problem, but they are aware of it and accept him the way he is.

The two most disturbing aspects of his reading problem are the extended hours he has to spend on his homework and the way he has been treated by most of his teachers. When Christian tries to do his homework, he inevitably begins daydreaming because he can't read the text passages. If there was one thing he could change about school, it would be to get rid of homework. Throughout the interview, Christian referred to the bad treatment he was subjected to by teachers. In particular, his first-grade teacher did nothing to help him and made it clear that all the students who completed their work were smart and the ones that could not were "dumb." In general, he wishes his teachers were more attentive to him, checking his understanding of subject matter. Two teachers who really made a difference were his dyslexia therapist at the clinic and his LRS remedial teacher, both of whom believed in his abilities and supported him. Christian clearly understands the importance of reading and knows his problem is significant (7/10).

Christian has a lot of interests including a fascination with trains. He is active in the local train club where he was invited to participate in adult club member excursions because of his expertise. His diverse interests are reflected in his possible vocational goals, which include demolition expert, politician, or train conductor.

CASE COMMENTARY

Christian's case tells the story of a boy with a severe reading disability who had to wait for three and a half years to receive a remedial program that helped him to acquire the phonological decoding skills to improve his reading. Although Christian has made progress, his reading speed remains at the first percentile, which severely impacts his reading comprehension. In the transparent orthography of German with a highly consistent grapheme-phoneme correspondence, dyslexic children show less of a deficiency in reading accuracy than in reading speed. The findings of an Austrian study showed that dyslexic children who received direct phonics instruction obtained high results in reading accuracy, but continued to exhibit extremely slow reading speed (Landerl, 2001). Dyslexic children were also found to have considerable spelling problems. Landerl noted that, although German dyslexic children do not have major problems translating graphemes into phonemes, their ability to use orthographic rules for spelling is insufficient. Thus, it is not surprising that Christian's spelling in the fourth grade was still very low. Suchodoletz (2006), who examined different remedial methods, found that only those that specifically addressed reading and spelling deficiencies were effective in performance improvement. Huemer, Pointer and Landerl (2009) compared evidence-based German reading and spelling programs in an effort to identify remedial reading components that have proven to be effective. The results revealed that very few of the remedial programs used in Germany met acceptable standards. However, there were several effective programs (those involving phoneme awareness, segmentation, letter-sound correspondences, etc.) that were recommended.

To help children like Christian improve reading speed, more research is needed to evaluate existing programs that specifically address this aspect of the reading disability. Huemer et al. (2009) suggested that reading speed is often a neglected area in remedial programs.

The fact that Christian made very little progress over a long period of time is also due to the deficient teacher training in the area of reading and spelling disabilities. Dummer-Smoch (1998) pointed out that teacher preparation in Germany is inadequate and that without effective teacher education, dyslexic children are missing the support they need from knowledgeable teachers. If Christian had been provided the remedial program used by the special education clinic and a dyslexia specialist from first grade on, he would likely be reading on a much higher level today.

Because of his persistent reading problem and lack of appropriate treatment, Christian experienced a lot of emotional stress. His mother described him as being fearful and desiring to exert excessive control. Research has suggested that children with dyslexia, particularly in grades 3–5 have significantly more academic stress and lower academic self-concept, which is manifested in emotions such as fear and physiological reactions (e.g., rapid heartbeat and nausea) (Alexander-Passe, 2007).

A few months after the interview, the outlook for Christian became unexpectedly brighter when his former clinical therapist explained to the school board that he was participating in an international study, in which his lack of progress would be reported. As a result of this attention, the school now provides remedial lessons on a one to one basis with a program that is aligned with Kossow's (1985) model, but provides a redesigned curriculum (Behrndt, Hoffmann & Koschay, 2009). The program contains all of the critical reading components required for successful treatment. Christian is currently enjoying the remedial sessions and the teacher who provides these. There is reason to be optimistic now that this bright child is finally receiving the attention and support he needs to improve his reading skills.

REFERENCES

Alexander-Passe, N. (2008). The sources and manifestations of stress amongst school-aged dyslexics, compared with sibling controls. *Dyslexia, 14*, 291–313.

Behrndt, S. M., Hoffmann, H., & Koschay, E.(2009). *Kompendium. Zum Abbau von Schwierigkeiten beim Lesen und beim Rechtschreiben* [Compendium for the reduction of difficulties in reading and spelling]. Rostock, Germany: Eigenverlag Greifswald.

Dummer-Smoch, L. (1998). Dyslexia in Germany- An educational policy for meeting dyslexic children's needs in the German school system. *Dyslexia, 4*, 63–72.

Huemer, S.M., Pointer, A., & Landerl, K. (2009). Evidenzbasierte LRS-Förderung. Bericht über die wissenschaftlich überprüfte Wirksamkeit von Programmen und Komponenten, die in der LRS- Förderung zum Einsatz kommen [Evidence based remediation of reading and spelling difficulties. Report about the evaluated efficiency of programs and components, which are applied in the remediation of reading and spelling difficulties]. Vienna: Bundesministerium für Unterricht, Kunst und Kultur.

Kossakowski, A. (1985). Worttafel. [Wordlist]. In H J. Kossow *Leitfaden zur Bekämpfung der Lese-Rechtschreibschwäche. Einführung und Kommentare.* [Manual for the fight against the reading and spelling weakness. Introduction and comments] (p.25). Berlin: Deutscher Verlag der Wissenschaften.

Kossow, H.J. (2000). *Das Lautwortoperationsverfahren* [Sound word operation technique]. Bochum, Germany: Winkler.

Kultusministerium (Hrsg) (1996). *Erlass zur Förderung von Schülern mit Lese-Rechtschreibschwierigkeiten und einer förmlich festgestellten Legasthenie.* [Regulations for the remediation of students with reading and spelling difficulties and for officially recognized dyslexia]. Mittl.bl. des Kultusministeriums Mecklenburg-Vorpommern vom 27.06 1996 . Schwerin, Germany, 401.

Landerl, K. (2001). Word recognition deficits in German: More evidence from a representative sample. *Dyslexia*, 7, 183–196.

Linder, M., & Grissemann, H.(2000). *Züricher Lesetest (6. Auflage)* [Zurich Reading Test (6th ed.)] (6.Auflage). Bern, Switzerland: Huber.

Ministerium für Bildung, Wissenschaft und Kultur des Landes Mecklenburg-Vorpommern (Hrsg.) (2005). *Förderung von Schülerinnen und Schülern mit besonderen Schwierigkeiten im Lesen, Rechtschreiben oder Rechnen* [Remediation of female and male students with specific difficulties in reading, spelling and arithmetic]. (Verwaltungsvorschrift vom 8. September 2005). Mittl. bl. des Ministeriums für Bildung, Wissenschaft und Kultur Mecklenburg-Vorpommern vom 08.09.2005. Schwerin, Germany, 1003–1005.

Petermann, F., & Petermann, U. (Hrsg) (2008). *Hamburg-Wechsler-Intelligenztest für Kinder-IV* (2., ergänzte Aufl.) [Hamburg Wechsler Intelligence Scale for Children-IV]. Bern, Switzerland: Huber.

Suchodoletz v., W. (2006). *Therapie der Lese-Rechtschreibstörung (LRS)(2. Aufl.)* [Remediation of reading and spelling disabilities (2nd ed.)]. Stuttgart: Kohlhammer.

Tewes, U., Roßmann, P., & Schallberger, U. (1999). *Hamburg-Wechsler-Intelligenztest für Kinder-dritte Auflage (Hawik-III)* [Hamburg Wechsler Intelligence Scale for Children] Bern, Switzerland: Huber.

Weiß, R.H.(1998). *Grundintelligenztest Skala 2* (CFT 20) (4. Aufl.) [Basic Intelligence Scale (2nd ed.)]. Göttingen, Germany: Hogrefe.

CHRISTIAN'S INTERVIEW

1. What do you want to be when you grow up?

     I don't know really. I have to see what's coming up. I'm interested in trains and in explosives and in building the scenery for a film and I'm a good story teller. I could be a train conductor, or a licensed blaster or a politician.

   Why do you think you would be good at that job?

     Because I'm interested in these things. I like to play with firecrackers. I could be a train conductor because I'm extremely interested in trains and I'm a member in a railroad club.

2. Tell me about a teacher who has been really important to you or one who has helped you: what did the teacher do to help you?

     Mrs. K. [the teacher in the remedial program in the clinic]. She encouraged me compared to the others who did the opposite. She said "you can do it, you can do it" and Mrs. B. also said, "you can do it and you're doing a good job." The other teachers who were supposed to help me said, "Oh, dear, he is not able to do anything."

3. Tell me about a teacher who didn't really help you that much or one who did not give you the help you needed.

   That was Mrs. W. in first grade. She said I was dumb. This was the typical teacher whom you shouldn't like . . . her favorite students who are good have the ability to perform and students who don't do well are stupid. And I didn't like my math teacher in my special education classroom. When you forgot your homework, she made a big deal out of it, the "show business" of shouting.

   What did you want the teacher to do to help you?

   I wanted the teacher to listen and that she does something for me and that she doesn't just say "you are really bad." She could have helped me with reading at the beginning of first grade by explaining things to me I didn't understand. Reading begins in first grade. She could have helped me with my written assignments because if you mess up first grade, you mess up the rest of your life.

4. Tell me what your mother thinks about your dyslexia. Does she talk to you about the problem?

   I've never thought about that up to now. She puts up with it and she supports me and she gets through all the problems with me.

   What does she say?

   She asks me about school and then I can tell her that the teachers were totally stupid again or that they got on my nerves or that the math teacher was terrible; she badmouthed me in front of the whole class. And then she says, "we have to check that out." And she addresses that with the teachers.

5. Tell me what your father thinks about your dyslexia. Does he talk to you about the problem?

   No.

   What does he say?

   He accepts me the way I am, but he doesn't talk to me about my dyslexia.

6. Tell me about something that makes you really happy.

   What makes me really happy is my spare time and that I have friends and a day all by myself. When I say today nobody should come here then I can relax here at home.

7. Tell me about something that makes you really sad.

   It makes me really sad that I had to leave second grade, the class I started school with.

8. When the work gets very hard at school and you think you can't do it, what do you do?

   I would say I try to do it as good as I can. Sometimes I ask a teacher to explain it to me or I ask a classmate.

9. What kinds of books do you like to read?
> *Non fiction books . . . and comic(s).*

What is your favorite book?
> *The book of the 100 major battles and the comic "Surrounded by Idiots."*

Do you read to yourself?
> *Yes.*

Who else reads to you?
> *Mum, most of the time in the evening when I'm in bed. I read to her and she reads to me.*

10. Do your friends know that you have dyslexia?
> *Yes.*

Do you talk to them about it?
> *No, we don't talk about it. They know it and they put up with it.*

What do you say?
> *Nothing really. Only when we are working in groups I ask them to slow down or I say, "could you please wait for me."*

What do your friends say to you about dyslexia?
> *Nothing, they accept it like it is. I'm completely normal to them.*

11. Do your siblings know that you have dyslexia?
> *Yes. Sometimes she says "hold on!"*

Do you talk to them about it?
> *No, she has known it from first grade on. You don't have to talk to her about that.*

12. Name three things you are really good at:
> *I'm good at sport activities, except for throwing. I can't do that well.*
> *I can tell stories well, but I'm not like Baron Münchhausen.*
> *When I'm watching a movie I pick out important things, which I can remember for years.*

13. Name three things you are not so good at:
> *Reading passages, reading instructions, fast and proper handwriting.*

14. If you are feeling bad about your reading, is there one person you can talk to who makes you feel better?
> *Mum and also Dad.*

What does that person say to you?
> *Go on, don't give up.*

15. Do computers help you with your reading?
> *Yes and no.*

If yes, how do they help you?
> *—If I have a passage about Queen Elizabeth and I want to know more about her I look it up in the internet.*

16. Do you usually have problems with your homework?
    Yes, I'm a dreamer. I'm sitting here and I look out of the window and then I'm daydreaming.

    Can you do your homework independently or does someone help you?
    Yes, I can, but most of the time somebody is helping me and that is Mum . . . Sometimes I'm daydreaming and sometimes I don't understand the text passages. And when I have to search for misspelled words I search the whole passage and can't find them. Then I need help. Also in math, I don't understand what I have to do because reading is so difficult.

17. If there was one thing you could change about school, what would it be?
    The first ting that I would do is: no more homework. If you pay attention at school, you could learn the subject material at school. And then you should be able to choose who is sitting next to you at school so that you don't have to sit next to somebody you don't like.

18. If you could have three wishes, what would they be?
    My first wish is to have three more wishes and then I have got five wishes. My first wish is that the teachers pay more attention to their students at school. Number two: the classes should be smaller. There are enough teachers. And my third wish: no more homework. Fourth wish that I don't live here so isolated. There is only one boy in this village who is my age and he lives close to the woods. Number five: I play soccer with him and I wish that the soccer field was O.K. There are lots of potholes in the field.

19. Tell me three things you would like your teacher to do to help you with your dyslexia.
    That the teachers pay more attention to me. Teachers want to force a lot of subject matter upon us and sometimes they don't understand that we don't get it. And a teacher should really ask me if I really understood. The teacher asks the class: "Did you all understand?" Then I think about it and all of a sudden I detect a missing part. I would like that he asks me personally if I understood.

20. Who is the best reader in your class?
    That is difficult. I can't really tell you. A good reader is Peter Schulze.

    How did he/she get to be such a good reader?
    Because the reading ability was put into his cradle. [he was born with it]. And because he likes to read and he wants to read.

21. Is it important to learn how to read? Why or why not?
    Yes, without reading you are stuck in the world. Without reading you couldn't do anything and the row of books over there [points to bookshelves] would just only be printed paper and you couldn't use a computer because most of the things there have to do with reading.

10 Jankó, a Case Study of Dyslexia in Hungary

Éva Gyarmathy

Jankó is a lively boy of 10 who is slight of build and possesses an inquisitive nature. He is very talkative and highly sensitive. He is an engaging child who selected his own pseudonym for his case study, which is also the name of a Hungarian folk tale hero, Erős (Strong) Jankó. During the break in the interview, Jankó played basketball using a crumpled-up piece of paper and aiming at the upper spring of the door. When the "ball" got stuck up there, he would not pull up a chair so as to reach it easily. He kept jumping up with a small stick he found in the room until he finally managed to push the crumpled paper out. His chances of success in this case were very low, but he was sure he could do it. It seems that whatever Jankó sets his mind on, he can accomplish. The only place this does not work is school.

BACKGROUND

Family History

Jankó's mother is a kinesiologist and his father is a chemical engineer. The family lives in a middle class neighborhood in a large city in Hungary. Jankó has a 6-year-old brother. The father, who is rarely at home, believes that Jankó would not have any difficulties if he paid more attention in school. The mother is aware that Jankó has true learning disorders and blames herself for not taking the appropriate steps to get him the help he needs. She also blames herself as she had learning difficulties in childhood. The mother reported that during her own school experience her memory was poor and she was always embarrassed during oral exams as she was afraid of failure. Thus, she developed self-esteem problems. Jankó's father, in turn, never liked to read. The mother thinks Jankó may have inherited dyslexia from his father and the related learning problems from her.

Medical History

Jankó was not a planned child. His mother, being unaware of her pregnancy, had an active social life that included frequent partying. When she became aware of the pregnancy, she was fearful and uneasy about the responsibility of having a child. The mother's labor was difficult and prolonged, eventually resulting in a cesarean delivery. At birth, the baby's heartbeat reportedly fell to a dangerous level, necessitating the administration of oxytocin. For the mother, Jankó's birth was a traumatic experience, which resulted in an emotional breakdown in the hospital that was so severe that she had to be placed in restraints. To this day the mother remembers the birth as a horrible experience.

Jankó has never been hospitalized nor had any serious illnesses. However, in recent years, he has begun to develop severe allergies. Not long ago, he exhibited such serious symptoms that his pollen allergy nearly progressed to asthma. He had been taking homeopathic medicine, when the family finally sought help from a specialist last year because of his allergy and his mental state. His anxiety increased to the extent that he could not go to school. The specialist diagnosed the allergy problem as being psychosomatic in nature.

Early Development

According to his mother, Jankó was always a challenging child. He slept very little and cried excessively. Frequent stomach aches were a cause of discomfort. He also had some behavioral problems. His mother described him as a "small rebel" as he seemed to want the exact opposite of everything his parents chose. She felt bad about all this and blamed herself for not being a good mother.

Jankó's development was adequate although a little uneven. His gross motor abilities were always very good. He moved very deftly at an early age, walking before he was 1 year of age. He learned to ski when he was about 4 or 5 years old and now at 10 years of age, he has learned to snowboard in a single day. Jankó also learned to ride a bike between the ages of 4 and 5 years. He had less interest in fine motor activities. Even as a young child, he did not engage in drawing.

He pronounced his first words when he was 1 year old. Thereafter, he was for the most part a friendly and loquacious child. He got on well with the children of family friends. He was adaptive and never dominant with children, but he preferred being with adults. Jankó particularly liked to act, dance, and entertain on top of the table from an early age.

SCHOOL HISTORY

Kindergarten

Jankó started kindergarten at the age of 3 years, but attendance was a problem from the beginning because he did not like school. His mother indulged him and did not force him to go as sometimes they traveled or visited relatives. Already at the age of 3 years, the child had the option to decide whether he wanted to go to the nursery school. Even though Jankó didn't have particular difficulties there, he didn't take a liking to either the teachers or his peers.

From the age of 5 years, kindergarten in Hungary is compulsory; however, there is no required curriculum. It is up to the individual teachers to determine whether children should have directed readiness experiences. If the teachers do not insist on these, children are virtually never engaged in developmental activities unless they appear to have serious problems. As Jankó wasn't in kindergarten very often, his early problems were not identified.

First Grade

At the age of 6, Jankó was eager to begin first grade. He and his mother even made a tour of the classroom in advance. However, this experience turned out to be a great disappointment as Jankó lagged behind in learning and could never do anything as well as the other children. His peers bullied and physically abused him, so much so that he began hiding from them out of fear. Then, after less than two months of first grade, his homeroom teacher slapped him in the face for noncompliance and making fun of her. This was a very humiliating experience for Jankó, but even after this abusive incident, the parents were reluctant to move him to another school. They felt that this might be interpreted as escapism. The mother reported that this was one of the hardest times of their lives. Eventually the school situation became unbearable for both Jankó and the parents. At mid-year they moved Jankó to a Waldorf School. The mother joined the parents' association and became active in the school to help with Jankó's integration, but it quickly became apparent that he was also going to have problems at his new school. The mother described Jankó as a "dreamer" who "is really not the type cut out for school." He was referred to a specialist in the school who assessed him, but did not give the parents any results. By the end of first grade, Jankó still could not read or write. Even though it was obvious that he had significant reading problems, no one at the school mentioned dyslexia.

In Hungary, dyslexia is still nonexistent as far as many teachers are concerned. They usually blame the children and the parents for learning failures. They consider the child lazy and/or obtuse, and they believe that the parents are responsible for either neglect or overprotection. This attitude is of no help in identifying and solving the child's problems. In a number of schools, they do not diagnose dyslexia because that would require the need for extracurricular training, for which there is insufficient funding. According to the law, pupils cannot be failed in the first four grades. Consequently, problems usually come to light only after four years at school. By that time, however, the gap between achievement and age has widened and the child has lost precious time, resulting in diminished self-esteem.

Second Grade

Second grade was not an improvement for Jankó, as he was unable to successfully master the curriculum. At the age of 7 years, his problems with reading and writing became progressively worse. He was very slow and had problems concentrating, problems which were exacerbated by the high number of pupils in the class (i.e., 30 or more). His mother was regarded as an impatient, interfering, and anxious parent because she was concerned with Jankó's lack of achievement. The homeroom teacher seemed unconcerned, thinking that he was simply a late developer. Jankó reported receiving some type of extra lessons at school, but the parents were not informed about the nature of these lessons and did not understand the purpose of this instruction. The fact that he received this support suggested that the school was aware of Jankó's problems, but chose not to refer him for evaluation. The philosophy of this Waldorf School was to extend considerable latitude toward developmental expectations, but this position had severe consequences for Jankó as necessary intervention was delayed.

Third Grade

Jankó's problems continued in third grade. He could not read sentences or correctly write letters, and he was still very slow. His learning frustration resulted in continued behavior problems at school. He was frequently sent out of the classroom for being disorderly, which Jankó felt was an injustice. His mother was determined not to complain to the school further so she did not intervene. The homeroom teacher finally referred Jankó to an education counselor because of his academic and behavior problems. The counselor told the family that he had no idea how Jankó could be motivated. At this point, Jankó was also tested and diagnosed as dyslexic. However, the mother rejected the diagnosis because she did not want him to have this label. She, therefore, only accepted the expert opinion with the condition that Jankó be described as "at risk" instead of dyslexic. The mother's attitude was related to the fact that in Hungary there is a general perception that dyslexia is some kind of mental illness. Parents are ashamed of the diagnosis and seek to avoid associated stigmatization. Hungarian parents are under no obligation to accept the opinion of experts; they can easily negotiate the diagnosis and may subsequently ask to change it. Because of this, a child's records may be altered substantially and therefore may not reflect the true nature of difficulties.

Fourth Grade

The gap between his grade level and actual achievement increased for Jankó as grade level advanced. To compensate, he misbehaved at school and vented his anger at his brother at home. Although Jankó tried hard to fit in with his peers, his efforts were in vain. The other children did not accept him socially and he seemed to disturb them. An "anti-Jankó" club was formed at his school, and these children actually beat him several times. During this time, Jankó often wet his bed and developed serious allergy and asthma attacks. The mother wanted to receive support for Jankó's learning, but she did not want him to be set apart and given different sorts of therapy. She wanted the school to accept him and to teach him in a way that he could learn. According to the mother the supplementary instruction that he received at school was of no help as it was basically "practicing the school work." The mother also took Jankó to a private reflexologist (i.e., a therapist who opens blockage of energy fields by pressures and movements), which Jankó detested as he found it to be boring and useless.

Finally, his mother took Jankó to a private psychologist to receive advice on how to help him. This psychologist tested him and informed the mother that the results of the assessment clearly indicated Jankó was dyslexic. In addition, his counting skills were found to be far below his high intelligence level. The psychologist recommended a private special needs teacher who could work with Jankó on a weekly basis to teach him reading and writing. The possibility of choosing a new school was also discussed, given that Jankó's situation was becoming worse. Subsequently the mother consulted the special needs teacher who started to work with Jankó. This teacher recommended a new school. Shortly thereafter, the mother changed her mind and did not take Jankó back to the special needs teacher nor did she change his school. As a result, there was no improvement. After this, Jankó's homeroom teacher began to work with him. The mother decided they should be patient and give this teacher a chance. However, the teacher suggested that Jankó give up sports and music so he could concentrate on learning instead of his hobbies. The teacher felt that these extracurricular activities made Jankó too tired in the afternoon and did not leave him with enough time and energy for learning. Jankó was thereafter deprived of his favorite activities. As in many other cases, this school had a misguided solution, which did not address the child's academic needs or interests (i.e., spending more time on the curriculum without exposure to specialized strategies designed to meet the needs of the dyslexic child).

DYSLEXIA DIAGNOSIS AND TREATMENT ISSUES

In Hungary, there is no uniform assessment procedure for identifying dyslexia. It is basically up to the specialists to select whatever tests they choose. Even committees of experts diverge in assessment procedures, and consequently, diagnoses are highly varied. If the assessment targets specific areas of the child's development, then the testing is carried out by the experts responsible for that particular area and individual testing methods differ greatly. There are very different sorts of methods and tools in use in the identification of dyslexia, but these can basically be divided into four groups: (1) intelligence tests, (2) perceptual-motor measures, (3) achievement tests, and (4) multicausal measures. There are also methods that use the teacher's evaluation of the children's achievement and behavior, which are basically structured observations. The results of these are rather subjective, but provide a detailed picture of the children's abilities (Kósáné, Porkolábné, & Ritoókné, 1987).

For Jankó, difficulties with school performances were not observed in kindergarten, but this is probably due to the fact that his attendance was erratic and there were few academic expectations at that level. Jankó's problems were initially noted in the first grade where he received his first assessment for learning problems. The results of this testing, however, were not released to the parents. A second assessment, on the parents' request and with the school's agreement, was carried out two years later, when Jankó was a third-grader. His third grade teacher was of the opinion that Jankó had difficulties with learning. She noted that his general speed was slow and he made many mistakes of form and mixed up letters in his writing.

Since the Hungarian language is a phonetic transparent language, it is not thought to be difficult for dyslexics, yet there are certain features that can cause problems. For example, Hungarian is an agglutinative language (i.e., prepositions do not stand alone, but are added to nouns) and word order is not fixed (i.e., suffixes serve as markers for sentence construction), which means that words can be very long and misreading endings can interfere with comprehension. Thus, it was not surprising that Jankó's reading was very slow and laborious. Also, the letters of the Hungarian alphabet are divided into three groups: standard characters, consonant combinations (e.g., sz, zs, gy), and vowels with diacritical markers (e.g., ő, á, ô), the latter two of which present particular challenges for dyslexic children because of confusions related to visual and phonetic similarities (Gyarmathy, 2004). These errors of letter identification and formation were observed in Jankó's reading and writing as previously indicated.

When Jankó was a third-grader he received his first professional assessment at the Educational Counseling Service, which is a state institution in every district in Budapest and in all Hungarian towns. The Ildkó Meixner test (Meixner, 1993) and the Meeting Street School Screening (MSSST) (Denhoff, Siqueland, Komich & Hainsworth, 1968) assessment methods were employed. Jankó's reading was found to be slow and erroneous, below developmental expectations of the test. His mistakes were consistent; he commonly mixed up letters (ő-ű, ty-gy-ny, b-d, sz-zs-cs) and he always halted when trying to identify the letters *b* and *d*. The results of this testing revealed that he exhibited sequential visual perceptual and visual-motor weaknesses as well as poor verbal memory. As previously mentioned, Jankó was diagnosed as dyslexic at this point; however, the diagnosis was changed to "at risk" for dyslexia at the insistence of the mother. The psychologists at the center recommended special education treatment. As a result of this testing, the special needs teacher at the school worked with him once a week for an hour. Jankó didn't like going to these sessions and no improvement was observed.

A year later in the fourth grade, Jankó was given the Gyarmathy-Smythe Cognitive Profile Test (Smythe, Gyarmathy & Everatt, 2002; Gyarmathy, 2009), which again confirmed his dyslexia. In addition, Jankó was found to have math problems, particularly in the area of counting. He also had serious difficulties in the area of spatial-orientation. His movement coordination was excellent, while his fine motor skills were somewhat below average. His counting, reading and spelling skills were all poor. The testing report described his need for intensive treatment as "urgent." In addition to the development of the relevant abilities, targeted reading development was also recommended, which meant that a specialist should reteach reading to Jankó. To address counting problems, it was suggested that the child learn to use the *soroban* (i.e., a Hungarian type of abacus).

After this testing, the mother chose to delay a remedial program to give the classroom teacher an opportunity to achieve results. She also believed this would provide Jankó with another opportunity to experience success and confidence in his classroom. Thus, the reading problems that he exhibited in first grade were becoming progressively worse as the last four years represented a series of missed opportunities that could have greatly changed the outcome for Jankó.

In Hungary, it is common for parents to seek private therapy solutions when the child's school progress is inadequate. While it should be the responsibility of the school and the education counselor to provide for the child on the basis of an appropriately designed individual education plan, this seldom occurs. The specialists at the official educational counseling centers (Nevelési Tanácsadó) have the responsibility to provide support for children with special needs and their parents; however, these counseling centers are overloaded so the staff spends most of the time and resources providing for children with much more severe disabilities than dyslexia. Thus, parents of children with dyslexia are generally left to fend for themselves and must seek help and information from independent sources. There are many well-trained dyslexia specialists in Hungary, but it can be difficult for families to find these specialists and provisions for remediation can be very costly.

PARENT PERSPECTIVES

Jankó's mother described him as a sensitive, independent child who has many talents. He is especially good at sports and is talented at table tennis, basketball, and climbing. Jankó also has talents in the areas of music and acting: even as a small child he was very precocious in his ability to entertain others and always enjoyed being the center of attention. In fact, his ability to entertain is so extraordinary that his mother believes he will become an actor. However, during the last few years these abilities have been less obvious as he has been bearing the burden of school failure, which has adversely affected all areas of his life.

The mother has some concerns about Jankó's social skills and behavior. When he is in the company of adults, he demonstrates excellent social skills as he is highly verbal, inquisitive, and ingratiating. However, when he is with peers his mother reported that he can be "manipulative, unsocialized, and thoughtless." She noted that he doesn't seem to realize when he is "pushing limits." When he hits someone, he doesn't understand that he is causing pain. However, the mother also described Jankó as a highly sensitive child, who cannot bear to see brutality on television shows. He even becomes overly emotional when watching cartoons, "which have a deep effect on him." She believes that he is subject to extremes of behavior. His mother reported that Jankó rarely reads independently at home, but his parents and grandparents read to him about five hours per week.

The mother defined dyslexia as "an ability disorder," in which a child "sees letters differently, and mixes them up." She also thinks he has a problem with motivation, meaning that if he is not interested in the topic, he cannot pay attention. She believes that dyslexia will influence her son's life by continuing to decrease his self-esteem and causing socialization problems. The mother reported the significance of her son's reading problem to be moderate, yet she believes that the effects on school and family life are severe. She also feels that Jankó's reading problem significantly interferes with his social life.

The mother stated that the most difficult aspect of Jankó's reading problem is that his "lack of success" affects his whole personality. She noted that he constantly experiences a feeling of being behind, which results in self-pity. He compensates for his poor reading by engaging in misbehavior, often resulting in his removal from the classroom, which puts him even further behind. His mother is also concerned about the way he mistreats his little brother. She reported that Jankó physically attacks and humiliates his brother, probably in an effort to relieve the accumulation of tension from school and the stress imposed by expectations he cannot meet.

For a long time, Jankó's mother refused to accept that he had significant reading problems. Two years earlier she would not allow an expert to include the diagnosis of dyslexia in the formal diagnosis after his testing. Today, she has finally accepted that Jankó needs help, but she is still ambivalent about confronting the problem and its consequences. She equates obtaining help for Jankó with conceding that this is a significant problem. She is reluctant to draw attention to him through his problems and oddly believes that providing her son with help may be "forcing him into this victim role." The father thinks it is the child's fault that he can't manage reading. He believes Jankó should pay more attention and work on improving his body posture while reading. The mother perceives that much of the problem may be due to Jankó's poor attention. This is why she continues to send him to reflex therapy even though she has not seen any results. The mother previously hoped that the school would solve Jankó's problem, but the Hungarian system does not have the capacity to provide this remediation. Supplementary lessons at school focus on the curriculum, not the remediation of specific learning problems, such as dyslexia. In spite of the latest diagnostic testing, which confirmed Jankó's dyslexia, his current homeroom teacher regards the situation as a question of motivation. He perceives the responsibilities of his role to be devoted to uncovering ways to motivate this child. And the mother seems willing to go along with this even though she knows that this particular teacher "tends to delegate the problems of the child to the family."

Jankó's mother loves her son and it is painful for her to see the child strain and struggle. He doesn't believe in himself because he keeps comparing himself to good students. Although he has made some progress in his reading, when compared to his peers the mother says it is "frightening" to see his lack of achievement. His homework creates a huge problem as he doesn't even know what he is supposed to do. She noted that he is at a disadvantage because he doesn't understand the lessons in class to begin with "so it is nearly impossible for him to do the homework, which is becoming an increasing problem."

If there is one thing that the mother could change about the way the school treats children with dyslexia, she stated ironically that there should be "no sweeping things under the carpet," which suggests that in spite of her ambivalence she wants help from the school. She also stated that "parents should not be left alone with their problems" as they need support. She wants small group classes, support for children with talents, greater attention to differences among children, and a special learning classroom where attention can be given to learning problems. The mother also sees the need for stress relief and self-esteem activities that might include "playful drama."

CHILD PERSPECTIVES

Jankó does not accept that he has dyslexia. In spite of his school problems and diagnosis of dyslexia, he unequivocally stated, "I don't have reading difficulties." He said that he loves books and is just getting "the hang of reading." He cannot, however, name a single book he likes. Although he is 10 years of age, he has only read one book on his own and is now in the process of reading his second. He admitted that his mother helps him when he cannot cope and family members read to him a lot.

While his mother rated the significance of Jankó's reading problem to be moderate, Jankó rated it as mild. He believes it only minimally interferes with school compared to his mother's perception that it causes significant interference. Likewise, his mother noted that the problem severely interfered with family life whereas Jankó minimized the influence of the problem. Characteristically, Jankó was unwilling to admit that his reading problem significantly interfered with his social life.

His interview responses relating to school were concise, and, again, full of inconsistencies. Although this is a child who is highly verbal, he shuts down when the topic of conversation relates to his learning problems. When asked to name things that he has trouble with, he first mentions learning, and then turns to much more specific things in the area of sports, such as swimming and dunking in basketball. In an answer to a question concerning his strategy for dealing with challenging work, he says that if he cannot cope with a task, he will try until he finally succeeds. However, he admits that sometimes he gets so frustrated that he slams his work to the ground and shouts "I won't learn this." Although, his mother reported that Jankó cannot do homework independently, he claimed that homework constituted only a "little" problem for him. On the other hand, if he could change something about school, "there would be no homework."

Jankó complained that teachers do not give precise instructions about their expectations. It is his opinion that they don't tell him exactly what he is supposed to do and therefore he cannot follow through. He perceives this to be a stumbling block to his success in the classroom. He would like his teachers to be more patient and to provide more demonstrations. Jankó says that if they would do that, it "would be enough, and I wouldn't need anything else."

Jankó doesn't seem to have any real friends. When he was asked to name his best friends, he answered, "there are none." He said his classmates consider him "stupid" and hurt him for no reason. He admits that he annoys them with his antics that are thinly disguised attempts to become more popular. Jankó thinks his peers find it amusing when he's funny. On the other hand, his peers often misunderstand his jests and take them seriously. This is when they start beating him, upon which he becomes angry and retaliates. Jankó reported that he doesn't get along well with his brother, either. He says his brother pesters him and he responds by beating him. Jankó considers it unfair that his mother scolds him when he gets physical as he is not the instigator. He doesn't seem to understand that it is inappropriate for a 10-year-old to physically attack a much younger and smaller child.

If Jankó could, he would run away from his failures and constant conflicts. His magical wishes indicate a desire for escape on the one hand, and a longing for success and achievement, on the other. His wishes of being able to fly and do anything with his magic wand or that of being able to dig himself in anywhere clearly show this. And of course, what would really make him happy would be "if I could do my work properly."

He also has, however, many diverse aspirations for future careers, even though he doesn't yet know precisely what he wants to be. He mentioned possibilities in sports (football player, basketball player, etc), music, blacksmithing, and chemical engineering, the latter being the profession of his father. In spite of all of his challenges and lack of confidence, Jankó possesses talents in sports and music that should be nurtured and appreciated.

CASE COMMENTARY

In many ways, Jankó's case is typical of a dyslexic child in Hungary, although in other respects his situation is unique. It is unfortunately typical that the identification of dyslexia and the risk of dyslexia, as well as the detection of deviations in abilities came late. Jankó was 9 years of age when he was diagnosed as dyslexic, which is a little later than typical, but there is also quite a bit of diversity in assessment practice because of extenuating circumstances. Some children will be screened for dyslexia during kindergarten and will be identified as "at risk" if problems are observed. Many of these children will later be diagnosed as dyslexic, probably at the end of first grade, which means that the child will be 8 years of age by the time treatment is received. Yet, it is also true that some very intelligent children can cover their weaknesses for a long time and will not be diagnosed until much later. Teachers are not trained to identify the symptoms of dyslexia, especially when the signs are not clear. All too often no one will notice there is a reading problem as the child may be compensating for this weakness through outstanding intelligence. Thus, a child that should be performing well above grade level will be functioning at an average or slightly below average level. Girls are particularly at risk of being overlooked because they tolerate frustration better. In the case of boys, constant failure often triggers aggression, as a result of which they are referred for behavior problems. It is at this point that the dyslexia or other specific learning difficulties are uncovered, which preferably happens sooner rather than later. Even after the dyslexia is identified, however, it is uncertain that the child will be provided with the necessary therapy. The support a child is provided always depends on local circumstances and the financial situation of the parents. In Hungary, the school is not responsible for providing remedial services to dyslexic students. The mental health centers for children are required to deal with dyslexics after the school refers the child for assessment and treatment.

The perception of dyslexia at school is also beginning to change, but the old view still has firm footing in some classrooms. Some teachers believe there's no such thing as dyslexia, only lazy children who want to be excused from hard work. Depending on the attitude, the teacher may rebuke the dyslexic child causing embarrassment in front of peers and/or perhaps even resort to violence such as in the case of Jankó who was slapped by his first-grade teacher. Other teachers may attempt to try to find ways to motivate the child, as Jankó's teacher tried to do at the Waldorf School. Unfortunately, however, neither impatience, nor patience is of any help when the child in fact should be provided with remediation to address the specific problems of dyslexia.

Due to the nature of confusion surrounding dyslexia, this learning disorder was excluded from the category of special educational needs in Hungary, which would have entitled these children to an increased per capita subsidy. Although dyslexics belong to the category of Special Education Needs (SEN), they can mostly receive only *dispensation* instead of services so they don't receive failing marks in school as schools do not receive extra money to support remedial needs with classes for dyslexic students. If a child has serious learning disorders, *dispensations* can be obtained from an official committee of experts. A *dispensation* allows a child to be excused from grading for problematic subjects (i.e., reading, writing, grammar, and second language). A *dispensation* also provides accommodations, such as additional time on written exams and oral administration. Consequently, only those who are diagnosed with another major SEN disorder, such as attention deficit with hyperactivity (ADHD) will obtain remedial support services. The dispensation process itself is problematic as it provides only a partial solution for students with dyslexia. The avoidance of failing marks is insufficient for these children. They can generally obtain full waivers in writing, reading, grammar, counting and learning foreign languages, but what they need is instruction to remediate their reading problems as opposed to accommodations. Due to their poor achievement, dyslexics will be at a disadvantage throughout their lives if they don't receive the help they need during their school years. For example, knowledge of foreign languages is indispensable in today's global society. In Hungary, performance on foreign language exams also exerts considerable influence on admission to higher education institutions and the awarding of degrees, which are given only to those who have passed at least one intermediate foreign language examination. Thus, if dyslexic students receive a waiver for foreign language, their chances for admission to certain university programs will be adversely affected.

In Jankó's case, there are a number of possibilities that might be suitable for meeting his educational needs, but each will require the assistance of a special needs teacher to help him cope with his difference in abilities, enhance his poor school skills and learn to use efficient learning methods. The first solution would be for Jankó to continue in his present school with the help of those teachers, but considering his current dire social situation and the meager experience of the teachers in teaching dyslexic students, this option could result in even greater tension leading to a further deterioration in Jankó's self-esteem. This is the fate of most dyslexics, who stay in mainstream education and obtain waivers in different subjects. As another alternative, the family could choose to obtain the status of a *private student*. This is a rare solution, as yet, and is used mainly in the case of a child who is unable to fit in due to emotional-behavioral disorders. As a *private student*, Jankó could have intensive support to overcome his disadvantage and the number of conflicts between him and his peers would also be reduced. Unfortunately, there is only a slight chance that a school will provide such an opportunity to a child like Jankó as dyslexia is not considered a severe enough disorder to attain this status even if it leads to behavioral and emotional problems. A third solution is for Jankó to go to a different school, which specializes in specific learning disorders, but in typical public school, dyslexics usually don't get enough help and individual support. It means that Jankó would find himself in the same situation he currently faces only in a different mainstream school. As none of these potential solutions seem ideal, it would appear that private remediation may be the only tenable answer for this child.

Jankó's case is also typical in that many dyslexics suffer from problems of low self-esteem and related behavioral difficulties due to continued school failure. Even a highly talented child, such as Jankó, can be deeply affected by the day-to-day struggle of not being able to live up to expectations. This frustration often turns to aggression as he tries to alleviate stress. Jankó will not accept that he has a reading problem. He resorts to self-deception and is constantly frustrated because he feels that there is something wrong with him. He uses his considerable willpower to deny and disguise his difficulties. He is angry at the world because he cannot achieve as his peers. What is unique in Jankó are his outstanding abilities and willpower. He has extraordinary achievement and outstanding success in activities he likes to do (i.e., sports, music, singing, and acting). These are areas where he has tremendous possibilities and should be used to facilitate his learning. Jankó's skill development could be best achieved through his artistic vein. His talent for acting and interest in literature could provide great opportunities for learning. Physical exercise and music also help learning. For example, he could learn literature through studying plays, prose, and poetry. These areas of strength must be emphasized as they are positive influences in Jankó's life, which will help him face the adversity that is imposed by his condition.

Jankó's plight is complicated by the mother's lack of willingness to make a decision about his treatment, which is in turn related to her concerns about calling attention to a disorder that she believes carries a certain stigma. As with all problems that families face, it is difficult to discern the dynamics that are preventing the parents from squarely addressing this problem with a reasonable solution. His current school and teacher, although of no help, are at least well-meaning. Apparently, in spite of the adversity that Jankó has faced, his family is not convinced that there is a preferable solution, at least not at this point in time. Jankó is a child with extraordinary abilities and talent who may well mature into a very successful adult. His chances of success will be greatly increased if he can manage to find a community where he is accepted and receives support for his dyslexia. Considering his strong determination and talents, he could be capable of outstanding achievements.

REFERENCES

Denhoff, E., Siqueland, M.L., Komich, M.P, & Hainsworth, P.K. (1968). Developmental and predictive characteristics of items from the Meeting Street School Screening Test. *Developmental- Medicine & Child Neurology, 10*, 220–232.

Gyarmathy, É. (2004). Research on dyslexia in Hungarian. In I. Smythe, J. Everatt, & R. Salter (Eds.), *International book of dyslexia: A cross language comparison and practice guide* (pp. 123–131). West Sussex: John Wiley & Sons Ltd.

Gyarmathy É. (2009). Kognitív Profil Teszt. *Iskolakultúra 3–4*, 60–73.

Kósáné, O.V., Porkolábné, B.K. & Ritoók, P. (1987). *Neveléslélektani vizsgálatok.* [Educational psychology examinations]. Budapest: Tankönyvkiadó.

Meixner, I. (1993) *A dyslexia prevenció, reedukáció módszere* [Method of dyslexia prevention and re-education]. Budapest: BGGYTF.

Smythe, I., Gyarmathy É. & Everatt, J. (2002). Olvasási zavarok különböző nyelveken: egy nyelvközi kutatás elméleti és gyakorlati kérdései. [Reading difficulties in different languages: Theoretical and practical issues of a cross-linguistic study]. *Pszichológia, 22*, 387–406.

JANKÓ'S INTERVIEW

1. What do you want to be when you grow up?
   I don't know. A football player, an NB1 basketball player, a musician, a blacksmith, or perhaps a chemical engineer.

   Why do you think you would be good at that job?
   Because then I could achieve what I want. My dad's a chemical engineer, too.

2. Tell me about a teacher who has been really important to you or one who has helped you. What did she do to help you?
   He was called Mr L. He helped me catch up when I fell behind, and he often told me what I had to do, and not how I had to do it.

3. Tell me about a teacher who didn't really help you that much or one who did not give you the help you needed. What did you want her to do to help you?
   Ms. H., she didn't specify the exercises as well as she should have. [In teaching eurhytmics.] *But she was fair.*

4. Tell me what your mother thinks about your dyslexia. Does she talk to you about the problem?
   Yes.

   What does she say? What's that?
   I don't have such a problem. I don't have reading difficulties.

5. Tell me what your father thinks about your dyslexia. Does he talk to you about the problem? He doesn't talk about it usually. What does he say?
   He only said I read differently. Because he thinks it's my body posture that's incorrect when I'm reading.

6. Tell me about something that makes you really happy.

    If I could do my work properly, be a singer, basketball player, and I would also have time to spend with my children. If I could fly, that would make me very happy.

7. Tell me something that makes you really sad.

    Mum thinks I pester my little brother, but I don't, and this really hurts me.

8. When the work gets very hard at school and you think you can't do it, what do you do?

    I keep trying until I finally succeed. Sometimes I'm so much frustrated that I slam it to the ground and say I won't learn that.

9. What kinds of books do you like to read?

    None of them. I've only just begun to get the hang of reading. I'm reading Nils Holgersen all on my own. My mum helps, when I get stuck. So far, I've only read PomPom on my own. I liked that.

    What is your favorite book?

    I don't have one, I like books.

    Do you read by yourself?

    Yes.

    Who else reads to you?

    Dad, Mum, my grandmothers. I've only just begun, but I enjoy it now. Writing, however, I don't like.

10. Do your friends know you have dyslexia?

    No.

    Do you talk to them about it?

    No.

11. Do your siblings know that you have dyslexia?

    No.

    Do you talk to them about it?

    No.

12. Name three things that you really good at:

    Table tennis, basketball, dodge ball.

13. Name three things that you not so good at:

    Learning, swimming, dunking in basketball.

14 If you are feeling bad about your reading, is there one person you can talk to who makes you feel better?

    My mother.

    What does she say to you?

    She says, try to concentrate on what you're reading, and don't pay attention to anything else.

15. Do computers help you with reading?
    No.

16. Do you usually have problems with your homework?
    Sometimes.

    Can you do your homework independently or does someone help you?
    I get help.

    Is homework a big problem or just a little one?
    Just a little one.

17. If there was one thing you could change about school, what would it be?
    There would be no homework.

18. If you had three wishes, what would they be:
    That I could fly.
    That I had a magic wand with which I could do anything.
    That I were good at digging, so that I could dig myself in anywhere.

19. Tell me three things that you would like your teachers to do to help you with your dyslexia:
    That they would be patient.
    That they would demonstrate things more times.
    That would be enough, I wouldn't need anything else.

20. Who is the best reader in your class?
    Péter.

    How did he get to be such a good reader?
    He once started reading and got to like it very much.

    If you did that would you be a good reader?
    Yes.

21. Is it important to learn how to read?
    Yes.

    Why or why not?
    If you're given a piece of paper you should read, it's not good if you don't understand what you're reading. If you can read, you will enjoy and understand it, which is very important.

11 Xavi, a Case of Dyslexia in Spain

Rosa Maria González Seijas

Xavi is a 10-year-old boy, who is currently in the sixth grade of primary education. He was diagnosed as having dyslexia at the age of 9, when he was in fourth grade. Xavi is a charming child who is highly social and very well behaved. During the interview, he seemed relaxed and enthusiastic about answering the questions. It was easy for the interviewer to establish rapport with him.

BACKGROUND

Family History

Xavi's parents have been divorced for five years and he lives with his mother in a middle class neighborhood in a coastal city of Spain. The mother works as a podiatrist's assistant and has a second job as a saleswomen in a clothing store. She completed two years of high school and an additional two years of professional training. His father is a salesman in a textile company, who travels frequently, but helps out whenever he can. The parents' relationship is very positive and they are good friends.

The boy sees his father on the weekends and any other time he wishes. When they are together, they play paddleball and, in the winter, they ice-skate or ski. On weekends, Xavi engages in activities such as hiking or playing basketball with his friends. He also enjoys excursions with his mother and grandmother. The maternal grandmother is a very important figure in his life. Xavi, the oldest grandchild, is often with his grandmother, who picks him up at school. They spend every afternoon and evening together. Xavi eats dinner with his grandmother and stays until his mother arrives to take him home at night. The grandmother is a 72-year-old retired nurse, who enjoys reading, painting, and traveling. She talks to Xavi about art and music, and has taught him to paint. The grandmother takes him to the opera, museums, and exhibitions. She also studies with him and helps with his homework.

Xavi's mother does not remember any cases of reading problems in her family. However, it is interesting that the grandmother reported that both

Xavi's aunt and his mother had reading problems during school. She noted that the aunt had "some dyslexia" and Xavi's mother had laterality and reading difficulties. She is not sure whether they received educational support for these problems at school.

Medical History

The pregnancy was normal and Xavi was a healthy full-term baby. There were no remarkable illnesses, hospitalizations, or required medications. Two years ago, Xavi complained that he could not see the blackboard well from his seat at school. On two separate occasions he was examined by an ophthalmologist who concluded that Xavi had normal eyesight.

Early Development

Xavi's development was typical; he achieved milestones within the expected parameters. He demonstrated normal language development and spoke his first words around 1½ years of age. He was a very talkative child whose language was clear except for problems associated with pronouncing the "r" (multiple vibrant). He began to walk when he was one year old and learned to ride a bicycle at an early age with no trouble. Xavi started to draw when he was very young and became quite accomplished with this hobby. When he was 6 or 7 years old, he won first prize in a painting contest at school. He has always liked to play with other children and has had no trouble relating to others. His mother noted that his development was normal in all areas except for reading. Xavi did not learn to read at the normal rate. The mother does not know whether his reading problems were related to a lack of support from his teacher or due to specific reading problems.

SCHOOL HISTORY

Preschool

In Spain, the curriculum plan for children up to the age of 6 (Infantil Educacion) has a dual purpose: (1) to promote, strengthen, and take advantage of children's development potential through educational action and (2) to provide the children with the competences, skills, habits, and attitudes that enhance their adjustment to Primary Education. More specific goals refer to promoting the capacities in the areas of motor, cognitive and linguistic development, interpersonal relations, social performance and adaptation, and personal equilibrium. The first cycle of Infantile Education covers 0–3 years and the second cycle 3–6 years (Ministerio de Educación y Ciencia. Diseño Curricular Base de Educación Infantil, 1989 [*Basic*

Curricular Design of Infantile Education, Ministry of Education and Science, 1989]).

Xavi began preschool at the age of 3. Although he cried on the first day of school, his mother remembered this stage as a good experience for her son. Xavi was highly verbal and seemed to really like school. He did a lot of drawing and handicrafts, activities that were particularly enjoyable for him. The mother was satisfied with the instruction that Xavi received as he met all of the standards without difficulties. Everything seemed totally normal and there was no indication of any problems.

Primary Education

Primary education in Spain is designed to contribute to the development of the capacities of children between the ages of 6 and 12 years. The organization of this level into three educational cycles of two years each facilitates adapting the teaching processes to each student's developmental and learning style, which is why teachers usually remain for an entire cycle with the same students (i.e., the first-grade teacher has the same group of children in second grade). Primary education includes the following work areas: knowledge of the environment, artistic education, physical education, Spanish language and literature, foreign language, language of the autonomous community, mathematics, religion/alternative activities. The ultimate goal of education in language and literature in the primary education stage is for the children to master the four basic language skills: listening, speaking, reading, and writing. Above all, the functional use of language, either oral or written, should be enhanced as an effective communication and representation instrument (Ministerio de Educación y Ciencia. Diseño Curricular Base de Educación Primaria, 1989 [*Basic Curricular Design of Primary Education, Ministry of Education and Science, 1989*]).

In Spain, the teaching of reading basically focuses on the grapheme-phoneme association. As Spanish is a transparent language, children are taught the association of consonants and vowels to form simple syllables: for example, *mo* and *to*, and their combination to form words, *moto* (in English, *motorcycle*). As these syllables and words are taught, they are made more complex, for example: *pan-ta-lon* = *pantalón* (in English, *trousers*). The process of reading and writing is taught in the first grade of primary education. In dyslexia, the main problem is the learning and automation of the rules of grapheme-phoneme conversion (Ramus, 2003), but in Spanish these rules are very simple. Thus, difficulties in reading speed and accuracy are more commonly observed as the main problems for Spanish children with dyslexia (Cuetos, 2008; Holopainen, Ahonen & Lyytinen, 2001; Jímenez & Hernández, 2000; Wimmer, 1993). These are the major reading difficulties that Xavi developed.

At the age of 6, Xavi began first grade of primary education in a class of 20 children, which was the first time that he began to have academic problems. The mother was surprised when Xavi had reading difficulty as he had demonstrated such strong oral memory skills (e.g., when they traveled by car, he learned songs, even in English, Japanese, or Chinese). He learned very slowly in all subjects and he did not receive any help. Xavi complained that his teacher shouted and insulted him when he did not do things the way she wanted. He also reported that this teacher hit him on the head when she was angry with him. The teacher treated others in the class similarly and regularly insulted them with name calling (e.g., "stupid" and "dummy"). Xavi said that one of his classmates was hit so hard that he had to go outside of the classroom and vomit. It is not surprising that Xavi hated this teacher. After several parents complained about the treatment their children received, she was suspended for three months.

Second Grade

Xavi started second grade at the age of 7 with the same teacher as the previous year. At the beginning of the school year the teacher again told the mother that Xavi was having problems and that he was not reading as well as the other students in the class. The mother remembers that the teacher's only recommendation was that Xavi should read a lot, which was the extent of the concern she showed during the entire year. The mother was very displeased as the teacher did not seem to be interested in Xavi or his lack of achievement. She did not request an assessment, nor did she plan more systematic support for him. Xavi's mother became very dissatisfied with the teacher and the school administration. The mother noted that the teacher never contacted her; it was the mother who always had to ask for conferences. As the mother was an alumnus, she wanted Xavi to attend the school as she had very good memories of her own experiences there. However, she clearly saw that the school was not providing her son with the education he needed.

A psychological test was administered to Xavi, but the mother was never told the name of the test or the results of this assessment. After this testing his mother was again informed that he had trouble reading, but no additional information was provided and no recommendations were given. His first- and second-grade primary education experiences were so negative that the mother decided to change schools.

Third Grade

When Xavi was 8 years old, he began studying at his new school, which is also his current school. As soon as he started this school, his reading problem was addressed and tutoring was provided. However, this support was very minimal as he only received five sessions of remediation over the course of the year from a part-time Hearing and Language teacher. These remedial activities included instruction that focused on syllable puzzles to form words, and visual memory and graphic representation exercises. The school did not assess him in-depth, although the tutor noted that the child had reading and maturity problems.

This first year at the new school was difficult for both the child and his mother. The academic demands of third grade were high for Xavi. It was also very stressful for the mother, who was very frustrated with Xavi because he always forgot his books, or his notes, or his homework. The first few weeks, he would come home empty-handed and his mother would have to call the school and return for his books or ask about the homework that had been assigned. In addition to dealing with Xavi's reading problems, the family was facing additional stress related to organization and attention problems. As a result of these demands, the school year ended with minimal improvement for Xavi.

Fourth Grade

At the age of 9, Xavi began fourth grade. He continued to have reading difficulties as well as organizational problems. His mother remembered this year as being particularly hard as his forgetfulness seemed to worsen, particularly with regard to his books and notes. At one point, his mother "threatened" that if he did not try harder, he would have to spend the entire summer in summer school (extra reinforcement classes after the school schedule) completing homework. During this year his mother decided to take him to academic support lessons twice a week (an hour each time) so they would help him with the homework assignments that she could not manage. Xavi was also having language problems with which his mother could not help. He is a Spanish speaker living in the autonomous community of Galicia that has its own official language (i.e., Galician), which is also transparent. Xavi had a very difficult time translating schoolwork from one language to another. For example: "I am a boy," is "yo soy un niño" in Spanish, and "eu son un neon" in Galacian. There were two subjects that were taught in Galacian and the rest were taught in Spanish. Xavi's difficulty was caused in translating words from Spanish to Galacian. His mother observed that whenever he learned a new Galician word, he forgot that particular word in his Spanish mother tongue. She hoped that the homework coaching would also assist with his language difficulties.

The experience in fourth grade was academically better, but his mother remembered it as being stressful and exhausting. She felt that she had to be very attentive to accommodate Xavi's problems, which put a great deal of pressure on her.

During this year, Xavi received his first in-depth assessment and, in addition, he received intensive instruction from a support teacher outside of the classroom. He attended the "Language" class (remedial reading-writing instruction in a small group) four hours per week, and additionally he received individual support lessons in reading and writing for two hours per week. The mother did not know what tests had been administered to Xavi, or what results he obtained, so it was necessary to obtain this information from the school. To assess reading, the school administered the Bateria de Evaluacion de los Procesos Lectores, Revisada (PROLEC-R; Cuetos, Rodríguez, Ruano, & Arribas, 2007). This battery was designed for children from first to sixth grade of Primary Education. It was administered individually and included nine subtests that explored the main reading processes. The PROLEC-R included subtests in phonics, word identification, and comprehension. The test results indicated that Xavi had some difficulty regarding accuracy of naming letters and reading words/ pseudowords. The speed scores revealed that he had severe difficulty in this area. He demonstrated a low level of automation in naming letters. He was also very slow for the tasks involving the identification of same-different words, reading words/pseudowords, and use of punctuation marks. In reference to the cognitive assessment, the results of the Bateria de Aptitudes Diferenciales y Generales (BADYG; Yuste, 2002) showed that Xavi has a normal general intelligence, but received "low" and "very low" scores in visual and auditory memory as well as "medium low" scores in sentence completion, number problems, and analogic relations. Xavi's auditory and visual memory problems appeared to be related to retrieval of letters and sounds associated with these as well as processing speed. The Evaluacion de los Procesos de escritura (PROESC; Cuetos, Ramos & Ruano, 2004) test was administered to assess spelling and writing skills. The results showed Xavi had difficulty in writing from dictation and application of orthographic rules.

Fifth Grade

During the fifth grade school year, Xavi participated in a special program, "Mentes Únicas" [Unique Minds] (Stern, 1999), for children with learning disabilities and their families, which was offered by faculty from a university in the city where he lives. The program offered a family support system, with the main objective of understanding the child's learning differences and special strengths. At the same time, the children acquire problem-solving skills and strategies to deal with self-esteem problems. Thus, the program focused on socio-emotional variables for both the children with difficulties and their families. Xavi was included in the pilot study with 12 participants: six children with difficulties, aged 9 to 11 years, and their mothers. The mother, sometimes accompanied by the grandmother, attended all of the eight weekly 1½ hour sessions. She thought that this was a positive experience as she felt close to the other families in the program. The mother said that the program established a bond of trust among the parents; she felt that she could say whatever she wanted and that the other parents understood her feelings. This program helped the mother during times when she felt "down" and gave her strategies to deal with problem solving in relation to parenting.

At school, fifth grade was similar to fourth grade only a little less stressful as Xavi was not forgetting as many things. He attended the educational support class with the specialist (outside the classroom) for one hour a week as the Language class group, which he had attended the previous course for four hours per week, was suspended due to administrative problems and time schedules. During this year, Xavi's academic results were generally good. He passed all subjects, although he failed some examinations. His mother felt sorry for him because even though he studied, his reading was very poor; he read so slowly that he could not complete a 15-question exam within the time limit. During this year, he began to train for basketball three days a week. He finished training at 8:00 p.m. and studied until 11:00 p.m., which was not enough time to complete his homework, but his mother would not let him stay up any later as he had to get up at 7:30 a.m. Xavi did not want to drop out of training and his mother realized that he was very motivated by basketball, so she tried to make his schedule work to include school and extracurricular activities.

His remedial reading teacher reported that although Xavi demonstrated good motivation, he made little progress in reading during that school year. His lack of achievement seemed to be related to the decrease in remedial support; one hour of support per week was insufficient to sustain the improvement that he had experienced in the previous year. He did not complete any of the homework that the school had assigned for the summer and, according to the remedial teacher in Hearing and Language, Xavi needed more reading help from his family.

Sixth Grade

Currently, Xavi only attends the remedial support class one hour a week. When reading words, he pronounces each syllable slowly. When he gets stuck on a syllable, he starts over, moving his finger along the text, and moving his head to follow the next row of words. He continues to complain of problems with his eyesight. Two years after the first assessment, his reading was once again evaluated with the PROLEC-R (Cuetos et al. 2007) to determine his current performance level. Comparing these results to those of the initial assessment revealed that there was improvement regarding accuracy in naming letters and reading words, but not in reading pseudowords and punctuation marks, which were assessed to be inadequate. The results regarding reading speed showed that Xavi was still in the "very slow" category.

DYSLEXIA DIAGNOSIS AND TREATMENT ISSUES

In Spain, there has been no diagnostic category that corresponds to the construct of specific learning disabilities as defined by the National Joint

Committee on Learning Disabilities (NJCLD; 1994) in the United Sates, but instead these learning problems have been considered in a broad sense and addressed under the term of "Necesidades Educativas Especiales" (NEE) (translated as Special Educational Needs or SEN). Learning disabilities are also covered by the Organic Law of Education (LOE), which mandates that students with special needs be provided with educational support. It is mandatory for schools to provide tutors to attend to these difficulties. If there are no counselors or psychologists available at the child's school, it is the responsibility of the tutor to determine assessment measures, remedial methods, supportive resources, and time required for remediation.

Although Xavi demonstrated reading problems from the first grade of primary education, he was not assessed and officially diagnosed until the age of 9 years, in the fourth grade of primary education. The use of the term *dyslexic* was avoided, but the possibility of this diagnosis was mentioned to the parents. In Spain, many professionals do not use the term dyslexia as they erroneously believe that if a child has dyslexia, there is nothing that can be done to help the child or address the problem. It is also avoided because the term is considered an "umbrella" under which various symptoms with no clear cause are included. Therefore, Xavi's diagnosis was delayed and his problems with dyslexia were not addressed until the age of 9 years. Xavi's main problem is reading speed, as he has trouble automating the grapheme-phoneme conversion rules, which results in very slow reading. When he received explicit, systematic, and intensive assistance from the specialized teacher, improvements were observed in his precision and speed, but as soon as the assistance decreased in intensity, this progress was no longer noted. Xavi's intervention program included phonemic awareness, naming speed, word identification, and passage comprehension. Writing and spelling instruction were also included. He will require more than the one-hour weekly reinforcement classes to make sufficient progress.

PARENT PERSPECTIVES

Xavi's mother thinks her son is an intelligent, well-adjusted child with excellent potential. She described him as a "good, responsible, respectful, and affectionate" child who loves painting, cooking, and watching movies. She observed that he is happy and motivated to go to school, and he makes an effort to do his homework. Xavi has many interests and hobbies and the mother believes that he can achieve whatever he wants, which is to become an archaeologist. Xavi reads a few hours per week at home and his mother also reads to him for an additional one to two hours. He particularly likes adventure books and everything related to archeology. Xavi has many friends and enjoys being with others. He loves music and drawing and watches television only on weekends during the school year. He prefers documentaries and programs about adventures and sports. The mother defined the term dyslexia as referring to a "slow learning process in both reading and writing" that will influence his life by causing him to be slow when he enters high school. The mother believes that Xavi's dyslexia is very significant and thinks that the problem interferes with school success. However, she does not think it affects Xavi's social or family life.

The mother stated that the most difficult aspect of Xavi's reading problems are related to the fact that he can't understand the reading material, thus he can't study independently or answer test questions. She thinks that his first school did not help her son at all and that may explain why the gap between performance and expected achievement, which began initially as a narrow gap, is now a wide gap. She stated that, at his current school, most of the teachers have helped him. The mother feels that Xavi would be doing better if he had received help from the beginning of his school experience. If there was one thing that the mother would change about the way schools treat students with dyslexia, it would be to provide testing at the beginning, give help to slow learners, and to provide more remedial classes.

CHILD PERSPECTIVES

Despite the fact that Xavi had some negative school experiences, he has enjoyed a positive social life that has been beneficial for his development. He has always felt supported by his friends especially when they have defended him from other classmates' mockery because of his poor reading. He does not consider the ridicule very important. In fact, it has decreased with time. He wants to learn to read well because it bothers him when he must read in front of the class. Xavi knows he is a poor reader and wants to do it well. This situation makes him very nervous.

He has always had his family's support and shares various leisure activities with his mother and his father (despite their being separated), and his grandmother. Xavi feels his family has encouraged him to improve and to do better. While his mother perceives dyslexia as a more significant problem that greatly interferes with school success, Xavi believes that it was initially significant (in first grade), but is now only moderately significant. This appears to be a common theme in Xavi's perceptions (i.e., he feels most of his school problems are behind him now). Although he doesn't feel that dyslexia interferes with his social life, Xavi stated that the most difficult thing about having a reading problem is reading in front of peers who may make fun of him.

He stated that he enjoys music, painting, and rock collecting. From an early age, with his grandmother's help, he has collected minerals from various places of the planet, which he patiently classifies and organizes. He does not read much, but archeology books are his favorites because he wants to pursue this profession. He thinks this would be a good job for him, which seems to be realistic as he has been preparing himself for this vocation since he was a young child. He also intends to continue to pursue basketball as a hobby.

Xavi's responses to the Sentence Completion questions of the interview revealed a profile of a child with a healthy personality, but one who has concerns regarding achievement. He has five best friends and enjoys his family and friends. He thinks that the best part of school is "the people in it" and sees nothing negative in his current school. He believes that what happened in the other school was because the teacher was a "bad person" but, in the current school, they help him to read and he thinks that the others value him positively because he doesn't "pick fights with anyone." In spite of his positive outlook, many of his responses revealed some insecurity. His response, "My classmates think I am a good person, even though I don't read well," is reflective of his concerns. In response to the sentence, "Sometimes I am worried about . . ." he answered, "knowing whether or not I passed an exam." When asked what makes Xavi sad, he responded, "I fail a test." There were several other responses that suggested he was sensitive to his peers making fun of him when he reads.

Xavi's strong family support was evidenced by his response to the sentence, "My parents are proud of me when . . ." to which he answered, "I do things well." Another sentence read "My parents are disappointed when . . ." to which he responded, "they are always happy, never disappointed—I try not to disappoint them." Xavi also stated that he was really happy when the family was all together.

Xavi identified the three things he is "good at" as basketball, drawing, and cooking while he could only identify reading as the one thing that he was "not so good at" even though he was asked to name three. He thought about this for a while and could not think of another area of weakness. Xavi's three wishes were for a healthy family, nicer teachers in his old school, and a shorter schedule at his current school so that he can work on his reading and realize his dream of becoming an archeologist. With regard to the last wish, it is interesting to note that Xavi believes that he needs more time to learn to read better and that he is personally responsible for improving his reading through independent work. He noted, "that's why I'm not making a wish to read better because I have to read okay by myself, not by wishing for it," which is an interesting attitude for a child with dyslexia. He seems to be taking responsibility for the remediation of his reading problems instead of relying on others.

In questions related to school and reading, his responses revealed a strong desire to be encouraged by his teachers and some animosity toward those who have refused to assist him. He is also somewhat concerned about the reaction of other children. After identifying the best reader in his class, he explained that this child does well because he "has been helped so much since he was a very little boy—teachers have helped him since the first grade, but I wasn't lucky enough to have the teacher he did." He identified his current tutor as the teacher who is always "encouraging him and teaching him to read words properly and to say them without pauses." He also named the specialized Hearing and Language teacher as one who has been the most helpful to him. When asked about the importance of learning how to read, Xavi said, "it eases many things . . . not thinking that someone is going to make fun of you because of a mistake." Xavi noted that if he could change one thing about school, he would have his first teacher fired and he would also change his current school schedule so he could begin at 9:00 a.m. and end at 1:00 p.m., leaving more time for homework and after school activities, which are now overwhelming to him. However, Xavi also said that homework does not cause many problems unless it is very complicated. His strategy for dealing with difficult work is to ask for help from his teacher or his parents.

In all the questions about his family, he revealed a strong tendency towards affection and respect. He stated that he tries not to disappoint them and is really happy when they are all together and joyful, and his family's health holds first place among his three wishes. Xavi seems unsure of what his parents think about his dyslexia, but he understands that they want him to keep trying and to work very hard. Xavi's interview suggested that he feels strong support from his social circle, but he is concerned about their perceptions of his competence and prefers not to openly discuss the problem with them.

CASE COMMENTARY

In Xavi's case, it was discovered from the maternal grandmother that his aunt may have had dyslexia and his mother had laterality problems and some reading difficulties that were never diagnosed or treated. It is interesting that the mother did not remember that she experienced reading problems. There are no indicators of abnormal prenatal, perinatal, or postnatal factors. The child's continuing complaints about eyesight problems are noteworthy, but detailed check-ups by two different ophthalmologists have revealed no problems. It is possible that Xavi has visual perceptual problems that are interfering with schoolwork. Xavi was assessed and diagnosed in fourth grade, although his reading problems were identified in first grade of primary education. This child suffered unnecessarily for many years because he wasn't given the help he needed. The situation was exacerbated by the horrendous experience he encountered with his first-grade teacher who was with him for two years. Even when he was finally identified as needing remedial reading, intensive assistance was only forthcoming for one year before the services were cut to one hour per week in fifth and sixth grades. Thus, he made very little reading progress after the intensive services were discontinued. Dyslexia research has long since documented that remediation must be intensive and consistent in order to make progress. When schools cannot make the commitment to the child to provide this support, there is little likelihood that the dyslexia will be remediated to the extent that successful achievement will be possible.

The reason Xavi did not receive an assessment when he started demonstrating reading difficulties and the reason why his intensive remediation was discontinued are one and the same: the school did not have the funds to provide these services. Xavi's situation was hindered because he attended a private school that received limited funds from the Public Administration and did not have their own funds to pay for two full-time specialists. Typically, remedial specialists in private schools only work part time (i.e., 13 hours per week) as opposed to the full time schedules that therapists work in public schools. The demand for provision of services for students with special learning needs usually exceeds specialists' availability, so that quite often, priorities must be established when structuring the schedules and attending to the cases that come up. Because of this, the specialists' work in Hearing and Language and Therapeutic Pedagogy usually focuses on the "more severe" cases, especially in the first cycle of primary education, where there is a higher prevalence of children who need intervention. The delayed assessment that Xavi received is most likely a function of the lack of resources for the specialists to attend children's needs. The work schedule of these professionals is usually overloaded, and they are overwhelmed, because there is normally only one or, at most, two professionals to attend the needs of all the children of infantile and primary education.

Xavi is a very bright child who has a tremendous amount of potential and should have a very bright future. Currently that future is in jeopardy if he does not receive the intensive and systematic support in reading that he requires. It is clear that when Xavi receives intensive services, his reading improves and when that support is withdrawn, that success diminishes. Considering the fact that all reports from teachers suggest that this is a child who is working as hard as he can to address his reading problem, he is receiving very little if any assistance from the school system. In light of this, it's almost heartbreaking to read Xavi's words that reflect his perception that he must learn to read better by himself, which unfortunately seems to be accurate in this situation.

Xavi is an optimistic child who is very well behaved and sociable. He receives strong support from his family and friends. Despite the fact that his parents are divorced, they have a friendly relationship, sharing interests, activities, and time with their child. Likewise, he has a very close relationship with his maternal grandmother, with whom he shares hobbies and diverse activities. In addition, Xavi is a highly motivated child who works hard to do his best. All of these factors are significant, but they are insufficient to insure his success. He needs intensive remedial services, which hopefully will be part of his future.

REFERENCES

Cuetos, F., Ramos, J.L., & Ruano, E. (2004). *PROESC evaluación de los procesos de escritura* [PROESC Assessment of Writing Processes]. Madrid: TEA Ediciones.

Cuetos, F., Rodríguez, B., Ruano, E., & Arribas, D. (2007). *Batería de evaluación de los procesos lectores, Revisada. (PROLEC-R)* [Battery of Assessment of Reading Processes, Revised. (PROLEC-R)]. Madrid: TEA Ediciones.

Cuetos, F. (2008). *Psicología de la lectura* [Pyschology of Reading]. Madrid: Wolters Kluwer España, S.A.

Holopainen, L., Ahonen,T., & Lyytinen,H. (2001). Predicting delay in reading achievement in a highly transparent language. *Journal of Learning Disabilities, 34,* 401–414.

Jiménez, J., & Hernández, E. (2000). Word identification and reading disorders in the Spanish language. *Journal of Learning Disabilities, 33,* 44–60.

Ministerio de Educación y Ciencia [Ministry of Education and Science] (1989). *Diseño curricular base* [Basic Curricular Design of Infantile Education]. Madrid: MEC.

Ministerio de Educación y Ciencia [Ministry of Education and Science] (1989). *Diseño Curricular Base* [Basic Curricular Design of Primary Education]. Madrid: MEC LOE. *LEY ORGÁNICA 2/2006, de Educación de 3 de mayo. BOE (Boletín Oficial del Estado), 4 de mayo de 2006* (Organic Law of Education 2/2006).

National Joint Committee on Learning Disabilities (NJCLD) (1994). *Collective perspectives on issues affecting learning disabilities: Position papers and statements.* Austin, TX: PRO-ED.

Ramus, F. (2003). Developmental dyslexia: Specific phonological deficit or general sensoriomotor dysfunction? *Current Opinion in Neurobiology, 13,* 212–218.

Stern, M. (1999). *Unique minds program for children with learning disabilities and their families.* New York: Unique Minds Foundation Inc.

Wimmer, H. (1993). Characteristics of developmental dyslexia in a regular writing system. *Applied Psycholinguistics, 14,* 1–33.

Yuste, C. (2002). *Batería de Aptitudes Diferenciales y Generales* (BADYG) [Battery of Differential and General Aptitudes (BADYG)]. Madrid: Ciencias de la Educación Preescolar y Especial.

XAVI'S INTERVIEW

1. What do you want to be when you grow up?

    To become an archaeologist and play basketball as a hobby.

    Why do you think you would be good at that job?

    Because I'm very interested in that. I have been collecting minerals since I was very little boy and it seems like a very good job to me.

2. Tell me about a teacher who has been really important to you or one who has helped you: what did the teacher do to help you?

    E. [the current teacher]. *He is always encouraging me. He helps me say the words the right way, without stammering. And L. [the* **Phonoaudiology** specialist teacher] *helps me a lot in reading. She helps me read fluently.*

3. Tell me about a teacher who didn't really help you that much or one who did not give you the help you needed. What did you want the teacher to do to help you?

> *None at this school because everybody has helped me so much.*
>
> *At my old school, my teacher A. wasn't interested in making us learn. She was so mad, always hitting people on the head and insulting them. She is not good.*
>
> *She insulted me and hit me on the head. Can you imagine that? You make a mistake any day and she walks by your side and hits you in the head or insults you.*
>
> *She hit hard with her open hand, on the head or on the back. Once a kid had to go outside to throw up because she hit him so hard that he got sick.*
>
> *That teacher would have helped more had she stopped insulting and hitting, and had she helped the kids more, and being interested to help us learn.*
>
> *She used to insult us by saying: "You dummy, stupid, dumb."*

4. Tell me what your mother thinks about your dyslexia. Does she talk to you about the problem? What does she say?

> *She says that . . . you'd better ask her. . . . that I have to get more involved and if I don't, things will be going the wrong way when I grow up.*
>
> *Sometimes she tells me that I shouldn't stop reading at all.*

5. Tell me what your father thinks about your dyslexia. Does he talk to you about the problem? What does he say?

> *He says the same as my mother. That you should work a lot.*

6. Tell me about something that makes you really happy.

> *That my parents talk to each other and get along together, so I can see them together. However, some of my friends are not that lucky.*

7. Tell me about something that makes you really sad.

> *When they argue sometimes and get angry at each other.*

8. When the work gets very hard at school and you think you can't do it, what do you do?

> *I ask my dad or my mom for help and they help me quickly, or study by myself, and if nothing results, ask for help. If I'm at school, I see the teacher and ask her if she can explain to me again.*

9. What kinds of books do you like to read?

> *Geography, Egyptian Archaeology, Atlas, the wonders of the world.*

What is your favorite book?

> *Let me think about it . . . one that my grandma has at home titled, The Mysteries of Egypt, it has all about archaeology in Egypt .*

Do you read to yourself?

> *I read to myself when I have free time and feel relaxed.*

Who else reads to you?

When I was a small boy my mom used to read for me, but not anymore.

10. Do your friends know that you have dyslexia? Do you talk to them about it?

They do know but I don't talk about with them because it is something almost forgotten.

What do you say?

I was embarrassed to read in class and make a mistake, so they'd make fun of me. In my old school all of them made fun of me, and because of that, I began to read so bad I used to hide behind other kids or hide my face with the book so the teacher could not see me and make me read.

What do your friends say to you about dyslexia?

Kids said that I read terrible. They said things like, "you are going nowhere reading like that, you silly boy," but my friends defended me.

11. Do your siblings know that you have dyslexia? Do you talk to them about it? What do you say? What do your siblings say to you about dyslexia?

N/A

12. Name three things you are really good at:

Playing basketball, drawing, singing—can I say another thing?—and cooking.

13. Name three things you are not so good at:

Reading [thinking for a while to find something else], *just reading.*

14. If you are feeling bad about your reading, is there one person you can talk to who makes you feel better? What does that person say to you?

Grandma, my whole family. All of them tell me: "Let's go! You can do it, you can improve."

15. Do computers help you with your reading? If yes, how do they help you?

No, I use the computer very little.

16. Do you usually have problems with your homework?

No, only if it is about something more complicated.

Can you do your homework independently or does someone help you?

No, I do it all by myself

Is homework a big problem or just a little one?

Homework is no problem. If I can, I try to find out when to play basketball also.

17. If there was one thing you could change about school, what would it be?

Right now: the schedule, if I could, I would begin at 9 and leave at 1, I could have more time for homework and after-school activities, and I wouldn't be overwhelmed.

Before: get the teacher fired.

18. If you could have three wishes, what would they be?

    I wish that my whole family stays healthy, that the teachers at my old school were better and nicer so the kids at my old school could be happier, and that classes at my current school were only in the morning because I want to become an archaeologist and read well, I have to do that by my own means. I need time, that's why I'm not making a wish to read better because I have to read OK by myself, not by wishing for it.

19. Tell me three things you would like your teacher to do to help you with your dyslexia?

    Right now nothing, they have helped me a lot. I used to want them to be more interested and pay more attention, and that they didn't have to get angry just because of a little mistake.

20. Who is the best reader in your class?

    A. G.

    How did he/she get to be such a good reader?

    He has been helped so much since he was a very little boy. Teachers have helped him since the first grade, but I wasn't lucky enough to have the teacher he did so I could not be at his same level.

21. Is it important to learn how to read? Why or why not?

    Yes, because it makes things easier for you. You should be relaxed not thinking that somebody is going to make fun of you because of a mistake. It is important to know that words sound differently.

12 João, a Case Study of Dyslexia in Brazil

Simone Aparecida Capellini, Giseli Donadon Germano, Fabio Henrique Pinheiro, Maria Dalva Lourencetti, Lara Cristina Antunes dos Santos, and Niura Aparecida de Moura Ribeiro Padula

João is a 10-year-old child who was diagnosed as dyslexic at the age of 7 when he was in first grade. João is a reserved child who is very interested in school. He is highly verbal, but has few friends. Throughout the interview, he responded enthusiastically to all the questions of the interviewer. João impressed the interviewer as being very expressive and eloquent in relation to his feelings and preferences.

BACKGROUND

Family History

João is an only child who lives with his parents in a middle-class neighborhood in a large city in Brazil. His father is a bus driver for city hall and his mother works as a maid in several private homes. Both parents reported having reading difficulties and neither graduated from high school. The mother achieved an eighth grade level of education while the father completed five years of schooling. The mother did not recall if other relatives had reading difficulties. This family typically does not read and the parents spend most of their time working.

Medical History

The pregnancy was considered to be normal, however the mother experienced a bladder infection in the last months. João was born in the hospital at 39 weeks of gestation. He was a healthy baby who has not required subsequent hospitalization. João has not had significant illness, but he has experienced recurring bouts of ear infections, which have required medication; he has had at least five of these middle-ear infections during childhood. The mother also reported that the child was sent to the neurologist at the age of 6 years old and was diagnosed with "brain immaturity." Tegretol, an anti-convulsant, was prescribed for this condition. After a year, Cintilan was prescribed as a substitute for the Tegretol. This is a drug that is sometimes prescribed for children with dyslexia because it has a peripheral vascular effect, which has been found to increase blood flow. These drugs were used because João was not ready to learn.

Early Development

João had a typical infancy and was somewhat normal in achieving developmental milestones, but he demonstrated some specific deviations. He spoke his first words at 12 months and began to put words together to make sentences at 18 months. João's mother noted that although he spoke a lot, he had some difficulty with vocabulary in that he substituted similar sounding words with different meanings, which resulted in confusion. According to the mother, his speech was not clear and he also had difficulty remembering the proper names of objects. With regard to motor development, João walked at 11 months and later learned to ride a bike without problems. However, João did not like drawing or coloring as he had a difficult time holding pencils and pens. The mother also commented that he played well with other children when she was in sight, but he was fearful of social rejection so he always wanted her to accompany him to the playground and ask other children if he could play with them. His mother reported that he was "guarded" in his social encounters and "afraid of being despised."

SCHOOL HISTORY

Kindergarten

João started kindergarten at the age of 5. In Brazilian kindergarten, the curriculum focuses on oral and written language. He experienced significant problems from the beginning. His drawings were very poor and he took too much time to write letters. With regard to socialization, the mother felt that kindergarten was a good time for João because he learned to socialize by himself and became a little more independent of his mother. However, with academics, João experienced considerable difficulty. She had to help him with his homework as he could not complete this by himself. The kindergarten teacher told the parents that João was different from the other children, particularly with regard to language skills. His speech continued to be unclear and impossible for the teacher to understand at times. According to the teacher, he did not appear to pay attention to the instructional activities. She had to separate João from the other students and explain the activity to him more than once before he understood. For example, if she asked the students to put their books on the shelf, João would put his pencils on the shelf instead. The teacher also reported that João had difficulties in visual discrimination and visual memory, time and space confusion and, as far as language was concerned, he did not know how to tell stories.

First Grade

By first grade, at the age of 6 years, it became increasingly obvious that João was experiencing significant difficulties in learning to read and write. The mother reported that he tried his best, but was very slow and could not learn beginning literacy skills. The first-grade teacher reported the same problems that the kindergarten teacher had identified (i.e., difficulties in visual and auditory discrimination, visual and auditory memory, letter discrimination as well as time and space confusion). He commonly confused letters and numbers that were similar (e.g., "6" and "9", "p" and "b", "q" and "d"). At the end of the first grade, the teacher noticed that João had not acquired the necessary skills for learning to read. He had not developed prereading skills and could not identify any of the letters of the alphabet. His language performance was below other students. For these reasons, João was not approved for promotion to second grade and thus failed the first grade. Because of these difficulties the school recommended that João be evaluated by a speech language therapist for phonological assessment at the Centre of Study of Education and Health (CEES/UNESP- Marília–São Paulo, Brazil) and for an interdisciplinary evaluation at the Ambulatory of Child Neurology of the Clinical Hospital of State University of São Paulo— FM/UNESP -Botucatu-São Paulo, Brazil).

The results of this interdisciplinary assessment revealed that João was dyslexic. On the neurological evaluation, he demonstrated sensory motor problems (i.e., he scored in the low range on measures of static balance, appendicular coordination, motor persistence, dynamic balance, torso-limb coordination, and sensitivity alteration). In the neuroimaging exam (Single Photon Emission Computed Tomography [SPECT]) hypoperfusion (lower activity) was identified in the region of the temporal lobe in the left brain hemisphere, which suggested that the auditory area of his brain was underactivated, and thus associated with poor auditory perception. It was this finding that resulted in the decision to prescribe the anticonvulsant medication. The results of the neuropsychological examination revealed that João was functioning within normal limits of intellectual ability with discrepant functioning between verbal intelligence (VIQ-83 points) and performance intelligence (PIQ-102 points) as demonstrated by performance on the Wechsler Intelligence Scale III- Revised (Wechsler, 2002). He also had problems with memory, reading, and writing. The phonological assessment identified deficits in the area of phonological awareness (i.e., phonemic, syllabic, rhyme, and alliteration), demonstrating auditory perception difficulty manipulating the sounds and graphemes of oral and written language. Additionally, his reading level and speed were found to be significantly lower than expected. Single word reading, nonsense word pronunciation, comprehension of text, and writing were also identified as areas of weakness.

When João was in the first grade for the second time, he started to have one-on-one reinforcement classes three times a week at school. The teacher reported that he presented difficulties in recognizing letters and wasn't able to copy from the blackboard. He was very slow and was unable to complete instructional activities. According to the teacher, João had difficulties in organizing his thoughts and comprehending oral instructions. He also presented dysgraphia because of his weak fine motor coordination. In contrast, João had good performance in arithmetic calculation when reading was not a requirement (i.e., story problems).

During this time his mother also took him to a speech language therapist at the University clinic twice a week for a year. As a procedure for remediation, the speech language therapist used the Play-On software (Magnan & Ecalle, 2006) adapted to the Brazilian Portuguese, which is part of a research project of a Post-Graduation Program in Education at São Paulo State University. This program was chosen because it is based on listening skills that foster the auditory perception of grapheme-phoneme association, which is necessary for learning the alphabetic writing system of the Portuguese language. The phonemes were addressed according to the order of development of speech and language sounds (/b/, /p/, /t/, /d/, /k/, /g/, /f/, /v/, /s/, /z/, /ʒ/, /e/, /ʃ/, /l/, /r/). The activities of the program included discrimination of phonemes in syllables, words, and phrases, as well as deletion of phonemes in monosyllabic, dissyllabic and trisyllabic words. The program was used in 13 individual sessions, lasting for 40 minutes on a biweekly basis.

The procedures for pre and post-testing included evaluation of auditory processing that focused on dichotic digits, dissyllabic words, and phonological awareness assessment. The results showed improvement in performance in all three areas. During the implementation of the phonological remediation program João showed lower performance in the sessions that involved discrimination of pairs of phonemes in logatomes (/t/ and /d/, /k/ and /g/, and /f/ and /v/), in words (/t/ and /d/, /f/ and /v/), and in phrases (/b/ and /p/ and /k/ and /g/). However, in the deletion task, it was observed that he had lower performance when he was required to delete phonemes in trisyllabic /ʃ/ and /ʒ/ words. Family and teachers were informed of these reading difficulties by the speech language therapist. The mother reported that she had not received any information from the school regarding João's diagnosis nor had the school provided any information about his remedial classes. It was very helpful for her to receive specific information on her son's reading problems.

Second Grade

When João entered second grade at the age of 8 years, he was still experiencing significant difficulties in learning to read and write. The mother reported that he continued to be a hard worker who was dedicated to improving his reading, but although he had achieved some progress, he was still lagging behind. He was promoted to the second grade in spite of the difficulties that persisted. His teacher noted that he had major problems with Portuguese. He had a limited reading vocabulary and thus was unable to comprehend paragraphs. His teacher was also concerned with his rate of reading, which was extremely slow. She also noted that João had difficulties in writing from dictation. However, she said that João was an active participant in oral activities in class and demonstrated much better performance in these activities compared to written work. João's mother reported that in spite of all of these problems, the school did not provide counseling support for the family to help them understand the nature of dyslexia. João received reinforcement reading lessons, but his classroom teacher did not provide any accommodations or support within the context of the classroom.

The family received support and counseling about dyslexia from the speech and language therapist at the Centre of Study of Education and Health (CEES/UNESP- Marília) in São Paulo, Brazil. The family went to the Centre twice a week where João received 80 minutes of direct remediation and the family received 20 minutes of counseling. This counseling provided information about the nature of dyslexia, such as patterns of inheritance and phonological problems. The activities performed by the speech therapist at the Centre included remediation with the use of controlled vocabulary books, syllabic manipulation and orientation to time and space. The reading therapy curriculum consisted of 18 stories, representing varying levels of difficulty. The foundation of this reading program was based on factors facilitating the acquisition of reading, such as word frequency, spelling regularity, and controlled vocabulary. The first level of the stories presented simple words consisting of monosyllables and disyllables of low complexity in short rhymed sentences. In the second level there was a predominance of simple sentences with minimal coordination of phrases. In the third level there was a predominance of phrases in direct order and simple sentences with occasional coordination and subordination of phrases.

As a result of exposure to this therapy, João improved his ability to recognize word structure and his understanding that vocabulary words are formed by different syllables that could appear in different positions of the word. As a result, his reading comprehension improved. He also demonstrated increased awareness of temporal concepts, such as days, months, and years.

Third Grade

At this grade, João continued to have the same difficulties in reading and writing, but there was some improvement. The teacher reported that he still had problems in activities that involved memory, such as recounting stories after reading. She also noted that he was very slow completing his work in the classroom so he seldom completed assignments and had to take them home to finish. The teacher accommodated him by allowing João to take his friends' notebooks home to copy the rest of the lessons. No specific activity was proposed by the school to help João with his difficulty in reading and writing.

João continued with the University clinic speech therapist twice a week and started to work on a remedial program of metatextual awareness (Spinillo & Ferreira, 2003). The objective of this program is to emphasize elements of text structure with story grammar markers that identified beginnings, development, and conclusions. The text is highlighted with the use of different colors that are related to various parts of the story. For example, the beginning of the story that includes the introduction of the characters and setting is highlighted in blue. The second part of the text that describes the action of characters, a description of problems and solutions is highlighted in red. The last part of the text, which is highlighted in green, provides the ending of the story including the resolution. In this program, particular emphasis is also given to story grammar conventions, such as introductory phrases ("Once upon a time . . .") and closing phrases ("lived happily ever after . . ."). The results of these activities were very positive as João acquired considerable awareness of text structure and also knowledge of the linguistic markers. Additionally, he improved his reading comprehension and started to write his own stories.

DYSLEXIA DIAGNOSIS AND TREATMENT ISSUES

As indicated in the preceding report of João's school experiences, he demonstrated severe characteristics of dyslexia from an early age, and was diagnosed when he was 7 years old. João was fortunate to have received his diagnosis of dyslexia at an early age largely due to the fact that he lived in Sao Paulo where the State University (UNESP) Centre of Study of Education and Health (CEES/UNESP-Marília) provides children with dyslexia and learning disabilities free treatment. Children who access these clinic services also have the opportunity to participate in research projects of graduate students who are pursuing Masters and doctoral degrees in education and who are members of the prestigious research group of the National Council for Scientific and Technological Development (CNPq): "Language, Learning and Schooling".

The school did not provide an evaluation of João's learning difficulties nor did it offer counseling support for the family or the child at any time. In Brazil, there are no official regulations for identification and treatment of dyslexia, thus, these children go undiagnosed unless their parents take them to a clinic, such as the one at the São Paulo State University.

Schools do not typically offer formal instruction for learning the rules of grapheme-phoneme correspondences, which is critical for the acquisition of literacy in the alphabetic system of Portuguese. João's school reinforcement classes offered only general reading instruction that was not specific to his needs. In order to learn to read and write independently, children require the prerequisite skill of interpreting sound units (i.e, phonemes) and understanding the complex relationship between phonemes and graphemes. If this instruction is not provided, children like João do not have the opportunity to overcome phonological processing deficits. In the absence of this instruction, difficulties in learning to read and write become progressively more severe and therefore more resistant to remediation. After being diagnosed with dyslexia João started receiving the services of a speech therapist when he was in first grade, which was very helpful. João received training in phonological awareness, text comprehension, text structure and text production. Over the course of the past three years, he has had great improvement in these areas, but it is very important that he continue with the therapy to sustain this growth and make additional progress.

PARENT PERSPECTIVES

João's mother feels that he is a very hard working child with a lot of potential. She describes him as "nice, reserved, happy, a little slow and funny." João enjoys playing video games at home, which his mother perceives to be a talent as he is apparently very good at this hobby. Although he seems to get along with other children, João has few friends. His mother reported that he reads about five hours per week; however, she did not indicate what materials he read, but she did say that he does not like "story books." Although neither she nor her husband likes to read, she spends approximately two hours a week reading to João to help him. João spends about eight hours per week watching television, mostly cartoons.

The mother understands that dyslexia refers to a "learning disability" that will cause her son to have "more problems than other children." However, the mother still has questions about the diagnosis, one of which is whether the problem of dyslexia can be "cured" or whether João will "have to live with that." She also understands that dyslexia will influence his school performance and socialization opportunities. On the Parent Perception Scale, the mother indicated that her son's problem with dyslexia is very significant and she believes it will continue to affect not only his school success, but also his family and social life, rating each of these areas as a "10" on a scale of "1" to "10" with "10" being the most significant. It is interesting to note that the mother seems equally concerned with the school problems and social difficulties, both of which she perceives to be related to dyslexia. When asked to identify the most difficult aspect of her son's reading problems, she answered that he would have greater difficulty in school as well as problems relating to other people and making friends.

The mother feels that school is the most negative aspect of her son's life, but she still believes that he is going to be successful because he is hard working and can develop other abilities. She also said that the speech language therapy has been very important as it has helped João to develop his reading and writing skills. She reported that this remediation has also had positive social consequences as it has improved his self-esteem, helping him to be less reserved and able to make new friends. Homework continues to be a significant problem as he needs help with the reading. He is very slow and has major problems with the completion of these assignments. The mother does not feel that the school has provided sufficient help nor does she feel that the teachers had the training to assist her son. The mother would have liked João's teachers to provide him more assistance and show more patience. In general, she does not feel that the country has adequate regulations to support programs for dyslexic children.

CHILD PERSPECTIVES

João is a hard-working child who is very reserved and has few friends. He has received little support from the school and his teachers, but has benefited greatly from the remedial program at the University clinic. At school he is grateful when his teachers have tried to accommodate his dyslexia (e.g., providing him with his classmates' notes to copy and content for class presentations), but they were not trained to give him the reading help he needed nor did they have the patience that he desired. His mother has helped him in every way that she could. João talks with her about his dyslexia and understands that he can count on her support. His father is less available to help him because "he doesn't have time" as "he works a lot." Although his mother indicated that João read five hours a week, he stated that he does not read independently, but he does enjoy his mother reading to him and is particularly fond of adventure books.

Although João has faced five years of school problems related to his dyslexia including the failure of first grade, his perceptions of his reading problem are very different from those of his mother; he feels that the problem is much less significant. In contrast to her high ratings ("10" out of "10") for the significance of the reading problem, João rated the magnitude of his reading difficulty to be a "4." Similarly, while his mother rated the magnitude of interference of the reading problem with school success, family life and social life to be "10" in all of these areas, João rated interference with school success as "4," interference with family life as "3" and social life as "2". Although he indicated that his social life is affected very little by his dyslexia, he later stated that he felt very resentful because his friends often make fun of him, saying that he is "slow." João indicated that the most difficult thing about having a reading problem is that he sees scrambled letters and can't follow what is going on in class. It is possible that his ratings on the Child Perception Scale reflect his true feelings and that he honestly does not believe that his problems are as severe as others perceive them to be. His career aspiration is to be a veterinarian and he understands that he must learn to read so he will "be able to go to veterinary college." He likes helping animals and believes he has strengths in science and mathematics. Perhaps with self-determination, he will achieve this goal in spite of the hurdles he faces with his reading.

João told the interviewer that he does poorly in sports as he does not have the physical coordination to play any games, like basketball and soccer. He said that he has difficulties in kicking and throwing and is the last to be chosen for sports teams. However, he is an excellent videogame player and enjoys playing with friends and family members. He revealed that he does poorly with writing texts and learning Portuguese. João looks forward to the time in the future when he won't have to study Portuguese.

João's responses to the Sentence Completion interview questions revealed a picture of a child who has low self-esteem and a poor social life with few friends. Although his frustrations with school continue to challenge him, he also has some positive feelings that are related to the school environment. He reported that the best thing about school is mathematics and that he likes it "when his teacher helps" him. He also feels happy "when I'm doing fine in Portuguese" and believes his parents are "proud of me when I get good grades." In contrast, he believes the worst thing about school is Portuguese and says he doesn't like his teachers to give him work that is too hard or scoring low on exams. He also becomes upset when his friends ridicule him for his slowness. João wishes "my friends would be nicer with me" especially at school. One area of school that exerts a particularly negative influence on his life is homework. Apparently there is quite a bit of stress involved with homework completion, which is typical for many families of children with dyslexia. João reported that he cannot do his homework independently and that he sometimes has arguments with his mother because he can't finish and gives up. Homework is challenging because João's reading level is very low, thus he needs intensive supervision and a lot of patience from those at home. This generates feelings of frustration and anxiety. He expressed this in his Sentence Completion response "sometimes I get worried when I don't know how to do my homework."

As indicated in the Child Interview (responses below), João continued to express frustration with school and reading, particularly where the Portuguese curriculum was involved. He becomes very upset when he talks about Portuguese and the required school activities of reading and writing. If there was one thing João could change at school, he would choose not to be required to take Portuguese lessons. In terms of dealing with his dyslexia in the classroom, João feels that computers would provide him with great assistance as the letters on the screen appear to be clearer than those in a notebook or on the blackboard. He also wishes that his teacher would teach the lessons slowly and spend more time with him individually.

CASE COMMENTARY

The history of reading and spelling problems in João's family is typical and corroborates previous findings (Capellini et al, 2007; Cope et al., 2005) regarding the hereditary influence associated with dyslexia. In this case, both the mother and the father had reading problems and neither achieved a high school diploma.

The case of this Brazilian child has many characteristics that are typical for the dyslexic population in general. In cases of dyslexia, there are usually phonological deficits and visual deficits. These phonological deficits are related to a difficulty in accessing and retaining phonological information, which is necessary to perform reading and writing tasks, and the visual deficits are related to a low temporal resolution, that is, confusion over symmetric letters. The findings of this study in relation to João's cognitive level corroborates previous findings (Swanson, Howard, & Saez, 2006; Capellini, Padula, & Ciasca, 2004), which were evidenced in studies with dyslexics with VIQ inferior to PIQ. This discrepancy has been observed in dyslexics, not only related to the verbal and performance quotient, but also between the quotients that indicate information processing speed and working memory, demonstrating that this would be a profile of dyslexia. Another characteristic of João was difficulty reading the mathematic problems as opposed to solving the actual calculations. According to the Brazilian literature (Capellini & Smythe, 2009; Germano & Capellini, 2008; Salgado & Capellini, 2008; Cardoso-Martins & Batista, 2005; Capellini et al. 2004; Capovilla & Capovilla, 2000) subjects with specific reading disabilities often present disorders in information processing, and as this processing is based on cognitive and linguistic skills, the comprehension of problems impairs performance in arithmetic.

After the specific intervention that combined phonological and metatextual instruction, João demonstrated improvement in phonological awareness and consequently obtained an increased reading level and better reading comprehension. These interventions showed improvement in the phonological perception in activities related to both reading and writing. However, João continued to struggle with fluency because of problems in phonologic processing and alphabetization. For children to understand what they read, they must be able to read words rapidly and accurately. The development of rapid and accurate word reading allows children to focus their attention on the meaning of what they read. Many things, including children's vocabulary, contribute to reading comprehension. The evidence demonstrates that when children are taught to manipulate phonemes and to learn the letters of the alphabet with an instructional approach that concentrates on learning one or two phonemes at a time, there is a greater likelihood for success (Capellini & Smythe, 2009).

A number of Brazilian studies (Germano & Capellini, 2008; Salgado & Capellini, 2008; Cardoso-Martins & Batista, 2005; Capellini et al. 2004; Capovilla & Capovilla, 2000) have shown the benefits of systematic, explicit phonics instruction on literacy levels in early grades. Phonics instruction has been seen as important because it improves children's word reading and reading comprehension. Despite these studies, not all schools use phonics instruction in the classroom, which causes problems for children with dyslexia who are trying to acquire the skills to read and write. Unfortunately, as previously indicated, there is no diagnostic category in Brazil for learning disabilities or dyslexia among the official categories that exist in the teaching system (auditory, mental, physical, and visual deficiency). As a result, there is no public policy to help children with dyslexia in the classroom. Cases such as João's are very common in classrooms in Brazil because services are not provided by the schools. The identification of dyslexia often occurs late and these children acquire other co-morbid problems such as anxiety, depression and low self-esteem. Although João was diagnosed relatively early, at the age of 7 years, he acquired these personality characteristics as a result of not receiving the assistance he needed at school. It is fortunate for João that he could access the no-cost remedial services of the University clinic, which provided him with the diagnostic and remedial support he needed. This reading assistance and the support of his family, particularly his mother, have had a positive influence on his life, which will hopefully enhance his opportunities for success in the years to come.

REFERENCES

Capellini, S.A., Padula, N.A., & Ciasca, S.M. (2004). Performance of school children with specific reading disabilities in a remediation program. *Pró-Fono, 16,* 261–274.

Capellini, S.A., Padula, N.A., Santos, L.C.A., Lourenceti, M.D., Carrenho, E.H., & Ribeiro, L.A. (2007). Desempenho em consciência fonológica, memória operacional, leitura e escrita na dislexia familial. *Pró-Fono, 19,* 374–380.

Capellini, S.A., & Smythe, I., (2009). Perspectives from Brazil (about dyslexia). *Perspectives on Language and Literacy, 35,* 17–21.

Capovilla, A.G.S., & Capovilla, FC., (2000). Efeitos do treino de consciência fonológica em crianças com baixo nível sócio-econômico. *Psicologia: Reflexão e Crítica, 13,* 1–28.

Cardoso-Martins, C., & Batista, A.C.E., (2005). O conhecimento do nome das letras e o desenvolvimento da escrita: Evidência de crianças falantes do português. *Psicologia: Reflexão e Crítica, 18,* 330–336.

Germano, G.D., & Capellini, SA. (2008). Efficacy of an audio-visual computerized remediation program in students with dyslexia. *Pró- Fono, 20,* 237–242.

Cope, N., Harold D., Hill, G., Moskvina, V., Stevenson, J., Holmans, P., Owen, M.J., O'donovan, M.C., & Williams. J. (2005). Strong evidence that KIAA0319 on chromosome 6p is a susceptibility gene for developmental dyslexia. *American Journal of Human Genetics, 76,* 581–591.

Magnan, A., & Ecalle, J. (2006). Audio-training in children with reading disabilities. *Computer & Education, 46,* 407–425.

Salgado, C.A., & Capellini, S.A. (2008). Phonological remediation program in students with developmental dyslexia. *Pró-Fono, 20,* 31–36.

Spinillo, A.G., & Ferreira, A.L. (2003). Desenvolvendo a habilidade de produção de textos em crianças a partir da consciência metatextual.In Maluf, R.G. (Org.), *Metalinguagem e aquisição da escrita. Contribuições da pesquisa para a prática da alfabetização* (pp. 119–148). São Paulo: Casa do Psicológo.

Swanson, H.L., Howard, C.B., & Saez, L. (2006). Do different components of working memory underlie different subgroups of reading disabilities? *Journal of Learning Disabilities, 39,* 252–269.

Wechsler, D. (2002). *WISC III: Wechsler Intelligence Scale for Children,* 3rd edition. In Figueiredo, V.L.M. Escala de Inteligência Wechsler para crianças. São Paulo: Casa do Psicólogo.

JOÃO'S INTERVIEW

1. What do you want to be when you grow up?
   A veterinarian.

   Why do you think you would be good at that job?
   Because I can help the animals.

2. Tell me about a teacher who has been really important to you or one who has helped you. What did she do to help you?
   My teacher helps me a lot. When I get late she gives me a sheet with the contents to do in my home.

3. Tell me about a teacher who didn't really help you that much or one who did not give you the help you needed. What did you want her to do to help you?
   I wish she would give me more time to do the activities. I am slow.

4. Tell me what your mother thinks about your dyslexia. Does she talk to you about the problem?
   Yes.
   What does she say?
   She talked to me a long time ago, I can't remember what she said.

5. Tell me what your father thinks about your dyslexia. Does he talk to you about the problem?
   No.

   What does he say?
   He doesn't have time, he works a lot.

6. Tell me about something that makes you really happy.
   When I get an "A" in a test, or when I spend more time with my family.

7. Tell me something that makes you really sad.
      When I get a bad grade in a test or when my parents can't stay with me on the weekends or when I can't play.

8. When the work gets very hard at school and you think you can't do it, what do you do?
      I do what I know and when I don't know I write "I don't know".

9. What kinds of books do you like to read?
      Adventure.

   What is your favorite book?
      The Bird of a Thousand Colors.

   Do you read by yourself?
      No.

   Who else reads to you?
      My mother.

10. Do your friends know you have dyslexia?
      Yes.

    Do you talk to them about it?
      No. [João doesn't have friends.]

11. Do your siblings know that you have dyslexia?
      [N/A, no siblings.]

12. Name three things that you really good at:
      Mathematics, science, videogames.

13. Name three things that you are not so good at:
      Portuguese, sports, writing texts.

14. If you are feeling bad about your reading, is there one person you can talk to who makes you feel better?
      No.

15. Do computers help you with reading?
      Yes. The letters appear to be clearer, different from notebooks or blackboard.

16. Do you usually have problems with your homework?
      Yes.

    Can you do your homework independently or does someone help you?
      My mother helps me because I can't do it on my own.

    Is homework a big problem or just a little one?
      It's a big problem, especially Portuguese.

17. If there was one thing you could change about school, what would it be?
      I wish that there weren't Portuguese lessons.

18. If you had three wishes, what would they be:
      (1) Play chess in school
      (2) I wish I didn't have difficulties

(3) I wish to have more recreation time

19. Tell me three things that you would like your teacher to do to help you with your dyslexia:
    (1) That she teaches the lessons slowly
    (2) I wish to have a computer in class
    (3) I wish the teacher spent more time with me

20. Who is the best reader in your class?
    I don't know.

21. Is it important to learn how to read?
    Yes.
    Why or why not?
    Because I would be able to study other things and to go veterinary college.

13 Yiannis, a Case Study of Dyslexia in Greece

Christos Skaloumbakas

Yiannis is an 11-year-old child who lives in a working-class neighborhood of a large city in Greece. He is an intelligent and polite child with an interest in learning that extends beyond the range of subjects covered at school. He is highly articulate, yet somewhat awkward and self-conscious in his social encounters. Yiannis is very perceptive and quite talkative with people he knows well or when talking about issues that interest him. He has been in a remediation program with the researcher for over two years so the interview was held in an informal and relaxed atmosphere.

BACKGROUND

Family History

Yiannis is the younger of two brothers (his older brother Kostas is 14 years old). The siblings live with their mother who works as a registered nurse at a large university-affiliated hospital as the parents divorced when Yiannis was 6 years old. The father is a biochemistry lab technician also working at a public hospital. The mother had experienced some difficulty in school particularly with reading, however she managed to improve her reading skills by practicing and feels quite comfortable with her ability at present. The father reported no learning difficulties even though he was left-handed and was forced by parents and teachers to switch hands in first grade. Both parents hold university degrees. The family of three is a tightly knit single-parent family led by a caring and resilient mother who tries her best to raise her two children. Relations between the parents are civil with the occasional tensions that are almost always contained. The family lives in the same building with the maternal grandmother, a common living arrangement even in urban areas of Greece. The grandmother is involved in the life of the family without, however, being intrusive.

Medical History

Yiannis was born after a normal full-term pregnancy. There were no complications at birth except a slight case of jaundice that receded after the baby was exposed to sunlight. The mother mentions no significant illnesses for the child apart from a few cases of bronchitis that were treated successfully with the use of inhalants. He does not have any hearing or vision problems.

Early Development

Yiannis went through infancy without major upsetting events although there was one sign of a developmental difficulty. He displayed nocturnal enuresis until first grade after which time the problem slowly disappeared. He began walking at the age of 1 year and rode a bike at the age of 5. Yiannis spoke his first words at the age of 1 and did not have any problems with naming objects, colors, or anything else. He possessed a very impressive vocabulary for his age, a fact that was often favorably commented upon by relatives and friends of the family, which is why the mother "never thought that something might be wrong." He attended preschool for one year and enjoyed it very much. All the teachers were very pleased with Yiannis even though he appeared to have some difficulty with handling scissors so he occasionally tried to avoid activities that involved cutting and pasting.

SCHOOL HISTORY

Kindergarten

The daily program in a kindergarten, which begins at age 5 for Greek children, involves activities that help social, language, and motor development. This is the time when children first encounter alphabetical and numerical symbols and are required to match the speech sounds that correspond to the graphemes and learn to express these in written form. Yiannis did not seem to enjoy any of the activities in kindergarten particularly those that required drawing, writing, or anything that involved the use of fine motor skills.

Yiannis had a very negative attitude toward school from the beginning of kindergarten. He refused to learn the letters of the alphabet despite the attempts of the teacher and also resisted the parents' attempts to introduce him to activities related to literacy. Eventually, the teacher suggested that the parents not pressure him as she believed he would eventually come around. The mother is unsure what exactly caused the child to refuse to cooperate. In retrospect, she believes that he may have been treated rudely by the teacher. Despite his negativity in school, Yiannis was an inquisitive child and learned the things in which he was interested. At the end of kindergarten, however, he was the only child who had not learned the alphabetic symbols. Additionally, he also had considerable difficulty with his pencil grip as well as his ability to cut shapes with a scissor. However, there were two other factors that may have had an effect on his behavior that year as well. Yiannis had to stay at school until 4:00 in the afternoon so he wasn't seeing his mother as much. This may have triggered feelings of anxiety, according to the mother. He also had to change classes mid-way through the year for administrative reasons, losing all the friends he had made by that time and having to readjust to a new environment.

First Grade

First grade was a disaster for Yiannis. At one point he refused to go to school. The mother reported that the teacher frequently insulted him in front of his classmates by making remarks that were demeaning (e.g., "you are an idiot"). He was yelled at on a daily basis because he failed to perform up to the teacher's standards. Yiannis was slow and could not finish most of the tasks performed in class; he struggled to catch up with written work while the teacher moved on at a rapid pace. Eventually, he would quit trying, resulting in more insults from the teacher. Every evening the mother would sit with the child so that he could finish his homework, a task that was often not completed even at 10:00 p.m. In the spring of that year, the mother decided to enlist the services of a tutor to assist Yiannis with his difficulties with written language. The tutor was an experienced general education teacher who came to the home three times a week and helped him with his homework, which reduced the stress induced by a heavy daily workload of assignments.

Second Grade

In second grade Yiannis had the same teacher and, thus, the same school problems. From the very beginning of the school year he found it increasingly difficult to keep up with the pace of the class as well as the homework. The mother decided to seek an evaluation by experts at a mental health center as the child was facing increasing difficulties. The assessment mainly relied on the results of a translated version of the WISC-III (Georgas, Paraskevopoulos, Bezevegis, & Giannitsas, 1997) and curriculum-based measures of reading and spelling as there were no standardized reading or spelling tests in Greek at that time. The WISC-III, which was administered by an experienced school psychologist, revealed Yiannis had a Full Scale IQ of 132 with a VIQ of 129 and a PIQ of 127. The tests of academic abilities were administered by an educational diagnostician who found that Yiannis' performance in reading and spelling was below the 10th percentile while his listening comprehension score was in the 80th percentile. His writing speed was very slow and his writing became illegible when completing timed tests. Yiannis was also examined by a child psychiatrist who confirmed the diagnosis of a reading disability.

These results were forwarded to the school, but despite the fact that the teacher knew Yiannis had dyslexia, she continued to be uncooperative. She frequently expressed the view that Yiannis was a difficult and stubborn child whose poor performance was due to his unwillingness to cooperate.

However, the mother could see that the child was trying very hard. The gap between his performance and the standards for his grade became so great that at some point the mother even considered having Yiannis repeat second grade in hope that the second time around he would have a better chance of succeeding. She consulted with the mental health center team who had performed Yiannis' diagnosis. They strongly objected to such an option as they saw no benefit to the child, only the distinct possibility of further undermining his already vulnerable self-esteem. In their opinion the child needed remediation in basic literacy skills, which he would not receive in the second grade curriculum because it was expected that children at this level had previously acquired these.

After the evaluation, he was placed at a special education class part-time. There he met a special educator who played a major part in Yiannis' future adjustment in school. He spent one hour a day three times a week for the entire year in the special class with the purpose of catching up in his lagging literacy skills. His special education teacher realized that Yiannis was an intelligent dyslexic child whose deficits in reading and writing were a serious obstacle to his academic success. His work with the teacher consisted mainly of improving his spelling and writing skills (visual and morphosynctactic). The work also focused on reading accuracy and rate as well as visual spelling. The reading program consisted of repeated readings of high-interest below grade-level texts that improved his fluency and readings of word-lists consisting of words that shared the same morphological root while differed in the ending. This allowed for a more accurate and fluent decoding of words. While this program was initially satisfactory, it lacked the sophistication and variety required to accommodate the learning difficulties of a child with such a high level of cognitive abilities. There were always at least three to four other students in class, most of them with learning disabilities while a minority had both learning as well as behavior problems. The remedial work became very tedious for Yiannis so the teacher slowly shifted her focus from a skills-remediation to a strengths-based approach.

The teacher cultivated a close relationship with the child and provided the source of support that Yiannis needed in school. She used his interest in science by asking him to look into different topics that would inspire him to write short passages. The mother claimed that his hours in the special class were the best during his school day. The special teacher's approach, however interesting, lacked the focus and intensity required for the type and severity of difficulties that Yiannis was facing. Overall, her help was invaluable in psychological terms, but it is doubtful whether it really helped the child academically.

Third Grade

In third grade Yiannis had a different teacher and tried even harder. However, it became apparent that he wasn't making any friends at school.

During recess he was sitting alone far from the playground and was very rarely seen chatting with other children. He didn't make any friends in class either. His interests, his remarks and his efforts to show off his knowledge on a number of subjects alienated his classmates who occasionally made snide remarks against him while others responded with sheer indifference.

His special education teacher had slowly but steadily dropped his remedial program in favor of tasks that were more attractive. Yet the teacher became the child's primary defender in school, consulted closely with his general education teacher, helped the child overcome his social awkwardness and inspired him with a new sense of self-esteem. Therefore, it was a huge loss to Yiannis when the teacher became pregnant and took a leave of absence. The governmental agency in charge of school staffing failed to ensure the prompt substitution of the teacher so for more than three months Yiannis received no remediation services and again his performance started to decline. The child was having problems with his sleeping patterns and was displaying high levels of anxiety over the completion of homework along with his lack of acceptance by his classmates. He was also picking any pimple that appeared on his face creating minor skin lesions. The mother decided to seek help for Yiannis from a psychologist in private practice who proposed that he be placed in a remediation program at a private treatment center twice a week. The mother followed this advice and Yiannis received special help for his reading and spelling problems. Additionally, he had private sessions with the psychologist in order to deal with his anxiety and low self-esteem.

Fourth Grade

In fourth grade Yiannis was still very slow in completing his homework assignments so his mother had to assist him almost on a daily basis in order to finish his work. Yiannis occasionally became frustrated and anxious because of his slowness, but overall, however, his schooling experience improved. His teacher made some important adjustments and assigned less homework to him, (i.e., half the text she assigned to other students for reading and half the text or list of words she assigned for spelling). This was a helpful practice as it enabled him to finish his homework earlier and always be well prepared. Thus, he was becoming more academically independent. The mother recognized the positive changes in the child's learning behavior, but was still anxious about his future success as school demands were becoming increasingly more complex. At that time she decided to seek additional help and was referred to a private special education treatment center.

Yiannis' literacy skills were re-evaluated at this center using the Logismiko Axiologisis Mathisiakon Dexiotiton kai Adynamion (LAMDA) [Software for the Screening of Learning Strengths and Difficulties] (Protopapas & Skaloumbakas, 2007a; Skaloumbakas & Protopapas, 2007), a standardized computer-based test measuring a number of skills relevant to the processing of written language. The test extensively measures skills in reading and oral comprehension. Performance in most of the sub-scales is timed and allows for a full description of the student's profile, thus producing a dual profile of the student's performance based on response accuracy and response speed. Yiannis' performance was typical of a dyslexic child in that he ranked below the 10th percentile in both accuracy and speed while his scores fell between the 10th and 25th percentile ranks in visual spelling. His speed in almost all tasks measuring reading or general verbal skills was below the 10th percentile, a fact which explains to a great extent his difficulty with written language even though his oral language skills are admittedly superior.

Based on the results of Yiannis' assessment, a specific remedial program was developed and implemented. This program focused on the use of spelling exercises based on a pictographic system where words with a high frequency are written in a way that the most troublesome parts are replaced by a picture drawn by the child, which alludes to the meaning of the word. In that way the meaning of the word becomes intertwined with its visual representation, thus, making it easier to remember. Reading intervention focused on repeated readings of selected texts below grade level as well as lists of words with the same root and varying endings. In that way both decoding and fluency purposes were served. Texts were used from a variety of sources with different purpose. Some of these were used for summarizing and others for reading comprehension while some would be used for improving syntactical and grammatical understanding.

DYSLEXIA DIAGNOSIS AND TREATMENT ISSUES

Before the year 2000 evaluation of learning difficulties in Greece was usually handled by the medical-pedagogical centers, mental health centers or hospital outpatient clinics offering child psychiatric services. All of these operated within the public sector under the supervision of the Ministry of Health, offering services at a negligible fee or no fee at all. There were usually long lists of children waiting to be evaluated and priority was typically reserved for students who were about to finish the lykeion (high school) who requested special testing accommodations for dyslexia for their university entry exams. As a result, students attending elementary school had to wait so long that they missed all of the benefits of early diagnosis and remediation. Quite often parents sought evaluation from independent clinics or help from private teachers or specialists without waiting for a formal diagnosis.

The situation did not change drastically after the passage of Law 2817 (Education of Persons with Special Educational Needs and Other Provisions, 2000) This law mandated the founding of Centers for the Diagnosis, Evaluation and Support (CDES) of children with special educational needs administered by the Ministry of Education and Religious Affairs. Despite the ministry's good intentions there was such a high demand for evaluations that waiting lists multiplied. However there was no visible improvement in the rate of providing school-based interventions. The special education classes became flooded with children displaying a diversity of problems most of which required an individualized approach.

Dyslexia is a well-established disorder with clear clinical features. In Greece, the disability refers to a deficient ability to read accurately and fluently while spelling is almost always affected. The Greek language is a highly orthographically transparent language (Seymour, Aro & Erskine, 2003) with a high degree of phoneme-grapheme correspondence (Protopapas & Vlachou, 2009). Furthermore, Greek letter names are also more easily attached to their phonemic counterparts much unlike the case in English. This allows for easier phonological decoding and more rapid automatization of the reading process compared to languages such as English which are highly orthographically irregular. Despite the relative ease with which most Greek children learn how to read, there are children, such as Yiannis, who achieve accurate and fluent reading at a slower pace, if ever. Phonological awareness skills as well as the ability to name stimuli at a rapid pace, an ability called Rapid Automatized Naming (RAN), explain most of the reading difficulties, whereas children deficient in both (i.e., double-deficit) exhibit the most severe problems (Papadopoulos, Georgiou & Kendeou, 2009). It appears that over time accuracy ceases to be the main problem and fluency becomes the major obstacle. Dyslexic children can learn how to read accurately and usually reach an acceptable level of fluency at the end of their first or second year in school if they are provided with intensive remedial support. Their slow reading rate may not appear problematic to the inexperienced listener yet their comprehension suffers when they have to perform within time limits or when they have to study content area subjects that are text-based such as history and geography. These are the problems that currently interfere with Yiannis' school success. Spelling skills are comparatively more affected and usually attract the teacher's attention more than their deficient reading performance. This is primarily due to the fact that a large part of spelling, called visual or "historical" due to the fact that it stems from more archaic forms of the Greek language, is not as orthographically transparent as reading where some of the vowels (i.e., the phonological equivalent of "ee" in *sheep*) have as many as six plausible alternative spellings. Because of that, it is usually visual spelling that suffers in the long range while rule-based spelling improves dramatically. In the absence of a rule, spelling is mainly visually based. Children acquire both morphological and visual spelling abilities at different paces. By the end of fourth grade they reach a sufficient level of morphological awareness to minimize spelling errors of a morphological nature (Nunes, Aidinis & Bryant, 2005) while visual type errors continue to plague some of the children particularly those with dyslexia.

Yiannis displayed severe learning problems before even starting elementary school, however, even though there was a system in place that would identify these difficulties and provide treatment options, his parents were not informed of this. Apparently, the school personnel were unaware of the existence of the newly founded CDES and of the type of services offered. Thankfully, the parents managed to find the Mental Health Center where Yiannis was eventually diagnosed with dyslexia. The early diagnosis saved him from further harassment at school, and helped secure the available school-based services. Even though his special education teacher was forced to leave midway through the year without being substituted promptly there were some benefits coming from the diagnostic process. Yiannis received a formal diagnosis and his learning disability received a name. This may have caused some stigma through the process of labeling, but on the other hand, Yiannis was placed in a special class where he gained an ally, his special education teacher, who became his advocate in school. It is not clear whether Yiannis would have made it through elementary school if not for her.

Nevertheless, the early age at which he was diagnosed (7 years old) is somewhat of a rare occurrence in Greece. Most parents seek evaluations for their children after third grade, approximately at the age of 8, with referrals peaking at fifth grade (when children are 10 years old) and first gymnasium (when children are 12 years old), perhaps due to the strain resulting from increased curricular demands. The diagnosis came as a relief to the mother who finally had her son's learning difficulties recognized and treated as such instead of being misinterpreted as signs of obstinacy and laziness. These were developments that benefited Yiannis in the long run. From then on there was a tendency by school personnel to view his problems with reading and spelling as secondary to content area achievement, a fact which allowed for improvement in the grades he earned. Writing assignments were marked for content and not for spelling errors or legibility, which allowed for a more accurate assessment of Yiannis' abilities and effort.

PARENT PERSPECTIVES

Yiannis' mother described her child as being "very responsible and very giving," but also quite obstinate and persistent, saying that "if he wants something, he wants to have it now." The mother reported that he is interested in crafts and mechanics, particularly robotic devices. He is quite imaginative in using different materials for making things. The mother stated that "he prefers robotics over reading because it requires brains as well as skillful hands." Because Yiannis does not like to read, he spends only one to two hours per week on extra-curricular reading. The mother noted that Yiannis did not have many friends as he enjoys playing alone. She observed that although he does seem to get along with the children of family friends and children outside of his class, he does not have any friends in his class.

Yiannis' teacher told the mother that he faces problems with other children, but it was not his fault. The mother stated that "for some reason children in his class do not make an effort to approach him and they end up rejecting him." He is not particularly interested in television, perhaps watching an hour per day, usually children's programs. He doesn't like scary programs or movies for grown-ups as he is afraid he might see something that will upset or frighten him. She also noted that he is afraid of the dark and worries a lot, which causes sleep problems.

The mother clearly understands dyslexia and is aware that Yiannis has a severe reading problem that exerts a strong negative influence on his school success. She stated that "the truth is that I'm quite anxious about the effects this would have in his life, in particular how it will affect his performance as a student in high school." His home life has not been affected as much as his social life and she claims that the teacher he had in first and second grade may have contributed to self-esteem problems with her demeaning remarks and overall rejecting attitude toward Yiannis.

The mother said that the most difficult aspect of her son's reading problem is the reading level of the texts at school. This is a particular problem that he faces in religious studies and history. She feels fortunate that, in spite of the reading problems, he enjoys history. His reading problem becomes more distressing when he has to study long passages that he has to reproduce almost verbatim in class. This practice is referred to as "parroting" (papagaleea), meaning the flawless recital of verbal material in the absence of deeper understanding of the text. In the past, this practice has been a trademark of parochial pedagogic practices, but it is slowly being cast aside by most educators in favor of more meaning-based assessment practices (i.e., question and answer formats).

Yiannis' mother is somewhat pleased with his progress particularly in the last three years. Overall, she expressed few criticisms of school practices, yet she is dissatisfied with some aspects of his education. She would like to have more remediation time for Yiannis' difficulties and is bitter about the first grade teacher's rejection of her son. The mother does not believe that most general education teachers are well informed about reading disabilities, thus, the system was not very sensitive to needs of children like Yiannis. She feels lucky that there was a special education class in the school and that the teacher was so helpful even though the services were insufficient to address his remedial needs. In general, the mother does not believe that Greece provides adequate regulations and support for children with dyslexia.

CHILD PERSPECTIVES

Yiannis has managed to keep a positive outlook in life despite his unfortunate early schooling experience. Although his reading problem is severe, he views this as a moderate obstacle that restricts his learning activities only marginally. It is interesting to note that his mother rated the significance of his reading problem as an 8 on a scale of 10 while Yiannis rated it as a 5. The same pattern of discrepancy is evidenced between the mother and son throughout the ratings on the Parent Perception Scale and the Child Perception Scale. With respect to perceptions regarding the influence of dyslexia on school success, the mother again rated this as an 8 while Yannis rated this as a 3. For the influence of dyslexia on friendships, the mother rated the variable as a 7 while Yiannis rated it as a 2. Although this suggests he does not believe his social life is influenced by his dyslexia, other comments he made contradict this. His social life is clearly a subject that upsets him occasionally, which is evident from his response that he is not very comfortable with people and feels that his classmates do not hold a high opinion of him (i.e., "they think I'm dumb"). Yiannis does not feel that his home life is affected by dyslexia (he rated this as a 1), but the mother viewed this differently, rating this as a 5.

Yiannis stated that the most difficult aspect of his reading problem is related to his inability to complete his homework in a reasonable amount of time as well as the effect that his poor reading skills have on his test-taking performance. His responses for the Sentence Completion interview revealed a child who maintains a positive attitude toward school in spite of his past history with some teachers who were unsupportive. He feels that getting good grades is important especially since it pleases his parents. Overall, Yiannis is a sensitive boy who is very fond of his family and counts on them for emotional support. However, when he talks with them about dyslexia, they tell him that the solution to his problem is to try harder. His parents' divorce is still a source of discontent for Yiannis that he frequently mentions, although much less than it was the first two years following their separation. These feelings are reflected in his three wishes: "that my parents hadn't separated, that I succeed in doing whatever I want in the future, and that I'm able to have a nice family of my own." The final wish may be a somewhat peculiar ambition for such a young a boy, but perhaps an aspiration that could make up for his negative experience as a child of divorced parents.

His interview shows someone with strong academic ambitions and an appetite for knowledge that seems unfettered by his dyslexia. He has ambition to learn and maintains a healthy criticism towards his school. Yiannis has specific proposals about how learning can become more enjoyable with technological support, such as computers and digital whiteboards. His favorite subjects (math, physics, and arts and crafts) require abstract non-verbal reasoning abilities, areas in which Yiannis excels. He uses his personal computer to type projects or stories he would enjoy reading, a habit which helps him to improve his reading and spelling. The only problem with his teachers is that they do not wait for him to complete his writing assignments in class particularly when they dictate something. Needing additional time for work is a challenge that he mentions several times during the interview. He is aware that hard work brings results by acknowledging that the best reader in class managed to become such by practice.

CASE COMMENTARY

Yiannis is a typical case of dyslexia in Greece in many respects. The attitude of his first and second grade teacher shaped his anxious and unenthusiastic attitude for school but, thankfully, not for learning. What is quite impressive is how helpless a parent and a child may find themselves in the educational system when there is no reliable school-based screening process to help identify children with learning problems and the educational law is not enforced. Yiannis' schooling experience, even though unpleasant at the beginning, improved with the passage of time and the help he received by his special teacher. Although in 2000 the state mandated a number of provisions for students with special needs and assigned the Center for Differential Diagnosis and Support a central role in that process, there appears to be a gap between the law's manifest intent and its actual enforcement on day-to-day educational practice. Despite the State's intentions, educational evaluations and everyday schooling practices remain separate and entirely different processes. This development came as a result of insufficient staffing of CDES and its inability to handle large and highly diverse caseloads. Thus, the initial idealized expectations were soon transformed into the unpleasant reality of long waiting lists and long awaited evaluations.

What is also striking is the fact that there are still teachers that treat children with learning difficulties in such an unprofessional and insensitive manner. It would appear that most general education teachers do not have an adequate understanding of the cognitive aspects of child development and frequently misinterpret low performance as laziness or unwillingness to cooperate. Their notion may sometimes operate as a self-fulfilling prophecy leading otherwise able children to perform and behave as failures. It is apparent that general education teachers in Greece have to become more informed about issues that underlie student failure and achievement, particularly with regard to reading disabilities. This knowledge could very well affect the quality of daily instruction and the future of at least 10–15% of their children who may benefit from differentiated teaching practices.

On the other hand, it was a good teacher who helped Yiannis adapt to the challenges of facing school as a dyslexic child. Her contribution was significant as she became a mediator with general education teachers and demonstrated a high level of sensitivity to Yiannis' psychological needs even though she was not able to provide the intensive remediation he required for reading and spelling. It is important to note that there is very little research on the effectiveness of different teaching methods regarding children with dyslexia in Greece. In the absence of such methods most teachers and practitioners have to improvise.

Yiannis was diagnosed quite early by Greek standards. Referrals for dyslexia assessments usually involve students in third grade or higher. This illustrates a recent downward shift in the average age of students requesting assessment from a few years ago when most students were assessed when entering gymnasium (12 years old; Protopapas & Skaloumbakas, 2007b). When Yiannis was assessed in his first years as a student in elementary school the only standardized test used was the WISC-R because at that time it was one of two existing standardized tests in Greece that measured cognitive abilities. The absence of other reliable indices of academic, language or cognitive performance frequently led to an overreliance on intelligence measures, a fact which may have inadvertently amplified the importance of intelligence and may have promoted the use and sometimes abuse of the discrepancy formula in the diagnostic process. This practice quite often led to the erroneous conclusion that many older students had difficulties due to "garden variety" learning problems stemming from low or borderline intelligence when it was their early untreated reading and spelling problems that led to the eventual drop in their intelligence, a phenomenon commonly referred to as the "Matthew effect" (Stanovich, 1986). This may be changing since last year when the state funded the construction of a number of tests that were completed recently and measured a diverse array of literacy-related skills. This development may eventually ensure a more balanced diagnostic process.

Yiannis is the case of a child with dyslexia who struggled to persevere in an often unfriendly and unresponsive school environment. As the author was writing the closing lines of this chapter, he was making excellent progress in school and his teachers were really impressed by his abilities. Yiannis seems to be on the road to a more rewarding future, one in which he will be able to further develop his skills, cultivate his interests, and excel in whatever area he chooses. However, it is important to remember that children like Yiannis with high intellectual ability and reading problems will continue to need support in order to achieve commensurate with potential.

REFERENCES

Education of persons with special educational needs and other provisions. (2000, 14 April). *Efimerida tis kiverniseos* [Official Government Gazette], 78 (tefxos A). (Law 2817).

Georgas, D.D., Paraskevopoulos, I.N., Bezevegis, I.G., & Giannitsas, N.D. (1997). *Elliniko WISC-III: Wechsler klimakes noimosinis gia paidia* [Greek WISC-III: Wechsler intelligence scales for children]. Athens: Ellinika Grammata.

Nunes, T., Aidinis, A., & Bryant, P. (2005). The acquisition of written morphology in Greek. In R. Malatesha Joshi & P.G. Aaron (Eds.), *Handbook of orthography and literacy*. Mahwah, NJ: Lawrence Erlbaum Associates, Inc.

Papadopoulos, T.C., Georgiou G.K., & Kendeou, P. (2009). Investigating the double-deficit hypothesis in Greek. Finding from a longitudinal study. *Journal of Learning Disabilities, 42,* 528–547.

Protopapas, A., & Skaloumbakas, C., (2007a). *Logismiko Axiologisis Mathisia-kon Dexiotion kai AdynamionLAMDA): Odigos Exetasti.* [Software for the Screening of Learning Strengths and Difficulties (LAMDA): User's guide]. Athens: EPEAEK II Action 1.1.3a, Ministry of Education and Foreign Affairs.

Protopapas, A., & Skaloumbakas, C. (2007b). Traditional and computer-based and traditional screening and diagnosis of reading disabilities in Greek. *Journal of Learning Disabilities,40,* 15–36.

Protopapas, A., & Vlachou, E.L. (2009). A comparative quantitative analysis of Greek orthographic transparency. *Behavior Research Methods, 41,* 991–1008.

Seymour, P. H. K., Aro, M., & Erskine, J. M. (2003). Foundation literacy acquisition in European orthographies. *British Journal of Psychology, 94,* 143–174.

Skaloumbakas, C., & Protopapas, A. (2007). *Logismiko Axiologisis Mathisiakon Dexiotiton kai Adynamion (LAMDA): Perigrafi Ergaleiou* [Software for the Screening of Learning Strengths and Difficulties (LAMDA): Description of instrument.] Athens: EPEAEK II Action 1.1.3a, Ministry of Education and Foreign Affairs.

Stanovich, K.E. (1986). Matthew effects in reading: Some consequences of individual differences in the acquisition of literacy. *Reading Research Quarterly, 21,* 360–407.

YIANNIS' INTERVIEW

1. What do you want to be when you grow up?
   I would like to be a robotics scientist.

   Why do you think you would be good at that job?
   Because I enjoy it and I would do my best to succeed.

2. Tell me about a teacher who has been really important to you or one who has helped you. What did the teacher do to help you?
   Mrs. K., you [the author] *and Mr. Z. They accepted me as I am and tried to help me become a better student.*

3. Tell me about a teacher who didn't really help you that much or one who did not give you the help you needed. What did you want the teacher to do to help you?
   There was no such teacher.

4. Tell me what your mother thinks about your dyslexia. Does she talk to you about the problem?
   Very rarely.

   What does she say?
   She insists that if I try hard enough the effects of dyslexia would become less important.

5. Tell me what your father thinks about your dyslexia. Does he talk to you about the problem?
   He shares the same point of view with my mom.

   What does he say?
   He says that nothing is too hard if I try and do my best.

6. Tell me about something that makes you really happy.
   Getting good grades at school.

7. Tell me about something that makes you really sad.
   Getting bad grades at school.

8. When the work gets very hard at school and you think you can't do it, what do you do?
   I concentrate hard so that I can get done as much and as soon as possible.

9. What kinds of books do you like to read?
   Funny books.

   What is your favorite book?
   Jeronimo Stilton. It's a book about a mouse that enjoys adventures.

   Do you read to yourself?
   Yes.

   Who else reads to you?
   I read to myself.

10. Do your friends know that you have dyslexia?
    Yes.

    Do you talk to them about it?
    Very rarely.

    What do you say? What do your friends say to you about dyslexia?
    They ask me how it is to have dyslexia, whether I find it difficult to read etc.

11. Do your siblings know that you have dyslexia?
    Yes.

    Do you talk to them about it?
    No.

    What do you say? What do your siblings say to you about dyslexia?
    They never mention it.

12. Name three things you are really good at:
    Mathematics, physics, and arts and crafts.

13. Name three things you are not so good at:
    Language, geography, and soccer.

14. If you are feeling bad about your reading, is there one person you can talk to who makes you feel better?
    My parents.

    What does that person say to you?
    They say that if I try really hard dyslexia will not affect me as much.

15. Do computers help you with your reading?
    They do.

    If yes, how do they help you?
    By reading and typing text. I sometimes write a funny story and then try to read it. That helps me.

16. Do you usually have problems with your homework?
    I do sometimes.

    Can you do your homework independently or does someone help you?
    In some subjects that I find hard to study I get some help from my mother.

    Is homework a big problem or just a little one?
    It's a little one.

17. If there was one thing you could change about school, what would it be?
    Having better [instructional] media in class, such as PCs or digital whiteboards etc. These are things that would make learning more interesting.

18. If you could have three wishes, what would they be?
    That my parents hadn't separated. That I succeed in doing whatever I want in the future and that I'm able to have a nice family of my own.

19. Tell me three things you would like your teacher to do to help you with your dyslexia
    It would help a lot if Mr. Z. and the school principal [who teaches religion] waited a bit longer for me to finish writing.

20. Who is the best reader in your class?
    Delia.

    How did he/she get to be such a good reader?
    She has read a lot of books.

21. Is it important to learn how to read?
    Yes.

    Why or why not?
    So that one can finish one's homework or read newspapers and magazines that he enjoys.

14 Taku, a Case Study of Dyslexia in Japan

Akira Uno and Jun Yamada

Taku is a 12-year-old first-year student of a middle school in Tokyo, Japan. He was given his diagnosis of learning disabilities (LD), Asperger syndrome (AS), and attention deficit/hyperactivity disorder (ADHD) when he was in second grade. In third grade, he was diagnosed as dyslexic with pervasive developmental disorders. His IQ is within the normal range, and he is a good player of *go* (a Japanese game played with black and white stones on a board), *shogi* (Japanese chess), and video games. Not surprisingly, however, his school records have been very poor mainly due to his poor reading and writing skills. During the interview he was attentive and responsive to the questioning.

BACKGROUND

Family History

Taku is an only child, who is given great affection by his parents. Both the father and mother graduated from technical college. The mother is a housewife having no reading and writing problems. The father, a computer instructor, has writing difficulties even now and says that Taku resembles him in this regard. He avoids handwriting and always uses a personal computer instead.

Medical History

The mother reported that she had an abnormal pregnancy at the early stage with the possibility of a miscarriage and was given an intravenous drip injection several times. Taku was born in the hospital at 37 weeks gestation. At the delivery, he did not cry and was given oxygen in the incubator for the first 24 hours. On the third day, he had phototherapy for hyperbilirubinemia. The mother said that after that difficult time, he had no serious diseases although he had an atopy, asthma, and a food allergy to fish, shellfish, *soba* (buckwheat noodles), and macadamia nuts. At present, he is in good health. As for his physique, he was a small boy until he was 3 years old, but since then has been around average in his height and weight.

Early Development

The first three words, "Mama," "Papa," and "Baaba" (nanny) appeared when Taku was around 1 year old. But after that, his vocabulary did not increase until he was 1 year and 10 months. This worried the parents who "turned off the TV." The mother began speaking to him as often as possible and also reading many picture books to him. His vocabulary then increased and he became very talkative around 3 years of age, but it is unclear if this was the result of the mother's intervention or due to normal developmental differences. Taku walked at 1 year of age and began riding a bike when he was 6. The mother reported that he was poor at jumping rope and playing ball. He started drawing early, but his pictures were indiscernible and his crayon grip was awkward.

Although Taku did not have significant behavioral difficulties early on, except for those related to his food allergies and atopy, he experienced sleeping problems. The mother sang him lullabies, read picture books, put him on her belly, and so on, for one or even two hours until he finally fell asleep. It should have been easy for Taku to sleep because he did not take a midday nap, but such was not the case.

SCHOOL HISTORY

Kindergarten

Taku started kindergarten at the age of 3 years. Various different seasonable toys and tools were available at kindergarten. The other children soon learned to play with these, but Taku was different. For example, around the New Year's days when top spinning was fun for children, the other kindergartners soon learned to master this activity whereas Taku could not as it was too difficult for him. He quickly lost interest and began running around the classroom while the other children were absorbed in spinning tops.

Taku attempted to color and draw pictures at around 1½ years but showed little or no interest in such activities after that. The crayons he had when he entered kindergarten remained almost the same, not used very much during his three years there. The mother remembered an episode involving a friend who was hospitalized. To prepare for a visit to the hospital to see a friend, Taku decided to draw a get-well picture for him. Even though he put great effort into the drawing, the picture he drew was described by the mother as "peculiar." His manner of holding crayons and pencils did not improve and his drawings continued to be incomprehensible most of the time.

During the kindergarten days, he was unable to learn to complete his daily tasks, which other children could do (e.g., hang the towel he used, put his schoolbag back in its place, give his teacher's message to the mother). He neglected the daily routines so often that female classmates began to look after him. Taku took such help for granted, and at home too, he failed to clean his room, which made his mother angry. When the mother asked the kindergarten teacher about Taku's progress, the teacher acknowledged his problems, but indicated that he would "become normal" and need less care as he grew older, which was a perspective that family friends also held. However, the mother felt that it would be more likely that he would need additional assistance as he developed.

First Grade

Because Taku was born early in February and school starts in the first week of April in Japan, he started first grade at the age of 6 years and 2 months. This meant that he was among the youngest children in the class as the average age for first graders in April is 6 years and 6 months, and those who were born in April were almost one year older than Taku. (The possible significance of early admission will be addressed in the Case Commentary section.) It was lucky, the mother thought, that the elementary school Taku attended was small, with only 16 students in his class compared to the average class size of 30 students for most schools in Japan. Moreover, the mother felt that all his classmates looked somewhat infantile like him. Her impression was that there were four out of the 16 students who had special needs; in fact, two of the four were treated in a special support program while the mothers of the other two were against the idea that their children should be taught in the program.

In the first term before the summer vacation, Taku suffered from a tic syndrome and his pediatrician recommended he see a doctor of psychosomatic medicine. Taku received play therapy at the Psychosomatic Medicine Department, Tokyo Kyosai Hospital. In the meantime, it turned out that he was sometimes bullied at school. The mother asked Taku's teacher for help to cope with this problem together. Their efforts seemed to be successful, and the tic syndrome soon disappeared. However, the physician that Taku saw at Tokyo Kyosai Hospital recommended that he be further tested during second grade.

Taku's academic achievement in this grade was within the range of the average. In retrospect, however, he must have had reading and writing problems although neither the mother nor the teacher was aware of them. According to the mother, Taku's problems were probably not identified because the progress of peers was also slow.

Second Grade

In second grade, Taku returned to Tokyo Kyosai Hospital for further testing. He was given the Japanese version of WISC III (Wechsler, 1998) and other tests (which, unfortunately, the mother did not remember). Taku's IQ was found to be well above average (i.e., PIQ = 104, VIQ = 134, FSIQ

= 123). According to the mother, the results of other tests showed he had LD, AS, and ADHD. The diagnosis of Asperger's was based upon behavioral observations. The LD diagnosis appeared to be based on the mother's report of problems as there was no record of a test battery administered at this time. Taku's reading and writing problems had become more apparent as he advanced in age. Also, the mother attempted in vain, to teach kanji to him by demonstration. When Taku began to cry, saying that he tried hard but couldn't write, the mother came to understand that his problems were very serious.

The doctor of the hospital told the mother that while Taku's learning disability was moderate considering literacy expectations at this level, social cognition seemed more problematic, and so it was better to try to improve his social skills. The doctor also said that it was necessary to check Taku's developmental progress regularly, but the mother didn't take that opinion very seriously. It should be noted that the doctor did not use the term 'dyslexia' but 'learning disability' instead. Probably the mother took the latter term lightly because Taku's intelligence was found to be normal.

At the end of the first term of the second grade, the family moved due to the father's job transfer. The new school, larger than the previous one, had three second-grade classes and the size of each class was as large as 40. The curricular standards of the class were higher, causing Taku embarrassment because he could not keep up with his peers. The mother thought he would soon get used to the new situation, but he did not. The classroom teacher asked the mother why he did not write anything in his notebooks and what he had been doing before in the former school. The mother replied that the students there were given handouts and that note-taking skills were not taught until the third grade. The mother then began to teach him how to take notes, but she found him to be almost hopeless. The mother was shocked when she realized how far he was behind his classmates.

Third Grade

When Taku became a third grader, the mother was told that an extra communication class (remedial reading and writing class) in which both social and academic skills were taught would be available at school. Thus, in addition to his regular classes, he went to that class on a regular basis, and began to write hiragana symbols little by little. His social problems diminished thanks to his teacher's effective treatment and to his friends' acceptance of his problems.

Taku and the mother also regularly visited the Psychosomatic Medical Department previously mentioned and a class at YMCA which offered support for children with learning disabilities. At home the mother continued to try to teach him how to write. However, this was somewhat of a struggle as Taku cried and said that although he tried hard to learn to write, he couldn't. This is when the mother realized that conventional teaching methods would not work for her son. The mother felt sorry for him and guilty for not taking his writing problems seriously. Around that time, a Dyslexia Center opened in Ichikawa City near Tokyo, and it was there that as a third grader Taku was for the first time diagnosed as dyslexic with pervasive developmental disorders. His cognitive potential and academic achievement were evaluated using the Standard Test of Reading and Writing (STRAW; Uno, Wydell, Haruhara et al., 2009; Uno, Haruhara, Kaneko et al., 2006), the WISC III (Wechsler, 1998), and other measures. The results of the STRAW indicated significant deficits in reading and writing; Taku's score was 18 out of 20 points (the third grade mean = 19.1, SD = 0.9) on the kanji word naming test and only two out of 20 points (the third grade mean = 19.0, SD = 1.6) on the kanji word writing test. Taku's intelligence was found to be well within normal limits (i.e., PIQ = 101, VIQ= 110, FSIQ = 112); however, it was significantly lower than the score obtained in the second grade. It is unclear why his VIQ was considerably lower at this grade as compared to that at the second grade (i.e., 134). The difference between PIQ and VIQ may be accounted for by the finding that Taku had few phonological deficits, while his immediate and delayed reproduction scores of the Rey-Osterrieth Complex Test (Rey & Osterrieth, 1993) were relatively low.

This was the first time that the mother heard the term *dyslexia*. The staff at the Center also explained the nature of the reading problem and provided the family with support.

Fourth to Sixth Grades

When Taku became a fourth grader he visited the Dyslexia Center on a biweekly basis. The mother was counseled not to be too nervous about her son's problem. She was also told how to handle his difficulties and followed this advice. Soon Taku was doing well completing the assignments given by the staff of the Center. The mother was happy even though it did not seem that he was making remarkable progress in learning to write.

Classes at school were changed in fourth grade so Taku had a new teacher and new classmates. He had some difficulty with them and began to say he didn't want to go to school. The difficulties were likely caused by the new teacher and classmates who did not accept him. His allergies and poor writing were negatively perceived by the other students. One day, he discovered that one of his classmates had written the words "Die!" on his schoolbag.

In spite of many challenges, Taku managed to finish fourth to sixth grades simply because, in the Japanese educational policy, virtually no children repeat the same grade regardless of their academic achievement. The mother said that even though Taku's school records continued to be very poor, her psychological burden was greatly reduced because she learned a lot about the nature of dyslexia at the Dyslexia Center.

When Taku was initially treated at the Center, his knowledge of hiragana was found to be weak as he was able to write only one half of these symbols. His long-term memory of auditory language (i.e., speech) was sufficiently strong. Therefore the teachers at the Center capitalized on this ability to teach hiragana and katakana symbols. They first had him memorize the order of syllables in the kana (i.e., hiragana/katakana) chart. After he memorized the order, he was taught to pair each syllable and its corresponding target hiragana/katakana symbol. This worked very well; he learned to read and write all hiragana and katakana symbols in a short period of time.

In fifth and sixth grades Taku made some progress, albeit slow. At the end of sixth grade, his reading problems had diminished although his writing problems remained. This developmental dissociation may be attributable to the possibility that (1) learning to write is in general more difficult than learning to read, in particular in Japanese and other languages that have Chinese characters in their orthographic systems, (2) Taku's perceptual and motor skills are deficient, and/or (3) children are given fewer opportunities to practice writing than reading, which will be discussed in the following section.

DYSLEXIA DIAGNOSIS AND TREATMENT ISSUES

Taku's dyslexia was not conspicuous in kindergarten because few, if any reading and writing tasks were given. The teachers at this level generally have considerable tolerance for individual differences in development. Taku was thus accepted by the children and teachers even though he was often only playing and running around alone. In first grade, no serious problems appeared to have arisen because reading and writing activities were limited and probably because oral communication was less demanding in his small class of slow achieving peers. But at the end of the first term of second grade, the family moved to another city and Taku began to attend a new class with 40 students. The reading and writing standard there was much higher than that of the former school, which upset Taku and the mother. Of course, Taku's reading and writing problems soon became obvious to his teacher. Although the classroom teacher noticed Taku's problem, she did not have any knowledge of dyslexia, which would have allowed her to address his problems and to help him cope. Thus, the gap between Taku's achievement abilities and the school curriculum expectations were very significant after grade 2. In third grade, Taku attended a special class in addition to his regular classes. He also went to a near-by YMCA class which focused on increasing communication skills for children with learning disabilities. Taku tried hard to overcome his dyslexia, but made no remarkable progress.

In summary, these and other results confirmed Taku's reading and writing deficits. It is noted that he is able to name individual hiragana (e.g., あ /a/) and katakana (e.g., ア /a/) symbols, which is comparable to the average naming skill of normal first graders. However, his writing skill of katakana fell far behind that of normal first graders. (Note that hiragana symbols are used to represent function words and the inflections of verbs, adjectives, and adverbs while katakana symbols are mainly loan words and often names for animals and plants. The symbol frequency is much lower for katakana than for hiragana.) More problematic is writing kanji characters which represent free and bound morphemes. Writing kanji is generally difficult because of the relationship between kanji and speech. Many-to-many relationships are typically observed for kanji characters and their pronunciations; for example, the kanji character <川> "a river" is pronounced /kawa/ and /sen/ whereas /kawa/ is represented by other characters (i.e., <皮> which means "a skin" and <革> which means "leather") and /sen/ is represented by many (e.g., <千> meaning "a thousand"). Further learning difficulty may occur because of the general orthographic and visual complexity of kanji.

From a practical point of view, the problem with kanji writing may be soluble in the future if Taku learns to use a computer keyboard because he now has sufficient knowledge of hiragana. That is to say, to use a computer to produce kanji requires two steps: one, converting speech syllables into hiragana symbols, and two, converting the string of hiragana symbols into the target kanji character. Thus, with good knowledge of hiragana and a minimum knowledge of target kanji characters, a dyslexic child could produce his speech utterances in written Japanese.

PARENT PERSPECTIVES

The mother described her son as energetic, intellectually curious, and tender-hearted. At present the mother does not seem very pessimistic about Taku's future partly because she has learned a lot about the nature of dyslexia, specifically because she knows that he is not mentally retarded, as the WISC III results indicate. She feels that dyslexia has caused him to suffer "from an inferiority complex" because of academic problems. She is concerned that he "hates school work." Yet he also had some special strengths. When he is interested in something, he learns quickly (e.g., memorizing phrases or playing piano by ear). Once when he was assigned his favorite role in a play at a school cultural festival, he quickly learned all of the lines in his role.

The mother reported that Taku's reading and writing problems only moderately affect his family life (rating this influence 4 out of 10 on the Parent Perception Scale). However, in the past homework has been an issue that has caused considerable stress. The mother stated that sometimes it has taken Taku three hours to complete homework that other children could finish in 30 minutes. As he could not complete the homework independently, she had to sit with him the entire time, which caused a lot of stress.

The mother noted that Taku has problems at school in addition to those that involve literacy. For example, Taku enjoys playing with other children, but he often couldn't wait for his turn to have a swing, and gives up waiting to play alone. He was also poor at rope jumping and throwing/catching a ball, and soon gave these up. The mother remembered that on a school sports day, he didn't join any of the games. According to the mother, Taku generally gets along with his classmates, but it is also true that he has been bullied or mocked frequently. The mother reported that Taku often fails to understand his classmates' communicative intentions in casual conversations, frequently taking the friends' words literally whereas other children would take them as a joke or white lie. Taku is well-known by his unusual or peculiar reactions and so his classmates continue to mock him. He has a difficult time understanding the perspectives of others, which is an autistic trait that may pertain to problems associated with theory of mind. The mother feels that Taku's reading problems adversely affect his social life, scoring this a 7/10 on the Parent Perception Scale.

Regarding Taku's school experience, the mother was satisfied with six of the seven teachers in that she appreciated their acceptance of Taku's reading and writing problems. However, only two teachers actually supported him by trying to teach him reading and writing while the others did nothing in particular. The mother also complained that even though Taku had enough knowledge, he could not score well on tests because of his poor reading and writing. She wished that the teacher would give oral exams to dyslexic children that would measure subject knowledge rather than reading and writing skills. She rated her son's reading problem to be a 7/10, which was the same rating she gave for its influence on school achievement. The mother is somewhat dissatisfied with the country's regulations and support for dyslexia as she does not believe that the concept of dyslexia is understood.

CHILD PERSPECTIVES

Taku does not seem to worry about his poor reading. Actually, he enjoys reading on a limited basis (e.g., comic books). He has problems reading more difficult materials, such as the instruction manuals for his video games, which are often written in small kanji characters and kana (hiragana and katakana) symbols. He is also well aware that writing continues to be his main problem. Even in sixth grade, he holds his pencil awkwardly and tries to avoid writing as much as possible.

His Sentence Completion responses suggested that school is sometimes very stressful for him. He mentioned several times that he doesn't like to study and finds it difficult to listen to the teacher in class. He rated his reading problem as an 8/10 on the Child Perception Scale and noted that its influence on school success was 7/10. Taku may have acquired some learned helplessness over the years as he has struggled in school. When asked how he deals with difficult work at school, he responded that he gives up and tries "to escape from reality." He also stated that he doesn't want to be compared with other children at school and becomes "scared when the teacher gets angry."

Taku's social problems have caused stress. Although he does have friends, he probably has more difficulty with socialization than he is willing to admit. Throughout his interview, there were frequent references to bullying. He noted that his classmates think he is "a pig and troublesome" yet girls in his class think he is "cute and popular." He named one best friend, who was a girl. He feels that his classmates harass him too much and he wishes his friends would invite him to "their houses to play," but yet he believes that his reading problem has only minimal influence on his social life (rating it a 2/10). In Taku's case, it could be that his social problems are more related to his Asperger's than his reading problems.

Taku has begun to understand his own problems, sometimes acknowledging that if something goes wrong, it's at least partly his fault. Indeed, Taku's autistic-like behavior appears to be mitigating or disappearing differentially. If so, one may ask if this tendency is attributable to spontaneous remission or some socio-educational effects in his everyday life. The latter effects, if any, may be related to video game playing which Taku has been fond of and good at for many years. He says he wants to have a job involving video games in the future and this may well be a realistic goal given his highly developed skill in gaming.

CASE COMMENTARY

It should be noted here that in Japan developmental dyslexia is included in learning disabilities under the Support Law for the Developmental Disabled enforced on December 10, 2002 (http:// www.mext.go.jp/a_menushotou/ tokubetu/05011301.htm). In this law, "developmental disability" includes autism, including Asperger syndrome, and other pervasive developmental disorders (PDD), attention deficit hyperactivity (ADHD), and similar brain functional disorders, which all emerge in young ages. In schools, however, much attention is paid to children with PDD or ADHD, but children with developmental dyslexia tend to be overlooked or neglected.

As in many other cases, it is difficult to determine what factors were involved with Taku's dyslexia. Aside from the possibility of the inheritance from his father, however, two interrelated factors are worth discussion from the viewpoint of the paucity of learning experience. A first factor may involve the delay of the verbal development in his second year as noted by the mother. The number of lexical items did not consistently increase after he began uttering the first three words, "Mama," "Papa," and "Baaba" (nanny) during the second year. The mother said that she attempted to increase the amount of linguistic input. As is well known, the manner and amount of linguistic input at early stages of life are of critical importance for the child's cognitive and linguistic development (Feldman, 2007; Hart & Risley, 1995). In this regard, the mother's attempt and effort are highly regarded. Unfortunately, however, the effects were not what she expected. A few possibilities for the failure are conceivable. One is the effect of Taku's attention deficit related to lack of social motivation or interest. Even though the amount of linguistic input from the mother might have been significant, the amount of intake might have been limited. It may also be likely that as a typical autistic child, Taku might have had difficulty recognizing the informative intent of the mother, and the mother-child conversational interaction might not have developed sufficiently or efficiently. If this mother-child communicative interaction is poor, it would be much more difficult to learn to communicate with a "silent and invisible interlocutor" through written language.

Another possibility is that the amount of utterances given to Taku by the mother and other caretakers might not have been sufficient although the mother stated otherwise. Although empirical data, such as mean number of the mother's utterances per hour (cf. Hart & Risley, 1995) is not available, the possibility of limited exposure to utterances would not be unlikely considering Taku's early developmental problems.

Taku's poor writing skills may partly be attributed to his avoidance behavior, which has prevented him from developing these skills further. This vicious circle may be inferred from the dissociation between hiragana and katakana writing scores (i.e., Taku's scores for hiragana writing were 85% mastery versus the 50% mastery for katakana writing). The hiragana-katakana relationship is characterized as a nearly perfect one-to-one correspondence, each corresponding symbol representing the same mora (or syllable). Although most katakana symbols are visually simpler than their corresponding hiragana symbols (e.g., hiragana-katakana: な―ナ /na/, わ―ワ /wa/, and は―ハ /ha/), Taku's scores were poorer for katakana than for hiragana probably because of his avoidance of writing which would suggest that he would have had far less opportunity to write words in katakana than those in hiragana. To extend this line of discussion on the lack of writing experience, the frequency of individual kanji characters in reading and writing is much less than that of hiragana and katakana symbols, which means that there are fewer opportunities for spontaneous learning for the former. And furthermore, the orthographic complexity is far greater for kanji than for kana symbols. Taku's limited amount of practice in writing kanji would naturally reflect such learning conditions. Not surprisingly, therefore, Taku's writing score for kanji in grade 3 was extremely low (i.e., 10% mastery compared to the 82% mastery for the third grade mean).

A second basic cause of Taku's dyslexia may pertain to his birth month: Taku was born in February and was always among the youngest students in his class. A great amount of research supports the hypothesis that among normal or even intellectually advanced children, a younger school entrance age leads to academic disadvantage in general, and reading problems in particular (Bedard & Dhuey, 2006; Bentin, Hammer, & Cahan, 1991; Carroll, 1963; Kawaguchi, 2006; Weinstein, 1968–1969; see also Morrison, Griffith, & Alberts, 1997). By contrast, positive effects of older entrance age seem evident. Older children tend to have better phonological awareness, a relatively greater amount of informal reading activity, and superiority complex which are combined to facilitate such children's development more than expected (Kawaguchi, 2006; Weinstein, 1968–1969). Older children's superiority to younger children may be even greater than generally believed. Unfortunately, Taku represents the opposite of such cases. He hates writing activities and a sense of his inferiority increases every time he has to write in the presence of peers in his class. He avoids writing, therefore the amount of writing practice is extremely limited.

If the lack of writing practice is the major cause of Taku's writing deficit, the challenge would be how to entice him to begin writing practice. One possibility is to use a personal computer even though at present he is not willing to accept this idea. But just as his father compensated for his handwriting problems by means of the personal computer, so would it be possible for Taku to do the same in the future.

Finally, a socio-educational implication may be worth considering. According to recent research (Boot, Kramer, Simons et al., 2008), video games may serve to improve basic perceptual and cognitive abilities involving attention, working memory, and executive control. It is thus likely that the video game 'training' that Taku has thus far had has contributed to his socio-cognitive development. Such being the case, appropriate video game training carefully selected for him may become a promising means to improve his attentional and cognitive abilities including reading and writing. Actually, at present, some companies market video games for educational purposes for schoolchildren. For example, Nintendo's Kanji Test DS and other software may turn out to be a good learning tool for Taku even though he believes that he is allergic to kanji writing.

Given this state of affairs, it is difficult to present a reliable prognosis of Taku's dyslexia. Yet, the first author, who has regularly been giving kanji writing training to Taku, would like to suggest that considering his present reading/writing achievement level, it will be very difficult for him to pass entrance examinations of high schools. However, given his video gaming interests and strengths, in the future he may be able to find a computer related job similar to that of his father's profession.

REFERENCES

Bedard, K., & Dhuey, E. (2006). The persistence of early childhood maturity: International evidence of long-run age effects. *Quarterly Journal of Economics, 121,* 1437–1472.

Bentin, S., Hammer, R., & Cahan, S. (1991). The effects of aging and first grade schooling on the development of phonological awareness. *Psychological Science, 2,* 271–274.

Boot, W.B., Kramer, A.F., Simons, D.J., Fabiani, M., & Gratton, G. (2008). The effects of video game playing on attention, memory, and executive control. *Acta Psychololica, 129,* 387–398.

Carroll, M.L. (1963). Academic achievement and adjustment of underage and over-age third graders. *Journal of Educational Research, 56,* 415–419.

Feldman, R. (2007). Parent-infant synchrony and the construction of shared timing: Physiological precursors, developmental outcomes, and risk conditions. *Journal of Child Psychology and Psychiatry, 48,* 329–354.

Hart, B., & Risley, T.R. (1995). *Meaningful differences in the everyday experience of young American children.* New York: Paul H. Brooks.

Kawaguchi, D. (2006). *The effects of age at school entry on education and income.* Economic and Social Research Institute, ESRI Discussion Paper Series No.162.

Morrison, F.J., Griffith, E.M., & Alberts, D.M. (1997). Nature-nurture in the classroom: Entrance age, school readiness, and learning in children. *Developmental Psychology, 33,* 254–262.

Rey, A. & Osterrieth, P.A. (1993). Translations of excerpts from Andre Rey's *Psychological examination of traumatic encephalopathy* and P.A. Osterrieth's *The Complex Figure Copy Test. The Clinical Neuropsychologygist, 7,* 4–21.

Uno, A., Wydell, T.N., Haruhara, N., Kaneko, M., & Shinya, N. (2009). Relationship between reading/writing skills and cognitive abilities among Japanese primary- school children: Normal readers versus poor readers (dyslexics). *Reading and Writing, 22,* 755–789.

Uno, A. , Haruhara N., Kaneko M., & Wydell N.T. (2006). *Screening Test of Reading and Writing for Japanese Primary School Children (STRAW).* Tokyo: Interuna Publishing.

Wechsler, D. (1998). *Wechsler intelligence scale for children,* 3rd ed. (Japanese version.) Azuma, H. et al., trans. Tokyo: Nihon Bunka Kagakusha.

Weinstein, L. (1968–1969). School entrance age and adjustment. *Journal of School Psychology, 7,* 20–28.

TAKU'S INTERVIEW

1. What do you want to be when you grow up?

   I want to work for a company which deals with video games.

   Why do you think you would be good at that job?

   I like video games.

2. Tell me about a teacher who has been really important to you or one who has helped you: what did the teacher do to help you?

   A teacher of social studies, because he listens to whatever I say. And a soccer coach.

3. Tell me about a teacher who didn't really help you that much or one who did not give you the help you needed. What did you want the teacher to do to help you?

   There is a teacher who I don't like. I am scared when the teacher gets angry. I want him/her not to be grumpy or not compare me with other kids.

4. Tell me what your mother thinks about your dyslexia. Does she talk to you about the problem?

   No.

5. Tell me what your father thinks about your dyslexia. Does he talk to you about the problem?
    No.

6. Tell me about something that makes you really happy.
    Video games, the internet, TV, comic books, and reading.

7. Tell me about something that makes you really sad.
    Studying, bullies, and those who commit suicide.

8. When the work gets very hard at school and you think you can't do it, what do you do?
    I give up that. I try to escape from reality . . . try to think about something else.

9. What kinds of books do you like to read?
    Adventure, fantasy, love, suspense, what life is, what human beings are, science, and music.

    What is your favorite book?
    No book in particular.

    Do you read to yourself?
    Yes.

    Who else reads to you?
    Mom sometimes reads to me.

10. Do your friends know that you have dyslexia?
    Yes.

    Do you talk to them about it?
    No.

    What do you say?
    Nothing.

    What do your friends say to you about dyslexia?
    They sometimes bully me.

11. Do your siblings know that you have dyslexia?
    I have no sibling.

12. Name three things you are really good at:
    Playing, escaping from reality, and eating a lot out of frustration.

13. Name three things you are not so good at:
    Studying, running, and being patient.

14. If you are feeling bad about your reading, is there one person you can talk to who makes you feel better?
    Yes.

    What does that person say to you?
    "Tell me what this means."

15. Do computers help you with your reading?
    No. I sometimes enjoy You Tube.

16. Do you usually have problems with your homework?
    Yes.
    Can you do your homework independently or does someone help you?
    Sometimes Mom helps me.
    Is homework a big problem or just a little one?
    A big problem. I hate studying.

17. If there was one thing you could change about school, what would it be?
    After lunch, I take a nap, but someone throws a ball at me. I want to have a room where I can take a nap safely.

18. If you could have three wishes, what would they be?
    To get rid of the bullies around me, to buy new video games, and to have a lot of money.

19. Tell me three things you would like your teacher to do to help you with your dyslexia:
    To put hiragana to difficult kanji characters. [Note: Hiragana symbols can be used as phonetic symbols. Smaller-sized hiragana symbols are put above or to the right of difficult kanji characters in children's books, Taku would like this for all of his textbooks.] *I want the teachers to realize that there are children who are poor at reading and writing. I want them not to deduct points for spelling on Science and Social Studies tests.*

20. Who is the best reader in your class?
    A girl whose name I don't know. She could read lines in a story fluently as if she were the character in the story.
    How did she get to be such a good reader?
    She is good at the Japanese language.

21. Is it important to learn how to read?
    Well, yes.
    Why or why not?
    Reading is necessary when I read books on video games. Writing is necessary when I have to write a report.

15 Vicente, a Case Study of Dyslexia in Chile

Arturo Pinto Guevara

Vicente is a 10-year-old boy whose reading problems were evident in kindergarten. He was subsequently diagnosed as dyslexic in first grade. This diagnosis was confirmed in fourth grade. At the beginning of the interview he appeared to be very restless and unfocused. However, as the interview continued, Vicente became friendly, relaxed, and cooperative.

BACKGROUND

Family History

Vicente lives with his parents and two siblings in an upper-middle-class neighborhood in Santiago. Both of his parents have university degrees. The father is an engineer and the mother is a former preschool teacher, but does not currently work. Neither of his parents experienced learning problems, however, Vicente's maternal uncle had reading problems, which required extra help from teachers and Ritalin to focus his attention.

Medical History

Nothing unusual was noticed during the mother's pregnancy and Vicente had a normal delivery. He has never been to hospital or involved in any serious accident. However, due to problems with focusing, attention, and concentration during school, his parents took him to a neurologist who diagnosed him as ADHD and prescribed Ritalin at the age of 10. The medication was later changed to Strattera. Vicente does not present any visual or hearing impediments.

Early Development

Vicente was somewhat delayed in his early language development, speaking his first words when he was 1 year and 5 months. At the age of 3 he started to put words together to form sentences and at the age of 5 he talked like the average children of his age. His pronunciation and elocution were clear and no special features were noticed, but his mother noted that he was slow in identifying colors and objects. Vicente learned to walk at 1 year and rode a bicycle by the age of 4. His mother described him as a "speedy learner." He started to paint and draw at the age of 2 and at the age of 4 he became quite prolific with this hobby. He experienced no problems holding pencils and showed interest in academic and social activities at school. His older sister spent a lot of time with him helping him study and taking him with her on social outings. He did not have any problems socializing with other children. The only problems in Vicente's early development were marked restlessness and sleep difficulties.

SCHOOL HISTORY

Kindergarten

In Chile, kindergarten is mostly a play experience that acts as a bridge or transition year for children who will then enter formal schooling. Curricular demands imposed on children in middle- and upper-middle-class schools include learning letters, numbers, and information about the natural and social world. In kindergarten students are required to complete homework which involves reviewing what has been learned during the day.

The beginning of kindergarten, at the age of 5 years, was a very good time for Vicente; he was a happy and sociable boy who played with all his classmates. However, after the winter holidays the child lost all interest and cheerfulness, which his mother attributed to the cold weather and being away from the garden and patio. She said that it became very difficult to send him to school after that. The mother was quite concerned so she spoke to his teacher who reported that Vicente was working more slowly than his classmates. The teacher had given him some extra homework to bring him up to the level of his peers, but this had resulted in no progress. He was given a remedial lesson book that consisted of exercises or assignments that he had to complete repeatedly in an attempt to achieve proficiency. The idea was that if the child did not learn the lesson when it was presented in the classroom, he would achieve this by repeating the same assignments at home. He was the last in the class to identify colors and objects and always the last one to finish his work.

First Grade

At the age of 6 years Vicente reluctantly started first grade. He resisted the fact that he had to attend school as the reading demands were too challenging for him. It was very hard work for him to learn how to identify letters and words. He was given a set of 40 cards with names of objects (e.g., table, pen, roof, door, etc.), in order to help him memorize the words. It was a difficult period as Vicente only remembered words for a short period of time. The mother tried to help him, but to little avail. The strategy of using sight words on flashcards was insufficient to address Vicente's reading problems.

Vicente was referred to the School Technical Staff who conducted an evaluation. He was given two standardized reading tests: the Prueba de Dislexia Específica [Test for Specific Dyslexia Evaluation] (TEDE; Condemarín, 1984) and the Reading and Progressive Comprehension Test (CLP; Condemarin, 1996). The results of the TEDE placed Vicente at the 5th percentile while the results of the CLP placed him at the 6th percentile. Therefore, the parents were informed that Vicente was dyslexic.

When the school authorities were asked for help by the family, they were unable to provide any due to school standards that did not allow them to make any accommodations or provide any remedial help. The school asked the mother to take her son to see a private special needs tutor to help him with reading, making it clear that Vicente's problems needed to be solved by the family, not the school. They communicated to the family that the curriculum was inflexible and unrelated to their child's needs. Thus, as his school-related stress increased, Vicente retreated. He became a shy child due to his difficulties and it was a hard year for him. The family complied with this recommendation and secured a private tutor who worked on reinforcement of the school curriculum on a biweekly basis, but very little progress was observed.

Second Grade

School attendance problems increased as Vicente's learning difficulties became increasingly obvious. His reading problems were worsening and he realized he was lagging further behind his classmates. Although he continued to attend private tutoring twice a week to reinforce the curriculum, this did not seem to be increasing school performance. The one positive aspect of this period was that he started playing basketball and began celebrating his victories with his teammates. The teachers reported the problem of disparity in relation to his performance and the class' reading levels. Vicente received no help, only criticisms pointing out he was not learning at the required speed expected by the school. At the end of the school year, the family was told that their son could not be promoted to third grade. The family accepted this decision on the basis of the school's counseling that led them to believe that repeating second grade would allow Vicente the necessary time to mature, which would solve his reading problems. Also, the school authorities pointed out that Vicente had failed to achieve the standard level for promotion required by all children, and therefore could not move forward at this point.

Vicente was very upset, becoming increasingly sensitive to his problems. Even though Vicente's private tutor had worked with him all year with the curricular materials provided by the school, this did not narrow the gap between the school's expectations and Vicente's achievement. The school's only solution was that he be retained in second grade. Although they knew he was dyslexic, they appeared to have little if any understanding of this condition and the specific problems involved. They recommended more of the same, which meant that Vicente would meet with additional failure the second time around.

Thus, when Vicente repeated second grade, his problems with reading and writing persisted without improvement. Although he continued to work with his private tutor who used the instructional materials provided by the school, his reading did not improve. However, he did make progress in mathematics and sports. It was during this time that Vicente became an outstanding basketball and football player.

Third Grade

Vicente was 9 years old when he began third grade, which was a very chaotic and difficult time for him. During this year the child's reading problems became even more persistent and the school had informed the mother that Vicente would need to repeat third grade. The biweekly private tutoring was insufficient to support the child's lagging school achievement. The mother decided to find another tutor who could more specifically address Vicente's reading problems. The mother also realized that she had to move her son to another school that had a different attitude towards children with learning problems. His current school had a negative and unsupportive attitude towards all children that could not comply with their specific demands. Upon learning of the mother's decision to move the child to another school, the school administration decided to give Vicente passing grades. The mother was told by the school authorities that Vicente would be able to pass to fourth grade with the lowest grades possible. The mother did not accept this change in policy as a remedy and continued to look for another school for her son. This was a challenging endeavor as all private schools in Chile have high entry requirements (including standardized testing) and long waiting lists, but the mother was able to find a school that accepted her son and had a support system for students with disabilities.

Fourth Grade

Vicente started fourth grade at a new school when he was 10 years old. During this time his classroom teacher noted that in addition to his reading problems, he was having difficulty paying attention. She recommended that the parents take him to a neurologist for evaluation.

The parents took Vicente to a multidisciplinary clinic where he was evaluated by a neurologist as well as an educational specialist. The neurologist diagnosed him as having ADHD and prescribed medication. The educational evaluation consisted of administration of the same two tests that he had taken in the first grade (i.e., the TEDE and the CLP). These results were lower, but similar to those obtained three years before; his scores ranked him at the 3rd percentile for both the TEDE and the CLP. Vicente was also given a standardized test of mathematics (the Prueba de Evaluación Matemática; Benton & Luria, 2000), which placed him at the 60th percentile rank. His full scale IQ was 110 as measured by the WISC- R. These test results confirmed his diagnosis of dyslexia.

The clinical diagnosis of dyslexia resulted in many changes needed to accommodate the child's requirements. Vicente's new school provided two hours of remedial support by a special needs teacher on a weekly basis. Initially Vicente was concerned that he would have to work with a teacher who was a stranger to him. However, this evolved into a very positive stage as he started to gain confidence when he began improving his reading. The mother was very enthusiastic about Vicente receiving this remedial assistance as she felt it was the first time he had been provided with support by the school.

DYSLEXIA DIAGNOSIS AND TREATMENT ISSUES

The country of Chile does not provide or consider any support for children with dyslexia who attend private schools so the parents are left without any guidance or support. However, in public education that caters to the lower-middle-class to the poor, there are remedial classes that provide differential instruction to small groups (four to six students) for two to four hours per week. A few private schools have a system in place to help students with dyslexia, but unfortunately almost all energies and resources are focused in teaching high achieving pupils with good academic results. Teachers focus most of their efforts on improving final scores on the national tests to improve the reputation of their schools. When schools realize that they have pupils with learning difficulties, these are neglected by the educational establishment and are handed back to their parents to care for their needs and education.

When Vicente began having reading problems in kindergarten, he did not receive the specific remedial support he needed even though it was obvious to all that he was struggling. In his particular school, which focused on high achievement, the children learned to read in the first few months of first grade. Vicente was made to feel that his reading problems were related to his own shortcomings instead of the school's inability to meet the needs of all students. Even though Vicente was diagnosed as dyslexic in the first grade, there was little understanding of his needs at school. In fact, the school's solution was recommendation of a private tutor who offered repetition of daily assignments to support the curriculum and grade retainment when curriculuar expectations were not met. For a dyslexic child reading at the 5th percentile in the first grade, it was impossible to meet the curricular expectations in a school that focused on high achievement and offered no accommodations. Vicente needed specific remediation techniques designed to address his phonological, vocabulary and comprehension problems. It is only when Vicente's parents moved him to another school that he received special education support for his reading problem.

After Vicente was moved to another school, his mother began to see changes in his reading and writing. With the school's cooperation, his new private tutor, the school's special needs teacher and the mother began working together adapting texts to support the reading and writing standards of the curriculum. To address Vicente's dyslexia, the private tutor continued to use a basic reading program to develop phonetic and comprehension skills in addition to supporting writing skills. Vicente was also taught strategies to promote self-monitoring. This remediation program began in the third grade and has continued until the present time at which Vicente is in the fifth grade. However, prior the the fourth grade, the program was not successful as there was no special needs teacher to support this content. Things have drammatically improved for Vicente as now the school special needs teacher and the private tutor work together to support Vicente's needs. Every new semester information shared by the school and special needs teacher is upgraded and checked, and there is a strategy agreed beforehand that is put into place to support him.

PARENT PERSPECTIVES

Vicente's mother understands that dyslexia affects the learning and reading comprehension capacity of her son. She is also aware dyslexia adversely influences his school progress. Yet in spite of the fact that his latest reading scores suggest that he is functioning in the 5th to 8th percentile ranks, she views his problems to be moderate (5 on a scale of 1 to 10) and their influence on school success to also be moderate (6 out of 10). It appears that the mother is very hopeful that the current system of support will help to ensure her son's school success.

The mother has faced many challenges to secure appropriate support for her child. As a former teacher, she has been clearly aware of Vicente's reading problems since first grade. Although she did not have a special education background, she knew that her child should receive special instructional assistance. However, even with this background, it took many years for her to understand how to secure appropriate assistance. She was very dissatisfied with many of Vicente's teachers and their lack of knowledge regarding reading problems. She stated that "there are few teachers who have supported" her son. Even those teachers who seemed to suspect that Vicente had a reading problem were unprepared or unwilling to give him the help that he needed. The school's remedial plan seemed to focus on two remedies: (1) additional homework practice and (2) retention. Through a series of negative experiences, the mother came to understand that it was not likely that Vicente would be helped by his school or teachers if he remained in that situation. Thus, the turning point for Vicente came when the mother decided to change schools.

Currently the mother is very satisfied with the educational situation as there is a special educator at the new school who works closely with Vicente's private tutor. The mother has now started to see improvement in his reading. She stated that the language, math, and head teachers in the new school have been very helpful. The parents have been positively surprised with their child's capacity for doing his homework independently in a systematic way. Before this process was put in place, it was almost impossible to have the child work on his homework without arguments.

Vicente and his mother have a very close relationship. She intuitively understands his nature and describes him as a tender and affectionate child who has struggled with a problem that has affected his self-esteem. When he started school and became confronted with academic problems, the mother watched him withdraw. However, over the course of time it became evident that he excelled in sports, which made all the difference. She believes that her son's athletic strengths provided him the balance he needed to maintain self-confidence. He gets along with his peers and has many friends with whom he engages in athletic activities. Thus, she feels that the dyslexia has exerted little if any influence on his social life. Likewise she does not believe that the problem has adversely influenced family life.

The mother expressed disappointment that her country does not provide the adequate school regulations for supporting children with dyslexia. She feels that the responsibility for helping dyslexics is left exclusively on the shoulders of families. She wished it was possible for schools to identify reading problems earlier and to provide the support that these children need so it would not be left to the parents, who do not have expertise in this area, to find solutions.

CHILD PERSPECTIVES

When Vicente was asked what he wants to do in the future he said, "I want to be a mechanic because I love cars." He believes he has the skills needed in technical activities, such as automotive or even possibly tailoring.

Playing video games is Vicente's favorite pastime. Vicente only reads a few times a week for up to two to three hours mostly with the help of his mother or grandmother. He doesn't like to read, but he does enjoy sports magazines or books depicting cars or basketball games. He watches an average of ten hours of television per week; his favorite shows involving car racing, boxing, basketball, and wrestling.

In spite of the fact that Vicente has struggled quite a bit in school, he believes (like his mother) that his reading problem is moderate (6 on a scale of 1 to 10) and the amount it interferes with school success is also moderate (6 on a scale of 1 to 10). His mother's strong advocacy for his needs has probably been very helpful for his self-esteem. For example, her decision to move Vicente from the school that wanted to retain him for the second time likely prevented further feelings of failure as Vicente reported that the worst thing about school is "that they retain you." He holds the perception that all of his teachers have helped him, which is inconsistent with the perception the mother has. While he does not bear grudges against his teachers, he expresses feelings of sadness associated with receiving low grades and reprimands from teachers in class. Homework does not present any problems for Vicente. If he doesn't understand an assignment, he knows he can ask for help. And if he struggles with schoolwork, his solution is to try harder. There are some things that he would change about school. He expresses a desire to learn how to study in a more efficient way. He would like his teachers to give him other types of tests (oral as opposed to written) and teach him "in a more direct way so they could help me with my dyslexia."

Vicente appears to be a well-adjusted child who enjoys socializing with his many friends. It has definitely helped his self-esteem that he excels in sports. In general, he feels that he is supported by his classmates, but complains that he is sometimes mocked by them for failing to "read correctly." Although his friends know he has dyslexia, he doesn't think they realize what it is like to have to study for "hours on end." He never talks to them about this problem and he doesn't feel that his dyslexia has significant influence on his social life.

As Vicente's family has demonstrated strong support and understanding of his reading problems, he does not feel that dyslexia has interfered with his family life. However, he admits that his mother finds it hard to deal with his dyslexia and sometimes becomes angry. And, like many children, he wishes that his parents would be less demanding about grades and homework. He reported that his mother talks to him about dyslexia and encourages him to pay more attention. Vicente's father also talks to him about the problem and provides additional encouragement. The grandmother is another strong source of support; when Vicente is feeling sad about his dyslexia, she is the person he turns to for consolation.

Vicente clearly understands the significance of reading and its implications for school and life success. He believes that it is very important to learn how to read as it makes a strong contribution to one's intelligence. He had no trouble identifying the best reader in his class and attributed this child's success to the enjoyment that student receives from reading.

CASE COMMENTARY

Vicente's case illustrates the need of implementing an early response system in schools to address possible cases of dyslexia. If these children are given the specific research-based instructional support that dyslexia requires, they will improve. Vicente's reading problems were obvious from the beginning of his school career, yet he was allowed to fall further and further behind. There must be a specific procedure to identify students with reading problems so they can be provided the support to learn and move forward with their classmates.

This case also vividly shows the problems that parents face in Chile where there are no enforceable laws that cover private schools. Middle-class and upper-middle-class families feel that they must send their children to private schools to secure the best education. However, most of these private schools do not feel an obligation to support a child's learning difficulties, which are viewed to be the child's problem, and the burden is set squarely on the shoulders of the parents. These private schools operate on the premise that their reputations of academic distinction must be upheld. Thus, they judge their pupils in reference to high academic standards. As soon as they become aware of a student that shows different or low academic results in their view, they believe the school's overall performance is compromised. From an ethical standpoint, it is the responsibility of all educational establishments to look after the well-being of all students. This must include the high achieving who display various talents as well as those who struggle for a variety of different reasons, including dyslexia. Educational establishments should not selectively determine to support only those who are high achieving. The only remedy these schools seem to have is to retain the student until the academic level is achieved. However, this remedy is ill conceived, particularly for students with dyslexia. This leaves the parents with no option other than removing their child from the school. The previously mentioned situation creates misunderstandings as the parents are not involved or informed and there is no clear information regarding the academic achievements or performance of the child. It is not helpful for parents to receive information from the school explaining that they are not capable of fulfilling the learning requirements of the student.

Another problem that children like Vicente face is the lack of help from teachers. The little advice that parents and children receive generally comes from a few teachers who point out the difficulties the student is having. These teachers recommend that the parents search for more suitable educational alternatives. Essentially they are shifting the problem (and the child) to another teacher or school instead of meeting the challenge themselves. However, Vicente's case also points out that there are Chilean schools whose goals demonstrate commitment to all learners. The second school where Vicente enrolled belongs to this category. When there is a coordinated effort between teachers, private tutors, and special educators who work together to create and implement a remedial plan based on the child's individual profile of needs, the result can bring improved achievement. Additionally, when the parents are included in the collaborative process, the tension endured by the parents and the child can be greatly alleviated. It is in the best interest of all to work toward clear communication of specific academic goals and desired outcomes.

As previously indicated, there are no government regulations for dyslexia that are imposed on private schools. But in public education, which caters to the lower-middle-class down to the lowest socioeconomic class, the law (Decreto n° 291 de 1999. Reglamento del Funcionamiento de los Grupos Diferenciales del país) requires schools to support students with dyslexia and other specific learning disabilities by providing small group instruction by highly trained specialists. However, the category of learning disabilities in Chile is often different from that of countries outside of South America. While in countries like the United States, sociocultural disadvantage may preclude the identification of learning disabilities, however, in the public school system in South America, poverty is a pervasive influence that affects learning and development and therefore cannot and should not be used as an exclusionary criterion for this category (Bravo-Valdivieso & Milicic Müller, 2001). Even though the provision of these human resources and services mandated by Chilean law probably has the capacity to help the student's special needs, there are very few middle- or upper-middle-class families who would take their children out of private schools to take advantage of the support provided by the Differential Groups as the public school system is considered to be less adequate for addressing their children's needs.

In reviewing Vicente's case, it would appear there may also be a need for special schools for dyslexic pupils in Chile. Supported by an early evaluation system and strong collaboration between parents and knowledgable teachers, these schools could provide the necessary remediation from the beginning so that the child does not experience self-esteem issues associated with reading problems and lack of achievement progress. These special schools could offer the appropriate research-based curricula for dyslexic pupils that could make a signficant difference in the lives of these children. Thus, if there are not sufficient private and public schools that are prepared to meet the needs of students like Vicente, it may be worthwhile to investigate the possiblity of establishing these to enhance opportunities for school success for all dyslexic children in Chile.

REFERENCES

Benton, A., & Luria A. (2000) *Prueba de evaluación matemática* [Mathematics skills test]. Santiago, Chile: Ediciones PUC.

Bravo-Valdivieso, L., & Milicic Müller, N. (2001). Learning disabilities studies in South America. In D.P. Hallahan & B.K. Keogh (Eds.), *Research and global perspectives in learning disabilities* (pp. 311–328). Mahwah, NJ: Lawrence Erlbaum Associates, Inc.

Condemarín, M. (1984). *Prueba de dislexia específica.* (TEDE) [Test of specific dyslexia (TEDE)]. Santiago, Chile: Andrés Bello Editores.

Condemarín, M. (1996*). Prueba Comprensión Progresiva de la lectura* (CLP). [Reading and Progressive Comprehension Test (CLP)]. Santiago, Chile: Andrés Bello Editores.

Decreto n° 291 de 1999. Reglamento del Funcionamiento de los Grupos Diferenciales del país. [Regulation of operation of differential groups in the country]. Mineduc. Chile

Ramírez, V., & Rosas, R. (2007). Estandarización del WISC-III en Chile: Descripción del Test, Estructura Factorial y Consistencia Interna de las Escalas. [Standarization of WISC-III in Chile: Test Description, Factorial Structure, and Internal Consistency of the Scales]. *PSYKHE, 16*, (1), 91–109, Edic. Pontificia Universidad Católica de Chile.

VICENTE'S INTERVIEW

1. What do you want to be when you grow up?
   I want to be a mechanic.

   Why do you think you would be good at that job?
   I like cars.

2. Tell me about a teacher who had been really important to you or one who has helped you. What did the teacher do to help you?
   He congratulated me and told me the right way to read some words.

3. Tell me about a teacher who didn't really help you that much or one who did not give you the help you needed. What did you want the teacher to do to help you?
   All teachers have helped me.

4. Tell me what your mother thinks about your dyslexia. Does she talk to you about the problem?
   My mom doesn't take the dyslexia so calm sometimes she gets angry.
   What does she say?
   She speaks to me about the dyslexia and says that it is necessary to pay attention.

5. Tell me what your father thinks about your dyslexia. Does he talk to you about the problem?
   My dad doesn't care about the dyslexia too much.

   What does he say?
   He says that it is a problem. He says that it's necessary to improve and that takes time.

6. Tell me about something that makes you really happy.
   Makes me happy to have friends and play with them.

7. Tell me about something that makes you really sad.
   When my classmates are reprimanded.

8. When the work gets very hard at school and you think you can't do it, what do you do?
     When work becomes difficult in the school, I try to think I can do it.

9. What kinds of books do you like to read?
     I don't like to read any book.

   What is your favorite book?
     I like mystery books. My favorite one is the "13 Mysterious Cases." I read them with my grandmother.

10. Do your friends know that you have dyslexia?
     My friends know that I have dyslexia.

   Do you talk to them about it?
     I don't. They don't say anything.

11. Do your siblings know that you have dyslexia?
     Yes.

   Do you talk to them about it?
     No.

12. Name three things you are really good at:
     Basketball, mathematics, soccer.

13. Name three things you are not so good at:
     The tasks where you have to write, talking about a topic in class, and singing.

14. If you are feeling bad about your reading, is there one person you can talk to who makes you feel better?
     I speak with Grandmother when I feel bad about reading.

   What does that person say to you?
     She says I'm a good boy at reading.

15. Do computers help you with your reading?
     The computers help me with the reading.

   If yes, how do they help you?
     They help me to understand the words.

16. Do you usually have problems with your homework?
     No.

   Can you do your homework independently or does someone help you?
     I don't need help.

   Is homework a big problem or just a little one?
     When I don't understand I request help.

17. If there was one thing you could change about school, what would it be?
     Improve how to study.

18. If you could have three wishes, what would they be?
    World peace, not to steal, and to be a good person.

19. Tell me three things you would like your teacher to do to help you with your dyslexia.
    I would like the teachers to give me other types of tests, to demand more of me and teach me in a more direct way so that they could help me with the dyslexia.

20. Who is the best reader in your class?
    The best reader in the class is Antonio.

    How did he/she get to be such a good reader?
    He reads books and he likes them.

21. Is it important to learn how to read?
    It is very important to learn how to read.

    Why or why not?
    Because it makes you more intelligent. It is always important.

16 Gwyn, a Case Study of Dyslexia in Australia

Christina E. van Kraayenoord

Gwyn is an 11-year-old child. At 8 years of age his difficulties with reading were diagnosed and named as dyslexia by a private educational psychologist. Throughout the interview Gwyn was animated and engaged. He provided thoughtful answers with a keen understanding of his uniqueness, abilities, and difficulties. He was able to "tell his story" with insight and a wonderful sense of humor.

BACKGROUND

Family History

Gwyn lives with his parents and older brother, Liam, in an upper middle class suburb of the Gold Coast, Queensland, Australia. He attends a private independent high school that is a co-educational, inter-denominational Christian day school for students from Early Education to Year 12. Both Gwyn's parents completed high school and obtained university degrees. They have their own software development business that they operate from their home. Gwyn's immediate family is very close and there is a great deal of love and affection as well as thoughtfulness and humor. Neither of the parents had learning problems, but the mother reported that her sister was dyslexic.

Medical History

Gwyn was a full-term baby, born with no apparent complications. Since birth he has had low muscle tone and hyperextensive joints, which according to his mother has meant that from an early age he has had "difficulty sitting still." Gwyn's only hospital visit occurred when he broke his arm at age 2 as a result of being accidentally pushed off the couch by his brother.

Early Development

Gwyn was somewhat slower in achieving language and motor milestones. He walked at 15 months and experienced laterality problems. The mother reported that he uses his left hand for eating and sports, but his right hand for writing. She also noted that he has fine motor problems that interfere with writing; holding a pen is something that "he has to physically work at, just to hold it in position." His mother stated that he is not really ambidextrous, "but much more left-right confused." He was toilet trained before age 2½ years. The family taught Gwyn to ride a bike at 6 years of age, an experience that was very challenging.

The mother reported that Gwyn spoke a little later than expected because his brother talked for him. As a baby he had recurring middle-ear infections that required the insertion of grommets (tubes) at around 14 months of age. After six months, there were no further ear infections. Developmental hearing checks during infancy and his school years revealed normal hearing. Other developmental milestones such as learning key concepts (e.g., color) were achieved without difficulty.

According to his mother, in the first five years of his life Gwyn greatly enjoyed spending time playing with his brother and with other children. Today, Gwyn is a healthy adolescent, although his mother reported that he is susceptible to more headaches than other children, which she attributed to stress associated with the effort he must expend to concentrate during the school day.

SCHOOL HISTORY

Until recently school-starting ages differed in the various states across Australia. This was the case for the states of Victoria and Queensland where Gwyn lived in his early years. The nomenclature for the various levels of schooling is also sometimes different across the states. Crèche (a form of childcare typically for children between 6 weeks and 3 years) and kindergarten (typically for children between 3 and 5 years) are not schools or part of the public school system. The programs are based on children's developmental needs. Preschool education (which is seen as separate from schooling) may involve attendance at a kindergarten (some of these are part of childcare services) for children between the ages of 3 and 5 years. Although it is not compulsory, most Victorian children go to kindergarten in the year before attending primary school, which is from 5 to 11 years. Kindergarten attendance is for a few hours from one to five days a week. The curriculum comprises activities focused on social, cognitive and physical skill development in preparation for school.

From the age of 1 year, Gwyn attended a private crèche three days per week. At 4 years of age he attended the crèche for one or two days per week and a community kindergarten two days a week. At that time his development was considered to be normal and he enjoyed his kindergarten experience. He interacted well with peers and had an extensive vocabulary for his age. He displayed no particular indicators of difficulty with learning although his mother pointed out "he had not come to text yet."

Preparatory Year

In Victoria, children start formal schooling at 5 years of age, which is when Gwyn entered the Preparatory Year (known as "Prep") at a state primary school. The school year starts in February and ends in December. Prep is the first year of school during which teachers focus on the development of foundational knowledge, skills, and behavior. The curriculum emphasizes literacy and numeracy skills, physical and creative skills, and information communication technology skills. According to his mother, his school experience was very enjoyable as his skills were not different from the other children (all boys) although he developed a "moderate stammer."

Year 2

The family moved to the state of Queensland to be closer to the maternal grandparents when Gwyn was 6 years old. At the time of Gwyn's school enrollment, there was some uncertainty as to the appropriate year level for him as school-starting ages were different in the states of Victoria and Queensland (i.e., at that time Queensland children started school 12 months later than their Victorian peers). His mother reported that since he could not read yet, there was debate as to whether he should enter Year 1 or 2. It was decided he would start in Year 1, but after two or three weeks, he was placed in Year 2. The mother noted that while he was socially and physically at the Year 2 level, it became obvious that with regard to academic skills, he was not performing similarly to his classmates.

Gwyn's stammer worsened after the move to Queensland. The mother felt it was the result of the academic demands that he faced at his new school and was a consequence of "his brain wanting the idea quicker than he could deliver it." He experienced many repetitions of sounds and phrases interspersed with apologies that were also repeated (e.g., "excuse me, 'scuse me"). At the school's suggestion, Gwyn's speech and language skills were assessed by a private speech pathologist and recommendations were provided to assist with his "mild dysfluency, his listening skills and his word-finding difficulties." The speech pathologist also suggested that the stammer was related to stress due to a combination of factors, including starting a new school and learning to read. She felt no intervention was necessary as Gwyn would improve if given time and attention. Therefore, the family tried to make a particular effort to listen to him.

In Year 2 the curricular expectations required the achievement of basic reading skills, which Gwyn had not yet acquired. In addition he had continued difficulty holding a pencil and writing. The teacher referred him to the school's Guidance Officer because of concerns about his social skills. She used a checklist for Autism Spectrum Disorder (ASD) and reading difficulties. The subsequent report stated that the ASD checklist had been used because "the teacher indicated there were minor social difficulties." However, it was concluded that, although Gwyn was experiencing some problems, the school did not have concerns for his ability to learn at this stage. Despite this conclusion, Gwyn attended reading sessions in a small group led by the school Principal and received some assistance from a Support Teacher. In Queensland Support Teachers (Learning Difficulties) assist students with literacy and/or numeracy difficulties. They may or may not have any additional training or qualifications above that of a classroom teacher. At the time, they typically worked in a remedial manner and often used a pull-out approach (separate classroom) that involved small group teaching mainly of decoding and comprehension skills. In the first two terms of Year 2 Gwyn was provided this instruction twice a week for 30 minutes by a Support Teacher, whom his mother regarded as effective, and in hindsight, perceived her to be one of the few educators who correctly diagnosed Gwyn's need to learn phonemes and phonics. However, this Support Teacher left the school and was replaced by a teacher who the mother perceived as less effective. The mother said the instruction in learning support comprised reading a series at a slower pace and more deliberately than children in the classroom. The mother met with the classroom teacher and Support Teacher at least once per term to monitor progress. The Support Teacher suggested that Gwyn was improving, which was also the mother's impression.

Year 3

Despite the mother's optimism about Gwyn's progress at the end of Year 2, he continued to experience problems in Year 3. His mother's visits to Gwyn's teacher and Support Teacher became more frequent. She believed that there was a lack of progress and a lack of structure in his reading instruction. The Year 3 teacher reported concerns about Gwyn's difficulties with learning early in the school year and he was referred by the school's Guidance Officer to a (state government) Community Child Health Services' Developmental Assessment Team (DAT). According to the DAT Report, Gwyn was referred "because of concerns about his motor coordination and his hand dominance." He was assessed when he was 7½-years-old. The Medical Officer who examined him noted that his general physical health was normal, but many of his joints were hyper-extensible. An occupational therapist evaluated his visual-motor skills with the Developmental Test of Visual Perception (Frostig, 1993). According to the physiotherapist who also assessed Gwyn, he achieved age-appropriately and above in most areas (e.g., balance, hand coordination, knowing left and right, visual perceptual skills), but experienced some difficulties with muscle tone and hyper-extensible joints, posture, scissors skills, pencil grasp, aspects of handwriting (e.g., posture, restricted finger movements), motor planning and short- and long-term visual and auditory memory. The report recommended that Gwyn be encouraged to use a molded pencil grip and to participate in sports to practice his skills, develop strength, and increase self-esteem and social skills. Gwyn's mother also recalled being given suggestions for physical exercises. His parents believed that these exercises would help his lack of coordination. They were grateful for the attention Gwyn received, but more concerned about his reading achievement, which had not been assessed by the DAT.

During this school year, Gwyn sat the Queensland, statewide mandated Literacy and Numeracy tests for all Year 3 students. With reference to literacy there are three separate tests. With respect to the domains of reading and viewing (the latter refers to the construction of meaning from and the use of visual symbols and signs, e.g., punctuation marks, traffic signs, illustrations), Gwyn's performance was below the average result for students in Queensland at this year level. The same was true for his performance in the domains of writing and spelling. An interpretation of these scores could have led the school to raise or to affirm concerns about Gwyn's literacy achievement. It appears, however, that the school believed that Gwyn's learning difficulties were mainly physical in nature associated with gross and fine motor problems.

Year 4

Early in Year 4, a school Guidance Officer assessed Gwyn's intelligence using the Wechsler Intelligence Scale for Children–Third Edition (Wechsler, 1991; WISC-III). According to the report, Gwyn was referred for assessment by his teacher and the school's Deputy Principal because of his reading and writing difficulties. The referral information indicated that his teacher reported that Gwyn's general knowledge was very good, but he had difficulty with reading and some mathematics. He did not have problems copying from the blackboard. There is no record that an assessment of reading and/or writing (or math) was undertaken at this time by the Guidance Officer, and it is suspected by the author that anecdotal information from the classroom teacher and Support Teacher was used to come to the conclusion about Gwyn's reading and math achievement.

The results of the WISC-III assessment revealed a Full Scale Score at the 45th percentile that was interpreted as average. His score was at the 61st percentile for Verbal Comprehension and at the 47th percentile for the Perceptual Organization Index, both interpreted as average. The interpretation also referred to difficulties with visual processing speed. The report concluded that Gwyn's reading skills (presumably based on the remarks of the Deputy Principal and teacher—see above) were not commensurate with his overall cognitive abilities. Thus, according to the report "Gwyn's profile was suggestive of a specific reading difficulty." The evaluation report also recommended that Gwyn might benefit from an assessment by a behavioral optometrist to address his visual processing problems.

During the year Gwyn continued with the biweekly small group learning support. The activities included the use of readers and activities such as reading and memorizing poems presented on projected hand-written transparencies. According to his mother there was no assessment of his reading, no monitoring of progress or intervention adjustments and, therefore, she became increasingly concerned about Gwyn's lack of reading achievement. She observed some of the support sessions and stated there was no systematic remedial program. The mother described the learning support as "useless" as the staff "weren't sufficiently qualified" and she felt he was just missing out on classroom time.

In the middle of the school year, Gwyn's mother took him again to see a private speech pathologist at the same practice where he had been assessed two years earlier. The speech pathologist assessed Gwyn using the Clinical Evaluation of Language Fundamentals-Fourth Edition (CELF-4: Semel, Wiig, & Secord, 2006), The Listening Test (Zachman, Barrett, Huisingh, Orman, & Blagden, 1992), the Queensland University Inventory of Literacy (QUIL; Dodd, Holm, Oerlemans & McCormick, 1996) and the South Australian Spelling Test (SAST; Westwood, 2005). The results of the assessment indicated that Gwyn did not have any dysfluency and he demonstrated age-appropriate language development. However, the report indicated that in spite of his strengths, Gwyn had a weakness in his ability to extract the main idea from information at the connected sentence level. The report also highlighted Gwyn's "impaired phonological awareness skills" and weak phonics skills, especially those involved in processing print.

Next, Gwyn's mother took him to an educational psychologist for a comprehensive assessment of reading, writing and spelling, who subsequently diagnosed him dyslexic. This psychologist began to work with Gwyn with a reading intervention program he had developed (i.e., *Understanding Words*, Wright, nd). This program "for struggling readers" involves synthetic phonics instruction in which the student is taught letter-sound correspondences, sight word reading, and whole text reading. These are taught through explicit instruction, decoding activities, spelling, word manipulation activities, passage reading, and comprehension exercises. The sequenced structure of each session involves: a review of previously learned skills, sight word teaching, sound-letter and decoding activities, spelling and letter-sound manipulation games, reading of the text passages, comprehension exercises, and dictation exercises.

The program was taught one-on-one in the evenings for 40 minutes twice per week for 12 months. The mother observed these instructional sessions so that she could undertake similar teaching at home, which she did five times a week during that period. After 12 months when the program was completed, the psychologist and mother used Spelling Mastery (Dixon, Engelmann, Meier, Steely, & Wells, 1998) to develop Gwyn's writing skills, with the idea of making connections between his reading and writing. It was used weekly and later fortnightly, for six months. However, Gwyn and his mother found it boring and prescriptive, and it was not successful. As part of the reading and writing program the psychologist monitored and documented progress in regular reports for the parents. For example the first Progress Report, written after two terms, stated that the improvements made in word reading, nonword reading and reading comprehension were "clinically meaningful and reliable," although reading was still an effort and spelling remained difficult. In the next report written approximately 10 weeks later, the "excellent progress" had been maintained.

The school indicated that they were pleased that Gwyn had seen an educational psychologist who had confirmed the diagnosis of dyslexia. The classroom teacher, Support Teacher and Deputy Principal were shown the program *Understanding Words,* but according to the mother, they showed little interest. In her view, the diagnosis and out-of-school intervention meant that she "was out of their face and they were delighted."

Year 5

Despite his mother's inclination to forgo the learning support classes, in Year 5, Gwyn continued to attend them. The instruction was a duplicate of the type of support received in Year 4, which again according to the mother was not based on Gwyn's instructional needs. His first semester school report recorded his performance in English as C (on a scale with a range of A (highest) to E (lowest)) in achievement and an A in effort.

Armed with confirmation of Gwyn's diagnosis, the mother requested that he be given an exam "reader" and additional time for taking tests. As a result, prior to sitting the mandated Year 5 Literacy Test (separate tests of reading and viewing, writing and spelling), the school was granted these accommodations from the Queensland Studies Authority (curricula and test authority). With respect to the Year 5 test in reading and viewing, and writing, Gwyn's scores were above the average result for students in Queensland at this year level. For spelling, the performance was below average for students in Queensland at this year level.

At the suggestion of the school the previous year, Gwyn visited a behavioral optometrist who recommended Gwyn wear glasses with colored lenses at all times when he was indoors. The family skeptically viewed this treatment as experimental based on their knowledge of the empirical literature. Indeed, according to Gwyn's mother they did not make any difference to his ability to see the letters more clearly while reading, thus, confirming the mother's perception that the school's recommendation was "misguided and unhelpful."

Year 6

In Year 6, Gwyn moved from the state primary school to the private combined primary, middle and secondary school that his brother attended in order to participate in the broader range of experiences the school offered. On enrollment, Gwyn's mother gave the school a detailed written report of his developmental and academic history, which also listed the accommodations his mother requested for his instruction and assessment needs. While some of these accommodations had been made by professionals who had assessed Gwyn over the years, the majority were suggestions that the mother herself believed worked best for his learning needs in the classroom and for homework.

Another reason for the move to the new school was that Gwyn's mother believed that he would be bullied less on the school bus. She felt that Gwyn was bullied because "he's different. . . . and he interacts differently." Gwyn's brother, Liam, who was aware that his brother was being bullied, was protective of him, but also embarrassed for him. Gwyn misinterpreted the attention that Liam's friends gave him as being related to the fact that he was "cool." According to his mother Gwyn was not "in the cool group" and in truth was more likely to be friends with children who were different (e.g., one good friend had Aspergers).

At the beginning of Year 6, an Appraisement by the school's Support Teacher was completed. This was a formal assessment undertaken to establish the nature of Gwyn's learning difficulties in literacy and/or numeracy and recommend the type and level of support he would need in the classroom. As well as documenting the findings of Gwyn's previous assessments, he was assessed using the South Australian Spelling Test (SAST; Westwood, 2005), the Middle Years Ability Test (MYAT; ACER Press, 2004) which is a group test that provides a measure of general ability and the Progressive Achievement Test-Revised Comprehension (PAT–R Comprehension; ACER Press, 2001), which is a group silent reading comprehension test. According to the report, the reasons for the Appraisement were the "parental concerns and Gwyn's past history of intervention and assessment." On the SAST Gwyn's spelling age was 10.5 years (his chronological age at the time was 10.4 years). Gwyn's performance on the MYAT was at the 4th percentile (Stanine 2) and his performance on the PAT-R Comprehension was at the 8th percentile (Stanine 2). The Report identified Gwyn as an oral/verbal learner and included recommendations (e.g., reducing the amount of copying from the board, using graphic organizers and color coding, enlarging electronically generated material and reading test questions).

Gwyn's Student Report for Semester 1 in Year 6 recorded Gwyn's Overall Assessment for English as a rating of C (range of A+ (high) to E) with an Effort rating of G (Good). The Student Report for Semester 2 indicated the same grades in English as for Semester 1.

Year 7

The mother met with Gwyn's homeroom teacher, who was also the Year 7 English teacher, at the start of the year to explain his learning preferences and accommodation requirements. The teacher was quite agreeable and suggested that in spelling, for example, Gwyn would learn 5 words (instead of 20) each week. During the first term of Year 7, Gwyn attended school-initiated remedial Math sessions (30 minutes) and English sessions (1 hour), one afternoon a week each, after school. The parents were also particularly keen for Gwyn to engage in a physical activity in which he could succeed and that did not rely on hand-eye coordination. Thus, Gwyn began swimming squad training once or twice a week after school. During the year he moved up 3 levels and became an excellent swimmer.

DYSLEXIA DIAGNOSIS AND TREATMENT ISSUES

For Gwyn, the formal identification of dyslexia did not come until Year 4 when he was 8 years of age. In Australia there is no recognized definition of "learning difficulties," the term that is most commonly used in this country to describe difficulties with literacy and numeracy. There is also no requirement or legislation that mandates that identification, support, or intervention be offered to students who have difficulty with literacy and/or numeracy.

It is clear that in the first year at school, Gwyn's parents, and from Year 2 (age 6), his teachers, were concerned with his lack of reading and writing progress. It was in Year 2 that the family moved from the state of Victoria to the state of Queensland. The issue of having different ages across Australia for school-start enrollment is one that has always been of concern to parents with children who move interstate. In the last two years the government has altered the school-start age so that Queensland is now aligned with other Australian states and in 2011 the country will adopt a national curriculum that should eliminate the problems that Gwyn experienced related to year-level placement.

Gwyn's assessment and diagnosis experiences were similar to many children with learning difficulties in Australia. While some school assessment of his reading may have occurred in the early years of schooling, the results were not shared with the parents. His stammer was obvious to both parents and teachers, which led to the school's suggestion in Year 2 that Gwyn visit a private speech therapist. His mother and the teacher identified problems in reading and writing, but the school seemed to believe that the writing difficulties were related to motor skills. The school also believed he had difficulties with social skills, leading to an assessment for ASD. Unfortunately, disparities between parents' and teachers' perceptions of children's problems are common and in this case led to delays in a comprehensive assessment of Gwyn's learning difficulties in reading. For example, in Year 3 the need for a formal reading assessment was overlooked by the school's Guidance Officer as evidenced by the suggestion that Gwyn be assessed by DAT, which focuses almost exclusively on development, health and physical concerns, such as motor movement.

Perhaps based on a common view in the literature at the time that learning difficulties could be identified by determining a discrepancy between intelligence and academic achievement (e.g., reading) in Year 4 the School's Guidance officer assessed Gwyn's intelligence and suggested his profile reflected a specific reading difficulty. As mentioned earlier, it is unclear as to the source of the information about Gwyn's academic achievement. An assessment made by a private speech pathologist indicated he had reading difficulties. The suggestion was made that his problems were the result of poor phonological and phonics skills.

It is interesting to note that from Year 2 the school provided learning support for Gwyn's reading. This instruction was provided by the Support Teacher and the school Principal. Again, because of the lack of documentation about the goals of the intervention and the lack of description of the intervention itself it is difficult to know exactly what was taught, how it was taught, and whether or not it was effective. Suffice it to say, the support was offered in a small group outside of the classroom. Again, this situation parallels the experiences of many children with learning difficulties in Australia. Learning support is often outside the classroom and unconnected to what occurs in it, the teaching is undifferentiated and often does not meet the specific needs of individual children, and on many occasions progress is not assessed to establish whether the intervention has been effective. The mother's perception that the learning support was not programmatic and lacked structure coupled with her son's lack of progress led to disillusionment and frustration with the school. The school's recommendation for a behavioral optometrist was further confirmation that the school had little to offer Gwyn by way of effective support for his reading difficulties.

Sadly, parents' feelings of anger and frustration, and often despair about the lack of support to effectively address children's reading difficulties in schools are common. Parents who have the financial means often turn to the private sector. At the same time, there is much skepticism about the claims made by some specialists offering assessment and intervention that are not directly related to education, such as the case of behavioral optometry.

The definitive diagnosis of dyslexia did not occur within the school system, but rather was provided by a private educational psychologist in Year 4. This is not a surprise, as the education system in Australia does not use the term dyslexia, viewing it as a medical term. However, the educational psychologist provided appropriate assessment and intervention. The results for the Year 5 mandated state test and his school report indicated that Gwyn's reading (and writing) performance had improved. While there is a need to be cautious in interpreting these results, it does appear that the combined work of the educational psychologist and the mother over 18 months improved Gwyn's reading. There were a number of elements of the program offered to Gwyn that are consistent with recommendations from various research groups and government agencies in Australia and internationally. These include the use of explicit or direct instruction of code-breaking skills such as phonemic awareness and phonics and of comprehension skills and strategies (Rowe, 2005; Snow, Burns, & Griffin, 1998). Allington (2009) has also called for intensive, sustained, expert-led and accelerated instruction for students with learning difficulties in literacy, which were features of Gwyn's program. The change in Gwyn as a result of this intervention was obvious and translated into increased confidence and self-esteem as well as an interest in reading for pleasure.

PARENT PERSPECTIVES

The mother reported that Gwyn has a very cheerful disposition. His favorite pastime was watching movies, especially during the family Friday and Saturday night movie ritual. The family did not watch much television, but they occasionally selected programs to watch together. She described Gwyn as good at cooking and swimming. When asked about Gwyn's talents, his mother stated: " . . . because his brain is wired differently . . . he has a unique view and I think one of his talents for us is that he shows us a different view than the normal left-brain thinker would."

The mother reported that while Gwyn did not have a great number of friends, he had a few very good ones he had maintained over the years and with whom he enjoyed spending time. Yet Gwyn was quite content playing imaginatively by himself for hours. In spite of the fact that he has had some negative social experiences (e.g., being bullied on the school bus) and has demonstrated what teachers have described as "minor social difficulties," she did not believe that his reading problem had exerted much influence on this aspect of his life, rating this 3/10.

Gwyn's mother rated his reading problem as being significant (8/10) and perceived that it adversely influenced his school success to a very great extent (10/10). She indicated that the most difficult aspect of Gwyn's reading problem had been the threat to his self-confidence. She has told Gwyn about various historical and contemporary figures with dyslexia and has encouraged him to view his condition as an opportunity. Gwyn's mother had educated herself about learning difficulties and understood the need for school staff to do more than the little they were doing for Gwyn. She was extremely persistent in her efforts to obtain a diagnosis of dyslexia and appropriate intervention. She understood that there is no cure for dyslexia and that reading would always remain difficult for Gwyn, yet she believed that the program provided by the education psychologist (i.e., *Understanding Words*), was very successful for her son. She reported that since Gwyn's participation in the program he had been reading extensively. The mother also felt that it was very important that she provide all his teachers with detailed written information about his reading problems with suggestions to meet his needs during classroom instruction and homework.

The mother's interview revealed that the family had instilled in Gwyn a deep sense of his own individuality, encouraged his personal aspirations, held positive expectations for his achievements, and was continually advocating for him.

CHILD PERSPECTIVES

Gwyn reported that he liked "reading a good book and eating nice food," and that reading and cooking made him happy. While at the time of the interview Gwyn continued to experience some difficulties with reading compared with that of his peers, he was an avid reader and rated the amount of reading he did as "high." He had a vast knowledge of his favorite authors and their books, especially in the fantasy genre. He also enjoyed audio books and listening to others read, signaling that one of his favorite family routines was his father's practice of reading aloud while having breakfast.

Gwyn reported that his parents perceived his dyslexia as a characteristic that made him "very unique" and "different to most people." He thought his parents were proud of him especially ". . . when I say 'I've finished a book'." Gwyn wrote "my siblings make me angry when they annoy me" and he wished that his brother would "be a bit more nice to me."

He rated the significance of his reading problem as moderately important (5/10), but did not believe that it interfered greatly with school success (4/10). Gwyn thought that the best thing about school was the "nice teachers." He believed that his classmates thought he was "cool." He also wrote, "Sometimes my classmates make me mad when they "joke around." In nominating the best readers in his class, Gwyn believed that these students excelled for various reasons, (i.e., one student was motivated to read, another was good at tests while a third was "smart").

When confronted with difficult tasks, he often sought clarification and sometimes referred concerns to his mother. He reported that occasionally his mother spoke to his teacher and then "my teacher would probably give me an easier thing to do." When asked how his teachers could assist him with the dyslexia Gwyn said he was uncertain, but he added that his uncertainty was because his mother had supplied his teachers "with a list of all the things that she thinks are important for the teachers to know about him." Gwyn confirmed it was important to learn how to read well "because reading is like a life skill that you should have."

Gwyn reported that problems with homework usually related to problem-solving in Math and his slow word processing. The family had tried to use Dragon Speak to assist with homework, but Gwyn reported it was not effective and so his mother often typed his homework for him. While Gwyn did not perceive homework as a major problem he disliked it intensely, arguing that time after school should be for relaxing and recreation.

Gwyn was able to name three friends stating he did not like it when his "friends joke around" and wished sometimes that they were more understanding of him. Gwyn reported that some of his friends knew about his dyslexia, even though he did not talk to them about it and he did not believe his reading problem interfered with his friendships (rating of 1/10).

Gwyn believed he has a positive future after high school. His career ambitions were to "be a cook and a story writer." He thought he would be a good chef because he was "good at reading instructions and making good foods." With respect to writing, Gwyn said he had a good imagination. In spite of his difficulties, Gwyn spoke of his enthusiasm for writing stories by hand when he had spare time. When asked to name three wishes, Gwyn laughed and paused in thought for a long time before stating, " I wish I was a bit smarter with my reading, just a bit better at reading, and no home-work, and I had a bit more money."

CASE COMMENTARY

There has been a long history of debate in Australia about whether or not learning difficulties or disabilities and specifically dyslexia should be for-mally recognized in legislation (van Kraayenoord, 2008). Even if such leg-islation had been in place, it is not known whether it would have improved Gwyn's situation. Legislation and associated policies do not always ensure access to assessment and intervention, or to effective support and enhanced outcomes. Nevertheless, for Gwyn much more should have been done to meet his learning needs on the grounds of equity and social justice.

In reviewing Gwyn's early development, there are several signals that might have suggested that he was at-risk of failing to acquire some of the skills necessary for the development of language, reading and writing. Such signals included: a family history of dyslexia, the late onset of walking and his low muscle tone and hyper-extensive joints, his right-left confusion, and the late onset of speech and his stammer. While none of these alone signals that a child will develop a learning problem, in combination they do sug-gest that aspects of learning might be difficult.

In Gwyn's case, even though he demonstrated problems early on, his reading disability was not identified until much later. The lack of focus on the early assessment of academic skills, in particular the failure to under-take detailed assessments of his reading and writing are a concern. It is not known how often schools make referrals or suggest that parents obtain out-of-school professional assessment for their child for ancillary concerns (e.g., motor skills) as opposed to specific academic problems. However, the author's experience of over 20 years of assisting families of children with difficulties and researching in schools in relation to literacy learning and learning difficulties suggest that this situation is quite common. It appears that in the early school years, there was insufficient attention paid to the need for a comprehensive and rigorous assessment of Gwyn's reading and writing knowledge and skills, either within the school or via a referral to an out-of-school educational expert or specialist.

The quality of intervention in schools offered to students with learning difficulties in Australia is unknown, although reviews of studies have revealed that it is often irregular, lacks intensity and is not aligned with classroom reading instruction (van Kraayenoord, 2008). Very few studies investigating the efficacy of intervention have been undertaken and most research has involved the description of intervention (see van Kraayenoord, Rohl, & Rivalland, 2005). Gwyn benefited from the diagnosis and the private tutoring by an educational psychologist who had developed his own program for struggling readers. The family paid for the assessment and subsequent intervention. Obtaining such private support requires the financial means to do so and this is often not available to many Australian families who have children with learning difficulties.

Gwyn's case clearly demonstrates the challenges of obtaining effective support for children with learning difficulties in Australia (see Louden, et al., 2000; van Kraayenoord & Farrell, 1998; van Kraayenoord & Elkins, 2009). The failure to address the concerns effectively from Gwyn's early years of school meant that preventative measures were not put in place nor were responses targeted or adequate. The lack of definitive and formal identification of Gwyn's academic difficulties meant that there was a lack of systemic, whole-of-school and whole-child response to his reading and writing needs (see Wyatt-Smith, Elkins, Colbert, Gunn, & Muspratt, 2007). It is unknown how knowledgeable or well-trained Gwyn's Support Teachers or his classroom teachers were or how able and/or willing they were to address his reading and writing difficulties in an appropriate, comprehensive, and concerted way. Australia's teachers need to be well trained in literacy development and also be able to meet the needs of students with learning difficulties in literacy. Teacher preparation courses in universities have a role to play here. In addition, there is a need for continued professional development for regular classroom teachers so that they provide good first instruction as well as supplementary instruction using effective methods.

Finally, it is a credit to his family, especially his mother, that Gwyn now, not only reads quite well, but also enjoys reading. In addition, Gwyn's personal characteristics suggest that he has overcome many of his difficulties in reading and sees his future as full of possibilities.

REFERENCES

ACER. (2004). *Middle Years Ability Test* (MYAT). Camberwell, VIC: ACER Press.

ACER. (2001). *Progressive Achievement Test-Revised, Comprehension* (PAT-R Comprehension). Camberwell, VIC: ACER Press.

Allington, R.L. (2009). *What really matters in Response to Intervention: Research-based designs*. Boston: Pearson Education.

Dixon, R., Englemann, S., Meier, M., Steely, D., & Wells, T. (1998). *Spelling mastery: Teacher presentation book level A*. Columbus, OH: SRA/McGraw Hill.

Dodd, B., Holm, A., Oerlmans, M., & McCormick, M. (1996). *Queensland Inventory of Literacy* (QUIL). Brisbane, QLD: The University of Queensland, Department of Speech Pathology and Audiology.

Frostig, M. (1993*). Developmental Test of Visual Perception—Second Edition* (DTVP-2). Austin, TX: PRO-ED.

Louden, W., Chan, L.K., Elkins, J., Greaves, D., House, H., Milton, M. et al. (2000). *Mapping the territory: Primary students with learning difficulties: Literacy and numeracy: Vol. 1–3*. Canberra, ACT: Department of Education, Training and Youth Affairs.

Rowe, K.J. (2005). *Teaching reading: Report and recommendations. Report of the Committee for the National Inquiry into the Teaching of Literacy*. Canberra, ACT: Australian Government Department of Education, Science and Training. Retrieved from http://www.dest.gov.au/nitl/report.htm

Semel, E., Wiig, E., & Secord, W. (2006). *Clinical Evaluation of Language Fundamentals-Fourth Edition* (CELF-4 Australian). Sydney: Pearson.

Snow, C.E., Burns, M.S., & Griffin, P. (Eds.). (1998). *Preventing reading difficulties in young children*. Washington, DC: National Academy Press.

van Kraayenoord, C.E. (2008). Research into learning difficulties in Australia: A selective review and suggestions for future research. *Australian Journal of Dyslexia and Other Learning Difficulties, 3*, 3–9.

van Kraayenoord, C.E., & Elkins, J. (2009). Literacies and numeracy. In A.F. Ashman & J. Elkins (Eds.), *Education for inclusion and diversity* (pp. 236–370). Frenchs Forest, NSW: Pearson Education.

van Kraayenoord, C.E., & Farrell, M. (1998). *Responding to students with severe and persistent learning difficulties in secondary schools*. Brisbane: The University of Queensland, Fred and Eleanor Schonell Special Education Research Centre.

van Kraayenoord, C.E., Rohl, M., & Rivalland, J. (2005). Intervention approaches for learning difficulties in literacy: An Australian approach. In P. Ghesquiére & A.J.J.M. Ruijssenaars (Eds.), *Learning disabilities: A challenge to teaching and instruction* (pp. 117–132). Leuven, Belgium: Leuven University Press.

Wechsler, D. (1991). *Wechsler Intelligence Scale for Children* (3rd ed.). Cordova, TN: Psychoeducational Corp.

Westwood, P. (2005). *South Australian Spelling Test*. In P. Westwood, *Spelling: Approaches to teaching and assessment, 2nd edition*. Camberwell, VIC: ACER Press.

Wheeler, R. (1992). *Learning Efficiency Test-II*. Novato, CA: Academy Therapy Publications.

Wright, C. (nd.). *Understanding words*. Mermaid Beach, QLD: Author.

Wyatt-Smith, C., Elkins, J., Colbert, P., Gunn, S. & Muspratt, S. (2007). *Changing the nature of support provision: Students with learning difficulties– interventions in literacy and numeracy project*. Canberra: Department of Education, Science and Training, Australian Government.

Zachman, L., Barrett, M., Huisingh, R., Orman, J., & Blagden, C.M. (1992). *The Listening Test*. East Moline, IL: Lingui Systems Incorporated.

GWYN'S INTERVIEW

1. What do you want to be when you grow up?
   I want to be a cook and a story writer.

   Why do you think you would be good at that job?
   Because I'm good at reading instructions and making good foods.

[story writer?]
Because I think I've a good imagination.

2. Tell me about a teacher who has been really important to you or one who has helped you.
I think it would be Mrs. N., my Maths teacher last year.

What did the teacher do to help you?
She was very helpful when I was trying to figure out a question . . . it was usually problem-solving. I'd ask her to read the question and if I didn't know how to do the sums and stuff I'd ask her how to help me with that, too.

3. Tell me about a teacher who didn't really help you that much or one who did not give you the help you needed.
I don't really have an answer for that.

What did you want the teacher to do to help you?
Well, read the question mostly. Because I usually have trouble reading what the questions ask me to do. When I understand the question I usually understand how to do the answer, get the answer.

4. Tell me what your mother thinks about your dyslexia.
She thinks it's very unique . . . that I'm very different to most people . . . because I have dyslexia.

Does she talk to you about the problem?
Yes.

What does she say?
I forget.

5. Tell me what your father thinks about your dyslexia.
He thinks mostly the same way as my Mum.

Does he talk to you about the problem?
Not very often, usually he doesn't.

What does he say?
I dunno. . . . probably asks me how's it's gotten—how my dyslexia's going.

6. Tell me about something that makes you really happy.
Reading a good book and eating nice food.

7. Tell me about something that makes you really sad.
Nothing.

8. When the work gets very hard at school and you think you can't do it, what do you do?
At school, I would go up to my teacher and then tell 'em.

9. What kinds of books do you like to read?
I like, you know the Guinness World Records, I like stuff like that. Yeah, fact books. I like the author Michelle Paver. Her books are pretty

good, like "Oath Breaker," that's set 6 thousand years ago, in ancient times, and the chronicles is called *Chronicles of Ancient Darkness.*

What is your favorite book?
> . . . *"The Chronicles of Ancient Darkness" books.*

Do you read to yourself?
> *Yep.*

Who else reads to you?
> *When I couldn't read that well my Mum used to read books to me.*

10. Do your friends know that you have dyslexia?
> *Yes, some of them.*

Do you talk to them about it?
> *No. I usually keep it to myself and my friends that I know.*

What do you say?
> *I've said that I have dyslexia and that's a reading and writing disability.*

What do your friends say to you about dyslexia?
> *They say they didn't know it 'cause they reckon I'm going really well in school.*

11. Do your siblings know that you have dyslexia?
> *Yes.*

Do you talk to them about it?
> *No.*

12. Name three things you are really good at:
> *Cooking, some Maths problems like I can get my head around really quickly, and I like P.E.*

13. Name three things you are not so good at:
> *Sometimes reading because I'm getting much better at reading, problem-solving Maths questions, and I like adjectives and stuff and to figure out what adjectives are and like adverbs and stuff.*

14. If you are feeling bad about your reading, is there one person you can talk to who makes you feel better?
> *Well when I'm feeling bad about my reading, I usually read.*

15. Do computers help you with your reading?
> *Yeah, because you have to type stuff up and research stuff so yeah.*

If yes, how do they help you?
> *Well it helps me with . . . we tried to get this thing working with writing, it like I speak into the computer and it types it up and it didn't work for me. It only worked for my Dad. [Q] Yeah, Dragon Speak.*

16. Do you usually have problems with your homework?
> *Well, it's usually on, it's sometimes on Maths because the Maths homework is pretty easy I reckon, but sometimes because there's*

like three problem-solving questions, I have to ask my Dad to help me with [it].

Can you do your homework independently or does someone help you?
. . . [mother helps] with the typing.

Is homework a big problem or just a little one?
Somewhere in between I reckon.

17. If there was one thing you could change about school, what would it be?
I reckon they should give you a bit more time to give you the time to do the homework that you need to do because when you get home it's like the time to just relax and it doesn't matter about doing any work.

18. If you could have three wishes, what would they be?
I wish I was a bit smarter with my reading, just a bit better at reading, and no homework, and I had a bit more money. Just a tiny bit because I don't have much money right now.

19. Tell me three things you would like your teacher to do to help you with your dyslexia:
I dunno.

20. Who is the best reader in your class?
There's Tracy, she's pretty good at doing work, and there's 2 other people in different classes.

How do you think that she got to be such a good reader?
I think she just uh, read when . . . she wanted to. Yeah.
Well there's [also] William Smith, he's really good at reading, and good at doing tests and stuff [Q] . . . because he has a crack at every book that looks good, I reckon.
. . . and Jack Brown, he's really smart too. [Q] Yeah, because he does really good on all the tests.

21. Is it important to learn how to read?
I think it's pretty important.

Why or why not?
Because reading is like a life skill that you should have and if you don't know how to read because it gives you ideas and stuff. Like watching a movie it gives you ideas. It's the same as reading.

17 Valeriy, a Case Study of Dyslexia in Russia

Olga Borisovna Inshakova
and Maria Arkhipova

Valeriy is an 11-year-old boy, who was diagnosed as dyslexic at the age of nine. He is a very social child who is talkative and fun loving. During the interview he spoke excitedly about his sport achievements. However, Valeriy's reading problems are upsetting to him. During the interview, when he spoke about these difficulties, he was obviously uncomfortable. He was reticent at these times, retreating from the conversation until the interviewer encouraged him to return again to the topic of dyslexia.

BACKGROUND

Family History

Valeriy lives with his mother and two elder brothers who are 14 and 16 years old in one of the largest cities in Russia. His parents were divorced soon after Valeriy's birth, but his father lives in the same city and visits the children several times a year. Valeriy is very close to his older brothers and spends most of his spare time going for walks and playing with them. His mother is a teacher in an Orthodox School. She did not experience any problems with school and has ten years of education. The mother always tries to help and encourages her son as she wants to give him the best education she can provide. There is a tradition in their family: every evening they choose an interesting book and read it aloud to one another. Although neither parents experienced learning problems, Valeriy's uncle on his father's side had delayed language development and reading difficulties. Valeriy's brothers do not have educational problems and do well at school. The older boys help each other and Valeriy as well.

Medical History

Valeriy's mother reported a normal pregnancy without problems. She delivered Valeriy in a hospital, however, there was some difficulty at birth as he suffered from asphyxia because his umbilical cord was wrapped around his neck and therefore he required special medical care. After the difficult delivery, he was kept at the hospital for an extended period. Valeriy had a healthy childhood without serious illnesses or hospitalizations, but he did have recurrent ear infections two to three times a year, which were treated with antibiotics (sulfonamide) and antiseptics.

Early Development

Valeriy's early development was characterized by delayed language development and some problems with fine motor coordination. He began speaking later than other children of his age; he did not speak his first words until he was 15 months old. He started to put words together to form sentences when he was three. Until the age of 4 years Valeriy often used syllables instead of words. He also had problems with visual orientation and coordination of finger movements. Valeriy did not start to draw or color pictures until the age of 5 because of difficulties holding pencils and crayons. He did not experience any problems with coordination or other physical development. In spite of Valeriy's language problems, he was a very communicative and social child. He enjoyed playing with other children and often communicated through gestures and facial expressions instead of words and phrases.

SCHOOL HISTORY

Kindergarten

When Valeriy was 3 years old, his mother realized that he needed special help for his developmental problems. He was referred for testing to a special committee, the Medical Psychological Pedagogical Commission (MPPC), which included teachers, doctors, speech therapists, and psychologists. They evaluated his auditory comprehension, phonemic awareness, and expressive and receptive language skills. He was also given a physical examination of the articulation organs. Valeriy was diagnosed as language delayed and subsequently placed in a kindergarten for children with speech problems. This kindergarten served only children with normal intelligence, eyesight, and hearing, who had problems with speech and language development. At this school Valeriy attended speech therapy sessions for development of his vocabulary and grammar, but he did not make sufficient progress. Valeriy's kindergarten teachers suggested his mother turn to a private speech therapist for help, because he needed individual sessions and more attention from a specialist. Valeriy attended kindergarten until midday. Three times per week the afternoons were devoted to remedial sessions with a private speech therapist. This therapist also helped to prepare Valeriy for the skills he would need in first grade. The additional therapy was effective as the private speech therapist coordinated her therapy with the speech remediation the child received in his kindergarten. As a result of this combined effort, Valeriy eventually showed progress regarding auditory discrimination and the acquisition of sound-letter correspondences.

In Russia kindergarten usually starts at the age of 3 and continues until the age of 6. The last year of kindergarten focuses on necessary skills for school success. This preparation includes lessons for the entire class as well as group lessons (i.e., dividing the class into two groups). During these studies the children receive primary grammar education, which usually required that children learn the alphabet and read short words. Although Valeriy had made some progress resulting from his speech therapy sessions it wasn't sufficient to meet the kindergarten requirements so he had to repeat the year. Thus, he was almost 8 years old by the time he entered first grade.

First Grade

When Valeriy started the first grade of the Orthodox School at the age of 7 years and 10 months, he immediately began to have difficulties in his studies. Though he intensively studied letters and their sounds at the therapy sessions in kindergarten, he had trouble with the identification of these at school. He also had problems with numbers and mathematical operations. He could not complete his homework without assistance from his mother or brothers. Because of these problems Valeriy was placed in a remedial class. The typical general education class size in Russia is approximately 25 to 30 pupils in contrast to the 8 to 12 students who are served in remedial classes.

In Russia remedial classes are offered in general education schools. In most schools, there are three typical classes and one remedial class. Children with difficulties in learning, adaptation and/or socialization and delayed speech and language development, are sent to such classes at the direction of the Medical Psychological Pedagogical Commission (MPPC). The curriculum in these remedial classes includes not only general educational content, but also remedial lessons. Usually teachers of these classes have special education training or are currently taking special courses. The remedial classes are only offered for a half-day so Valeriy was dismissed from school mid-day. Although he earned very low marks in first grade, he was promoted to the second grade.

Second Grade

At the age of 8 years and 10 months, Valeriy entered second grade where his difficulties with studies became even more pronounced. Valeriy did not understand the mathematical problems and began having problems with the formal Russian language curriculum. The teacher tried to help him, but she did not have enough experience or training to understand the problem of dyslexia. The teacher recommended that the mother take Valeriy to a special center that could address his problems or transfer to a special school for children with speech difficulties. The Centre of Science for Health of Children is an independent scientific medical organization that is under the supervision of the Russian Academy of Medical Sciences. The experts at this center provide diagnostic services for learning problems, consultation for the parents, and remedial classes. However Valeriy's mother ignored the teacher's advice as she believed that her son had been given all the help he needed.

At the end of the year Valeriy showed gains in math. He learned how to solve calculation problems, but still he could not solve mathematical problems that involved words or reasoning as he could not read the task properly and understand it.

Third Grade

After the second grade, Valeriy's remedial class was disbanded. Former students were sent to the Institution of Pediatrics for testing. Valeriy's cognitive potential was determined to be within normal limits, but his reading was significantly lower than expected. Thus, he was diagnosed as dyslexic. In Russia there are several techniques for assessing dyslexia, but measuring word recognition and comprehension are considered obligatory. Silent reading can also be investigated. Examination of word recognition focuses on the technical aspects of reading including speed, accuracy, and fluency for letters, words, word-combinations, and sentences. Valeriy's oral reading was slow and labored as he read syllable by syllable with numerous errors. Assessment of comprehension included both listening comprehension (independent summarizing of a text that was read to the child) and reading comprehension. Valeriy was given comprehension questions concerning the structure of the text, separate words and word-combinations, selection of synonyms to the word in the text, a choice of words used in the text, and the timing and sequence of events. As Valeriy experienced significant problems with word recognition and comprehension, he was diagnosed as having "combined dyslexia." The experts in this center explained to his mother that the term dyslexia was applied in situations when children with normal intelligence have problems with reading. As a result of this assessment and diagnosis, Valeriy was sent to a typical general education class for third grade and was provided with additional classes with a speech therapist for 45 minutes three times a week. He enjoyed the classes with the speech therapist. He particularly liked writing from dictation. These sessions helped Valeriy to become more successful in reading and comprehending text.

Though he still could not yet read as well as his classmates, he worked very hard. Valeriy's mother spent less time helping him with his homework. His general education teacher knew about his problems and tried to accommodate his special needs. Valeriy said that she was a strict but understanding teacher.

Fourth Grade

Fourth grade became the most successful in Valeriy's educational experience. The speech therapist continued to help him, delivering services on the same schedule. As a result, Valeriy seemed to become more successful with his studies. His mother reported that for the first time, he was able to complete his homework independently. He made considerable progress in math and has fewer problems with reading and writing. These improvements have helped to make Valeriy more self-confident; however, the mother noted that in spite of these improvements, he still has major problems in both reading and writing.

DYSLEXIA DIAGNOSIS AND TREATMENT ISSUES

Predisposition to dyslexia can be found before a child enters school with the help of special methods of testing and studying the early development of the child. In Russia, it is considered to be very important to monitor the development of early problems in speech and language as these may be precursors of later reading and writing problems (Inshakova, 2004). There are recognized neuropsychological and pedagogical methods that are widely accepted; however, these are not always used. Valeriy's case is an example of what typically occurs in the Russian system: before entering kindergarten he was tested by the MPPC and diagnosed with delayed language development predictive of later reading and writing problems. Thus, he was subsequently placed in a special school. Reading and writing problems can be found together or separate from each other. In Russia writing problems are much more common than reading problems with a ratio of 4:1. In Valeriy's case, he experienced both reading and writing problems.

Typically, dyslexia diagnosis in Russia is attempted at the end of second grade. This is considered to be an optimal time for two reasons. First, many children have delayed development of reading skills, but most of these disappear in the second grade. Secondly, in the first grade reading problems may not be detected due to successful correction at the speech treatment sessions in kindergarten and the minimal demands of the first-grade curriculum. The problems associated with dyslexia become evident when the curriculum imposes increased demands on the child.

Although the actual diagnosis of dyslexia is formally attempted at the end of second grade, the screening of possible problems begins in the first grade. Twice a year (in the beginning and in the end) the school speech therapist tests all the children. Children who are identified as having the most serious problems are then provided with speech therapy. Each therapist is limited to helping only 25 children per year, though there may be many more who need such assistance. In the four grades of the primary school there can be anywhere between 120 and 400 children. Valeriy did not receive this service in first and second grade because of the limited number of students who were accepted in this program.

The teacher in the special class in first grade tried to provide the necessary help for the child, but it was not enough. She did not provide individual sessions because she believed that the commonly used method was sufficient to resolve his reading problems. However, this was a misjudgment as this method was not effective for Valeriy's needs. Lessons in the special class helped him overcome dyscalculia, which is why this difficulty was not diagnosed. It was not until the third grade when Valeriy was sent to the Institution of Pediatrics that he began to receive effective reading instruction. This dyslexia correction technique was complex in nature. It included work on development of oral speech, memory, attention, thinking, representations of space and time, visual-motor coordination and reading accuracy. To address reading and writing, the "merge" method was used. Merge refers to a combination of a consonant and a following vowel. Thus, any Russian word can be divided into confluences that are small visual units such as бе-л-ка, и-г-ла, ра-ке-т-ка. The confluence method helps to organize visual perception as the child is marking the confluences with a pencil while reading a text passage independently. It appears that this method has been successful as Valeriy and his school therapist have been using it for the acquisition of writing and reading with good results.

In the Russian language there are 33 letters including 8 vowels, 23 consonants and 2 silent letters and 42 phonemes. The Russian orthography is relatively regular with a few exceptions (e.g. the hardening or softening of the preceding consonant by adding a silent grapheme). Russian morphology is highly complex with difficult conjugation and declension patterns. The majority of Russian words consist of two or three syllables of the CV or CVC structure but multiple consonant clusters like CCCCVC are also part of the Russian orthography. These combinations can be challenging, thus, even in the regular classroom the first two years are devoted to syllable reading and writing.

Additional complications are due to the fact that the spelling sometimes doesn't reflect the pronunciation of a word. In the Russian language the order of subject, verb and object is not as strict as in the English language (i.e., SPO) in the formation of a sentence. Therefore, the reader has to rely on inflectional endings and accuracy in decoding becomes vitally important for reading comprehension. Valeriy would have needed an intensive individualized remedial intervention from first grade on to be successful with the demands of his language, but this was not provided.

PARENT PERSPECTIVES

Valeriy's mother described him as a boy who is cheerful and kind. She reported that he has a special talent in the area of sports, particularly football and basketball. He enjoys the companionship of his brothers and playing with toy cars. Valeriy does not read at home unless he is doing his homework, but his mother reads to him about six to seven hours per week. He spends approximately two hours per week watching television, mostly cartoons and children's shows. Socially Valeriy does very well; he has lots of friends with whom he plays frequently. However, the mother noted that because of his language problems, he has some difficulty in these social situations when the children are discussing serious topics.

The mother described dyslexia as meaning "a child cannot read properly." She rated his dyslexia as being significant (8/10) on the Parent Perception Scale and feels that it has a major impact on school success, rating this problem 10/10. However, it is interesting to note that the mother is sure that his reading problems will not affect his future, believing he can achieve everything that he wants. She does not think that dyslexia seriously affects Valeriy's social life (rating this 2/10) or family life (3/10). In general, the mother expresses satisfaction with the progress her son has made in school and the help that has been provided. She feels that his teachers and speech therapists have provided both understanding and assistance. However, she would have preferred that her son had been given speech therapy in the first grade as a continuation of the services that he was given in kindergarten. The mother reported that there is a problem with a lack of specialists for dyslexia in the schools. And if she could change something about the treatment of dyslexia in Russia, there would be more Study Centers. In Russia these are special centers where children with speech, reading and writing problems can get necessary help, usually after school in addition to the school lessons, but there are currently not enough of these centers to serve all of the children who need this assistance.

Although Valeriy completes his homework independently, the mother reported that he makes a lot of mistakes because he does not understand the required tasks and he reads very slowly so it takes an excessive amount of time to finish the work. She believes that homework is a significant problem. It is also interesting to note that the mother reported that Valeriy's only fear was coming to school without his homework completed.

CHILD PERSPECTIVES

Valeriy has a rich social life and enjoys being with other children, especially with his two best friends. He said that his classmates always try to support him, but other responses indicated that he perceives his reading problems to have adversely affected some of his social experiences. Valeriy is keen on sports and plays both football and basketball so it is not surprising that his favorite subject in school is physical education. The boy has a good sense of humor, which was very obvious in this interview. But it was clear that problems with reading and writing upset him very much. However, his responses on the Child Perception Scale were very different from those of his mothers. Whereas his mother rated the significance of his reading problem to be very high, Valeriy rated it a 6/10. Valeriy reported that dyslexia has only a moderate influence on school success compared to his mother's perception that it greatly affects school achievement. And interestingly enough, the mother does not perceive dyslexia as an influential problem in his social life, but Valeriy apparently believes that it has a very significant impact on social experiences, rating it 10/10.

Valeriy's responses on the sentence completion activity revealed some of the stresses he faces in his school, family, and friendships. He enjoys school when the teacher talks about interesting things, but he does not like when he is asked to come to the blackboard and complete tasks in front of the class. He said that it is very difficult for him to read and summarize texts, and he is always happy "when it's a break" during the school day. Valeriy believes that his classmates think that he is a good friend, but his difficulties with language comprehension affect these relationships. He would like to have more support from his classmates. In his completion responses to "Sometimes kids make fun of me because . . ." he answered, "I asked a silly question." Many of his responses were related to his homework difficulties: "When I do my homework, I feel bad." He is often worried about his homework and would like to have more assistance from his parents. He also becomes angry when his brothers prevent him from doing his homework. But when he succeeds in doing some difficult tasks he is very happy and he knows that his mother is proud of him.

In the future Valeriy wants to be a paratrooper in the army. He thinks he would be good at this job as he is strong and he does not believe it would involve any reading. His favorite book is "Prehistoric Stories" and he enthusiastically speaks about the Stone Age. But when he was asked who reads to him, he got very confused and quickly answered, "no one." However, his mother indicated that she reads to her son every day. Valeriy's friends know about his reading problem and "they try to help me when I am reading." Although he is close to his brothers and they know he has dyslexia, they don't talk about it and Valeriy would prefer to keep it that way. He could not name the best reader in his class and said that all his classmates read well. He does not seem to understand how these students became such good readers. He is also unsure about the importance of learning to read. Throughout the interview Valeriy complained about the stresses of homework. His three wishes were to study well, to complete his homework faster and for nothing bad to happen to his family When asked to name three things that his teacher could do to help him with his dyslexia, he could only think of one thing: "to answer my questions." If he could change one thing about school, he would "ban the lessons of Russian." Valeriy does not have access to computers so he has not received assistance from this technology.

CASE COMMENTARY

The latest longitudinal research shows that dyslexia is divided into three types: semantic, technical and combined (Inshakova, Suhanova & Shashkina, 2009; Inshakova, 2008a; Inshakova, 2008b). Technical dyslexia is connected only with the problem of reading speed. Pupils who have this type of dyslexia cannot learn how to read fast in spite of the education that they receive during primary school. They understand the text, can retell it and answer all the questions. Children with semantic dyslexia can read fast from the first year of education but have problems with understanding of the given text. The most difficult type is combined dyslexia. Children with combined dyslexia cannot read fast and do not understand the given text. Valeriy has this type of dyslexia, which is one of the most typical for Russia.

Valeriy's problems in the acquisition of language were apparent even before he entered kindergarten. He spoke in syllables instead of whole words. Because of his mother's initiative he was evaluated by a committee of experts and then placed in a special kindergarten where he received assistance from a speech therapist. The curriculum in this special kindergarten included primary grammar education, which usually requires that children learn to identify letters of the alphabet and to read short words syllable-by-syllable before going to school. Additionally Valeriy went to see a private speech therapist who coordinated her program with the instruction he was given in kindergarten. It is interesting to note that Valeriy could not apply the skills he learned in kindergarten when he progressed to first grade. He immediately experienced problems in letter and sound identification. In Russia all dyslexics with normal intelligence study in schools of general education. Speech therapists, teachers, and parents do their best to help these children overcome their problems. Special correctional classes and Schools of Health are provided for such children. Here correctional studies are combined with the special healthcare environment. In Schools of Health children are given better nourishment, extra sport lessons, physician care, and lessons on sanitation. Valeriy did not go to a School of Health because his mother wanted him to stay at the Orthodox school, but he was transferred to the correctional class for first and second grade where there was half the number of children compared to the regular education class and where the curriculum was easier. Although Valeriy was in a special class the program of the second grade was complicated for him and he could not cope with the tasks. The teacher's method was not geared to his reading and writing problems, which is why Valeriy did not improve. If he had been diagnosed earlier or if his mother had followed the teacher's advice and sent him to the Center of Science for the Health of Children for a consultation, he may have done better. After he was diagnosed as dyslexic he was sent to the sessions of the school speech therapist. The speech therapist's method included correction of reading, writing and speaking problems in the group of four to five pupils. The sessions were regular (three times a week for two years). Valeriy improved his reading and writing skills but was still not performing at grade level. As Valeriy was able to identify letters and sounds at the end of kindergarten, but not in the beginning of first grade it would have been important to continue with speech therapy lessons in first and second grade to establish a sound knowledge in phonics to aid his reading acquisition process. Instead he received regular reading instruction in a remedial classroom which was not sufficient. In order to help children like Valeriy it is important that teachers who offer remedial work are qualified to recognize reading and writing disorders and are educated in using appropriate methods of treatment.

REFERENCES

Inshakova, O.B. (2004). Problems of dyslexia in Russia. In I. Smythe, J. Everatt and R. Salter (Eds.), *International book of dyslexia* (pp. 173–178). West Sussex, England: John Wiley & Sons.

Inshakova, O.B. (2008a). Различные типы дислексии и их взаимосвязь с нарушениями речевого развития у младших школьников [Various types of dyslexia and their interrelation with infringements of speech development in younger pupils]. *The Bulletin Kostroma: The State University of N.A.Nekrasov*, (4), 190–196.

Inshakova, O.B. (2008b). Динамика Овладения технической и смысловой сторонами чтения школьников [Dynamics of mastering technical and semantic parts of the reading of pupils]. *News of the Russian State Pedagogical University of A.I.Herzen*, 38 (82), 64–68.

Inshakova, O. B., Suhanova A.G., & Shashkina L.I. (2009). Взаимосвязь различных типов дислексии с нарушениями зрительного и речевого развития школьников [Interrelation of various types of dyslexia with infringements of visual and speech development of pupils]. Materials for international conferences of the Russian Association of Dyslexia-M., 64–69.

VALERIY'S INTERVIEW

1. What do you want to be when you grow up?
    Paratrooper.
   Why do you think you would be good at that job?
    Because I am strong.

2. Tell me about a teacher who has been really important to you or one who has helped you: what did the teacher do to help you?
    My class mistress helps me to speak properly.

3. Tell me about a teacher who didn't really help you that much or one who did not give you the help you needed. What did you want the teacher to do to help you?
    They all helped me and I want that the teacher answers my questions.

4. Tell me what your mother thinks about your dyslexia. Does she talk to you about the problem?
    Yes.

   What does she say?
    Be attentive when you read and do not be afraid.

5. Tell me what your father thinks about your dyslexia. Does he talk to you about the problem?
    No.

   What does he say?
    I don't know. My father doesn't live with us.

6. Tell me about something that makes you really happy.
    Playing games and going in for sport.

7. Tell me about something that makes you really sad.
    A lot of homework.

8. When the work gets very hard at school and you think you can't do it, what do you do?
    I ask my classmates to help.

9. What kinds of books do you like to read?
    About the Stone Age.

   What is your favorite book?
    Prehistoric stories.

   Do you read to yourself?
    Yes.

   Who else reads to you?
    No one. [seemed very confused]

10. Do your friends know that you have dyslexia?
    Yes.

   Do you talk to them about it?
    No.

   What do you say? What do your friends say to you about dyslexia?
    They try to help me when I am reading.

11. Do your siblings know that you have dyslexia?
    Yes.

   Do you talk to them about it?
    No, I don't want them to know.

   What do your siblings say to you about dyslexia?
    They don't talk about it.

12. Name three things you are really good at:
    Playing sport, games, writing.

13. Name three things you are not so good at:
    English, retelling. [he could not name the third thing]

14. If you are feeling bad about your reading, is there one person you can talk to who makes you feel better?
    Classmate.

    What does that person say to you?
    Give me a piece of advice.

15. Do computers help you with your reading?
    No, I don't have one.

16. Do you usually have problems with your homework?
    Sometimes.

    Can you do your homework independently or does someone help you?
    My brother helps me.

    Is homework a big problem or just a little one?
    It's very difficult.

17. If there was one thing you could change about school, what would it be?
    I would ban lessons of Russian.

18. If you could have three wishes, what would they be?
    Study well.
    Make my homework faster.
    Nothing bad to happen to my family.

19. Tell me three things you would like your teacher to do to help you with your dyslexia.
    To answer my questions.

20. Who is the best reader in your class?
    All my classmates read well.

    How did he/she get to be such a good reader?
    I don't know.

21. Is it important to learn how to read?
    Maybe.

    Why or why not?
    Because my mother says so.

18 Jim, a Case Study of Dyslexia in the United States

Peggy L. Anderson

Jim is an 11-year-old child who was diagnosed with a reading disability at the age of 7. It was easy to establish rapport with this child who was highly verbal and responsive to the interview process. He was also very energetic, frequently leaving his chair to walk around throughout the questioning.

BACKGROUND

Family History

Jim was born in a Colorado mountain community where he lived with his family until he moved to Denver two years ago. He currently lives with his younger brother and parents in a middle-class suburb. His father owns a retail ski shop in the mountain community and makes the 95-mile commute several times a week. His mother is a homemaker. Both parents have bachelor's degrees and neither experienced any learning problems. However, other family members on both sides of the family have had reading difficulties. The paternal grandfather, who is now 68, reported that he had dyslexia and was retained in first grade. The mother's brother had expressive language difficulties and reading problems that affected his school achievement. Jim also has a cousin who was diagnosed with a reading disability.

Medical History

The mother reported that there were no complications associated with her pregnancy or Jim's birth. He did not experience any significant illnesses nor has he had any serious accidents. His hearing and visual acuity are normal, but Jim experienced visual tracking problems for which he had two years of therapy that did not produce benefits, according to the mother's report. He currently takes Zoloft (50 mg.) daily for generalized anxiety problems.

Early Development

Jim did not have any problems achieving language milestones. He spoke early (9 months), and quickly began to put words together to form sentences. He was talkative with clear speech. Although he walked at 13 months and learned to ride a bike at 6 years, his mother noted that gross motor activities were always challenging for him. Jim also experienced some fine motor problems; he never liked to color or draw as these were difficult for him.

No feeding problems were present until the age of 3 when Jim began to restrict his diet. Gradually he stopped eating all foods until it came to the point that he would eat only bread and peanut butter. Crying problems were present from an early age and increased as he grew. It was difficult for the parents to determine the cause of his excessive crying. For example, at his 4th birthday party, he fell off his bike and could not stop crying. The crying was unrelated to any injury, but rather seemed to be associated in some nonspecific way to the party commotion. Even though their pediatrician had frequently told them not to worry, they decided to seek a psychiatric evaluation at a university-affiliated medical center where Jim was subsequently diagnosed as having a generalized anxiety disorder at the age of 5. Play therapy was recommended for treatment. This therapy continued for three years, but the parents decided that it was insufficient for his problems so Jim began to take medication (Zoloft), which they believe has been very beneficial.

In addition to Jim's crying and eating challenges, he also experienced some tactile issues. From an early age, he complained that certain clothing and shoes "felt funny." These problems were fairly significant and prompted the mother to obtain sensory motor integration therapy for him, which lasted for five years (from age 4 to 9). The mother believes that this therapy was beneficial for his tactile defensiveness and excessive crying as well as his self-imposed dietary restrictions. While Jim is still a "picky eater," he now enjoys a much wider variety of foods.

SCHOOL HISTORY

Preschool

Jim began preschool at the age of 3 years for two days a week. Preschool focused on socialization, language, and motor development as well as early academic activities. He experienced some difficulties with socialization that were mainly related to sensory overload when there were too many children around. For example, he had some problems with circle time because of interpersonal spatial needs (he often sat on a chair at the periphery of the circle instead of on the floor with the other children). The academic activities centered on learning the names of the letters and associated sounds.

Learning to write one's name was also expected. During the three years of preschool, Jim was not able to attain these skills. Socially the mother reported that he got along fairly well with the other children. She received occasional calls from the teachers about "hitting," but did not perceive these to be significant.

Kindergarten

When Jim started kindergarten at the age of 6, his mother indicated that "he wasn't out of the norm for expectations." However, at the beginning of the year, the mother requested a meeting with the teacher as she anticipated that he would have problems. She told the teacher that Jim was behind in his achievement, but the teacher was unconcerned and suggested that they "wait and see." In January, he was placed on an Individual Literacy Plan (ILP), which provides extra support for students in general education who experience reading problems. This ILP involved pull-out services (i.e., the child is taken out of the classroom and provided with supplementary instruction on a one-to-one or small group basis) that focused on learning letter sounds. Jim did not object to leaving the classroom for these services. The mother saw limited improvement that she described as proceeding at a "snail's pace." He experienced some socialization problems that seemed to be related to his need for defined personal space. In February, it was determined that Jim had not made sufficient progress and the school initiated a full evaluation with referral reasons as follows: "[Jim] has exhibited unusual behaviors in class, including little or no eye contact, self-stimulation, high anxiety, overt concern for a large amount of personal space, slight aggression when angry, difficulty with associating letter names, sounds and form, spatial awareness and perception, weak fine motor skills" as well as achievement scores that indicated severe needs.

The school team completed a comprehensive assessment that included evaluations from the special educator, the speech/language therapist, and the school psychologist. The results of the psychological evaluation revealed that Jim's intelligence as measured by the Wechsler Intelligence Scales for Children-IV (WISC-IV; Wechsler, 2003) fell in the average range. The psychologist estimated his full scale IQ to be 102; he did not give the actual full scale as there was significant variation between the index scores, which would have adversely affected the total score. His Verbal Comprehension Index fell in the high average range (standard score of 112), but his visual Processing Speed Index fell into the low average range (standard score of 83). The psychologist noted that Jim demonstrated strength in the areas of verbal and reasoning comprehension and weakness in visual motor processing speed. The speech and language report revealed strong expressive and receptive language skills, but noted a need to develop pragmatic and social skills, particularly with regard to increasing eye contact. The special educator administered the Woodcock Johnson Tests of Achievement III (W-J

III; Woodcock, Schrank, Mather & McGrew, 2007), which showed that Jim scored below expectancy in academic skills (18th percentile rank) compared to his math skills (27th percentile rank) and his oral language skills (70th percentile rank). He was also given the Test of Early Reading Ability-Third Edition (Reid, Hresko & Hammill, 2002), which placed him at the 1st percentile. Based on the results of his assessment, Jim was diagnosed as having a specific learning disability in the area of reading. An individual educational plan (IEP) was developed to meet his instructional needs for reading and writing. His IEP stated that he would receive resource support for two hours per week in addition to one hour of supplementary support in the classroom. His general education teacher would also receive 30 minutes of consultation from specialists to help her provide appropriate support for Jim. These services commenced immediately.

First Grade

The mother reported that this school year was a satisfactory experience for Jim as he had a "really good teacher who was a good combination of a mother figure and a teacher." Even though Jim was pulled out for remedial reading, he did not perceive himself to be different. The children in this class demonstrated a wide variety of academic and social abilities. Thus, in a classroom situation of this type, Jim's reading difficulties were perceived as just another variation. This first-grade classroom was somewhat calmer than his kindergarten experience so the mother felt that Jim was doing "okay" socially. At the end of the school year, the teacher reported that Jim was still behind the other children in reading, but she was pleased with his progress and his effort. The teacher recommended summer tutoring for two to three hours a week so he would continue to improve. The mother complied with this recommendation, but she is uncertain if it had any effect.

Second Grade

At the age of 8, Jim started second grade, which turned out to be the worst school year thus far. The mother described the teacher as "young and well-meaning," but not having "a lot of empathy for kids who were struggling." In this teacher's classroom, Jim became very aware that he "wasn't measuring up" and began acting out. He started aligning himself with children who were frequently in trouble, and began talking back to the teacher and becoming oppositional. After two months into the school year, Jim told his parents that he hated school and didn't want to attend any longer. His anxiety seemed controlled by the medication he was taking, but he started having attentional problems in addition to his behavioral difficulties. The special educator at the school told the parents that the attentional difficulties were most likely related to sensory integration problems. His difficulties with visual motor processing made writing tasks increasingly difficult. The mother reported that although Jim was receiving a lot of support from the school, his reading progress continued to be very slow and his "self-esteem was getting put through the wringer." She thought to herself "if this continues, he'll never get anywhere." Homework was also an enormous struggle, generally ending in tears. Because of his weak reading and handwriting skills, a single worksheet could become a seemingly insurmountable hurdle that caused exhaustion and frustration. He worked an hour and a half most evenings to keep up. The mother was somewhat perplexed that no one at school considered the homework expectations in light of Jim's problems. He was required to do the same work as the other children, who probably completed the tasks in 15 to 20 minutes.

At this point, the parents began to discuss possible solutions. One of the therapists who had worked with Jim in the past had recommended a private school for children with learning differences/disabilities in Denver. This private school provided expertise for a student population with average to above average potential and learning differences, such as dyslexia or ADHD, or nontraditional learning styles. Although this school had an excellent reputation for meeting the needs of students with dyslexia, it was located 95 miles from their home. This seemed like a drastic step, but the family was willing to investigate all possibilities so they visited the school. They spent the day observing classrooms and talking with teachers and administrators. The visit convinced the parents that this private school would be a preferable alternative, but they left the decision largely up to Jim, who decided in favor of the transfer.

As part of the application process for the new school, Jim was required to have another psychoeducational evaluation. He was once again given the WISC-IV (Wechsler, 2003), which identified the same pattern of strength in verbal comprehension (standard score of 106) and weakness in processing speed (standard score of 80) that was noted in kindergarten. The W-J III Tests of Achievement (Woodcock et al., 2007) were also repeated, revealing continued weakness in reading (Broad Reading Cluster Score 4th percentile) and growth in mathematics (Broad Math Cluster Score 48th percentile).

Third Grade

The decision to move Jim to the new school created all sorts of family challenges. The parents decided against selling their home and moving the entire family until they knew for certain that the private school was a good match for Jim. The grandparents agreed to move to the mountain community and take care of Jim's younger brother while the mother and Jim moved into an apartment in Denver. The father spent half of his time in Denver and the other at home in the mountain community.

As it turned out, the family's decision to change schools was a good one. Almost immediately Jim began to do better in school. The mother said "it seemed like the greatest thing in the world." He had two teachers, both of whom he liked, and he made friends right away. The curriculum at the private school was specifically tailored for his needs and he was supported with increased individualized attention. His reading program, the F.A.S.T. Reading System (Tattum, 1998), used a multi-sensory approach that focused on auditory processing, phonics and literature-based instruction that was aligned with the National Reading Panel's (2000) five essential components of reading instruction (i.e., phonemic awareness, phonics, vocabulary, comprehension, and fluency). In addition, the homework demands dramatically decreased. Jim was given the same amount and type of homework every night so the parents knew what to expect. He had approximately 20 minutes of homework and an additional 20 minutes of reading on a daily basis.

At the end of the school year, the parents felt Jim had made improvement in reading, but perhaps less in writing. They were favorably impressed with the school. Jim's self-esteem had definitely improved and he wanted to return for the following year.

Fourth Grade

Jim is currently in fourth grade at the private school and is continuing to make slow, but steady progress in both reading and writing. Although the mother recognizes that he is still behind in reading, she feels like "he is in a good place" and is pleased with his progress. She believes he is benefiting enormously from the individualized attention that the private school is providing, but she has realistic expectations for her child. The private school offers a K–12 program so Jim will be able to continue until he graduates from high school, which is his desire. He does not want to return to the public school setting and his parents are in agreement. Although the family is still split between two separate communities, they are committed to arranging their lives so that Jim can be in the best educational setting possible.

DYSLEXIA DIAGNOSIS AND TREATMENT ISSUES

In the United States, federal law (i.e., Individuals with Disabilities Education Act) mandates a free and appropriate education for all students with disabilities in the public school system. While in some countries dyslexia is considered a learning difference, in the United States it is a disability that is covered under the special education category of specific learning disabilities (SLD). The Individuals with Disabilities Act (IDEA) requires particular evaluation procedures to meet eligibility requirements for all disabilities. However, individual states and local education agencies (LEA) are allowed to interpret these rules and regulations within certain parameters. Prior to the 2004 reauthorization of IDEA, all states were mandated to use the discrepancy definition for identification of learning disabilities, requiring a significant discrepancy between ability and achievement in one or more of seven areas (i.e, oral expression, listening comprehension, written expression, basic reading skill, reading comprehension, math calculation, or math reasoning) (USOE, 1977). Originally the USOE (1976) had proposed that a severe discrepancy must be documented by achievement in one or more areas falling below "50% of the child's expected achievement level, when age and previous educational experiences are taken into account" (USOE, 1976, p. 52405). However, due to considerable objection by the public, including parent advocacy groups, the formula was deleted from the regulations and individual states were given the authority to develop their own discrepancy criteria for SLD eligibility. When IDEA was reauthorized in 2004, the government changed its position, requiring States to permit the use of response to intervention (RTI) or other alternative research-based procedures for identifying learning disabilities. The law allows States to continue to use the discrepancy definition, but it can no longer be required. In Colorado, new State regulations have been developed to adopt the exclusive use of the RTI model for evaluation of students with SLD. Thus, use of the discrepancy formula was prohibited after 2009 (Colorado Department of Education, 2008).

The discrepancy formula was used in Jim's case as he was diagnosed before the new Colorado regulations were implemented. As demonstrated by the evaluation data, Jim's profile was a "textbook" case that could be construed as support for the validity of this method for children like him. Kavale (2002) as well as others have suggested that the discrepancy formula should not be eliminated as it is a legitimate and psychometrically defensible method for identification that helps to define the SLD construct. Nevertheless, Colorado and seven other states of the 50 have chosen to do so (Zirkel & Thomas, 2010). One of those criticisms lodged against the discrepancy criterion, which has particular bearing on this case, concerns the premise that young children in lower grades have a difficult time meeting the criteria because there is insufficient reading required at that early level (Hallahan, Kaufman & Pullen, 2009). Such was not the case for Jim whose reading quotient on the Test of Early Reading Ability-Third Edition (standard score of 66) was 36 points below his estimated full scale WISC-IV quotient of 102. Thus, he easily met the eligibility requirements of the discrepancy definition at the age of 6, enabling him to access special education services to support his reading needs, which may or may not have happened with the RTI model. While some researchers have suggested that the IQ-achievement discrepancy approach is a "wait to fail" model (Lyon & Fletcher, 2001) as young children cannot be reliably measured until the age of 9, this was not the situation for Jim, who may have been an exception. In spite of the criticism against the discrepancy definition (Fletcher et al., 2002), many professionals have advocated for its continued use in addition to other methods of evaluation (Scruggs & Mastropieri, 2002). In any case, overreliance on intelligence testing for purposes of fulfilling the discrepancy model requirements seems ill advised and the role of intelligence testing for identification of children with dyslexia has been questioned (Vellutino, Fletcher, Snowling & Scanlon, 2004). Certainly helpful information may be obtained from an IQ test regarding a child's verbal and visual-motor performance, but unfortunately this data is rarely used for those purposes. And in Jim's case, it would be difficult to defend why professionals required three administrations of the Wechsler Scales over a four-year period (note: he was give his first Wechsler when he was diagnosed with generalized anxiety at the age of 5).

In examining Jim's school records and interviewing the mother, it would appear that this child was very carefully monitored by the public school. The mother informed the kindergarten teacher of her concerns in the beginning of the school year, and by January the school had agreed to begin the evaluation process. Although the mother had wanted the school to move more quickly as she strongly felt that Jim had a learning disability that was "not magically going to get better," it would be hard to fault the kindergarten teacher for waiting a semester to observe the child. The school conducted a comprehensive evaluation of Jim that included input from a variety of relevant disciplines with full reports that were shared with the family. Throughout the process everyone involved appeared to be extremely conscientious about meeting designated responsibilities.

Following the evaluation and identification of his needs, an IEP was developed to address specific reading and writing difficulties. The school immediately implemented the plan, as opposed to waiting until the beginning of the following school year, which unfortunately often happens in the United States. The support plan included pull-out remediation, supplementary in-class instruction, and teacher consultation, all of which seemed very appropriate for Jim's needs. While this combination of services seemed to be ideal, Jim did not make progress. The instructional approach itself may not have been a good match for Jim or intensity may have been insufficient, but since the specific intervention is not listed on Jim's IEP and the mother is unsure, it is not possible to evaluate the remediation. However, it is clear that effective early remediation must include intervention that provides explicit emphasis on phonological processing and alphabetic instruction with sufficient intensity (Torgesen, 2002). The fact that Jim's performance on the WJ-III Letter-Word identification subtest at the end of kindergarten placed him at the 18th percentile compared to the results of retesting at the end of second grade, which placed him at the 6th percentile is concerning. It is not surprising that the mother decided to seek a different educational setting. Even when everything seems to have been put into place for a child, conventional special education often fails to achieve the desired results (Hanushek, Kain, & Riukin, 1998; Swanson, 2008). As there have been no standardized test scores since Jim started the private school, recent progress cannot be verified, but both the mother and Jim have a strong sense that he has made significant strides. It is possible that he has greatly benefitted from the multisensory reading program at the new school, and that it has been implemented with significant intensity to bring about positive results. Also the private school's requirement of 20 minutes of reading five times per week could bring about increased achievement (Anderson, Wilson, & Fielding, 1988), but Jim is sometimes resistant to practice because it is not enjoyable. Like other children with significant word-level reading problems, he reads slowly with many errors and admits to frequent guessing because he wants to "get it over with." As Schatschneider and Torgesen (2004) observed, this common pattern of inaccurate reading and diminished practice can result in slow growth in sight word vocabulary.

PARENT PERSPECTIVES

The mother described her son as "kind, smart, strong-willed, and caring with a good sense of humor." Although Jim has had behavioral problems associated with his anxiety since early childhood followed by academic problems, his mother perceives his strengths to outweigh his challenges. She noted that he is particularly good at conceptual math and surprisingly introspective. And even though he doesn't like to read, he is very adept at using all sorts of compensatory skills to comprehend text when he is highly motivated (e.g., when he is shopping online). He watches little television (an hour or less a week), and when he does, it's usually as a social event.

In spite of all the challenges Jim has faced with his reading, she perceives this to be a moderate problem (6/10 on the Perception Scale) that has exerted a moderate influence on his school success (4/10). It appeared that her perceptions may have been related to the fact that Jim is now in a school that is meeting his needs so his problem has been minimized. Even though addressing Jim's needs has necessitated family separation and a major move, she perceives Jim's problem to have affected family life only minimally (3/10). Likewise she believes his social life has been affected very minimally (2/10). Yet, at the same time, she is very aware of how his need for personal space can sometimes create problems with other children.

In general, the mother believes that the U.S. has adequate laws and regulations for meeting the needs of students with dyslexia, but the problem seems to be in the implementation. With the current system, she does not think that it is possible to provide the necessary remediation to achieve significant progress. She does not hold any grudges against the public school system; she noted that all of Jim's teachers have helped him, but "it just wasn't enough." When she reflects on the disparity between Jim's private school and the public school, she has observed a number of differences. In the private school there is an emphasis on patience, individualized attention, and recognition that every child wants to succeed whereas in the public school there seems to be a lack of understanding of individual differences, which encourages teachers to judge all children by inflexible standards.

The mother believes that the culture of the public school doesn't promote a valuing of differences; instead children are made to feel that something is wrong with them if they are different. When she talked about the family's challenges to secure an appropriate education for Jim, she raised the question, "in a perfect world, we wouldn't be forced to choose and sacrifice, but how do you change the public school system?" And then she realistically identified problems that would be involved in attempting to do this (e.g., the lost remedial time waiting for more appropriate or more intensive support). In the end, it seemed preferable to move Jim to the private school and pay for the expensive private school tuition.

The mother is now satisfied with the progress her son is making in reading and his more positive social/emotional situation. She noted that he no longer cries when he reads and is able to do his homework without major problems. Yet she is very realistic about the future as she knows there is a long road ahead for Jim. She is confident that he will be able to successfully complete college with support, but she understands that his professional choices may be limited by his disability.

CHILD PERSPECTIVES

Jim is a loquacious child who demonstrated enthusiasm for a variety of interests. He wants to be a fighter pilot when he grows up because he likes "being up in the air." This professional aspiration is consistent with his strengths in technical areas; he reported that he is very good at the use of computers, cameras, and fixing electronics. It is also interesting to note that Jim mentioned he would not be a good interior designer because of his spatial difficulties, which is rather insightful for an 11-year-old.

Many of Jim's perceptions of his reading disability are referenced to his different school experiences: he discusses his feelings in terms of before (at the public school) and after (at the private school). Currently his school is meeting his needs with sufficient remedial support, thus he perceives his reading problems to be of minimal significance (3/10). At his previous school, he thought his reading problem exerted significant influence on his school success (7/10), but at his present school, it has minimal influence (he asked if he could mark 1.5 instead of 1 or 2). Throughout his interview he frequently referred to his negative experiences at the public school. For example, although homework is still "the worst thing about school," at the public school it presented a huge challenge whereas now it is "just a little one."

Socially, Jim seems to be doing somewhat better, particularly considering the problems he experiences with anxiety and interpersonal space. He reported that his reading disability had little to no impact on his social life (1/10). He has several friends at his new school and believes other children like him, but he wishes they would pay more attention to him. Many of his interview responses reflected an underlying current of social difficulties. He frequently referred to having been unfairly blamed by teachers, classmates, and his brother. Jim also mentioned concerns about others teasing him for his reading problem, particularly at his previous school. His perception that his social life is not impacted by his reading problems seems somewhat inconsistent with his actual experiences.

Jim and his family are very close and he perceives his reading problems to have had little or no impact on family life (1/10), but his responses reveal that he may be minimizing this influence because of the strong support provided at home. When he is feeling bad about his reading, he goes to his mother for consolation as she encourages him to believe in himself and keep trying. His parents take turns reading with him, but he prefers reading with his mother as he finds her more supportive. Reading with his father is sometimes stressful. Jim worries that his problems make his father's "life harder when we get into fights about reading" and "maybe the fighting kind of makes him depressed." He imagines that his father might be asking himself "why did this have to happen?" When Jim senses his father's frustration, he becomes tense and asks himself "why do I have to be like this?" Jim does not talk about his reading problems with his brother as he doesn't want him to begin teasing him. When his brother asked him why he went to a special school, Jim replied "that's kind of personal."

Jim does not read for pleasure, but he enjoys having others read to him. He reported that he does not read independently unless he is on the computer searching for information related to a product he wants to purchase (e.g., an application for his Ipod Touch). He clearly knows the importance of learning to read and understands that more reading is likely to bring improvement, and yet, it is so difficult for him that he tries to avoid it whenever possible. Jim has faced academic challenges for a number of years now and he easily identified factors that would improve his performance. Throughout the interview he expressed the wish that all teachers could demonstrate more patience and provide extra help, critical variables that he needs to be successful in the classroom. Of all of the teachers he has had in the past, he named his current teacher at the private school as the best because "she's really patient" and gives him the help he needs. Teachers who are not supportive are those who "yell" and "scream" if he forgets something or fails to fulfill other expectations. And, as with all children, he feels very happy when someone at school tells him he has done a "good job."

CASE COMMENTARY

Neither of Jim's parents had reading problems, but it is not surprising that there were other family members on both sides (i.e., the paternal grandfather, a maternal uncle, and a cousin) who were affected. The heritability of dyslexia was informally observed over 100 years ago (Hinshelwood, 1907) and formally documented for the first time over 50 years ago by Hallgren (1950). Since this historic research, there has been a steady stream of scholarly work that has strengthened understanding of the strong relationship between genetics and reading disabilities.

Jim's excessive crying, self-imposed dietary restrictions and tactile defensiveness in early childhood were signs that he was facing psychological challenges before he began to have reading problems. There is strong evidence to suggest that reading disabilities are comorbid with a variety of other conditions, the strongest link connecting dyslexia with ADHD (Maughan & Carroll, 2006). Usually when anxiety is observed in dyslexic children it is the result of challenges associated with the reading problem, which can result in depression and diminished self-concept. Thus, literacy problems constitute a risk factor for both generalized anxiety and school-related anxiety (Carroll, Maughan, Goodman & Meltzer, 2004), but there is insufficient research at this time to suggest that anxiety and dyslexia are biologically linked. There is a relationship between Jim's anxiety and his problems with sensory motor integration. His anxiety, in part, appears to be related to over-arousal that is triggered by crowded, noisy situations, such as those that occur at school or other social events, resulting in agitation and aggression, which are common reactions for children facing sensory processing dysfunction (Eide, 2003). In spite of the sensory motor integration therapy he has received, these problems continue to plague Jim.

Jim was identified in kindergarten and provided with special education support to address his reading, but he did not make the anticipated progress and may actually have been losing ground. Research has demonstrated that early intervention and intensive remediation, at least with regard to experimental research, has resulted in strong gains for most at-risk students at the beginning of their school years (Torgesen, 2000). In his review of intervention studies, Torgesen found that although the rate of success varied, 50% or more of these students made appreciable gains (close to normal growth), yet 2 to 6% did not. He concluded that knowing "what kind of instruction is most effective is not the same thing as knowing how much of that instruction, delivered under what conditions" (p. 63) will lead to adequate reading development. Early intervention for Jim began at the age of 6, but with little apparent benefit. It could be suggested that all of the time and energy expended for his testing may well have been better spent on the development of his remedial program. As Vellutino et al., (2004) recommended, priorities need to be shifted from attention to psychometric activities to the complex challenges of instruction and remediation. All children with reading problems should be provided with programs that reflect best practices to achieve gains instead of the inadequate or inconsistent intervention that many have received in special education programs (Hanushek et al., 1998; Swanson, 2008). In fact, as Torgesen (2005) commented, one of the greatest challenges is to obtain high quality intervention for all children. It is a source of pride that the U.S. has had federal and state laws mandating services for all children with reading disabilities for over 30 years, yet it is disconcerting to contemplate the strong possibility that these efforts have not substantially helped the children for whom they were designed. Over the course of time, there has been a growing concern that the special education system may be seriously flawed.

If the system isn't working as it should, public schools and higher education must both shoulder responsibility. Those responsible for preservice education should be producing teachers who have the knowledge and expertise to generate significant gains in the children they serve. This responsibility must be shared by general educators as well as special educators. As Jim's mother noted, she did not feel that teachers were aware of student's individual differences, a sentiment voiced by Lyon et al. (2001) who noted that teachers are often not trained "to address individual learning differences in general and specifically are not prepared to teach reading to students" (p. 280) with a wide range of abilities, which was this mother's concern. It is hoped that the RTI movement will provide benefit to both general and special educators by promoting a partnership of shared responsibility for students with reading disability. In any event, teacher preparation programs must emphasize the current knowledge base of reading research and provide sufficient practical experiences to prepare candidates for the challenges that await them in the classroom. Public schools must then support these teachers with ongoing inservice education to keep them highly trained so they can achieve consistent results with the children they serve.

Finally, it is noteworthy to comment on this family's commitment to secure an appropriate education for their child. When they came to realize that special education was an empty promise, they "moved mountains" to secure the help their child needed. While it is gratifying to consider this outcome with optimism, at the same time, it is difficult to ignore the fate of other children similar to Jim whose families do not have the education or means to obtain this assistance.

REFERENCES

Anderson, R.O., Wilson, P.T., & Fielding, I.G. (1988). Growth in reading and how children spend their time outside school. *Reading Research Quarterly, 23*, 285–303.

Carroll, J., Maugham, B., Goodman, R., & Meltzer, H. (2005). Literacy difficulties and psychiatric disorders: evidence of comorbidity. *Journal of Child Psychology & Psychiatry, 46*, 524–532. doi: 10.1111/j.1469–7610.2004.00366.x

Colorado Department of Education (2008). Guidelines for identifying students with specific learning disabilities. Retrieved from http://www.cde.state.co.us/cdesped/download/pdf/SLD_Guidelines.pdf

Eide, F. (2003). Sensory motor integration-current concepts and implications. *Sensory Integration Special Interest Section Quarterly, 26* (3), 1–5.

Fletcher, J.M., Lyon, G.R., Barnes, M., Stuebing, K.K., Francis, D.J., Olson, R.K., Shaywitz, S.E., & Shaywitz, B.A. (2002). Classification of learning disabilities: An evidenced-based evaluation. In R. Bradley, L. Danielson, & D.P. Hallahan (Eds.), *Identification of learning disabilities: Research to practice* (pp. 185–250). Mahwah, NJ: Lawrence Erlbaum Associates.

Hallahan, D.P., Kauffman, J.M., & Pullen, P.C. (2009). *Exceptional learners: an introduction to special education (11th ed.)* Boston: Allyn & Bacon.

Hallgren, B. (1950). Specific dyslexia (congenital word-blindness): A clinical and genetic study. *Acta Psychiatrica et Neurologica*, 65 (Suppl.), 1–287.

Hanushek, E.A., Kain, J.F., & Riukin, S.G. (1998). *Does special education raise academic achievement for students with disabilities?* National Bureau of Economic Research Working Paper No. 6469.

Hinshelwood, J. (1907). Four cases of congenital word-blindness occurring in the same family. *British Medical Journal*, 2, 1229–1232.

Individuals with Disabilities Education Improvement Act of 2004 (IDEA), Pub.L.No.108–446, 118 Stat. 2647 (2004), [Amending 20 U.S.C. § § 1400 et seq.].

Kavale, K.A. (2002). Discrepancy models in the identification of learning disability. In R. Bradley, L. Danielson, & Daniel Hallahan (Eds.), *Identification of learning disabilities: Research to practice.* Mahwah, NJ: Lawrence Erlbaum Associates.

Lyon, G.R., Fletcher, J.M., Shaywitz, S.E., Shaywitz, B.A., Torgesen, J.K., Wood, F.B., Schulte, A., & Olson, R. (2001). Rethinking learning disabilities. In C.E. Finn, Jr., A.J. Rotherham, & C.R. Hokanson, Jr. (Eds.), *Rethinking special education for a new century* (pp. 250–287). Washington, DC: Progressive Policy Institute & The Thomas B. Fordham Foundation.

Lyon, G.R., & Fletcher, J.M. (2001). Early warning system. *Education Next, 1(2)*, 23–29. Retrieved from www.educationnext.org/20012/22.html

Maughan, B., & Carroll, J. (2006). Literacy and mental disorders. *Current Opinion in Psychiatry*, 19, 350–354. doi: 10.1097/01.yco.0000228752.79990.41

National Institute of Child Health and Human Development. (2000). Report of the National Reading Panel. *Teaching children to read: An evidence-based assessment of the scientific research literature on reading and its implications for reading instruction* (NIH Publication No. 00–4769). Washington, DC: U.S. Government Printing Office.

Reid, D., Hresko, W., & Hammill, D. (2002). *Test of Early Reading Ability (third edition).* Austin, TX: PROED.

Schatschneider, C., & Torgesen, J.K. (2004). Using our current understanding of dyslexia to support early identification and intervention. *Journal of Child Neurology*, 19, 759–765.

Scruggs, T.E., & Mastropieri, M.A. (2002). On babies and bathwater: Addressing the problems of identification of learning disabilities. *Learning Disability Quarterly*, 25, 155–168.

Swanson, E. (2008). Observing reading instruction for students with learning disabilities: A synthesis. *Learning Disability Quarterly*, 31(3), 115–133.

Tattum, S. (1998). *F.A.S.T. reading system.* Denver: F.A.S.T. Learning.

Torgesen, J.K. (2000). Individual differences in response to early interventions in reading: The lingering problem of treatment resisters. *Learning Disabilities Research and Practice*, 15, 55–64.

Torgesen, J.K. (2002). Lesson learned from intervention research in reading: A way to go before we rest. *Learning and Teaching Reading*, 1, 89–103.

Torgesen, J.K. (2005). Recent discoveries from research on remedial interventions for children with dyslexia. In M. Snowling and C. Hulme (Eds.), *The science of reading: A handbook* (pp. 521–537). Oxford: Blackwell Publishers.

U.S. Office of Education (USOE). (1976) Assistance to states for education of handicapped children: Proposed rulemaking. *Federal Register, 41,* 52404–52407. Washington, DC: U.S. Government Printing Office.

U.S. Office of Education (USOE). (1977). Assistance to states for education of handicapped children: Procedures for evaluating specific learning disabilities. *Federal Register, 42,* 65082–65085. Washington, DC: U.S. Government Printing Office.

Vellutino, F.R., Fletcher, J.M., Snowling, M.J., & Scanlon, D.M. (2004). Specific reading disability (dyslexia): What have we learned in the past four decades? *Journal of Child Psychology and Psychiatry, 45,* 2–40.

Wechsler, D. (2003). *Wechsler Intelligence Scale for Children* (4th ed.), San Antonio, TX: Psychological Corporation.

Woodcock, R.W., Schrank, F.A., Mather, N., & McGrew, K.S. (2007). *Woodcock-Johnson III Tests of Achievement.* Rolling Meadows, IL: Riverside Publishing.

Zirkel, P.A, & Thomas, L.B. (2010). State laws for RTI: An updated snapshot. *Teaching Exceptional Children, 42* (3), 56–63.

JIM'S INTERVIEW

1. What do you want to be when you grow up?
    Fighter pilot.
   Why do you think you would be good at that job?
    I love flying in planes. I just like being up in the air.

2. Tell me about a teacher who has been really important to you or one who has helped you: what did the teacher do to help you?
    Probably my music teacher, Mr. L. He's really nice and he just helped me a lot through the year. He's also patient. You know he'd give me some extra help if I was having a hard time getting something. I felt like he was giving me some extra support, but then yet again I feel like he would help anyone.

3. Tell me about a teacher who didn't really help you that much or one who did not give you the help you needed. What did you want the teacher to do to help you?
    My other music teacher at my old school. If you were not singing, she would yell at you. She'd just scream at you. She'd say "why aren't you singing?" Well, I forgot the lines and she would say "you shouldn't forget the lines." If it's something I don't like, I generally forget it, but if it's something I do like, I remember it pretty good. The best educational teacher I've ever had is probably the teacher I'm having now. She's really patient. You know it's extra help. She helps me write because I'm a really messy hand-writer.

4. Tell me what your mother thinks about your dyslexia. Does she talk to you about the problem?
    Yes.

   What does she say?
    She definitely thinks I'm different. Sometimes I get really strange ideas that pop in my head. It's harder with my dad than it is for her. I

get frustrated when he makes me go back and reread a word because some of the words I know, but I just guess at it because I just want to get over reading. [My mom] says maybe you can try it again tomorrow night. Maybe you should tell Dad that he's doing this wrong. Sometimes he'll say "no, that's not right" with a kind of an attitude. I don't really like it because I feel like he's kind of saying "anyone can get that." My mom says "can you please try that again?"

5. Tell me what your father thinks about your dyslexia. Does he talk to you about the problem? What does he say?

    He definitely doesn't like it because it makes his life harder when we get into fights about reading and stuff. It usually goes on for 15 minutes and then Mom comes in and stops us. Maybe the fighting kind of makes him depressed. I think he thinks "why did this have to happen?" I get frustrated with myself when I can't read a word and I get all tense and I ask "why do I have to be like this?" because I just don't like it when I guess at words . . .

6. Tell me about something that makes you really happy.

    Remember how I said I got those strange ideas? When I get those sometimes they work and they really turn out to be like a great idea actually that is what makes me happy the most.

7. Tell me about something that makes you really sad.

    When my dad says "no" about stuff like I asked him if I could buy something and he said "no". I asked "why not?" and then they tell me and then I say "okay." Then I just walk away. I can say (to myself) I wouldn't have liked that anyway.

8. When the work gets very hard at school and you think you can't do it, what do you do?

    You know if it's a test I'll use the multiplication charts to help. If it's writing I'll generally go up to the teacher and say "can you help me with this?"

9. What kinds of books do you like to read?

    Scary mystery books.

    What is your favorite book?

    This one called Lightening Thief. It's a Greek mythology book.

    Do you read to yourself?

    No, only if it's something I'm really interested in and I want to get information. That's like the only time . . . when I was looking into buying this app [application] for my Ipod Touch . . . something online . . . different kind of reviews about it.

    Who else reads to you?

    My mom and dad, they both alternate nights.

10. Do your friends know that you have dyslexia?

    Most of them because I kind of struggle when I'm reading stuff in class. Because most of them at this school, we all have something like a learning difference. At [previous school] I used to get teased a lot about that. They'd say "ha ha, you can barely read something." It was annoying, that's why I left . . . they started doing it in second grade.

11. Do your siblings know that you have dyslexia?

    I don't think he knows, but I don't want him to know. He may know, he may not . . . I'm worried that when he gets angry he'll tease me like they did at [previous school].

    What do your siblings say to you about dyslexia?

    [When his brother asks why he goes to a special school, Jim explains to him] *That's kind of personal.*

12. Name three things you are really good at:

    Musical . . . drums, marching band stuff.
    Technical . . . like I'm good with computers, cameras, stuff like that.
    Good at figuring out stuff like what's happening . . . by that I mean, say that the microwave was having a problem, a little thing fell out of it and my mom didn't know where it went and I put it back in.

13. Name three things you are not so good at:

    Writing, reading, spatial . . . I guess what I mean by that I would not be a good interior designer . . . they need to be good at picturing stuff . . . for example, they need to picture where stuff will go and whether it will look good or not.

14. If you are feeling bad about your reading, is there one person you can talk to who makes you feel better?

    My mom.

    What does that person say to you?

    Like for example, if I'm doing a test and it has a lot of reading, she'll say just "think you can do it."

15. Do computers help you with your reading?

    Yes.

    If yes, how do they help you?

    Because if you have a special setting, you can make the print bigger and smaller. Computers also help with my writing because I can type stuff.

16. Do you usually have problems with your homework?

    Depends on how hard it is, like spelling is and comprehension is pretty good.

    Is homework a big problem or just a little one?

    [At previous school it was a problem], *but now just a little one.*

17. If there was one thing you could change about school, what would it be?

   More time for specials. [At previous school] that they would believe you more: because they would never believe me when I told on somebody.

18. If you could have three wishes, what would they be?

   To have unlimited amount of money.

   Have people be a little more nice to me, like not teasing me, not making fun of me, not give me attitude.

   Have a really big house.

19. Tell me three things you would like your teacher to do to help you with your dyslexia:

   To maybe give me a little bit more extra help.

   Probably to let me sit by my friends a little bit more, because that helps me . . . I guess I know if I ask my friend for help, he'll help me.

   Maybe not make me read as much because I have to read a 100 minutes per week and we have a lot of things going on.

20. Who is the best reader in your class? How did he/she get to be such a good reader?

   It would probably be mostly the girls because a lot of the girls are really good readers. Probably the shortest girl in our class . . . she reads a lot at night, like she'll stay up and read 30 minutes a night. Most of the boys usually get distracted including me and then wonder off to try to avoid reading or make jokes about the book and how the people look.

21. Is it important to learn how to read?

   Yeah.

   Why or why not?

   Because in your life, you're going to be doing a lot of reading in your life when you grow up . . . like you'll be reading a grocery list, or how much something costs.

19 Cross-Case Analysis and Reflections

Peggy L. Anderson and
Regine Meier-Hedde

"In the middle of difficulty lies opportunity."

—Albert Einstein

The most significant results of this international study are found in the interpretive analyses of the individual cases that are provided in this volume. The voices of these children and their mothers clearly articulated their challenges, accomplishments, and concerns. The most indelible impression that has emerged from these conversations with the children is one of remarkable perseverance and resilience. While it is true that they sometimes spoke of sadness, frustration and disappointments related to their dyslexia, there was no culture of self-pity or despair. More often, the children expressed positive feelings and a genuine desire to move ahead. As one child said in regard to his three wishes, "I'm not making a wish to read better because I have to read okay by myself, not wishing for it." Likewise, the mothers were resolutely positive in their approach. They may have regretted the lack of school and teacher support and misperceptions of their children's reading problems, but they viewed their children as more capable than disadvantaged. In general, they were philosophical about the failings of the educational system, preferring not to waste time and energy complaining, but rather focusing attention on what was often incremental progress in their children's reading.

A secondary objective of this study was to examine summary data for purposes of identifying possible trends that might serve as a beginning point for future cross-cultural research of dyslexia. In order to ensure that these interpretative cases represented the stories of the children and their mothers with fidelity, voluminous data were collected. However, it is clearly beyond the scope of this chapter to summarize and comment on all of this data, which would also place disproportionate emphasis on the quantitative aspect of the study. Thus, this cross-case analysis focused on selected case characteristics for purposes of providing insight and recommendations that will hopefully be of value for families, teachers, and future researchers.

FAMILIAL CHARACTERISTICS

The age of the 17 children in this study ranged from 10 to 12 years of age with the average being 10 years-11 months. The majority of the children came from middle-class households. Most of the children lived with both parents with the exception of three who lived with their mothers as a result of divorce. Fourteen (82%) of the 17 children had family members with dyslexia, which is consistent with Hallgren's (1950) classic study in which 88% of his sample had relatives with the same condition. Additionally, seven of the children in the current study had more than one relative with dyslexia.

MEDICAL PROBLEMS

Birth Complications

Birth complications were reported in the cases of 82% of the children in this study, which included both pregnancy and delivery problems. These complications were diverse and included maternal infections, anoxia, jaundice, gestational kidney failure, and breech birth. There were also two children who were born at 37 weeks, but none who were designated as premature. Studies that have investigated the significance of birth complications for prediction of dyslexia and/or learning disabilities have revealed inconsistent results. Colletti (1979) examined the birth records for a group of children between 7 and 12 who were later identified as having learning disabilities and found that these children had a significantly higher number of birth complications than would be expected. She noted that in the United States, 85% of the population of newborns were designated as healthy compared to the 34% of her sample. She also discovered that the Apgar scores of her study group were significantly lower than the norm. Badian (1986), in a later study, found that children with a history of birth complications lagged behind peers in reading achievement early in their school careers, but eventually (by third grade) caught up. She concluded that poor birth history appeared to be associated with early problems in reading, but were not significantly associated with later reading disability. However, Saviour, Padakannaya, Nishanimutt and Ramachandra (2009) more recently discovered that prenatal/postnatal risk factors clearly play a significant role in nonfamilial types of dyslexia.

Table 19.1   Relatives with Dyslexia   (N= 14)

First Degree	Second Degree	Third Degree
12	11	2

Medication

Thirty-five percent of the children in this study were taking medication on a regular basis. Three of the six children took medication to control symptoms of Attention Deficit/Hyperactivity Disorder (ADHD), which is the most frequent psychiatric disorder associated with reading disabilities (Maughan & Carroll, 2006) and is also commonly associated with learning disabilities (Mayes, Calhoun & Crowell, 2000). There is some research that has demonstrated that medication can increase reading achievement for children who have significant problems sustaining attention (Scheffler et al., 2009; Kupietz, Winsberg, Richardson, Maitinsky & Mendell, 1988), while other research has found a weaker link (Forness, Cantwell, Swanson, Hanna, & Youpa, 1991). The parents of the three children in this study who took medication to control ADHD symptoms were satisfied with the effects. The other three children took medication for different reasons, including anxiety (Zoloft), "mental state," and "brain immaturity" (Tegretol).

Ear and Eye Problems

The mothers all reported that their children had normal hearing acuity, but there was a significant number who experienced recurrent bouts of otitis media. Forty-one percent of the study sample experienced two to five (or more) episodes of otitis media with effusion (OME). Most of these children were treated with antibiotics and only one child had tubes inserted surgically (i.e., myringotomy). The literature on reading problems and middle-ear infections has not established a definitive link between these. Earlier research revealed a relationship between otits media and educational achievement (Silva, Chalmers, & Stewart, 1986) while other research has not documented this relationship. One of the largest studies was conducted by Peters, Grievink, van Bon, and Schilder (1994) who studied a cohort of 946 children and found that reading was not affected by the recurrent bouts of middle-ear effusion, but a small effect for spelling was uncovered. These researchers concluded that OME evidently is not a major factor that explained children's language or learning problems. However, considering the magnitude of the spelling problems that children with dyslexia have and the fact that 7 out of 17 children in this study had these infections, a probable relationship appears likely. It would also seem to be a good idea for pediatricians in particular to be aware that OME may be associated with later reading and spelling problems so that parents could be advised of this possibility if difficulties occur.

Fifty-three percent of the children in the study had visual difficulties of some type. Of these nine children, only four had problems related to abnormal visual acuity, all of which were caused by refractive errors corrected with glasses. In addition to these problems, one child consistently complained of difficulty seeing the board and reading materials. He had several eye exams with acuity judged to be normal in each of these. Four other students had eye therapy as a recommended remedy for tracking problems and/or reading difficulty. Three of these therapeutic treatments involved orthoptic exercises and one involved the use of tinted lenses. None of the mothers found this therapy to be beneficial. The relationship between vision and dyslexia has been fraught with controversy. However, in the United States, the American Academy of Pediatrics, the American Academy of Ophthalmology, and the American Association of Orthoptics (2009) recently issued a joint statement indicating that "scientific evidence does not support the efficacy of eye exercises, behavioral vision therapy, or special tinted filters or lenses for improving the long-term educational performance" (p. 837), concluding that none of which should be endorsed or recommended. In 2000, the United Kingdom College of Optometrists commissioned a study on behavioral optometry, concluding that there were insufficient clinical trials to support this type of therapy for dyslexia as well as for a number of other conditions (Barrett, 2009). It might be helpful if international medical organizations, such as the World Health Organization, could establish positions on this therapy so parents who are seeking guidance could have additional expert advice to consider before undertaking this controversial treatment.

EARLY DEVELOPMENTAL PROBLEMS

The mothers in this study were asked to assess their children's early development in terms of speech/language, motor, and socialization. Speech/language interview questions focused on acquisition of milestones, such as first words and putting sentences together, as well as general and specific observations of performance. About half of the children (47%) had delayed speech and/or language while 24% showed marked difficulty with naming of objects. These children were likely at a disadvantage when they started school as the literature suggests they would be much more apt to experience difficulties learning to read (see Scarborough, 2003 for a review of related studies). Early motor competence was addressed in the interview with questions concerning milestones. In addition, specific questions regarding fine and gross motor skills were asked. Sixty-five percent of the children demonstrated early fine motor difficulties and 47% had gross motor difficulties. Fine motor problems were manifested in problems with coloring, drawing, and writing while gross motor problems were observed in late walking, difficulties learning to ride bikes, and participation in sports activities. It was not surprising that motor problems were observed in high frequency as research has demonstrated a strong relationship between these difficulties and reading problems (Iversen, Berg, Ellertsen & Tønnessen, 2005; Fawcett & Nicolson, 1995; McPhillips & Sheehy, 2004). In fact, research has suggested that early motor problems may well be a possible sign for a wide range of developmental problems (Missiuna, Rivard & Bartlett, 2003). In terms of early socialization, the mothers were asked questions regarding playing with other children. Only three children (18%) had social problems that restricted play activities. There was also a high percentage (41%) of children who had early sleep difficulty and several who had extreme eating problems that included pica, frequent vomiting, and self-imposed dietary restrictions.

SCHOOL HISTORY, DIAGNOSIS AND REMEDIATION

The children in this study attended both public (53%) and private (29%) schools, and sometimes a combination (18%) of these. The average age of dyslexia diagnosis for the 17 children in this study was 8 years, 0 months, which was 2½ years after the problem was first noted (i.e., at the age of 5 ½). In the majority of cases, the child's problems were observed from the beginning of the first school experience. In some countries, children were expected to begin reading at the age of 4 while in others reading was not required until the age of 7. Regardless of age or language, the problems began as soon as letters (or characters) and sounds were first introduced. Often there was a noticeable change in the child's attitude toward school once it was clear that he was not achieving commensurate with peers. School avoidance was cited in a high number of cases (47%) and in many instances, the mothers did not initially understand the reason for the child's sudden change in attitude. For example, one child from South America became depressed in the second half of his first school year, which the mother attributed to the bad weather that kept him from playing in the garden. However, soon after the first signs became evident, the mothers became very aware of the problem. Although the teachers understood these children were struggling, they often misperceived the significance of the reading problems. In nine of the 17 cases, the mothers were the ones who initially suspected the problem and requested an evaluation. Sometimes the mothers had to repeatedly ask for testing. Only six of the referrals were initiated by the school. One was initiated by the child's pediatrician and the remaining child was referred cooperatively by the parents and school. There were only two cases of early referral, which occurred within the first six months of the first year of formal schooling, and in one case the mother had previously requested the referral. Nine of the children (53%) were provided reading remediation before the official diagnosis of dyslexia, but these programs appeared to have little if any impact on the reading problems, which invariably became more severe. Grade repetition was a popular strategy to deal with reading underachievement as six of the children (35%) were retained, which is similar to that which has been identified in other research on learning disabilities (Karande, Satam, Kulkarni, Sholapurwala, Chitre & Shah, 2007). For one of these children who repeated, a second retention was recommended by the school and subsequently refused by the mother. In addition to the six repeaters, it was recommended that two other children repeat grades, but their mothers also refused. Retention did not help any of these children and had the deleterious effect of causing additional stress and erosion of self-worth. This result is not an exception as the research on grade retention suggests it is counter-productive and more likely to produce a negative impact on social-emotional well being without providing long term academic gains (Brophy, 2006). One child summed up this negativity by saying that the worst thing about school is that "they retain you."

Diagnostic methods (including specific tests) were varied and impossible to reliably categorize. In some countries, the speech and language therapist was responsible for the testing while in other countries it was an educational psychologist, and in others still it was a team that included a variety of professionals. After the diagnosis of dyslexia, 16 of the students were provided with some type of remedial program. Only one child did not receive remediation from the school, but this boy's mother attended training classes for dyslexia and provided him with successful multisensory remediation at home. There was a tremendous difference in the services that were received by the other children. It was not possible to make generalizations about the remedial programs as few mothers were given specific information about the content. In reviewing the case studies, it appeared that most did not provide the necessary content and/or intensity to achieve desired results as the majority of the children did not make significant achievement gains. This finding was not particularly surprising as efficacy studies have shown that school-based remedial programs, whether "pull-out" or inclusive, have not been effective for helping poor readers at grade 2 and after (Lyon et al., 2001). Lyon and his colleagues identified a number of obstacles to remediation success including insufficient teacher preparation, large class size, and lack of appropriate instructional program. Inadequate instruction in specific reading component areas has also been identified as a problem in remedial programs (Swanson, 2008).

In addition to the school remediation, 11 students had private tutoring, which was also varied. Some tutoring was devoted exclusively to supporting the child's curriculum while other tutoring focused on helping the child complete homework. Only a few tutors provided the children with a highly specialized remedial reading program. While it is gratifying to report that so many children received additional instruction before and after the diagnosis, it is disappointing to review the outcome of this support. These children made improvements, but only in a few cases did these gains appear to be significant enough to close the gap between grade level and achievement. This lack of progress over time supports the case for the establishment of data bases that would allow professionals to determine what constitutes acceptable and unacceptable achievement toward educational goals (Stone & Doane, 2001).

As a group, the children in this study demonstrated marked dysfluency in reading, which is one of the more prominent characteristics of dyslexia as the child develops. Early problems with word analysis can lead to later slowness and dysfluency as "fluency forms the bridge between decoding and comprehension" (Shaywitz, 2003, p. 231). As the text becomes longer, there are more words to decode, and, thus, more obstacles to gaining meaning from text. For 82% of the children in this study, there were persistent complaints of slowness and for approximately 50% there were problems related to accuracy in reading. There are many reasons why children are dysfluent and sometimes improvement of decoding skills is insufficient to produce accurate and fluent text reading or reading comprehension (National Reading Panel, 2000; Share, 2008; Shaywitz, Morris & Shaywitz, 2008). It does not appear that the majority of children in this study received adequate early phonemic awareness and decoding training to develop these skills, but even if they had, this intervention may have produced accuracy without gains in speed, which is a common characteristic of dyslexia in languages that have consistent orthographies (Share, 2008). The lack of systematic fluency instruction also appears to represent an instructional weakness (Kuhn & Stahl, 2003). Current treatment efforts to address fluency are further complicated by other problems, including a lack of consensus regarding the meaning of fluency in relation to other terms such as rate, automaticity, and processing speed, which need to be addressed to inform diagnosis and intervention (Wolf & Katzir-Cohen, 2001). Additionally, when children have fluency problems, there is a spillover effect in other academic work, such as reading in the content areas and writing in class, which was observed to be a problem in this study.

In spite of the fact that most of the children in this study did not make significant gains, the majority of mothers (70%) stated that they were satisfied with their child's progress in reading. However, it should be noted that five of the twelve mothers who indicated that they were satisfied were equivocal in their responses. Two of these mothers explained their satisfaction in reference to the fact that their children were no longer crying when reading. Two other mothers noted that they were satisfied even though their children had actually made very little progress and one mother noted that although handwriting and spelling had improved, her child hated to read and write. The mothers who were dissatisfied with progress were largely worried about the slow rate of improvement and voiced concerns, such as "he has made progress, but compared to the others, he's not making progress" or "he's getting better, but I can't say I'm pleased with the progress." In general, most of these mothers seemed to focus on positive aspects of progress even when they clearly had nagging concerns and questions about the slow rate of improvement. They also seemed to connect the question of progress to their children's efforts, perhaps more so than with actual achievement. This positive attitude was very likely communicated to their children, which would have been valuable psychological support.

PERSPECTIVES ON INSTRUCTION AND SUPPORT

Teacher Support

When the mothers were asked if their children's teachers had provided sufficient support, 31% felt they had, 50% felt that they had not, and the remaining 19% were unsure. The satisfied mothers explained their responses in terms of seeing higher grades, less frustration, and more teacher-initiated help. One mother explained that although she believed that the teachers had provided sufficient help, it was insufficient to meet the needs of her child, thus indicating that she felt her child's reading needs might be beyond what could reasonably be expected from a teacher. The parents who did not believe that teachers had provided sufficient help expressed frustration in their need to "push" or "fight" with the schools to get the help for their children or to take the remediation on them-selves. Some of these parents who were dissatisfied complained about specific teachers who were unkind or incompetent and a general lack of knowledge of children's reading problems. One dissatisfied parent added that although teacher support was insufficient, it was not the fault of the teachers as they had been inadequately trained. Inadequate support/neglect was one of the negative experiences that applied to all case studies in Edwards' (1994) research.

The issue of instructional support was addressed in several different questions. One of these questions asked the children to identify "three things you would like your teacher to do to help you with your dyslexia." While two children indicated they did not know, and one child said, "the things she is doing for me right now," most had specific ideas about assis-tance that would help them. Their ideas mainly focused on increased individualized support and accommodations. In terms of individualized support, some children referred to needing more reading instruction, but most wanted increased personal attention. Comments such as "pay more attention to me," "be more interested," "spend more time with me" and "answer my questions," suggested that these children often feel neglected in the classroom. In terms of accommodations, the children primarily wanted less reading (e.g., "don't make me read as much," and "have teacher read instructions"), less writing ("not give me lots to write" and "allow me," to dictate answers to teacher"), and more time to complete in-class and

Table 19.2   Assistance Children Wanted from Teachers

Individualized Support	25
Accommodations	11
General Instruction	6

homework assignments. Additionally, some children had general requests, such as "be patient," "teach lessons more slowly," and "don't get angry at mistakes." This question and the responses revealed important information as these children clearly expressed ideas about the type of help they needed to be successful in the classroom.

School Support

The mothers were asked the following question to help identify ways in which schools could be more supportive of children with reading problems:

"If there was one thing you could change about the way the school treats children with dyslexia, what would it be?"

Problems associated with insufficient special education services were noted with high frequency. The mothers wanted improvement in terms of the quantity and quality of special education, which they found wanting. This message was consistent with the desires the children expressed on the previous question. One mother stated that children with dyslexia need "empirically tested and proven programs that would teach them what the gaps are . . . but also allows them to demonstrate their potential," which she did not feel were available in her country. Another mother stated "I want there to be measurable goals for the work . . . and a time table for achieving these goals." It is also clear from these answers and from other interview responses that mothers do not believe that their children's individual differences were appreciated, understood, or given sufficient attention. One mother voiced her concern by saying "There doesn't seem to be any valuing of differences so kids are made to feel that something is wrong with them when they are different," while another mother spoke of wanting her son to be taken "more seriously," and for teachers to "find out how

Table 19.3   School Changes Mothers Wanted for Dyslexia Treatment

Increased Time & Quality of Special Education Services	5
More Acceptance & Knowledge of Individual Differences	4
Early Diagnosis & Intervention	4
Psychological Counseling for the Child & Teacher	1
Help for Parents	1
Respect for Children and Elimination of Punishment	1
Accommodations	1
Don't Know	1

Table 19.4   School Changes Children Wanted   *N=17

Decreased Homework /Studying	6
Elimination of Language Lessons	3
Increase Recess & Extracurricular Time	2
Teacher Issues	3
Social Concerns	2
Decrease Reading & Writing	1
Media in Class	1

One child gave 2 responses

he learns." Mothers also wanted earlier diagnoses and immediate attention after the problem was identified. McNulty's (2003) research on the life span of individuals with dyslexia speaks to the importance of these mothers' concerns; children need repeated explanations of their learning differences that emphasize strengths to combat the concern that "something's wrong with me" and to promote adaptation and positive self-image.

Children were also asked a similar question about identifying one thing they could change about school. The most frequent response they gave concerned homework, which they would like to have decreased. Three students expressed a desire to have better teachers and/or to remove poor teachers. Wanting to eliminate the language lessons and increasing break time were also mentioned. One child's explanation of the problems was particularly reflective of the frustration he was facing with school demands:

> I wish I could change the curriculum that I could not have to read and write. When I do homework, I can ask my parents, classmates, and teachers. But nobody will help when I take examinations. When I fail, both my parents and I will be very upset.

Homework

The issue of homework was investigated by asking both the mothers and children whether it caused problems, and if so, were these significant or minor problems. According to the mothers, homework was a problem for 65% of the children, and for ten of them it was a significant problem. One of the mothers indicated that homework was "sometimes" a problem if unexpected assignments came up, which heightened the child's anxiety. The other mothers reported that homework was not a problem and many of these indicated that their children could handle the work independently. One mother explained that homework had previously been an enormous problem, but

Table 19.5 Mothers' Perceptions of Homework N= 17

	Yes	No	Sometimes
Does child have problems with homework?	11	5	1
Is problem significant?	10	1	1

since the child had moved to a private school there were fewer problems even though he was still not independent in completing these tasks.

When the children were asked about homework, 53% said that it was problematic and most indicated it was a significant problem. Two of the students reported that "sometimes" homework was a big problem and one student indicated that it was a problem before he changed schools. Only three students reported that they could consistently complete their work by themselves while another three students reported that sometimes they could and sometimes they could not. The largest number of students reported that they needed help to complete this work.

It is clear from the interview data in this study that homework presented a significant challenge to the children and their families. The data in the tables do not reveal the true story of the challenges homework imposed on these children and their families. The mothers described in detail the frustration that their children encountered when trying to complete homework and the negative influence on the family life. It was not unusual for the homework to stretch on for hours, and for there to be tears of frustration associated with this time of the day. Many of the mothers talked about the lack of understanding and sensitivity that teachers showed the children. For example, in one case study the teacher decided that it would be a good idea to assign a semester's worth of homework for the child to complete over a holiday break. In addition to this type of misperception, there were generally three major problems that occurred: (1) misunderstandings about the assignment itself, (2) length of assignment, and (3) difficulty of the assignment. The children often did not understand the oral instructions or could not write quickly enough to record the assignment before the teachers erased the board. Then there were associated problems with getting the assignment materials (books, workbooks, notebooks, etc.) from school to home, and additional problems getting the finished assignment back to

Table 19.6 Children's Perceptions of Homework N=17

	Yes	No	Sometimes
Do you have problems with homework?	9	5	3
Is problem significant?	7	3	2
Can you do your homework independently?	3	11	3

the school. One mother told of elaborate plans in which she had parties or bought gifts for other children in the hopes that her son would be able to call these children on the phone to receive clarification of assignments. While the length of these homework assignments may have been appropriate for the average child at that age, the children with dyslexia required three to four times longer to complete the work. Sometimes parents would resort to completing the work for the child "just to get it over with." One mother said "I don't think there was ever any consideration given to what it is like for a child with a reading problem to complete homework." That is probably very accurate as few teachers would assign three hours of homework to a 10-year- old on a daily basis. The final problem with homework was the difficulty level. For whatever reason, many children were required to copy huge amounts of letters or characters as part of the homework. Sometimes they had to copy the lengthy instructions or in other situations, the copying itself was part of the homework. For children with fine motor problems in addition to reading difficulties, the writing demands created an exhausting situation. Seldom could the content subject exercises be completed without the assistance of the parents because of reading problems. Even children who were very good at math could not complete their work as they could not read the problems.

Since there is inconsistent evidence that homework improves the academic performance of children in the elementary school years in the United States (Cooper, Robinson & Patell, 2006) and international studies actually show an inverse relationship between achievement and homework (Baker & Letendre, 2005), it would seem reasonable to question the practice for all students (Kohn, 2006), but particularly for those with reading problems. Assigning perfunctory homework without consideration for the characteristics of the learner with reading problems constitutes punishment for both the child and family.

Computer Support

Almost all of the children in this study had access to computers and many of them made reference to technology supports, such as books on CDs, iPods, and computers, in their interviews. However, only 59% of the children reported that computers helped them with reading. These children referred to the benefits of internet research, reading/spelling software programs, reading support web sites, increasing font size for easier reading of material, and the advantages of writing on the computer. Some of the children who indicated that computers did not help seemed unaware of the possible applications. For example, one child said that computers could not help with reading because "they don't read for me," which suggests that this child has not been introduced to assistive software that could be very beneficial for his reading needs. It is unfortunate that all children with reading disabilities do not have access to technology, such as text-reader software, that would allow them to read grade-level text independently, an enormous breakthrough as these students would not have to depend on their teachers or peers for assistance (Hasselbring & Barusch, 2005). Research has demonstrated that computer-assisted instruction has been highly effective for children with reading problems as it provides specific instruction in phonological awareness, word identification, and passage comprehension (Torgesen & Barker, 1995; Olson & Wise, 2006) as well as supportive instruction and opportunities for practice (Hall, Hughes & Filbert, 2000). In this study, the lack of computer-assisted instruction and applications did not appear to be related to economics, but rather seemed to be connected to a lack of instructional knowledge on the part of teachers and schools. It would be very helpful for teachers to make recommendations to parents for the use of computer support for reading at home. There are numerous reading software programs in many languages that have user-friendly versions for home use. In addition there are numerous web-based instructional programs that could also be beneficial.

Educational Policy for Instructional Support

When mothers were asked whether they felt that their country provided "adequate regulations and support for children with dyslexia," nine of the 17 (53%) said "no." These mothers expressed concerns about the lack of awareness of dyslexia, the lack of special education services, and the amount of responsibility that parents must undertake to secure help for their children. As one mother said, "the work falls on the shoulders of the parents—there are regulations, but if the parents don't push . . . nothing will happen." Three mothers declined to answer the question because of insufficient knowledge and one mother was ambivalent. There were only three mothers who answered affirmatively, and two of these indicated that the implementation of the laws was problematic. Thus, there was only one mother who was pleased with the country's laws and implementation.

PERSPECTIVES ON READING PROBLEMS

Significance of the Reading Problem

From the results of the Perception Scale responses (see Appendix), there were differences in regard to how the mothers and the children perceived reading problems. When asked to rate the significance of their child's reading problem, the mothers' scores ranged from 5 to 10 with an average rating of 7.8 while their sons' scores were somewhat lower, between 3 and 9 with an average rating of 5.7. Results were similar for rating the impact of the reading problem on school success with the mothers giving an average rating of 7.7 and the children giving an average rating of 5.8. When the mothers were asked to identify the "most difficult aspect" of their child's reading problem, they were likely to name more than one factor. Social and emotional consequences were named more than any other aspect. They voiced concerns such as "school success is so important for self-image" and dyslexia was a "threat to self-confidence." One mother summed her concerns with the statement "he is suffering." Mothers also mentioned the need to better understand the nature of the reading problem so that they could understand their sons. For example, one mother expressed the desire to "always stay aware of how difficult reading is for him." When the children were asked about the most difficult aspect of the reading problem, they were more likely to describe specific problems, such as "scrambled letters," "recognition of characters," and the need "to guess at words." The second greatest concerns for the children were the social consequences of the reading problem, such as thinking that the other children would make fun of them or being identified as "stupid" by teachers.

Importance of Reading

In an effort to understand the children's attitudes about reading, they were asked whether it was important to learn how to read, and why or why not. The overwhelming majority (88%) answered affirmatively. The most commonly cited reasons for the importance of reading were of a practical nature (e.g., reading grocery lists, newspapers, participating in an election, etc.). Only one child indicated that reading was "not so important" because he felt that there would not be much reading required after leaving school while another child expressed ambivalence about the importance of reading.

Another item on the Perception Scale asked the children to rate the amount of reading they did on a scale of 1 to 10; their average rating was 5.1. On a similar item, the mothers were asked how much they read to their children, the average of which was 5.3. There were avid readers in this study, but some of these children were actually reading very little if any at home. All of them were watching more television on a daily basis (i.e., 57 minutes) than they were reading. Only six children were reading independently (corroborated by mothers' report), and three of these also read with their family. These children read a wide range of reading materials with regard to difficulty level. For example, one child's favorite book was *Three Little Pigs*, while another child was reading the series *The Chronicles of*

Table 19.7 Children's Reasons Why Reading Is Important	N=15
Practical Applications	11
Gain Knowledge	2
Read Faster & Better	1
Avoid Ridicule	1

Ancient Darkness, which is approximately at the 9 to 12 year reading level. In addition to those children who read independently, seven other children read at home regularly with the assistance of their parents (usually the mother) or grandparents. The mothers of the reading children reported that they read anywhere from 20–70 minutes daily, with an average of 25 minutes, which is quite high as some research has reported that 10-year-olds typically spend 15 minutes per day reading (Taylor, Frye & Maruyame, 1990). However, it would be difficult to draw comparisons as most of the children in the current study were not reading independently. Since four of the children rarely, if ever, read at home, the average daily reading for this entire group was 16 minutes. While this figure may be consistent with that reported for typical readers, it may not be sufficient to increase achievement for these children or to address specific problems. On one hand, it is understandable that children who struggle with reading would read less as it is so arduous. However, the benefits of reading practice are considerable (Anderson, Wilson & Fielding, 1988; Lewis & Samuels, 2005). It has also been reported that assisted reading practice is even more beneficial (Shany & Bielmiller, 1995; Topping, Samuels & Paul, 2007). With regard to fluency problems, the time that these parents and grandparents spent in partner reading or monitoring reading aloud is likely to be very helpful for these children over the long run, more so than the independent reading. Paired reading appears to be a promising practice that may be particularly helpful in producing gains in fluency (Huemer, Landerl, Aro & Lyytinen, 2008) as does guided repeated oral reading (Chard, Vaughn, & Tyler, 2002; Report of the National Reading Panel, 2001) neither of which requires a teacher. In addition to the children reading to themselves and reading with or being read to by family members, many of them were also listening to books on CDs or tapes, which is another form of literacy that is beneficial and should be encouraged (Chard et al., 2002).

Influence of Dyslexia on Life

To gain insight into perceptions of outcomes, the mothers were asked the question "How do you think your child's dyslexia will influence his life?" The mothers expressed two major areas of concern: they worried about the implications of poor school performance on life and how their children's learning differences might affect their futures. These mothers, like most, placed a high value on school success and were concerned that lack of achievement would set the stage for further problems in life. Many mothers saw school problems as the first domino falling. One mother expressed her concerns in the following way, "Because of his poor academic performance, he may not go to a good school . . . he may not get a better job because he will perform badly on public examinations." Another mother voiced this concern in terms of vocational preferences, "I think he will have to change his wishes; he will not get the job he wants." Some mothers were concerned about their children "fitting in" to society as one mother said, "I think life will be difficult for him because he is different than others." Yet other mothers were more philosophical about the challenges imposed by dyslexia. As one mother said, "All people are limited in some way and this will be his limitation." And, finally, a couple of mothers were very optimistic as illustrated by the following observation: "I think over the years he will improve with time . . . I am positive about his future . . . there will be no problem." By and large when the mothers spoke of influences that might interfere with development and adult success, they were far more positive than negative.

PSYCHOLOGICAL PERSPECTIVES

Social and Emotional Aspects

The literature concerning social and emotional aspects of dyslexia largely suggests that children with this condition are likely to face problems with adjustment and diminished self-esteem (Edwards, 1994; McNulty, 2003; Riddick, 2010; Terras, Thompson & Minnis, 2009). Most of the children in this study had been consistently teased about their reading and for two of these children, the problems rose to the level of bullying. These results are also consistent with the findings of Singer's (2005) research that investigated strategies that children with dyslexia use to maintain their self-esteem in the face of teasing and bullying. Yet, in spite of this maltreatment at school, only nine of the 17 children experienced social acceptance problems as disclosed by the child and/or reported by the mothers. Five of the children in the study also specifically expressed anxiety in relation to their reading difficulties. Some research has reported a relationship between anxiety and dyslexia (Willcut & Pennington, 2000; Carroll, Maughan, Goodman, & Meltzer, 2005), but the sparse work in this area limits conclusions that can be drawn. Four of the children had been verbally and/or physically abused by teachers, which was a problem that was documented by the case studies of Edwards (1994) and Riddick (2010). However, in spite of the teasing and

Table 19.8   Mothers' Concerns: Influence of Dyslexia on Life   *N=17

School	7
Individual Differences	7
Vocational	2
Social/Self-Esteem	2
No Problem	2

Two mothers expressed more than one concern.

abuse, only four of the children in the study had persistent social problems that continued to 10 or 11 years of age. It appeared that the other five had passed through the worst phases of peer and teacher ridicule to emerge as socially accepted children. The early school years (i.e., grades 1 to 6) may be the most difficult for children with dyslexia as they initially face the stigma associated with the condition, but later express fewer negative feelings of self-worth (Ingesson, 2007). The ability to compartmentalize the condition is seen as one important aspect for successful adjustment.

Even though most of these children did not experience continuing social problems, almost all of them expressed some feelings of diminished self-worth related to reading problems. Dyslexia was perceived as a distinct liability that many (41%) were reluctant to discuss with others. The "three wishes question" was asked to gain information about the children's feelings; it is conjectured that wishes concerning challenges children are experiencing have the potential to provide a "window into the child's emotional experience" (Nero & Hinton, 2003, p. 97). Since the children were being interviewed about dyslexia, it was perhaps not surprising that one third of the wishes concerned dyslexia and school problems. These wishes were made almost three times more than any other category of wish; for 11 of the 17 children, one or more of the wishes focused on school/dyslexia issues, which reflects the influence of this condition on their lives. These wishes included desires to "wish my dyslexia away," "be smarter in reading," have "smaller classes," and "no homework."

Self-Efficacy

Children with dyslexia encounter difficult situations every day at school. How they respond to these challenges may predict more or less successful outcomes. In this study, the children were asked the following question,

"When the work gets very hard at school and you think you can't do it, what you do?"

Seven (41%) of the children explained that they asked for help from teachers, parents, or classmates, which has been identified as a successful strategy for students with learning disabilities (Goldberg, Higgins, Raskind & Herman, 2003). Another seven children gave answers that could be classified as demonstration of perseverance, such as, "it is always difficult, but I am not going to give up because it's hard," "I concentrate so hard that I can get done as much and as soon as possible," and "I try to think I can do it." The ability to sustain efforts in the face of difficulty has also been established as a success attribute in students with learning disabilities (Goldberg, et al., 2003). Sometimes children put forth considerable effort, but then succumb to frustration; as one child noted that he tried very hard to succeed, but then he admits that "I become so frustrated that I slam it to the ground and say I won't learn it." Only two children in this study gave up when the work became too difficult. One of the two explained, "I leave it. I don't do anything. Then Mummy writes it." While the other one said, "I give up . . . I try to escape from reality." There was also one child who first asked for help and gave up if it was not forthcoming; this child said, "I ask my teacher and if she refuses to help, I put it at the corner of my desk and fall asleep." Some research (Burden, 2005) shows that students who believe that they can be successful when confronted with a task have an appropriate level of self-efficacy, which according to attribution theory is based on a strong internal locus of control. These students attribute their success to internal factors like effort and ability (Humphrey & Mullins, 2002). In the current study, the majority of students had proactive ways of handling difficult situations in school, either by asking for help or persevering. This behavior is the opposite of learned helplessness in which negative events are attributed to internal, stable and global causes that cannot be changed (Joiner & Wagner, 1995). In Burden's (2005) study of adolescent boys attending a private school for dyslexics, a high degree of self-efficacy and internal locus of control was observed along with a low degree of learned helplessness as the administrators and teachers engendered these attributes. Despite the fact that many children in the current study faced adversity, teasing and an absence of support from teachers in the beginning of their school careers, the majority now demonstrate an emerging strength in self-efficacy, which could, in part, be explained by the mothers' strong support (e.g., constantly communicating with their schools, finding appropriate schools, initiating testing, securing school-based and private remediation, helping with homework, etc.). The assistance of significant others, particularly mothers, has been identified as an influential factor in the success of children with dyslexia (Burden, 2005). Terras et al. (2009) apply a "resilience perspective to the psycho-social dimension of dyslexia," (p. 319), which supports movement away from the deficit model to promotion of understanding of factors associated with both success and failure. Within this framework, dyslexia is perceived as a risk factor, but not necessarily a predictor of a negative outcome. This perspective is consistent with the findings of the current research: these children were not incapacitated by dyslexia.

In order to examine the children's perspectives on how a person could become a good reader, they were asked a two-part question,

"Who is the best reader in your class?" and "How did he/she get to be such a good reader?"

Burden and Burdett (2005) stated that attitude toward a learning task or learning in general is one key element in that individual's motivation to learn. Five of the 17 children reported that a "good reader" is someone who "likes to read" and/or one who "wants to read," thus, attributing competence in reading to the attitude of the reader and hence to that individual's motivation. Two of those children also mentioned ability in addition to motivation. Two other children named ability as the sole reason for reading success while four others attributed success to effort. Five students did not have any idea how other children became successful readers. In fact, one child said, "If I had known, I would have done the same thing!" Another child explained that the good reader in his class has been helped a lot by his teachers, but that he wasn't lucky enough to have a teacher who helped him. It would appear that these children could benefit from teacher support that would focus on understanding the relationship between practice and reading improvement. Spending more time with guided reading practice at home and at school could help these children see a link between their effort and reading gains.

REFLECTIONS

In summary, the most important cross-case conclusion from this study is that these children with dyslexia, from all over the world, waited too long to receive what was usually insufficient special education services that were secured in large measure by the tremendous energy that mothers expended to that end. There were some children who made significant strides in reading achievement, but not enough considering our knowledge of dyslexia treatment. We can do better for the children and their parents. We can develop policy for earlier diagnosis so teachers and parents no longer have to fight the system to secure early referrals and testing. We can improve our teacher preparation programs to give general classroom teachers the working knowledge they need to address reading problems, treatment, and suitable accommodations in relation to curricular expectations. We can also improve our special education preparation programs so that these teachers better understand the science of remediation and know how to consistently apply it in practice. We can help all teachers understand how technology can be implemented to increase specific reading skills and access content area curricula so that these children can experience learning success as they move ahead to whatever educational level they choose for themselves. We can provide assistance to navigate through the anticipated social and emotional stressors related to school expectations so these children can emerge with confidence and self-reliance. And finally, as Olson (2005, p. 232) encouraged in his Norman Geschwind Memorial Lecture on dyslexia, "maybe we can also do a better job of recognizing the basic value and dignity of all children with learning disabilities who are often neglected in our society."

The voices in these cases are those of only 17 children, but their messages, individually and collectively, reflect what the dyslexia literature has been telling us for decades. These children may be separated by great distance, but they are connected by their similar stories. Five years down the road, will these children, who will then be teens, face the same struggles they are challenged with today or will their futures be brightened by significant changes in the way we treat dyslexia? It would not take a miracle to effect change in this direction, only a renewed commitment to the lives of those we all serve.

REFERENCES

American Academy of Pediatrics (2009). Joint statement—learning disabilities, dyslexia, and vision. *Pediatrics*, 124, 837–844. doi:10.1542/peds.2009–1445

Anderson, R.C., Wilson, P.T., & Fielding, L.G. (1988). Growth in reading and how children spend their time outside of school. *Reading Research Quarterly*, 23, 285–303.

Badian, N.A. (1986). Improving the prediction of reading for the individual child: A four-year follow-up. *Journal of Learning Disabilities*, 19, 262–265. doi: 10.1177/002221948601900502

Baker, D.P., & Letendre, G.K., (2005). *National differences, global similarities: World culture and the future of schooling.* Stanford, CA: Stanford University Press.

Barrett, B.T. (2009). A critical evaluation of the evidence supporting the practice of behavioural vision therapy. *Ophthalmic & Physiological Optics*, 2, 4–25. doi: 10.1111/j.1475–1313.2008.00607

Brophy, J. (2006). *Grade repetition.* Paris: IIEP/IAE.

Burden, R.L. (2005). *Dyslexia and Self-Concept: The search for dyslexic identity.* London: Wurr.

Burden, R.L., & Burdett, J. (2005). Factors associated with successful learning in pupils with dyslexia: A motivational analysis. *British Journal of Special Education*, 32 (2), 100–104. doi: 10.1111/j.0952–3383.2005.00378.x

Carroll, J., Maugham, B., Goodman, R., & Meltzer, H. (2005). Literacy difficulties and psychiatric disorders: evidence of comorbidity. *Journal of Child Psychology & Psychiatry*, 46, 524–532. doi: 10.1111/j.1469–7610.2004.00366.x

Chard, D.J., Vaughn, S., & Tyler, B.J. (2002). A synthesis of research on effective interventions for building reading fluency with elementary students with learning disabilities. *Journal of Learning Disabilities*, 35, 386–406. doi: 10.1177/00222194020350050101

Colletti, L. (1979). Relationship between pregnancy and birth complications and the later development of learning disabilities. *Journal of Learning Disabilities*, 12, 659–663.

Cooper, H., Robinson, J.C., & Patall, E.A. (2006). Does homework improve academic achievement? A synthesis of research 1987–2003. *Review of Educational Research*, 76, 1–62.

Edwards, J. (1994). *The scars of dyslexia.* London: Cassell.

Fawcett, A.J., & Nicolson, R.I. (1995). Persistent deficits in motor skills of children with dyslexia. *Journal of Motor Behavior*, 27, 235–240.

Forness, S.R., Cantwell, D.P., Swanson, J.M., Hanna, G.J., & Youpa, D. (1991). Differential effects of stimulant medication on reading performance of boys with hyperactivity with and without conduct disorder. *Journal of Learning Disabilities*, 24, 304–310.

Goldberg, R.J., Higgins, E.L., Raskind, M.H., & Herman, K.L. (2003). Predictors of success in individuals with learning disabilities: A qualitative analysis of a 20-year longitudinal study. *Learning Disabilities Research and Practice*, 18, 222–236.

Hall, T.E., Hughes , C.A. , & Filbert, M. (2000). Computer assisted instruction in reading for students with learning disabilities: A research synthesis. *Education & Treatment of Children*, 23 (2), 173–193.

Hallgren, B., (1950). Specific dyslexia ("congenital word blindness"): A clinical and genetic study. *Acta Psychiatrica et Neurologica, 65* Suppl., 1–287. doi: 10.1080/01411920701609380

Hasselbring, T.S., & Baush, M.E. (2005). Assistive technologies for reading: Text reader programs, word-prediction software and other aids empower youth with learning disabilities. *Educational Leadership, 63* (4), 72–75.

Huemer, S., Landerl, K., Aro, M, & Lyytinen, H. (2008). Training reading fluency among poor readers of German: Ways to the goal. *Annals of Dyslexia, 58,* 115–137. doi:10.1007/s11881–008–0017–2

Humphrey, N. & Mullins, P.M. (2002). Personal constructs and attribution for academic success and failure in dyslexia. *British Journal of Special Education, 29* (4), 196–203.

Ingesson, S.G. (2007). Growing up with dyslexia: interviews with teenagers and young adults. *School Psychology International, 28,* 574–591. doi:10.1177/0143034307085659

Iversen, S., Berg, K., Ellertsen, B. & Tønnessen, F.-E. (2005). Motor coordination difficulties in a municipality group and in a clinical sample of poor readers. *Dyslexia, 11,* 217–231. doi: 10.1002/dys.297

Joiner, T.E. & Wagner, K.D. (1995). Attribution style and depression in children and adolescents: A meta-analytic review. *Clinical Psychology Review, 15* (8), 777–798.

Karande, S. Satam, N., Kulkarni, M., Sholapurwala, R., Chitre, A., & Shah, N. (2007). Clinical and psychoeducational profiles of children with specific learning disability and co-occurring attention-deficit hyperactivity disorder. *Indian Journal of Medical Sciences, 61,* 639–647. doi: 10.4103/0019–5359.37784

Kohn, A. (2006). Abusing research: The study of homework and other examples. *Phi Delta Kappan, 88,* 9–22.

Kuhn, M., & Stahl, S. (2003). Fluency: A review of developmental and remedial practices. *Journal of Educational Psychology, 95,* 3–21.

Kupietz, S., Richardson, E., Winsberg, B.G., Maitinsky, S.,& Mendell, N. (1988). Effects of methylphenidate dose on behavior, cognitive performance, and reading achievement in hyperactive, reading-disabled children: I. Behavior and Cognition. *Journal of the American Academy of Child and Adolescent Psychiatry, 26,* 70–77.

Lewis, M., & Samuels, S.J. (2005). *Read more—read better? A meta-analysis of the literature on the relationship between exposure to reading and reading achievement.* Minneapolis: University of Minnesota.

Lyon, G.R., Fletcher, J.M., Shaywitz, S.E., Shaywitz, B.A., Torgesen, J.K., Wood, F.B., Schulte, A., & Olson, R. (2001). Rethinking learning disabilities. In C.E. Finn, Jr., A.J. Rotherham, & C.R. Hokanson, Jr. (Eds.), *Rethinking special education for a new century* (pp. 250–287). Washington, DC: Progressive Policy Institute & The Thomas B. Fordham Foundation.

Maughan, B., & Carroll, J. (2006). Literacy and mental disorders. *Current Opinion in Psychiatry, 19,* 350–354. doi: 10.1097/01.yco.0000228752.79990.41

Mayes, S.D., Calhoun, S.L., & Crowell, E.W. (2000). Learning disabilities and ADHD: Overlapping spectrum disorders. *Journal of Learning Disabilities, 33,* 417–424.

McNulty, M.A. (2003). Dyslexia and the life course. *Journal of Learning Disabilities, 36,* 363–381. doi: 10.1177/00222194030360040701

McPhillips, M., & Sheehy, N. (2004), Prevalence of persistent primary reflexes and motor problems in children with reading difficulties. *Dyslexia, 10,* 316–338. doi: 10.1002/dys.282V

Missiuna, C., Rivard, L., & Bartlett, D. (2003). Early identification and risk management of children with developmental coordination disorder. *Pediatric Physical Therapy, 15* (1), 32–38.

National Institute of Child Health and Human Development (2000). Report of the National Reading Panel. *Teaching children to read: An evidence-based assessment of the scientific research literature on reading and its implications for reading instruction* (NIH Publication No. 00–4769). Washington, DC: U.S. Government Printing Office.

Nereo, N.E., & Hinton, V.J. (2003). Three wishes and psychological functioning in boys and Duchenne Muscular Dystrophy. *Journal of Developmental and Behavioral Pediatrics, 24*, 96–103.

Olson, R.K. (2006). Genes, environment, and dyslexia: The 2005 Normal Geschwind Memorial Lecture. *Annals of Dyslexia, 56*, 205–238.

Olson, R.K., & Wise, B. (2006). Computer-based remediation for reading and related phonological disabilities. In M. McKenna, L. Labbo, R. Kieffer, & D. Reinking (Eds.), *Handbook of literacy and technology*, vol. 2 (pp. 57–74). Mahwah, NJ: Lawrence Erlbaum Associates.

Peters, S.A.F., Grievink, E.H., van Bon, W.H.J., & Schilder, A.G.M. (1994). The effects of early bilateral otits media with effusion on educational attainment. *Journal of Learning Disabilities, 27*, 111–121.

Riddick, B. (2010). *Living with dyslexia* (2nd ed.). London: NASEN Routledge.

Saviour, P, Padakannaya, P., Nishanimutt, S. & Ramachandra, N.B. (2009). Familial patterns and biological markers of dyslexia. *International Journal of Human Genetics, 9* (1), 21–29.

Scarborough, H.S. (2003). Connecting early language and literacy to later reading (dis)abilities: Evidence, theory, and practice. In S.B. Neuman & D.K. Dickenson (Eds.) *Handbook of early literacy research* (Vol. 1, pp 97–110). New York: Guilford Press.

Scheffler, R.M., Brown, T.T., Fulton, B.D., Hinshaw, S.P., Levine, P., & Stone, S. (2009). Positive association between attention-deficit/hyperactivity disorder medication and academic achievement during elementary school. *Pediatrics, 123*,1273–1279. doi: 10.1542/peds.2008–1597

Shany, M.T., & Biemiller, A. (1995). Assisted reading practice: Effects on performance for poor readers in grades 3 and 4. *Reading Research Quarterly, 30*, 382–395.

Share, D.L. (2008). On the Anglocentricities of current reading research and practice: The perils of overreliance on an "outlier" orthography. *Psychological Bulletin, 134* (4), 584–615. doi: 10.1037/0033–2909.134.4.584

Shaywitz, S. (2003). *Overcoming dyslexia*. New York: Knopf.

Shaywitz, S.E., Morris, R., & Shaywitz, B.A. (2008) The education of dyslexic children from childhood to young adulthood. *Annual Review of Psychology, 59*, 451–475. doi:10.1146/annurev.psych.59.103006.093633

Silva, P.A., Chalmers, D., & Stewart, J. (1986). Some audiological, psychological, educational, and behavioral characteristics of children with bilateral otitis media with effusion. *Journal of Learning Disabilities, 19*, 165–169.

Singer, E. (2005). The strategies adopted by Dutch children with dyslexia to maintain their self-esteem when teased at school. *Journal of Learning Disabilities, 38*, 411–423. doi: 10.1177/00222194050380050401

Stone, C.A., & Doane, J.A. (2001). The potential for empirically based estimates of expected progress for students with learning disabilities: Legal and conceptual issues. *School Psychology Review, 30*, 473–486.

Swanson, E.A. (2008). Observing reading instruction for students with learning disabilities: A synthesis. *Learning Disability Quarterly, 31*, 115–133.

Taylor, B., Frye, B., & Maruyame, G. (1990). Time spent reading and reading growth. *American Educational Research Journal, 27*, 351–362.

Terras, M.M., Thompson, L.C., & Minnis, H. (2009). Dyslexia and psycho-social functioning: An exploratory study of the role of self-esteem and understanding. *Dyslexia, 15*, 304–327. doi: 10.1002/dys.386

Topping, K.J., Samuels, J., & Paul, T. (2007) Does practice make perfect? Independent reading quantity, quality, and student achievement. *Learning and Instruction, 17,* 253–264.

Torgesen, J.K., & Barker, T.A. (1995). Computers as aids in the prevention and remediation of reading disabilities. *Learning Disability Quarterly, 18,* 76–87.

Wolf, M., & Katzir-Cohen T. (2001). Reading fluency and its intervention. *Scientific Studies of Reading, 5,* 211–238.

Willcut, E.G., & Pennington, B.F. (2000). Psychiatric comorbity in children and adolescents with reading disability. *Journal of Child Psychology and Psychiatry, 41,* 1039–1048.

Appendix
Interview Protocol

INTERNATIONAL CASE STUDIES OF DYSLEXIA
PARENT INTERVIEW

Mother's Name _____

Date _____

Mother's Occupation _____

Spouse's Occupation _____

Years of School for Mother _____

Years of School for Spouse _____

Phone _____

Email Address _____

Child's Name _____

Child's Date of Birth _____

Age _____

Language _____

GENERAL QUESTIONS:

1. What is your child's favorite thing to do at home?
2. Does your child read at home?
   If so, how many hours a week?
   Does anyone read to him?
   If so, who?
   How many hours a week?
   What kinds of books does he like?
3. Does your child have a lot of friends or does he prefer to play alone?
4. Does your child have any problems getting along with other children?
   If so, please describe:
5. Does your child have any special talents?
   What kinds of things is he good at?
6. Does your child like television?
   How many hours a week does he spend watching TV?

What are his favorite shows?
7. Does your child have any special fears (animals, darkness, etc.)?
8. What words would you use to describe your child?
9. As you know, this interview is about your child's dyslexia. Can you tell me what the term "dyslexia" means?
10. How do you think your child's dyslexia will influence his life?

MEDICAL HISTORY:

1. Was there anything unusual about the pregnancy with your son? Was this a full-term pregnancy?
2. Did the child require any special medical care, or hospitalization, at birth or during the first two months after birth?
3. Has your child ever been in the hospital or been seriously ill at home? If so, what were these illnesses and what was the age at the time of illness?
4. Has your child ever been in a serious accident? If yes, please explain:
5. What other illnesses has your child had since birth? Any ear infections? If so, how many and how were they treated?
6. Does your child currently take any medication? If so, what type and for what purpose?
7. Has your child had any difficulty with hearing or vision? If so, what were these problems, when did they occur, and how were they treated?
8. Are there any other family members who have had reading problems? If so, please describe the nature of the difficulty:

DEVELOPMENTAL HISTORY:

1. At what age did your child speak his first words? When did your child begin to put words together to make sentences? How would you describe your child's language from 1 year of age to 5 years? Did he speak a lot or just a little? Was his language clear? Did you notice any peculiarities with his language? Did he have any difficulty naming objects, colors or anything else?
2. At what age did your child begin to walk? When did your child learn to ride a bike? Did he have difficulty learning to ride a bike? At what age did your child start coloring or drawing pictures? Were these early drawings good or did he have problems holding crayons and pencils?

3. Did your child enjoy playing with other children during this time? Did your child experience any problems getting along with other children?

If yes, what kinds of problems did he have?

4. Is there anything else that you can tell me about his early development?

SCHOOL HISTORY:

(Be sure to record the child's age and grade for all of the events below.)

1. The next section of this interview deals with your child's school history. I would like to know about your child's progress (e.g., when he first encountered difficulty, and what help he received, etc.). We're going to go through each year of schooling separately starting with kindergarten.

Kindergarten: (narrative description of experiences)

Was this level of schooling a good experience for your child? Why or why not?

First Grade: (narrative description of experiences)

Was this level of schooling a good experience for your child? Why or why not?

Second Grade: (narrative description of experiences)

Was this level of schooling a good experience for your child? Why or why not?

Third Grade: (narrative description of experiences)

Was this level of schooling a good experience for your child? Why or why not?

Fourth Grade: (narrative description of experiences)

Was this level of schooling a good experience for your child? Why or why not?

2. To review your child's school history, the first time he had difficulty was in which grade?

And the problem was:

(The parent may have answered this above, but check to make sure your understanding was accurate.)

3. Did you experience any problems getting the school to test your child for his reading difficulty?

   If so, please describe these problems and explain how they were resolved:

4. How old was your child when he was diagnosed as dyslexic?

   What grade was he in?

   Did the school explain what dyslexia was?

   What did they say?

5. Did you and your husband understand what they told you about dyslexia?

   Did you have any questions?

6. When he was evaluated for reading problems, what tests was he given? Do you have the test results? (If yes, researchers should record the relevant results):

   > Reading tests and percentile scores:
   > Spelling tests and percentile scores:
   > Math tests and percentile scores:
   > Other academic tests and percentile scores:

   IQ tests and scores (If WISC, include performance, verbal, and full scale):

7. Was he diagnosed as dyslexic the first time he was referred for evaluation?

   If not, please describe what happened after the first evaluation and then the results of the second evaluation, etc.:

   First Evaluation Results:

   Second Evaluation Results (if applicable):

   Third Evaluation Results (if applicable):

SPECIAL EDUCATION TREATMENT AND RESULTS:

1. After he was diagnosed as dyslexic, did he immediately receive instruction help from the school?

   If not, how long did it take for your child to receive help from the school?

2. Please tell me about the help that your child received at school for his dyslexia:

First year of special instruction:

Did he receive special instruction (that which was different from what was provided to the other children) during the school year he was diagnosed as having dyslexia?

If so, please describe the nature of this assistance:

Was this instruction provided in the child's classroom or in another room by a different teacher?

How many minutes a day did your child receive the instruction?
Was there a special name for the instruction?
What was the focus of the instruction (e.g., phonics, vocabulary, etc.)?
How long was this service provided?

In addition to this assistance, did he receive any other assistance in the school or outside the school (private tutoring)? If so what was the nature of this service?

Did your child make progress with this help?

How much did he improve (test scores or statements from teachers, or parent observations)?

Did he like receiving this special help? Why or why not?

(Note: In the actual interview the above section was repeated up to four years after the diagnosis)

3. Are you satisfied with the progress that your child has made in reading since his diagnosis?
4. Do you feel that the teachers have provided sufficient help for your child?
   Why or why not?
5. Does your child have problems with homework?
   If so, please describe these:
   Is this a minor problem or a significant problem?
6. Do you think that your country provides adequate regulations and support for children with dyslexia?
   Why or why not?
7. If there was one thing you could change about the way the school treats children with dyslexia, what would it be?

INTERNATIONAL CASE STUDIES OF DYSLEXIA
PARENT PERCEPTION SCALE

(This interview is read to the parent. The examiner instructs the parent to answer the following questions about the child's reading problems on a scale from 1-10, with 10 being the highest and 1 being the lowest.)

Sample Item: How much do you like sweets (e.g., cakes and candy)?

LOW 1   2   3   4   5   6   7   8   9   10 HIGH

(Examiner checks understanding by asking if parent really likes sweets or doesn't care for them.)

1. In general, how significant do you think your child's reading problem is?

LOW 1   2   3   4   5   6   7   8   9   10 HIGH

2. How much does the problem interfere with school success?

LOW 1   2   3   4   5   6   7   8   9   10   HIGH

3. How much does the problem interfere with family life?

LOW 1   2   3   4   5   6   7   8   9   10   HIGH

4. How much does the problem interfere with your child's social life (friendships)?

LOW 1   2   3   4   5   6   7   8   9   10   HIGH

5. How much do you read to your child?

LOW 1   2   3   4   5   6   7   8   9   10   HIGH

6. As a parent, what do you think is the most difficult aspect of your child's reading problem?

INTERNATIONAL CASE STUDIES OF DYSLEXIA CHILD PERCEPTION SCALE

These questions are read to the child. The examiner instructs the child to answer these questions on a scale of 1-10, with 10 being the highest and 1 being the lowest.

Example: How much do you like ice cream?

LOW 1   2   3   4   5   6   7   8   9   10   HIGH

(Examiner checks understanding by asking if the child really likes ice cream or doesn't like it.)

1. In general, how significant do you think your reading problem is?

LOW 1   2   3   4   5   6   7   8   9   10   HIGH

2. How much does the problem interfere with school success?

LOW 1   2   3   4   5   6   7   8   9   10   HIGH

3. How much does the problem interfere with family life?

LOW 1   2   3   4   5   6   7   8   9   10   HIGH

4. How much does the problem interfere with social life (friendships)?

LOW 1   2   3   4   5   6   7   8   9   10   HIGH

5. How much do you read?

LOW 1   2   3   4   5   6   7   8   9   10   HIGH

6. What do you think is the most difficult thing about having a reading problem?

CHILD SENTENCE COMPLETION & ELABORATION

School

1. The best thing about school is _____.

2. I like it when my teacher _____.

3. The worst thing about school is _____.

4. I don't like it when my teacher _____.

5. My classmates think I am _____.

6. Sometimes my classmates make me mad when they _____.

7. It makes me sad when _____.

8. It makes me happy when _____.

Social

1. Other kids like me because _____.

2. My best friends' names are _____.

3. Sometimes kids make fun of me because _____.

4. My favorite thing to do is _____.

5. Sometimes I get worried _____.

6. I don't like it when _____.

7. My friends don't know that _____.

8. Sometimes I wish my friends would _____.

Family

1. My parents are proud of me when I _____.

2. When I do my homework, I feel _____.

3. My parents expect me to _____.

4. I wish my parents would _____.

5. My siblings make me angry when _____.

6. My parents are disappointed when _____.

7. I wish my siblings would _____.

8. I'm really happy when _____.

(Note: The Child Interview is not provided here as it is included at the end of each case study chapter.)

International Case Studies
Contributor Biographies

PRINCIPAL INVESTIGATORS/EDITORS

Peggy L. Anderson, PhD, is Professor in the special education program of the Teacher Education Department at Metropolitan State College of Denver, Colorado, USA. Her research interests are reading disabilities, curricular accessibility, and on-line learning experiences in teacher preparation. Her publications include *Case Studies for Inclusive Schools* (ProEd, 1997, 2005) and the *Streamlined Shakespeare Series* (Academic Therapy, 1999, 2000, 2004, 2006).

Regine Meier-Hedde, Dipl.Päd., M.Ed. (University of New Orleans, LA), is a dyslexia therapist in Hamburg, Germany with over 25 years of experience in private practice. For the past few years, as a wingwave (EMDR) coach, she has additionally specialized in treating dyslexic and other children with school related anxiety. Her research interests include case histories of dyslexia and outcome studies.

INTERNATIONAL RESEARCHERS/CONTRIBUTORS

Australia

Christina (Christa) E. van Kraayenoord, PhD, is an Associate Professor in the School of Education at The University of Queensland, Brisbane, Queensland, Australia. Her research interests are related to literacy development and literacy education, learning difficulties and disabilities, especially in literacy, and whole school reform and teachers' pedagogical change in literacy. Christa is the President-Elect of the International Academy for Research in Learning Disabilities and is the Editor of the *International Journal of Disability, Development and Education*.

Brazil

Simone Aparecida Capellini, Speech Language Therapist, PhD in Medical Sciences, is Professor in the Speech Language and Hearing Pathology

Department at São Paulo State University, Marília, São Paulo, Brazil. She is Coordinator of the *Evaluation and Intervention of Language, Fluency and Learning Disabilities Laboratory.* Her research interests are reading disabilities, dyslexia, learning disabilities, attention deficit disorder with hyperactivity, evaluation, and intervention. Her publications include *Neuropsycholinguistic Perspectives on Dyslexia and other Learning Disabilities* (2007).

Giseli Donadon Germano, Speech Language Therapist, M.Ed., is a doctoral student in the Post-Graduate Program in Education at São Paulo State University, Marília, São Paulo, Brazil. She is a member of the *Evaluation and Intervention of Language, Fluency and Learning Disabilities Laboratory.* Her research interests are reading disabilities, dyslexia, learning disabilities, attention deficit disorder with hyperactivity, evaluation, and intervention.

Fabio Henrique Pinheiro, Speech Language Therapist, M.Ed., is a doctoral student in the Post-Graduate Program in Education at São Paulo State University, Marília, São Paulo, Brazil. He is a member of the *Evaluation and Intervention of Language, Fluency and Learning Disabilities Laboratory.* His research interests are reading disabilities, dyslexia, learning disabilities, attention deficit disorder with hyperactivity, evaluation, and intervention.

Maria Dalva Lourencetti, Psychologist in the Child Neurology Ambulatory of the Clinical Hospital at the Medical School of São Paulo State University, Botucatu, São Paulo, Brazil. She has an M.P.H. from Sacred Heart University. Her interests are dyslexia, learning disabilities, attention deficit disorder with hyperactivity, and neuropsychological evaluation.

Lara Cristina Antunes dos Santos, Child Neurologist, is a Master's student in the Post-Graduate Program in Education at São Paulo State University, Marília, São Paulo, Brazil. She is Coordinator of the Child Neurology Ambulatory of the Clinical Hospital at the Medical School of São Paulo State University, Botucatu, São Paulo, Brazil. Her interests are dyslexia, learning disabilities, attention deficit disorder with hyperactivity, gifted child, and child neurological evaluation.

Niura Aparecida de Moura Ribeiro Padula, PhD in Medical Sciences, is Professor in the Psychiatry, Psychology and Neurology Department at São Paulo State University, Botucatu, São Paulo, Brazil. She is Chief of the Child Neurology Discipline. Her interests are dyslexia, learning disabilities, attention deficit disorder with hyperactivity, epilepsy, and child neurological evaluation.

Canada

Ronald W. Stringer, PhD, is an Associate Professor in the School Psychology program of the Department of Educational & Counselling Psychology at McGill University in Montreal, Canada. His research interests include early reading acquisition and reading disabilities, as well as the experiences of students with learning difficulties, and Métis education. He is also a practicing psychologist in Montreal.

Barbara Bobrow, M.A., is a founder and Coordinator of Professional Services at the Learning Associates of Montreal, a not-for-profit centre that offers psycho-educational assessment, academic tutoring, remediation and unique after-school and summer-camp programs for children with learning difficulties. She also consults with Cree, Inuit, and other native school boards.

Brenda Linn is a reading specialist who has worked with dyslexic children as a teacher, principal, and psycho-educational consultant, in classroom and clinical settings. She is also a reading researcher, who has conducted studies at the University of Oxford and at McGill. Her research interests include the effect of the recent synthetic phonics initiative on literacy instruction in England and Wales, and the influence, or lack of influence, of scientific studies of reading on literacy programmes in the primary grades.

Chile

Arturo Pinto Guevara, Ed.D., is Professor and researcher in the Department of Special and Differential Teacher Education at the Universidad Catolica del Maule, Chile. He conducts research in the areas of cognition, language, and special educational needs associated with specific learning disabilities. His publications address the learning dynamics (2007), evaluation and treatment of dyslexia (2000–2008) and transitional curriculum specific to educational needs (2009, 2010). He has developed undergraduate and graduate degree programs in national and international universities. He has participated in numerous conferences and seminars focusing on specific learning disabilities.

China

Steven S.W. Chu, M.A., is a first-year doctoral student at the Hong Kong Institute of Education with an emphasis in special education. For more than 10 years, he has been working as a frontline language teacher at a primary school. He is currently involved in research concerning the self-concepts of Chinese children with dyslexia. His primary interests include developmental dyslexia, autism, second language acquisition, literacy learning, and instructional strategies.

Kevin K.H. Chung, PhD, is Associate Professor and Associate Dean (Research), School of Education Studies, The Hong Kong Institute of Education. His main research interests are developmental dyslexia, reading and writing acquisition, applied neurosciences in language learning, and other learning disabilities in Chinese. His publications include *The Hong Kong Test of Specific Learning Difficulties in Reading and Writing for Junior Secondary School Students (HKT-JS)* (Hong Kong Specific Learning Difficulties Research Team, 2007) and *The Hong Kong Behaviour Checklist of Specific Learning Difficulties in Reading and Writing for Junior Secondary School Students (BCL-JS)* (Hong Kong Specific Learning Difficulties Research Team, 2009).

Fuk-chuen Ho, PhD, is Assistant Professor in the Department of Special Education and Counselling at the Hong Kong Institute of Education. His research interests are reading and writing problems, autism spectrum disorders, and professional development for teachers of special schools. His publications include *QEF Thematic Networks Scheme—Serving Students with Dyslexia* (Quality Education Fund, 2008) and *Theory of Mind II: Teaching Children with Autistic Spectrum Disorders Emotions* (Hong Kong Education Bureau, 2009).

Egypt

Soad A. Shahin received her PhD from Utah State University, USA. She was formerly an Associate Professor of Genetics at Ain Shams University, Cairo, Egypt and the College of Education, Jeddah, Saudi Arabia. In her current role as President of the Egyptian Dyslexia Association, she trains teachers and parents to teach dyslexic students. She is an active contributor to several projects that serve dyslexic children in the schools and raise public awareness of dyslexia in Egypt.

France

Liliane Sprenger-Charolles is a senior research scientist (Laboratory of the Psychology of Perception, CNRS and Paris-Descartes, France) who works on reading acquisition and developmental dyslexia. She is widely published (e.g., 30 papers in peer-reviewed journals, 30 chapters, and 6 books) and she has been an invited speaker at a number of international conferences. She also acts as a reviewer and consultant for several journals, research councils (e.g., Natural Sciences and Engineering Research Council, Canada), and national and international institutions (e.g., the World Bank, IIEP-UNESCO, Research Triangle Institute, USA). She is also involved in teaching activities for psychologists, speech therapists, physicians and teachers, in France and abroad (e.g., Canada, Italy, Spain, USA).

Gilles Leloup is a PhD student in the Laboratory of the Psychology of Perception (CNRS and Paris-Descartes, France). He is also a speech therapist, and is involved in teaching activities for speech therapists. His clinical and experimental research is focused not only on developmental dyslexia but also on aphasia and epilepsy, topics on which he has published a book (*Les aphasies: Evaluation et rééducation*, Chomel-Guillaume, Leloup, & Bernard, 2010) and a chapter ("Interventions orthophoniques et conduites de remédiation chez l'enfant avec épilepsie," Leloup, 2008; in Jambaqué, Ed., *Epilepsies de l'enfant: Troubles du développement cognitif et socio-émotionnel*).

Greece

Christos Skaloumbakas, PhD, (special education), works as a learning disabilities specialist in the Hyperactivity, Attention & Learning Disorders Unit, Department of Child Psychiatry of Aglaia Kyriakou Children's Hospital, Athens, Greece. His research interests include dyslexia, instructional modifications for children with LD, preschool ADHD and training of parents who have children with ADHD.

Hungary

Éva Gyarmathy, PhD habil., is senior researcher at the Research Institute for Psychology of the Hungarian Academy of Sciences. Her research interests focus on gifted individuals with specific learning difficulties. She is a lecturer at the Eotvos Lorand University and at the University Budensis. She regularly gives lectures and leads workshops on specific learning difficulties, ADHD, autism and behavior difficulties. She is a consultant to private schools that serve high achieving children and adolescents who are dyslexic and hyperactive. She is also a psychotherapist. Her publications include *Holistic Learners* (Whurr Publishers, 2000) and *Diszlexia. Specifikus tanítási zavar* [*Dyslexia. Specific Teaching Difficulties*] (Lelekben Otthon, 2007).

India

Sunil Karande received his M.D. (Pediatrics) from Seth Gordhandas Sunderdas Medical College & King Edward VII Memorial Hospital, Mumbai, India. Currently he is Professor of Pediatrics and In-Charge of the Learning Disability Clinic at the Department of Pediatrics, Seth Gordhandas Sunderdas Medical College & King Edward VII Memorial Hospital, Mumbai, India. His recent research is on quality of life of children with specific learning disabilities and on recollections of learning disabled adolescents of their schooling years.

Rukhshana F. Sholapurwala received her M.Ed. from Shreemati Nathibai Damodar Thackersey Women's University, Mumbai, India. Currently she is Special Educator at the Learning Disability Clinic, Department of Pediatrics, Seth Gordhandas Sunderdas Medical College, and King Edward VII Memorial Hospital, Mumbai, India. Her recent research is in devising a screening tool to identify children with specific learning disabilities during their primary schooling years. She runs a private clinic for children with learning disabilities and is the Course Coordinator for the Postgraduate Diploma Course in Special Education at South Indian Education Society College, Mumbai, India.

Israel

Talya Gur, PhD, is a faculty member in the Special Education Department of Oranim Academic College of Education, Israel. Her research interests are reading acquisition, and diagnosis and treatment of reading disabilities.

David Share is Professor and Head of the Department of Learning Disabilities in the Faculty of Education, University of Haifa, Israel. His main research interests focus on cognitive and psycholinguistic aspects of early reading development and reading disabilities. His major publications include his exposition of the self-teaching model of reading acquisition (*Cognition*, 1995), and a critique of Anglocentrism in current reading research and practice (*Psychological Bulletin*, 2008).

Japan

Jun Yamada, PhD, is Professor of Graduate School of Arts and Sciences, Hiroshima University, Hiroshima, Japan. His research interests are developmental dyslexia, stuttering, and perception and production of speech in English and Japanese. His publications include *Kotoba o Shinri-suru* [The Psychology of Language] (Tokyo: Yuuhikaku, 1983) and *Kodomo no Kotoba* [Child Language] (Tokyo: Yuuhikaku, 1985).

Akira Uno, D.Med.Sc., is Associate Professor of Graduate School of Comprehensive Human Sciences, University of Tsukuba, Japan. He is also Vice President of Japanese Dyslexia Research Association, and President of Non Profit Organization 'LD/Dyslexia Centre'. His research interests are cognitive neuropsychology, especially for developmental dyslexia, specific language impairment and childhood aphasia. His publications include *Reading and Writing* (2009), *Cortex* (2009), *Kotoba to Kokoro no Hattatsu to Shougai* [Development and Disorders of Language and Mind] (Tokyo: Nagai Pub, 2007), and *Shougakusei no Yomikaki Sukurihningu Tesuto* [Screening Test of Reading and Writing for Japanese Primary School Children] (Tokyo: Interuna Pub Inc., 2006).

Russia

Olga Borisovna Inshakova, PhD, is Professor of the special education program of the Department of Speech Pathology at Pedagogical State University of Moscow, Russia. Her research interests are reading and writing disabilities of students of grades 1–4 of comprehensive school, readiness of children for education, training students to work with pupils who have dysgraphia and dyslexia and who study not only in public schools, but also in special schools for children with serious speech problems. Her publications include the results of four years of studies of mastering reading and writing skills of children with dysgraphia and dyslexia (2004, 2007, 2008, 2009) and studying dysgraphia and dyslexia of bilinguals (2005, 2006).

Maria Arkhipova, is a student of Department of Speech Pathology, Pedagogical State University of Moscow, Russia. Her research interests are reading and writing disabilities of students of grades 1–4 of comprehensive school.

Spain

Rosa Maria González Seijas, PhD, is professor of the Department of Developmental and Educational Psychology of the Faculty of Education Sciences at the University of A Coruña, Spain. Her research interests are the prevention and intervention of learning disabilities in reading and writing. She has published in Spanish *Poder escribir: Programa de entrenamiento de los procesos cognitivos de la escritura* (2002) [Able to write: writing cognitive processes training program] and *Actividades para el aprendizaje de la lectura y la escritura* (2008) [Activities for learning how to read and write].

Sweden

Gunnel Ingesson, PhD, is an Associate Professor in the Department of Psychology at Lund University. She is a specialist in clinical psychology and neuropsychology. Her research interests are cognitive and psychosocial aspects of developmental dyslexia.

Index